Nature Contained

Environmental Histories of Singapore

Nature Contained

Environmental Histories of Singapore

Edited by

Timothy P. Barnard

NUS PRESS
SINGAPORE

© 2014 Timothy P. Barnard

Published by:

NUS Press
National University of Singapore
AS3-01-02, 3 Arts Link
Singapore 117569

Fax: (65) 6774-0652
E-mail: nusbooks@nus.edu.sg
Website: http://www.nus.edu.sg/nuspress

ISBN 978-9971-69-790-7 (Paper)

National Library Board, Singapore Cataloguing-in-Publication Data

Nature contained : environmental histories of Singapore / edited by Timothy P.
   Barnard. – Singapore : NUS Press, 2014.
   pages cm
   ISBN : 978-9971-69-790-7 (paperback)

   1. Human ecology – History – Singapore. 2. Singapore – History –
      Environmental aspects.   I. Barnard, Timothy P., 1963-

GF13
304.2095957 -- dc23   OCN859513265

Front cover: A supertree, and trees, at Gardens by the Bay, Singapore (Courtesy of Christopher Yong).

Back cover: Poster for the special stamp collection "Wayside Trees of Singapore", 1976 (Courtesy of the Postal Services Department, Singapore, and the National Archives of Singapore).

Typeset by: Forum, Kuala Lumpur, Malaysia
Printed by: Mainland Press Pte Ltd

Contents

List of Illustrations

FIGURES

Chapter 1

PLATES

Chapter 2

Chapter 3

Chapter 6

TABLES

Acknowledgements

Any book, particularly an edited volume, requires the unseen efforts of many people. The editor and all of the authors wish to express our appreciation to the numerous staff in libraries, archives and other depositories for their help in gathering materials. The institutions consulted for this book range from the Natural History Museum in London to the National Archives of Singapore, as well as libraries throughout the world. The tireless efforts of these curators make visits not only productive, but also pleasant. Among the people that we would like to specifically acknowledge from these institutions are Christina Soh from the Library of Botany and Horticulture at the Singapore Botanic Gardens and Kelvin Lim from the Raffles Museum of Biodiversity Research.

Other individuals, by generously giving their time for interviews and explanations, also greatly influenced the research in this book. They include Leo Tan, Peter Ng and Ilsa Sharp, as well as Richard Corlett, P.N. Avadhani, Michael Daly, Christopher Yong, Kevin Khoo, Vidya Murthy and Puah You Kai, who described their experiences and provided advice on facts and figures that helped shape this work. In addition, institutions such as the Nature Society of both Singapore and Malaysia have been generous in their support. Without the help of all of these friends and colleagues, and we apologize for those left unmentioned, this volume would not have been the rewarding experience it has turned out to be. To all, we would like to express our thanks for their support.

Timothy P. Barnard
Singapore, April 2014

An Introduction

Timothy P. Barnard

Singapore is a small nation-state, an island, at the tip of the Malay Peninsula. Located at the southern end of the Melaka Straits, it has always been a strategically located entrepôt for funnelling goods between South and East Asia as well as within Southeast Asia. The trade that flows past Singapore, and the economic and political control over it, has often been the cornerstone of studies of the Singaporean past.[1] The development of trade, politics and economics, however, has taken place within an environment that is part of a larger tropical zone of incredible biodiversity. This book is an attempt at understanding how this environment has influenced the history of Singapore since the early 19th century.

Modern Singapore reflects much of this tropical biodiversity through governmental efforts to create a "Garden City," making it one of the greenest urban centers in Asia. This designation originated in efforts that began in the early 1960s, when Lee Kuan Yew proposed a tree-planting program to ensure that Singapore would become an "oasis in Southeast Asia."[2] Government agencies, including the Singapore Botanic Gardens, were enlisted in this effort, which, despite constant economic development and change, has resulted in a city that is "clean and green." In the 1970s, Lee took great pride when visitors would compliment the city-state he ruled for its greenery, as occurred when he met a visiting French minister. As recounted in his autobiography, Lee could not understand the full content of the praise from the visiting official, as he did not understand French.

---

[1] Hong Lysa and Huang Jianli, *The Scripting of a National History: Singapore and Its Past* (Singapore: NUS Press, 2008).

[2] Lee Kuan Yew, *From Third World to First—The Singapore Story: 1965–2000* (Singapore: Singapore Press Holdings, 2000), p. 199.

The one word he could make out in the European language, however, was "verdure," conveying not only the idea of a city that was green, but one flush in environmental assets.[3]

A description of Singapore as a site of flourishing, vibrant vegetation did not solely come out of government campaigns in the late 20th century. As early as 1856, John Crawfurd—the British Resident of Singapore from 1823–26—described Singapore as an island wrapped in "continual verdure."[4] This picture of Singapore as a place of tropical fecundity, however, is a complicated one. The natural environment in Singapore has constantly undergone change. When Crawfurd oversaw the administration of Singapore in the 1820s, it was mainly an island covered in tropical rainforest. By the mid-19th century, the spread of gambier and pepper plantations led to an almost complete deforestation of the island, except on hilltops and the steepest of slopes. Replacing much of this primeval vegetation, as well as gambier and pepper, was *lalang*, a common blade grass (*Imperata cylindrica*), which is difficult to remove from the soil due to its root structure. This transformation in the floral cover of Singapore also led to a vast change in the types of fauna present in the forest. Large jungle animals, such as tigers, soon found little cover or useable habitat. This change was drastic, leading biologist Richard Corlett to estimate that up to 50 percent of the species native to Singapore have disappeared since the mid-19th century.[5]

Into the ecological system of Singapore, new flora and fauna also were introduced. Many of the early transplants, such as gambier and pepper, or nutmeg, were planted in the hope of developing viable export crops. The result was numerous, often small, plantations stretching into the interior that fed into global industries. The initial crops of spices were replaced in the early 20th century with the expansion of rubber plantations, which quickly

---

[3] Lee, *From Third World to First*, p. 203; Harvey Neo, "Challenging the Developmental State: Nature Conservation in Singapore," *Asia Pacific Viewpoint* 48, 2 (Aug. 2007): 186–99.

[4] See the first excerpt, following this chapter, in this collection. John Crawfurd, *A Descriptive Dictionary of the Indian Islands and Adjacent Countries* (London: Bradbury and Evans, 1856), p. 396.

[5] Richard Corlett, "Vegetation," in *The Biophysical Environment of Singapore*, ed. Chia Lin Sien, Ausafur Rahman, and Dorothy Tay B.H. (Singapore: Singapore University Press, 1991), pp. 134–54. See also the notes on this in John van Wyhe's contribution to this volume.

came to dominate the non-urban landscape of Singapore up to the Japanese occupation. To feed the growing population, there were also farms providing vegetables and meat, particularly the domesticated pig (*Sus domesticus*), for local consumption. These new products transformed our understanding of what was possible from the local environment as well as the appearance of the landscape. For example, the agricultural development that these pigs represent led to a focused program of food production following the Second World War in which Singapore became self-sufficient (or extremely close to it) in pork, eggs, and poultry until the 1980s, something that seems unimaginable in the 21st century.

All of these various flora and fauna are part of an environmental history of Singapore, in which plants and animals are as important as any human that shaped the nation-state, pointing to alternatives for under-standing and appreciating the past of the island. History goes beyond the (often air conditioned) offices of government officials, or stevedores of the port. The history of Singapore, thus, is more than a story of trade, immigration and nation-building. While these are important factors in the development of the island, they all occurred in a natural environment in which the interaction of humans with the flora and fauna determined how we understand a small state in Southeast Asia. This book is an attempt to begin an exploration of this aspect of its past. Each of the chapters examines the interaction of humans with the Singaporean environment, often focusing on how it has influenced our understandings of events in the larger eco-nomic, political, social, and intellectual history of the island. In this regard, this book reflects much of the diversity, and dynamism, of environmental history globally.

Environmental History and Singapore

Environmental history is the study of how the environment has influenced humans, and humans the environment. It arose as a subfield within historical studies in the 1960s, as part of larger global social movements that opened the investigation of a variety of social and cultural fields. As a subject of research, it draws upon the humanities and natural sciences to investigate, and better understand, the past. In the United States, scholars such as Donald Worster led the early development of the field through their studies of the American frontier and national parks. Currently the field is quite broad in scope, and has become influential in historical studies of agriculture, exploration, imperialism, technology, and urban areas. Environmental history has also become popular among those interested in issues such as global sustainability, climate change, and urban development.[6]

While environmental history is a field of growing importance globally, in Southeast Asia it is still in its infancy. Many works on Southeast Asian history do have an environmental component, however, as factors such as shifting trade winds and expansion of rice fields often played a role in the regional past. In addition, in an area in which works of anthropologists and other scholars often filter over into the historical, it is common for researchers to reach across artificial disciplinary divides that often separate research in other areas of the world. Works, such as Clifford Geertz's *Agricultural Involution*, or Michael Adas' *The Burma Delta*, while not written specifically with an environmental history background, can easily be interpreted within the subfield and greatly influence our understanding of the interaction of humans and the environment over time.[7] The cross-fertilization of different academic disciplines continues into the 21st century, and external influence of global studies of the environment and Southeast Asian approaches continue to influence studies of the region.

Despite the role that environmental studies of the past can play in our understanding of Southeast Asia, there have been few important figures and works. One exception is the role that Peter Boomgaard has played in the development of the study of environmental history in Indonesia. While acting as the Director of the Royal Netherlands Institute of Southeast Asian and Caribbean Studies (KITLV) in Leiden, the Netherlands in the 1990s, Boomgaard oversaw the EDEN (Ecology, Demography and Economics in Nusantara) project, which resulted in numerous monographs, edited works and articles that focus on the Indonesian environment in historical perspective.[8] With his focus on the largest nation in Southeast Asia, and

---

[6] Donald Worster, *The Wealth of Nature: Environmental History and the Ecological Imagination* (Oxford: Oxford University Press, 1993); Donald Worster, ed., *The Ends of the Earth: Perspectives on Modern Environmental History* (Cambridge: Cambridge University Press, 1988); Richard White, "Environmental History: The Development of a New Historical Field," *Pacific Historical Review* 54 (1985): 297–335.

[7] Clifford Geertz, *Agricultural Involution: The Process of Ecological Change in Indonesia* (Berkeley, CA: University of California Press, 1963); Michael Adas, *The Burma Delta: Economic Development and Social Change on an Asian Rice Frontier, 1852–1941* (Madison, WI: University of Wisconsin Press, 1974).

[8] There are numerous works, although a good starting point would be *Paper Landscapes: Explorations in the Environmental History of Indonesia*, ed. Peter Boomgaard, Freek Columbijn, and David Henley (Leiden: KITLV, 1997).

access to research funds, Boomgaard was influential in developing a group of researchers that considered how the environment has influenced, and been influenced by, humans. Much of this work, however, has not spilled across national boundaries into other areas of Southeast Asia. It is with this work that initial steps are taken in a path that Worster, Boomgaard, and others have cut in the historical relationship between humans and nature that this work hopes to emulate.

While there are a number of excellent works on the Singaporean environment, as well as the political and social history of the nation-state, this volume is an introduction to the possibilities of combining these environmental studies and the Singaporean past. The authors come from a wide range of backgrounds, from botanists to historians. The chapters roughly follow a chronological order. In between each of these essays are short excerpts from documents, interviews, and accounts of the events that influenced the chapters. These "sources" provide a brief taste of the wealth of accounts and documents available for the study of the environmental history of Singapore. Beyond this chronological order, the chapters focus on two major aspects of the Singaporean past: how a consideration of plants and animals allow us to better understand larger issues in studying the history of Singaporean society.

The first of these chapters, by Tony O'Dempsey, focuses on the broad changes in the Singaporean ecological landscape over the past 200 years, and provides a survey of many of the developments that the subsequent chapters will examine in greater detail. Through his study of how an island transformed from one covered in tropical rainforest and swamps to gambier and pepper and then rubber plantations before transitioning into the secondary forest cover of a "green" Singapore, he explains how larger economic policies and products have influenced the environment surrounding Singaporeans.

The effects of rapid gambier and pepper plantation growth influenced the plant and animal ecology of Singapore, and this is the focus of the next two chapters in this book. With regard to animal life, Timothy P. Barnard and Mark Emmanuel survey the role that tigers played in changing 19th-century ecological landscape. As gambier and pepper proliferated, the disturbance to the forest provided an ideal habitat for tigers, which attacked Singaporeans—mostly Chinese agriculturalists—living in the frontier between the town and forest for the first half century of the existence of colonial Singapore. On the edge of these plantations, the British scientist Alfred Russel Wallace also began his exploration of nature in Southeast Asia. John van Wyhe provides an examination of Wallace and his time in

Singapore, and the role that it played in the development of his theories of natural selection in the next chapter in this book.

Singapore was a key location for scientific research on the environment, as can be seen in the work of Wallace. This theme continues in Nigel P. Taylor's discussion of the role that the Singapore Botanic Gardens have played in this development of economic botany in the region. This contribution can be most famously seen in the development of techniques for the processing of rubber and oil palm, two products that transformed the landscape of Singapore and the Malay Peninsula for over a century, as well as the transformation of "green" Singapore under the post-1965 government. As the Director of the Singapore Botanic Gardens, Taylor provides the insight of both a botanist as well as an administrator who has to oversee the creation of functional green space in the heart of the island, and is able to place the development over a century and half in a historical perspective.

Although tigers haunted Singapore in its first few decades, deforestation and the expansion of the municipality led to a distancing of the links between animals and the larger society as much of the island's flora and fauna was "tamed." This distancing between humans and nature, and the control of the environment, becomes the focus of several later chapters. Singapore's role as an entrepôt not only involved the export of rubber; it also included the export of exotic animals. Fiona Tan turns her attention to the links between the port and animals from the larger Malay World during the late colonial period by focusing on legislative attempts to control the animal trade flowing through the harbor. The inability, or lack of desire, of the colonial government to handle the issue, helps provide insight into the role of personalities in environmental matters, as well as the role that trade played in the development of public policy, as her chapter ventures into the city, with a particular focus on bird shops located along Rochor Road in the 1930s.

The role of animals such as birds, and how a modern, urban populace can understand them, is the focus of the next chapter, which follows the development of the Raffles Museum natural history collection, and its fate following Singaporean independence in 1965. Natural history museums, much like Botanic Gardens, allowed for research into the environment of the region. The discovery and collection of new species, as well as their presentation to the public, helped the colonizer visualize its empire at the level of nature. As science and empire changed in the second half of the 20th century, however, the issue of what to do with the massive collection of preserved animals in the Raffles Museum became a concern for government officials and scientists in Singapore. As this colonial era collection did not fit into understandings of a modernizing and technologically advanced nation-state, the fate of all of these animals, as well as Singaporeans relationship with the natural world, came into question. Through the dedicated efforts of a handful of scientists, they were able to preserve the collection, while continuing to try and make it relevant to young Singaporeans who were growing more distant from their natural surroundings.

These natural surroundings included a vast number of farms up until the 1980s. Agricultural food production in Singapore was one of the early triumphs of the independent government, and from the 1960s until the 1980s Singapore experienced a high level of food security. A number of key products that the citizens consumed, ranging from pork to eggs, were produced on the island. Cynthia Chou, a Singaporean anthropologist living in Europe, explored many of these farms in the 1980s, and discusses the relationship between farmers and government officials, and changing understandings of what the former can contribute to society, in Chapter 8. When government policy called for the closing of these farms in the mid-1980s, and began to focus on agro-technology, it was the end of an era of food self-sufficiency in the nation, pointing to the role that government officials also played in the long-term relationship between the population and the natural environment.

The role of these government officials, and their relationship to nature and civil society, in a global context is the focus of the final two chapters in this book. Goh Hong Yi examines the often-contentious relationship between members of the Nature Society and government officials in the early 1980s with regard to the exotic animal trade, which also harks back to Tan's earlier chapter, and culminated in Singapore joining the Convention on International Trade in Endangered Species of Wild Fauna and Flora (CITES) in 1986. The process, however, was one in which the loyalty of civil society activists to the state was often called into question, and even resulted in a diplomatic row with the United States. Goh argues that this was a key early moment in not only the development of civil society in Singapore, as well as environmental activism, laying the foundation for the future relationship between the government and activists that has resulted in a number of green spaces being designated reserves and national parks.

In the final chapter, Timothy Barnard and Corinne Heng place the efforts of the modern Singaporean government to promote a "clean and green" environment in historical perspective. While the results of this program have been extraordinary, they also reflect a growing technocratic approach to the environment. Singaporean nature, much like its political, economic, and social policies, was to be controlled and quantified. While this led to a much greener environment, it has also led to calls from various environmental groups, including the Nature Society, to allow for more "natural" growth. These developments, however, are the culmination of over 200 years of interaction between humans and the natural environment in a small port in Southeast Asia. They are part of its environmental history.

While this volume covers the past 200 years of Singaporean environmental history, it is an introductory work. There are still many other areas that other scholars could explore in much greater detail. The urban environment, and even medicine and health, for example, provide a richness of resources that wait for the curious. Hopefully, this work will spur others to look into alternative approaches to examining Singaporean history, and its environment. This is a first step, and, beyond any enjoyment and insight the chapters provide, may it allow others to ask different questions of, and view from different perspectives, the Singaporean past.

SOURCE 1

John Crawfurd's Singapore: An Excerpt from *A Descriptive Dictionary of the Indian Islands and Adjacent Countries* (1856)[1]

John Crawfurd

SINGAPORE, correctly SINGAPURA, from the Sanscrit singa, lion, and pura city. This is the name of an island, which with the exception of a single village of poor and predatory Malay fishermen, and that only formed in 1811, was covered in a primeval forest down to the 6th day of February, 1819, and is now the fourth in rank of the European emporia of India, ranking after Batavia. De Barros gives a whimsical etymology of the name "Anciently," says he, "the most celebrated city which existed in the land of Malacca, was called Cingapura, which in the language of the country signifies 'false delay' (falsa demora)." This derivation must have come through the Malays who, no doubt were then, as they now are, ignorant of the true meaning of the name, and indeed, even of the fact that it is derived from the sacred language of the Hindus.

Singapore is the most northerly of the large islands of the almost countless group that in a great measure blocks up the eastern end of the strait which divides the Peninsula from Sumatra, leaving but narrow channels for navigation, and forming as it were, a region of straits. It is about thirty miles distant from the southern extremity of the Asiatic continent, and separated from the mainland by a strait generally about a mile broad, but in some parts little more than three furlongs. This is the Sâlat tambrau (strait of the tambrau fish), of the Malays and the "old Straits of Singapore" of European navigators. It was the old passage into the China Sea, but has long been abandoned for that by the southern side of Singapore. I went through it in a ship of 400 tons, and found the passage tedious but safe. Singapore in its greatest length

---

[1] John Crawfurd, *A Descriptive Dictionary of the Indian Islands and Adjacent Countries* (London: Bradbury and Evans, 1856), pp. 395–400.

from east to west, is 25 miles long, and in its greatest breadth 14, having an area of 206 square geographical miles, which will make it 70 miles larger than the Isle of Wight. To the north, it is bounded by the territory of Jehore, the limit between being the continental shore of the narrow strait already mentioned. Everywhere else, the British settlement extend to 10 miles from the shore of the main land, and within this distance are contained no fewer than 75 islets of various sizes, embracing an area of 17 square miles, so that the superficies of the entire British settlement amounted to 223 square miles.

Viewed from a distance, Singapore presents no marked elevations, but has the unvarying aspect of one continuous forest. The surface, however, is undulating; consisting, generally, of rounded hills of 80 to 120 feet high, with narrow valleys not above 15 or 20 feet above the sea level. A chain of rather higher hills runs through the island from east to west, making the water-shed in one direction to the north, and in the other to the south. The culminating point of the land is a hill, nearly in the centre of the island, called Bukit-timah, that is, "tin-hill", and this rises to the height of 519 feet above the low water-mark spring tides.

The geological formation of Singapore consists of the same rocks as the Peninsula generally, and is plutonic and sedimentary; the first consisting of granite, and the last, which embraces the greater portion of the island, of sand-stone, slate, and clay iron-ore. The only metallic ore that exists in abundance, and this is very rich, is that of iron. The island lies also in the formation most favourable for the existence of tin, namely, between the junction of granite and sand-stone, but no ore of it has as yet been discovered. The blue clays furnish an excellent material for bricks and tiles; and the decomposed feldspar of granite the finest kaolin which has yet been seen in India, but it has not been applied to the manufacture of porcelane. Some portion of the island, as that which is the site of the town, is of alluvial formation, chiefly sand with a very thin covering of vegetable mould.

The climate of the island is well described by Mr. Thomson, in the Journal of the Indian Archipelago. "Singapore," says he, "though within 80 miles of the equator, has an abundance of moisture, either deposited by the dews or gentle refreshing showers, which keeps its atmosphere cool, prevents the parching effects of the sun, and promotes continual verdure. It never experiences gales. If more than ordinary heat has accumulated moisture and electricity, a squall generally sets in, followed by a heavy shower of rain; such squalls seldom exceeding one or two hours in duration. According as the monsoon blows, you will have the squalls coming from that direction. But the most severe and numerous are from the south-west, called 'Sumatras,' and these occur, most frequently, between 1 and 5 o'clock in the morning. The north-east monsoon blows from November to March; after which the wind veers round to the south-east and gradually sets in the south-west, at which point it continues to September. The north-east blows more steadily than the south-west monsoon. The temperature is by one or two degrees cooler in the first than in the last." The average fall of rain is found, from the observation of a series of years, to be 92.697 inches;

and the average number of days a year in which rain falls is found to be 180, thus dividing the year almost equally between wet and dry; the rain not being continuous but pretty equally distributed through the whole year, January, however, being the month in which the greatest quantity falls. The mean temperature of Singapore is, at present, 81°.247, the lowest being 79°.55 and the highest being 82°.31, so that the range is no more than 2°.76. It would appear from this that the temperature on the island is by 9° 90' lower than that of many other localities at the same latitudes. Comparing the temperature now stated with that which was ascertained 20 years earlier, and in the infancy of the settlement, it would appear that it had increased by 2° 48', a fact ascribable, no doubt, to the increase in buildings, and to the country having been cleared of forest for three miles inland from the town, the site of the observations. The general character of the climate as to temperature is, that the heat is great and continuous, but never excessive, and that there is little distinction of seasons; summer and winter differing from each other only by one or two degrees of the thermometer. Thunder showers are of frequent occurrence, but the thunder is by no means so severe as I have experienced in Java, and seldom destructive to life or property. "That interesting and wonder phenomenon, called a water-spout," says Mr. Thomson, "is often to be seen in the seas and straits adjacent. They ought more properly to be called whirlwinds charged with vapour. They occur, generally, in the morning between the hours of eight and twelve, and rise to the height of half a mile, appearing in the distance like large columns supporting the heavy masses of cumuli above them. I noticed in October, 1841, six of these attached to one cloud, under action at the same time. In August, 1838, one passed over the harbor and town of Singapore, devastating one ship and sinking another; and carrying off the corner of the roof of a house in its course landward. No other atmospheric disturbances of any moment occur. The typhoons of the China Sea and Bay of Bengal do not reach those parts, nor are there hot winds to parch the land. The equable and quiet state of the atmosphere and seasons of these regions, consequently create analogous properties in the face of indigenous vegetation. Evergreens abound; few trees shed all their leaves at the same time; and many of the fruit trees produce all year round. Such as have their seasons of fruit will produce crops out of season, bearing small irregular ones at intervening times. This continual verdure is, perhaps more grateful to the stranger than to those who have been accustomed to it. To the former it bears the pleasant appearance of exuberance and fecundity—of a region where the lofty forest not only hangs over the beach, but clothes the mountains to their tops, so unlike the sterile barrenness of higher latitudes. To the latter, the continual sameness palls the senses. They want variety, and call for a sterile winter, only that they may renew, with doubly keen perception, their acquaintance with the beauties of returning summer, a season that always here reigns."

Notwithstanding its heat and its monotony, the climate of Singapore is even remarkable for its salubrity; and with, perhaps, the exception of a few little-frequented spots in the interior, it is certainly free from the malaria which often infects countries, apparently more favourably circumstanced. This advantage it seems to owe to its perfect ventilation by the monsoons—by land and sea-breezes—and by frequent squalls. That this is the main course is proved by the eminently pestiferous air of a land-locked harbor at the western end of the island, and not above two miles distant from the town.

A popular view of the botany of Singapore has been given by Dr. Oxley, a man of science, and long familiar with the place. "If nature," says he, "has been frugal in her gifts of the higher orders of the animal kingdom in Singapore, she has lavished with unsparing prodigality, the riches of the vegetable one. Notwithstanding the infertility of the soil, climate more than compensates for the loss: heat and moisture cover the lean earth with unceasing verdure; and we realize, what fancy paints as the most desirable of all climates—an eternal spring. But independently of its position, the botany of this place possesses several other interesting considerations. Being a connecting link between the Indian and Australian forms, we have types of both, and many genera of either region. We observe the Indian forms in the natural families Palmae, Scitamineae, Aroideae, Artocarpeae, Euphorbiaceae, Apocyneae, Guttiferae, Convolvulaceae, Leguminosea, all numerous. The natural families Casuarineae, Myrtaceae, particularly Melaleucae, and Proteaceae, connect us with Australia."

"The plants," he observes, "which usually spring up when the primeval forest has been cut down; and where the bane of all the rest of the vegetable kingdom, the Andropogon caricosum, or Lalang grass, has not taken possession, belong to the following genera: Melastoma, Myrtus, Morinda, Solanum, Rubus, Rottlera, Clerodendrum, Commersonia, Ficus, and Passiflora. The jungle, with the exception of its outskirts is unexplorable, without great risk, from the number of tigers; but I have collected between forty and fifty orchideous plants, including epiphytal and terrestrial, and about the same number of ferns. Fici are extremely numerous. Of palms, I have not seen more than twenty species, although, I believe, there are a much greater number. The most interesting of these in an economic point of view, are the coco-nut, the Areca catechu or pinang, the Areca sigillaria or nibung, the Sagus laevis or râmbuja, the Nipa fruticans, or nipa, and the Gomutus or iju. Of the natural families which most abound, the Asclepiadeae, Euphorbiceae, Scitamineae, and Urticaceae are the chief." The forest contains an immense number of species of timber trees, most of them of great height and growth. Above two hundred have been collected, and of these about half-a-dozen afford good timber for house and boat building. The teak is not of the number. The forest, also, produces the two species which yield the useful gutta-percha, and a fig which affords an elastic gum. But for use these articles, as well as timber, are not obtained from Singapore itself but from the wider and more accessible forests of the neighboring continent.

The zoology of Singapore is that of the neighboring continent, to the exclusion of some of the larger animals, as the elephant, the rhinoceros, the tapir, and the ox. The largest feline animal indigenous to the island is a small leopard, called by the Malays arimau-däan, that is the "the branch" of climbing tiger. But the tiger, an animal unknown to the island in the earlier years of British settlement, made its first appearance five or six years after it was formed, and is now too abundant. It seems to have crossed over from the continent, attracted no doubt by the sound of human voices and lowing of cattle. It has multiplied greatly, and is supposed to destroy, yearly, from two to three hundred persons, proving the greatest bane of the settlement. Large rewards have been offered for the destruction of tigers, and a good number have been captured in pitfalls, but all attempts at their extermination have been unsuccessful and are likely long to prove so in this still forest-clad island, parted from a region in which the tiger is abundant by a channel of no more than few furlongs broad. The channel between Penang and the main is two miles broad, and this has been sufficient to exclude the tiger, for although there have been examples of individuals having crossed over, it has been in an exhausted state, and they have been immediately destroyed.

Of the natural family of Mustelidae, there are two in Singapore, the musang of the Malays, Paradoxus musanga, and the binturang, Ictides ater, of the size of a badger. Otters are occasionally seen along the coasts, but are rare. The wild hog is frequent, and there are five species of deer, the usual ones of the Peninsula and Sumatra, from the Rusa of the size of a heifer to the kanchil, which is hardly as large as a rabbit. Among mammals, one species of bat is often to be seen, the same which is so frequent in almost all parts of the Archipelago, the kalong or Pteropus javanicus. This is about the size of a raven, and a troop of them in flight has very much the look of a flock of crows, and by a stranger may be easily mistaken for one. "I may add," says Dr. Oxley, "In rendering a sketch of the zoology of Singapore, several species of the bat tribe, and among them that most destructive one to all fruits, the flying fox or Pteropus. Fortunately, however, they are at yet scarce, but at no distance from us they are numerous beyond count. I have seen a flock of them while anchored in the Straits of Malacca, so large as to take several hours in passing. A colony is at present located in a mangrove creek at the head of the estuary of the Jehore river. In the day they are seen asleep hanging in millions from the branches of the mangrove. At sunset they begin to stir, and presently they ascend into the air and wing their way to the south-east in one vast uninterrupted cloud. They pass the whole night in the jungle and plantations devouring fruit, and as soon as dawn begins to appear, they mount the air again and return to their roosting-place at the head of the estuary. Their flesh is eaten by the natives, but no real fox smells to my mind half so rank as they do. Methinks a rat would be palatable food compared with them." These bats, in so far as the orchard is concerned, are the locust of the country, in which flights of the insect itself as far as I am aware are unknown. The Ptermonys, or flying squirrel, the krawak of the Malays, is very frequent in Singapore, and so are three different species of monkey.

As with the larger quadrupeds, the larger birds of the Peninsula and Sumatra are not found in Singapore. It has neither their peacocks nor their pheasants, and the only birds of the Rasorial family which exist in it are two species of quail. Nearly all the web-footed birds, whether indigenous or of passage, are not to be seen. There are six different species of pigeon, from the size of our wood-pigeon to that of a thrush.

Parrots are frequent, but the species only two or three. The only bird that can be called game is the snipe, which seems a stranger to no country in the world that has marshes. The birds of prey of four different genera are sufficiently numerous, and Dr. Oxley remarks that among birds of this family, is "that perfect type of true falcons, the beautiful little Falco caerulescens, which, although not much larger than a sparrow, will kill and carry off a bird the size of a thrush."

Among reptiles, alligators are common in the salt water creeks, and along the shores of the island, but having an abundant supply of fish, are not troublesome to man. The Iguana lizard, the bewak of the Malays, is not unfrequent, but the noisy house lizard or tokay, the tâké of the Malays, so common in Penang and so much more so in Siam, is not found in Singapore. The esculent turtle is very abundant along the shores of Singapore and the neighboring islands, and being, as food, restricted to the European and Chinese population, is the cheapest animal food in the market, one of the largest weighing several hundred weights selling for six or seven shillings. "Snakes," says Dr. Oxley, "are not numerous. The most common is the dark cobra. I believe this with a trigonocephalus are the only well-authenticated venomous species on the island. The first possesses the peculiar property of ejecting venom from its mouth. The Malays say there is no cure for its bite. I have seen it prove fatal to a fowl in two or three minutes, but have not observed its effects on large animals. Those I have killed have measured from 4½ and 5¼ feet in length. This reptile being slow and sluggish is easily overtaken and killed. When attacked, it erects the body and dilates the skin on either side of the head, uttering a noise like that of an irritated cat. If attacked it throws, to the distance of six to eight feet, a venomous fluid or a most poisonous quality." Fish and crustaceans are in great plenty, and Dr. Oxley has enumerated forty species of them as seen by himself. About half-a-dozen of these are excellent for the table, fully equal to the best fish of our own coasts. Among these the best is the white pomfret of Europeans, the bawal-puteh of the Malays, of richer flavor than our soles and less luscious than the turbot.

The agriculture of Singapore, although conducted with sufficient spirit and activity, is limited to a small number of objects, and nearly excludes all the cereal grasses and pulses constituting the staple articles of human food. The soil of the island, with very few exceptions, is like that of the adjoining peninsula, unfertile—and there is no natural, and therefore no cheap source of irrigation, and hence the land is incapable of furnishing a cheap supply of the main necessaries of life, which are yielded only within the Archipelago by rich volcanic or alluvial soils, assisted by a copious perennial irrigation. For such plants as rice, the sugar-cane, the indigo-plant, pulses, maiz, tobacco, cotton, the soil must be considered as ill-suited. Besides want of fertility of soil, Singapore wants sufficient elevation to give a climate fit for the production of coffee. Even the nutmeg thrives only when forced by rich dressings, and the clove does not succeed at all. On the other hand, all plants which depend on heat and moisture than on soil, flourish luxuriantly, such as the coco and areca palms, with the Uncaria gambir, which is indigenous. Black pepper, which is a long-naturalised exotic, although it answer well, yet even it requires some manuring. In 1854, the quantity of pepper produced amounted to 3,116,533 pounds, and the betel or areca nuts to above 40,000 cwts. Among the plants congenial to both soil and climate are most of the intertropical fruits, whether indigenous or exotic. Among these the most easily reared, and even cheaper than the banana is the pine-apple, equaling in size and flavor the finest productions of our hot-houses. Besides fruits, the soil and climate are well adapted to the production of the yam and igname, and to that of the coarse pot-herbs which belong to the latitude.

The following judicious remarks are made by Mr. Logan on the soil of Singapore: "The soil is much more varied than it was supposed to be in former years, and so far from consisting entirely of decomposed sandstone and clay-iron ore, it contains a plutonic (granitic) tract of about sixty square miles, and another in which shales predominate. Although the soils have not the fertility of the volcanic and calcareous ones which occur in many parts of the Indian Archipelago, they are covered with an indigenous vegetation of great vigour and luxurance, supporting numbers of animals of different species. The hills of plutonic rock support dense and continuous forests composed of more than 200 species of trees, many of which are of great size. So long as the iron is not in such excess as to recompose the clay into stone, or render it hard, those soils which contain most iron are most fertile. The purely, or highly felspathic are the worst. But even felspathic soils, when intermixed with a sufficient proportion of quartz, are, in this estimate, capable of producing an abundant vegetation. Although it is obvious to every observer that there is no kind of soil in the island for which nature has not provided plants, that flourish luxuriantly in it, yet it must not be hastily concluded, as some have done, that this exuberant vegetation indicates a general fertility in the soil. It is found, on the contrary, that there are very few soils in which cultivated plants not indigenous to the region, but whose climatic range embraces it, will flourish spontaneously. While the coco-nut, areca, sago, gomuti, and the numerous Malayan fruits succeed with little care, the nutmeg and clove are stunted, and almost unproductive, unless carefully cultivated and highly manured. Yet the climate is perfectly adapted to them. Place them in the rare spots where there is naturally a fertile soil, or create one artificially, and the produce is equal to that of trees in the Molucca plantations. With respect to indigenous plants, gambier, pepper, and all the fruits flourish on the Plutonic hills, provided they are not too deficient in iron and quartz. The hills of violet shale, where they are not too sandy, are equal to the best Plutonic soils, — those, namely, in which there is a sufficient proportion of hard granules to render them friable, and sufficient iron to render them highly absorptive to water, without becoming plastic. Of all the sedimentary soils, the sandstone and very arenaceous shales are the worst. Of the alluvial soils, the sand, particularly when it contains a mixture of vegetable matter, or triturated shells, is the proper soil of the coco-nut and the vegetable mud of the sago. When the country has been better and longer drained and cultivated, the latter soil will become a rich mould. At present it is too wet and sour to make fertile soil. Rice is grown on some patches of it. The bluish sea mud contains good ingredients, but the clay is in excess, and the animal matter in it appears to assist in rendering it hard and intractable, when it is not saturated with water. Even for such soils, however, nature has provided plants useful to man, for the area and some of the indigenous fruit trees grow well in it with little cultivation. Although there are cultivated plants adapted to every kind of soil in the island, and it has indigenous tribes of man who can live exclusively on its yams, sago, fish, and wild animals, it is incapable of feeding a population of the more civilised races, and the latter must always be dependent on other countries for the great necessary of life—rice."

In the husbandry of Singapore, neither plough, harrow, nor spade are employed. All is done with the hoe and mattock. The whole is, in fact, a garden culture, in which no great crop is cultivated giving scope for the plough, and which is perhaps best performed by the hoe, the congenial and habitual implement, for this purpose, of all Asiatic nations. With respect to tenures, wild lands, when alienated by the government, are granted in fee simple, on payment of thirty shillings an acre, if within two miles of the town, and of one-half that amount, if beyond this distance. At this simple arrangement the government arrived at last, after the higgling and blundering of a quarter of a century, and the expenditure of vast quantities of ink and paper.

The only manufacture deserving this name that is carried on in Singapore, is that of sago, and for this, it is a workshop of nearly all that at present appears in commerce. This amounts to about 8000 tons yearly, of the value of about 30,000£. Great quantities of tools, implements, swords, and wall-pieces are manufactured by the Chinese, and there is some manufacture of furniture, with some boat and shipbuilding, but not to any great extent, for wet and dry docks remain yet to be constructed, although there be localities well adapted to them.

But ever branch of industry is merely subsidiary to trade. Singapore is, in fact, a great commercial emporium, in which are warehoused for future distribution, the staple products of Europe, Asia, and America. The town, the seat of this commerce, lies in the north latitude 1° 17′, or only seventy-seven miles from the equator, and in east longitude 103° 50′ 47″. Its locality on the southern side of the island, on a salt creek, into which falls the brook called the river of Singapore; the commercial part of it being on the western bank, and the public buildings and private houses on the eastern, which spreads into a sandy plain, a little above the level of the sea. There is properly, no harbour, but the bay which fronts the town, and which is also the highway through the Straits of Malacca, is a roadstead equivalent to a harbour in a region never vexed by storms. Ships of the largest burdens lie in good anchoring-ground at the distance of two miles from the shore, those of moderate draught of water, within a mile, and small craft close to it. The salt creek, which has a quay on the commercial side, is navigable at all times for lighters up to the warehouses of the merchants.

In 1826 …

CHAPTER 1

Singapore's Changing Landscape since c. 1800

Tony O'Dempsey

At the time of Sir Thomas Stamford Raffles arrival in 1819, the island of Singapore was not totally pristine. Although there had been a significant trade port in Singapore in the 14th century, over the subsequent 400 years small groups of *orang laut* (sea people), who occupied the coastal and mangrove river inlets, became the main occupants of the island. Their settlement on the land is thought to have been limited in extent and mainly at the mouth of the Singapore River. Elsewhere, on the southern part of the island *orang Kalang* lived at the mouth of the Kalang River, while in the north *orang Johor* and *orang Selat* lived in the estuaries of the Ponggol River and Seletar River, where the remnants of their communities remained into the 19th century. As fishing was the main occupation of these groups, their impact on the landscape would have been marginal. They certainly utilized mangrove timbers and Nipah palms in the construction of their abodes and possibly utilized some of the lowland rainforest trees in boat-building. Beyond the harvesting of timber for construction, it is thought that they did not venture inland further than the need for fresh water, medicinal plants, and forest fruits required.[1]

In a pristine state, Singapore featured three significant ecological habitats (see Figure 1.1). The first of these was lowland dipterocarp forest, which T.C. Whitmore defines as a type of forest within the lowland rainforest formation

---

[1] John N. Miksic and Cheryl-Ann Low Mei Gek, eds., *Early Singapore 1300s–1819: Evidence in Maps, Texts and Artifacts* (Singapore: Singapore History Museum, 2004); Kwa Chong Guan, Derek Heng, and Tan Tai Yong, *Singapore: A 700-Year History: From Early Emporium to World City* (Singapore: National Archives of Singapore, 2009).

on dry lands up to 1,200 meters in which the family Dipterocarpaceae dominates the upper and emergent canopy; it was the most extensive forest type in Singapore.[2] These dipterocarp forests vanished fairly quickly during the first hundred years of colonial rule due to uncontrolled harvesting of timber as well as destructive agricultural practices. The influence of tides and water characterized the second and third major habitats in Singapore. The first of these habitats was the freshwater swamp forest, which is typically found on the low lying coastal alluvial plains and associated with river and stream systems, and mangrove forest, which occurred within the areas of tidal influence. Freshwater swamp forests originally covered a significant portion (approximately 65 square kilometers) of Singapore and have since suffered significant depletion through land conversions. Freshwater swamp forests come about due to flat low-lying land close to the coast and above the limit of the spring high tide becoming inundated due to rainfall runoff, inflow from surrounding elevated terrain, and the tidal effects restricting outflow of water from the streams. This periodic inundation gives rise to a habitat that is floristically distinct from the surrounding lowland dipterocarp forest. The alluvial soils, upon which this forest type grew, however, would become highly desired agricultural land during the colonial period in Singapore, when most of it was converted for the growing of vegetables. Mangrove forests are the third ecological habitat in Singapore. These forests formed within the intertidal zone. During colonial times, these forests were valued for firewood and charcoal production, poles for fishing platforms (*kelongs*), and timber for boat-building.[3] As will be seen, during the first hundred years of colonial rule, poor land administrative practices led to the destruction of most of these forest habitats along with the dependent fauna.

In the late 18th century Chinese clan wars in the Riau Islands forced some Teochew planters to flee to Singapore Island. They most likely settled in remote river estuaries, such as that of Sungei Seletar as well as close to the mouth of the Singapore River, which was nothing more than a primitive trading post at the time. These Teochew planters continued the only occupation they knew—gambier and pepper planting. As such, 20 gambier plantations existed in Singapore at the time of Raffles arrival in 1819. This

---

[2] T.C. Whitmore, *Tropical Rain Forests of the Far East* (New York: Oxford University Press, 1984).

[3] *Sonneratia* species were sought after for use in struts in boat construction, while *Rhizophora apiculata* is preferred for charcoal production.

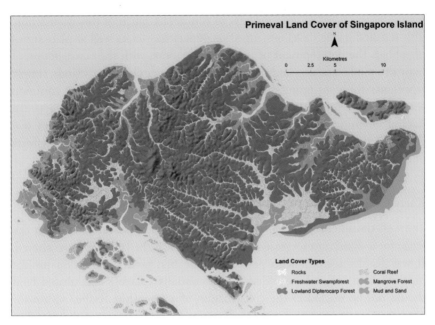

Figure 1.1 Primeval vegetation of Singapore

number is unlikely to have included plantations in remote parts of the island that escaped official attention until as late as 1846, when one such plantation was discovered accidentally along a branch of the Sungei Seletar.[4]

The presence of small settlements in the swampy coastal areas of an island largely covered in dipterocarp forest, however, caused little change in the vegetative cover of Singapore. This would largely occur with the arrival of British imperial rule in the early 19th century. This chapter will trace the changes that Singaporean vegetation has undergone since approximately 1800. The massive deforestation of the landscape for plantations characterizes the first of these periods. This was followed in the late 19th century by a period during which the colonial government attempted to develop

---

[4] James C. Jackson, "Chinese Agricultural Pioneering in Singapore and Johore, 1800–1917," *Journal of the Malayan Branch of the Royal Asiatic Society* 38 (1965): 77–82; K.W. Pitt, "From Plantations to New Town: The Story of Nee Soon," in *The Development of the Nee Soon Community*, ed. L.G. Lim How Seng (Singapore: The Grassroots Organisations of Nee Soon Community and National Archives, Oral History Department, 1987), pp. 193–225.

nature reserves and water reservoirs to counteract much of this destruction. This resulted in the development of secondary forests, as well as plantations of rubber. The development of modern Singapore, with the construction of high-rise public housing and movement into former plantations lands, simply represents the continuing transformation of the landscape. The common theme for the past 200 years, thus, is constant change. The Singaporean natural environment has been both preserved and transformed, and will continue to transform, from an imagined pristine state through the efforts of man.

Early Colonial Influence on Vegetation

The well-documented arrival of Sir Stamford Raffles arrival in 1819 set the scene for a significant increase in the rate at which the landscape was altered. It was Raffles himself who performed the first land reclamation project on the island, when he decided that potentially valuable agricultural land should not be wasted in the construction of a township. Raffles' vision for Singapore was not only as a tax free port and establishment of the island as a trading hub. He was also interested in developing other economic activities as were already in progress in Penang where sugar cane and other crops were established and considered successful. He ordered that excavated soil from a nearby hill be used to fill nearby mangrove swamps.[5]

Spices, particularly nutmeg and mace, cloves, and pepper, had been the cornerstone of most European trade in Southeast Asia up to that time, and had fueled much of the British-Dutch rivalry in the region over the previous two centuries.[6] Merchants and administrators in the English East India Company in the early 19th century were keen to establish commercial plantations within their holdings to gain better control over the trade. As part of these efforts, Raffles established experimental botanical gardens of nutmeg and cloves next to his residence at Fort Canning in 1819. Subsequently, well-off British and Chinese residents planted nutmeg plantations near the town. These plantations thrived for the next 40 years, until an infestation of parasites wiped them out in the 1850s and 1860s. The early failure of the

---

[5] Munshi Abdullah, *The Autobiography of Munshi Abdullah*, trans. W.G. Shellabear (Singapore: Methodist Publishing House, 1918), pp. 142–3.
[6] For an accessible history of this period, see Giles Milton, *Nathaniel's Nutmeg: How One Man's Courage Changed the Course of History* (London: Hodder and Stoughton, 1999).

nutmeg crop meant that it did not have a substantial impact on the total native vegetation coverage of the island, as the plantations were within the extent of the municipality.[7]

The early Teochew immigrants (Chaozhou people, a dialect group originating from Chaoshan in eastern Guangdong Province, southern China) not only brought their agricultural practices to Singapore in the late 1700s, but also their "*kangchu*" system of social organization, which would influence how the landscape was exploited over the first century of colonial rule. The fundamental unit of organization was the "*kangkar*," the riverine village headquarters for the *kangchu* (head man). The typical *kangkar* village consisted of substantial central buildings essentially comprising the *kangchu*'s residence and operational center, around which were scattered shops and stores, often including an opium den and gambling house. Radiating out from these villages were pigsties, vegetable farms, and orchards. Traces of this land tenure system remain to this day in the names of various localities in Singapore. Places such as Lim Chu Kang, Yio Chu Kang, and Choa Chu Kang ("*chu kang*" meaning "river owner" in Teochew) are geographic markers for these gambier production centers of the 1800s.

The *kangkar* contained a number of *bangsals*, which were areas cleared and usually cultivated with gambier and pepper, and also included the processing facilities and "coolie lines" (accommodation). Typically, nine or ten men would work a single *bangsal* in what we might today call a share-farming arrangement. As *bangsals* became depleted after 15–25 years, the planters moved outward within the *kangkar* to establish new *bangsals*, leaving the abandoned areas to revert to *belukar* (secondary forest) and *lalang* grass.[8]

Rivers and streams were the main avenues for moving into interior Singapore in the early decades of colonial rule, as roads to Bukit Timah, Kranji, Serangoon, and Seletar were only established several decades after 1819. Reliance on river transport meant *kangkars* were close to navigable river systems and were typically located at the point of tidal influence. This inevitably meant that the development of these remote areas began along the rivers, expanding outward from the central village. An added advantage of these intertidal locations would have been the ready supply of

---

[7] Thomas Oxley, "Some Account of the Nutmeg and its Cultivation," *Journal of the Indian Archipelago and Eastern Asia* 2, 10 (1848): 641–60.
[8] James C. Jackson, "Chinese Agricultural Pioneering in Singapore and Johore, 1800–1917," *Journal of the Malayan Branch of the Royal Asiatic Society* 38 (1965): 77–82.

the back mangrove palm *Nypa fruticans*, the Nipah palm, fronds of which were commonly used for roof thatching, while other parts of the palm were harvested for other domestic uses. Hence, for many years after the arrival of Raffles, remote areas were accessible only via navigable waterways. As the road system became established, *kangkars* were found in inland areas devoid of the opportunity for river navigation. An example of this phenomenon is Bu Ko Kang, which covered an area between the Bukit Timah and Seletar Roads during the latter half of the 19th century.[9]

Gambier and pepper were typically grown together on these *bangsals* for crop management reasons since neither was economically viable in its own right. Although pepper was lucrative, it was seasonal and thus did not require workers to be constantly on hand. In contrast, gambier required almost continuous attention, so this crop ensured that a workforce was onsite when occasionally needed for the harvesting or maintenance of the pepper vines. Additionally, the waste runoff from the gambier-boiling process provided fertilizer for the pepper plants. After a period of 15–20 years, the gambier and the pepper crops would exhaust the nutrients in the soil and would start to decline. At this point, the plantation would be abandoned and fresh land would be cleared to continue the activity. As such, gambier and pepper plantations practiced what we would describe today as method of shifting agriculture.

By the late 19th century, the great majority of gambier and pepper plantations were concentrated in northern and western Singapore, mainly due to better soil conditions. Neither crop could thrive in ponded water (swampy ground) nor on steep hillsides or at altitudes greater than 200–300 feet (61–91 meters).[10] This explains their relative absence from eastern Singapore as well as the retention of native forest stands on hilltops in the hilly central part of Singapore Island. The crop also would not have been planted within the swampy lands of alluvial streams; for this reason, some retention of riverine and swampy forest along certain streams is evident even today, though some of these were eventually converted for vegetable and fish farming. Further evidence that gambier was not planted within swampy areas

---

[9] Shawn Lum and Ilsa Sharp, *A View from the Summit: The Story of Bukit Timah Nature Reserve* (Singapore: Nanyang Technological University and the National University of Singapore, 1996); Peter K.L. Ng and N. Sivasothi, eds., *A Guide to the Mangroves of Singapore, Volume 1: The Ecosystem and Plant Diversity* (Singapore: Singapore Science Centre, 1999).

[10] Henry N. Ridley, *Spices* (London: Macmillan, 1912), pp. 254–7.

is obtained from the *Annual Reports of the Forest Department*, in which H.N. Ridley reports that in 1889 the interior forest reserves, such as Ang Moh Kio and Sembawang, still contained "good swampy forest."[11] This also explains the existence of primary forest on hilltops and within many of the swampy streams of the Central Catchment Nature Reserve in modern Singapore.

Both gambier and pepper are destructive in the sense that they require huge amounts of timber to process (see Table 1.1). Gambier involved the constant boiling of the leaves, while pepper required kiln drying; this resulted in the destruction of surrounding forests for firewood. These crops also denuded the ancient and leached soils of their nutrients resulting in the practice of shifting agriculture leaving in its wake total destruction of forest. Timber resources within the confines of any *bangsal* commonly were fully consumed during the time that it was occupied.

In a report submitted in 1883, the Superintendent of the Botanic Gardens, Nathaniel Cantley, reported that a typical *bangsal* consumed approximately 2,500 pounds of timber each day in pepper kilns as well as for boiling gambier. Based on these very approximate calculations, we are able to validate the anecdotal estimate that a *bangsal* consumed an area equal to that planted with gambier and pepper for the purpose of firewood. In fact, this is probably a very forgiving estimate as it is not known if the stakes were obtained from timber originally cleared for the *bangsal* or if that original clearing had been completely burned, and stakes taken from surrounding forest—an even more destructive scenario. Little is known about the fate of the saleable timber felled for gambier plantations. Alfred Russel Wallace mentions the presence of Chinese timber cutters in the Bukit Timah and Bukit Panjang areas when he stayed at the Jesuit mission on Bukit Timah Road, and Ridley mentions in his notes that the timber being cut was sold in China where it was considered scarce.[12] We also learn from the papers of the day that woodcutters were active in whatever jungles remained during the 1800s and that this was a distinct industry from the gambier plantations. It is, therefore, possible that some of the lands cleared for gambier could have been previously logged for valuable timber species within reason of accessibility.[13] Based on estimates, an original clearing removed approximately 7,000 cu

---

[11] H.N. Ridley, "Annual Report of the Forest Department" (1889).

[12] H.N. Ridley Notebook HNR-3-2-2, p. 187. Much of the material on Ridley in this chapter is taken from his personal notebooks, labeled "HNR," which can be accessed at the Library of the Singapore Botanic Gardens.

[13] "Decrease of Rigers," *The Straits Times*, 16 Apr. 1864, p. 1.

Table 1.1 Estimates of amount of forest cover needed for gambier and pepper
production

Estimate volume of timber in 1 ha of dipterocarp forest	Average tree diameter: 1.5 m DBH Average Tree Height: 20 m PI* R* R* H = 11 cu m / tree Average number of trees per hectare: 20	**220 cu meters / hectare**
Estimate timber required for stakes in a 30 ha *bangsal*	1 Stake: 20 cm x 20 cm x 4 m = 0.15 cu m 400 Stakes: @ 5 m spacing over 1 ha = 64 cu m	**1,920 cu meters**
Estimate timber usage for firewood over 15 years within a 30 ha *bangsal*	Usage at 2,500 lbs/day = 1.4 cu m / day 15 years * 365 * 1.4 = 7,665 cu meters	**7,665 cu meters**
Estimate amount of forest required for firewood and stakes	(7,665 cu m + 1,920 cu m)/220 cu m / ha	**43.6 ha**

meters of timber of which 2,000 cu meters was required for stakes upon
which gambier and pepper were grown; the remaining 5,000 cu meters was
either sold or burned; and, for the 15 years a gambier and pepper plantation
operated, there was a demand for almost 8,000 cu meters of fuel, which the
surrounding forest supplied.

The destructive nature of gambier and pepper planting became clear to
residents of Singapore by the 1840s. In an article published in 1843 in the
Singapore Free Press and Mercantile Advertiser, which deserves to be quoted
in length, Halbert Eestalrig criticized the government land occupation policy
and agricultural system as follows:

> … behind Bukit Tassie [Province Wellesley] and at other places great
> plains covered with lalang and studded at intervals with weather-
> beaten lifeless trunks of trees exhibit the natural results of free and
> unconditional occupation. In Singapore the same course has from the
> first been allowed and is now in operation over a larger surface than was
> ever abandoned to this destructive system in the northern settlement.
> The greater part of the lands in the vicinity of the town were, soon after
> the establishment of Singapore, occupied by Chinese gambier and pepper
> planters who with an indifference, on the part of the local authorities to
> a practical evil under their eyes with which is strangely out of keeping

with the industry with which regulations have been coined, clipped, and recast, have been always allowed to take procession of as much forest land as they chose, without the slightest acknowledgment of the proprietary right of the Government. The general mode in which these planters proceed is gradually to withdraw labour from their plantations as the plants from increasing age lose their luxuriance. The lalang which so long as the plantation is in its prime is repressed with some care rapidly gains upon the gambier and is at last suffered to choke it. Before the squatter has ceased to gather the feeble foliage of the worn out plants he has already opened a fresh location in the jungle, and the former scene of his labours is abandoned to the dominion of the lalang which with the old gambier plants forms an excellent tiger cover. Hence when the European capitalists sought localities accessible by public roads for space for plantations they were obliged to be satisfied with the scourged and rejected lalang grounds which marked the wake of the Chinese who made them pay large sums to relinquish their pretended possessory rights. Large tracts of land in this state may be seen to the west of the town [Tanglin]. The interior of the public forests when explored exhibits a succession of gambier and pepper fields scattered throughout the jungle many already abandoned and all progressing to the same useless and noxious condition ... The quantity of ground that has undergone or is undergoing this process cannot be estimated under 50,000 acres. The evil does not simply consist in the exhaustion of the soil but in the serious bar that is placed in the way of really useful planters who are desirous of extending permanent cultivation by the heavy outlay required to extirpate the lalang. This according to the texture of the soil is between thirty and forty dollars an acre and it is an expenditure of absolute necessity for not an inch of lalang root can be safely left.[14]

As gambier plantations expanded throughout the island, clearing of forest rapidly reduced the available habitat for native fauna, many of which depended on the forest habitat for survival. As a result, some species became extinct. An example is the Oriental Pied Hornbill (*Anthracoceros albirostris*), which is reliant on native forest fruits such as nutmegs and became extinct in Singapore during the late 19th century. Other species such as deer, colugo, and porcupine managed to hang on in small numbers of remaining small patches of forest. The banded leaf monkey (*Presbytis femoralis femoralis*) is another example where a very small number remained confined within forest reserves that became part of the Central Catchment

---

[14] Halbert Eestalrig, "Notes in the Straits," *The Singapore Free Press and Mercantile Advertiser*, 28 Sep. 1843, p. 3.

Nature Reserve.[15] Some species, such as wild pig (*Sus scrofa*), adapted to the new order with their numbers increasing during the gambier period to the extent that they became a nuisance to the gambier planters. No doubt the opening up of jungle and planting of vegetables about the *bangsals* provided extra foraging opportunities for these animals. Gambier planters actively trapped and hunted pigs in an attempt to control their numbers.

Tigers also adapted to the new situation. No longer able to obtain sufficient food within the small patches of remaining natural habitat, these animals turned to predating on domestic livestock, dogs and most famously human beings, and it was during the 19th century that Singapore became famous for its tigers. They were thought to visit Singapore from Johor by way of the intermediate islands of Pulau Ubin and Pulau Tekong and reaching the main island via the sandy shores that are interspersed between mangrove swamps between Punggol and Changi. Henry Ridley is credited with reporting that the tigers came to Singapore for breeding and that cubs were produced in the early part of the year. Their favorite locations were the slopes of Bukit Timah Hill, as well as the sandy forests of Changi. These tigers remained on the island until April by which time their food sources would be depleted and the family would scatter, roaming about Singapore or if the young were old enough, swim back across the Johor Straits.[16] An analysis of the geographic extent of tiger incidents as reported in the daily newspapers, however, indicates that it is likely that a population of tigers did exist on the island and that their distribution was homogeneous; this is apparent from the records of Pasir Panjang, Bukit Timah, Seletar, Chua Chu Kang, and Pandan from which tiger incidents are recorded over the majority of the 19th century. It is also noteworthy that these localities retained some of the larger patches of retained forest, much of which were included in the Forest Reserves in the later 1800s. There is not a remarkable preference among tigers for Bukit Timah or Changi from these records.

It was their predation of humans that caught the attention of the citizens, leading to exaggerated reports that a tiger killed a person every day in 19th-century Singapore (see Figure 1.3). Based on newspaper accounts, it is interesting that the highest rate of human casualty was during the peak

---

[15] While these species may still be found in the nature reserves today, it is with a substantially degraded genetic legacy. A. Ang, et al., "Low genetic variability in the recovering urban banded leaf monkey population of Singapore," *The Raffles Bulletin of Zoology* 60, 2 (2012): 589–94.

[16] H.N. Ridley, "The Mammals of the Malay Peninsula," *Natural Science* 6, 35–37 (Feb. 1895): 89–91.

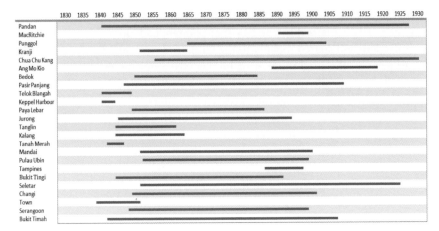

Figure 1.2 Geographic distribution of tiger incidents between 1840 and 1930 (based on newspaper accounts)[17]

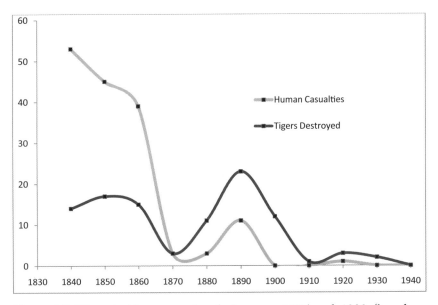

Figure 1.3 Tiger incidents per decade between 1835 and 1930 (based on newspaper accounts)

[17] NewspaperSG (http://newspapers.nl.sg/) is a digital archive of newspapers between 1831 and 2009 provided by the National Library of Singapore.

period of gambier and pepper planting. The falloff in human deaths after 1870 may be partly explained by the fact that planters had almost run out of land in Singapore and started moving to the virgin soils of Johor. By the end of the "tiger period," the total number of human casualties reported in the papers was 145 deaths while the number of tigers killed is only 99. Even if the ratio of 5:1 is applied to the highest incidence of reported human casualties in a year, we get nowhere near the reported value of 365, pointing toward a mythic role tigers played in the first century of colonial rule in Singapore.[18]

In his excellent study of early agriculture in Singapore, James Jackson reports that toward the end of the gambier era, timber resources had declined to such an extent that it was difficult to find even the simple stakes needed for growing gambier and pepper vines.[19] This was one of the reasons for the eventual decline of these crops in Singapore, as well as a reduction in native fauna, such as tigers. There were, of course, other reasons for the decline of gambier plantations, including the colonial government's move in the mid-1850s to enforce a land title system, which made shifting cultivation more difficult, as well as the falling price of the crop. Gambier, and the important role it played in shaping the Singaporean landscape, had passed. The land was exhausted and almost completely deforested. The total amount of land under gambier cultivation continued to drop throughout the rest of the 19th century. By the late 1800s, gambier and pepper plantations were concentrated in the north and west, and two significant *kangkars*—Yio Chu Kang and Chan Chu Kang—were devoid of gambier and pepper *bangsals*. Ang Mo Kio was covered with vegetable farms and fruit orchids. By 1910, less than 1,000 acres (404 ha) of land in Singapore was under gambier cultivation.[20]

Government Intervention in the Landscape

In search of more timber and fresh soil, planters of gambier and pepper in the second half of the 19th century moved to Johor, where they continued their agricultural activities under the instrument of a "*surat sungei*" (river

---

[18] John Cameron, *Our Tropical Possessions in Malayan India: Being a Descriptive Account of Singapore, Penang, Province Wellesley, and Malacca; Their Peoples, Products, Commerce, and Government* (London: Smith, Elder, 1865), p. 106; See also Timothy P. Barnard and Mark Emmanuel's contribution to this volume.

[19] James C. Jackson, "Chinese Agricultural Pioneering in Singapore and Johore, 1800–1917," *Journal of the Malayan Branch of the Royal Asiatic Society* 38 (1965): 77–82.

[20] Ibid.

letter), documents officially from the Johor ruler entitling them to occupy and develop the inland areas of the southern reaches of the Malay Peninsula. Here they continued with their *kangchu* system with river systems remaining the principle channel of communication for transport of produce to market as well as the import of materials and consumables not available within the *kangkar*.[21]

In Singapore, the land and soil were exhausted by the mid-18th century. Realization of the problem first arose in the 1840s when Europeans began venturing to Bukit Timah to visit the highest point in Singapore. To reach the hill, they traveled through deforested countryside. To counter the destructive nature of the Chinese agricultural practices, the government reserved the hill, albeit with no distinct boundary set aside, for "climatic purposes." At the same time, a road was established to the summit of Bukit Timah and soon after that a government bungalow was built at the summit.[22] Despite these initial concerns, little else was done to counter the loss of forest and vegetation for several decades.

In the late 1870s, the government of the Straits Settlements began to look into the state of the natural forests. At this time, the Colonial Secretary instructed J.F.A. McNair—Colonial Engineer and Surveyor-General for the Straits Settlements—to furnish a report on the principle forest trees indigenous to the Straits Settlements and Native States of the Malayan Peninsula.[23] The report that McNair submitted on 21 June 1879 was divided into two sections. Section A consisted of a table detailing the known species of forest trees and providing native name, botanical name, geographic context, dimensions, growth rate, value, abundance and other pertinent remarks about subjects such as strength and use. Section B provided specific answers to questions the Colonial Secretary posed (see Table 1.2).

McNair's report provided the wake-up call for the government whose inaction to date had resulted in almost complete destruction of the native forests in Singapore. As a result, Governor Sir F.A. Weld commissioned

---

[21] Carl Trocki, *Prince of Pirates: The Temenggongs and the Development of Johor and Singapore, 1784–1885* (Singapore: NUS Press, 2007).

[22] See John van Wyhe's contribution to this collection for more details on this era, and the Bukit Timah region.

[23] Report by the Colonial Engineer on the Timber Forests in the Malayan Peninsula; J.F.A McNair, Colonial Engineer and Surveyor-General, Straits Settlements. Correspondence of the Colonial Engineers office, Singapore 21st June 1879. An accessible copy of this report may be found appended (E1) to Nathanial Cantley's report on the Forests of the Straits Settlements.

Table 1.2 Return B of McNair's 1879 Report

#	Secretary's Question	McNair's Answer
I	What are the kinds of timber trees produced in the country and to what uses are they generally applied? (state botanical name where known)	Vide Return A.
II	Are the forests or lands producing the trees owned by the Government or by private persons?	Owned by Government chiefly.
III	What is the approximate extent of timber-producing for land at the present time?	acres In Singapore 22,000 In Penang and P. Wellesley 130,000 In Malacca 45,000
IV	Is this area increasing or diminishing?	Diminishing.
V	If diminishing from what causes?	From the sale of land and extension of cultivation and too often from illicit felling, and from charcoal burning.
VI	Are any steps taken for the prevention of waste or for the re-planting any area which has been cleared?	The Government has one forest ranger at Singapore and two at Penang, and frequently men are brought before the police and punished for felling trees on Government land, but no steps are taken to re-plant any area with fresh trees which has been cleared. The Eucalyptus and Acacia of Australia are being tried at Singapore on a small scale.
VII	What is the quantity of timber which might fairly be cut every year without permanent injury to the forests?	The Government can spare no more in either of the settlements. At Singapore a reserve is kept round the principle hill for climatic purposes, and at Penang, Province Wellesley and Malacca there are also belts reserved for the same purpose, but it is feared that trees are often felled by Chinese, for want of a larger staff for supervision.
VIII	What is the quantity actually cut every year?	It is impossible to say.

Table 1.2 (continued)

#	Secretary's Question	McNair's Answer
IX	What is the proportion for home consumption and for export?	None for export; mangrove is used for firewood, of which there is an abundant supply, but all timbers for building purposes are imported into the settlements. Mangrove bark is exported to a limited extent.
X	What have been the annual exports of each kind of timber during the past ten years; stating the proportions to each country and the value of such exports?	No exports during the last ten years.
XI	What are the reasons for, or causes of, the increase or diminution of quantity or value in the exports	Do.
XII	(If it be so) what are the causes of the small exportation in comparison with the capability of production.	Do.
XIII	Have any observations been made or conclusions arrived at as to the climatic influence of forests or the effect of their clearance on the rainfall, floods, &c.?	It is found in Singapore that although the Crown lands have been greatly denuded of trees, there has been no marked diminution in the rainfall. I attach a minute sent in by me to Government last year, when the subject was under consideration.
XIV	Forward any reports made by departments or societies, or any Acts of Legislature bearing on the subject.	There are no Acts of the Legislature bearing on this subject, but there can be no doubt that it would be desirable that there should be attachéd to the Land Department, a small Forestry Department, for the purpose of preserving our reserves, and restoring our forest by the establishment of nurseries for young trees.

Nathaniel Cantley to prepare a report on the Crown Forests of the Colony, and to make recommendations for the creation of a Department for their preservation. Cantley had arrived in Singapore in 1880; however he fell ill and returned to England for recuperation.[24] It was not until 1882 that he was able to undertake a tour of the various districts comprised within the Straits Settlements. Cantley finished the report in late 1883 and, with respect to the state of forests in Singapore, he was quite scathing:

> It is apparent that no sufficient attempts have been made to conserve the Government forest lands, and that nothing has been done towards utilizing the extensive grass wastes that are to be seen throughout the settlements. The present state of affairs is the result of reckless, migratory cultivation carried on by the Chinese, and this extensive deforestation has brought with it its attendant evils. Our timber supply has fallen far short of the demand, and the climate of the colony is becoming sensibly affected ...
>
> It has been said that, at home as well as in their colonies, other nations pay earlier attention to the conservation of forests, than the English; and it is hard to conceive a more short-sighted policy than that which has suffered these Settlements to drift into their present condition of scarcity of forest and forest produce.[25]

To support these assertions, Cantley provided detailed descriptions of the state of the forests in Singapore. He described an island on which the remaining uncut forests were widely distributed in isolated patches. These forest patches were of various sizes from one-half acre to approximately 25 acres in size and of no particular shape. The distance between forest patches averaged ¼ mile (½ km) and often exceeded one mile (1.6 km). Cantley described the areas between these forest patches as wasteland containing mainly *lalang* grass; and, it is clear that these lands were former gambier plantations.

Cantley made nine recommendations at the end of his report (see Table 1.3). The government wasted no time in implementing these recommendations, and by 1884 had established the Forestry Department under Cantley's leadership. As part of these actions, officials were appointed to oversee the forests of Penang, Malacca, and Singapore (D.C. Young was the

---

[24] Walter Fox, "Report on the Gardens and Forests Department, Straits Settlements, For the Year 1894;" for more on Cantley, see Nigel P. Taylor's contribution to this volume.

[25] Nathaniel Cantley, *Report on the Forests of the Straits Settlements* (Singapore: Government Printing Office, 1883).

Table 1.3 Cantley's recommendations for forest lands in the Straits
Settlements (1883)

* Preventing the felling of forest and the clearing of forest lands.
* The redemption, by exchange or otherwise, of such land as is selected for planting with forest trees.
* The survey and demarcation of such Crown forest lands as are still undetermined, and the preparation of good and reliable maps shewing [*sic*] the forests and topographical features of the various lands throughout the settlements. This is a desideratum that should be looked upon as a first duty of the Survey Department.
* The formation of local forest reserves for the supply of wood and general purposes; and mountain and river reserves for protection where necessary.
* The establishment of a Forest Department to take charge of all Crown Forests whether proclaimed as reserves or otherwise.
* The marking out of certain blocks of forest near the chief towns of each settlement of a sufficient size to serve as reserves for the supply of fuel and small building wood.
* The appointment of a body of Forest Guards for protective purposes, to be quartered in the country districts throughout the Settlements.
* The immediate collection of seeds of the best indigenous timber trees, and the formation of nurseries for the propagation of such seeds.
* The introduction of an ordinance for better conservation of the Crown Forests.

first overseer of the Singapore forests). Each of these executives supervised subordinate staff who oversaw the work of forest watchmen and laborers engaged in forest work. Forest watchmen were established as a body separate from ordinary employees; they were assigned uniforms and their chief duties were to patrol the forest reserves to protect them from illegal harvesting and to keep open the boundary paths. Laborers, also known as coolies, were employed in numbers ranging from 200–600 throughout the year depending on the demands of projects being undertaken. Typically, these laborers marked and cleared boundary paths in the reserves, and constructed bridges over streams and swamps. They were also engaged in replanting native species into the *lalang* infested former gambier lands that were included within the forest reserves.

Forest reserves were delineated such that they included as many of the remaining patches of primary forest as possible, and as a result also included areas of land that were previously planted with gambier that lay between the target forested areas. These forest patches were only to be found on hilltops toward the center of the island and likely were left due to difficulty of access for gambier planters as well as timber collectors. For mangrove areas, the reserves were demarcated about the tidal reaches of the major river systems—Pandan, Jurong, Seletar, Serengoon, and Kranji.

During these initial efforts, Cantley classified the forest reserves in Singapore into three categories. The first of these categories was "Town Reserves," which were located at Bukit Timah, Pandan, and Military; the second category was "Coastal Reserves," which were located at Blukang, Murai, Kranji, Seletar, Changi, and Jurong; and, the final category was "Interior Reserves," located at Sembawang, Bukit Mandai, Chua Chu Kang, Bukit Panjang, and Ang Mo Kio. These forest reserves, particularly the interior ones, were demarcated to include significant patches of primary forest; however they were also known to contain substantial areas of brushwood and *lalang*, indicating that they were previously under gambier cultivation. Based on surveys conducted for the 1889 *Annual Report of the Forestry Department*, we are able to determine estimates of timber, brushwood, and *lalang* for each of the forest reserves as follows:

Table 1.4 Summary of forest reserves in 1889, forest cover, and classification[26]

Forest Reserve	Total Area (ha)	Timber (ha)	Brush- wood (ha)	Lalang and Fern (ha)	FR Type
Blukang	612.7	566.6	46.1	0	Coastal
Murai	127.2	121.4	5.8	0	Coastal
Kranji	301.9	226.5	2.5	72.9	Coastal
Seletar	603.9	404.7	0	199.2	Coastal
Ang Mo Kio	117.5	81.0	0	36.5	Interior
Changi	563.8	364.3	0	199.5	Coastal
Bukit Panjang	47.5	7.0	0	40.5	Interior
Military	44.1	13.8	23.8	6.5	Town
Chua Chu Kang	329.3	81	81	167.3	Interior
Bukit Mandai	164.7	40.5	81	43.2	Interior
Sembawang	378.8	153	40.5	185.3	Interior
Bukit Timah	342.4	121.5	88.2	132.7	Town
Pandan	874.9	291.4	17	566.5	Town
Jurong	166.7	55.4	42.9	68.4	Coastal

[26] H.N. Ridley, *Annual Report of the Forestry Department* (Singapore: Government Printing Office, 1890).

The area of Forest Reserves was eight percent of total land area of the main island, which was approximately 54,000 ha at this time. Or, to look at it another way, after half a century of gambier cultivation, 90 percent of the forest cover of Singapore was gone. The late action by the Straits Government in establishing forest reserves was truly a case of closing the stable door after the horse had bolted. By this time, *lalang* (*Impertina cylindrica*) and brushwood, which was made up mainly of species such as *tiup tiup* (*Adinandra dumosa*) and silverback (*Rhodamnia cinerea*), both of which can survive on the denuded soils that covered abandoned gambier lands.

Henry Norman Ridley replaced Nathanial Cantley when the latter passed away in 1887. Although he later became famous for his role in establishing the rubber industry in Malaya, Ridley was occupied in his early years in Singapore with getting the forest reserves in order and this involved clearing and establishing their boundaries. It was early in his tenure as Director of Singapore Botanic Gardens and Forest Department that Ridley discovered that many of the forest reserve boundaries had been incorrectly laid out and much time, energy, and cost was expended in putting them right. In some cases, the corrected boundaries passed through Chinese gardens (small plantations typically consisting of pepper and other plants of commercial value) and occasionally houses, thus requiring the eviction of the occupants. Ridley's approach was to implement what was known as the "Dutch Plan" where the encroaching garden or plantation was allowed to remain with the payment of some quit rent and responsibility to plant and maintain seedlings of forest tree species until the crop had matured and was harvested. By that time—usually two or three years later—the seedlings had grown enough to survive competition from weeds and vermin.[27] Ultimately, the Land Officer, who pointed out to the government that he alone had the right to collect rents, foiled this pragmatic plan to reestablish cleared forest about the margins of the reserves. The Chinese planters apparently did not think much of the Land Office, and promptly abandoned the land resulting in the loss of seedlings due to lack of maintenance.[28]

In managing the Forest Department, Ridley took the time to investigate the nature of the timber industry at that time and fully understood the true value of native forest species, as well as the ability of contractors to pay, and had set prices accordingly. Most timber sales transactions were for

[27] H.N. Ridley Notebook (HNR-3-2-2), p. 194.
[28] Ibid., p. 196.

firewood, which came from the *bakau* timbers of the mangrove reserves. The growing population of Singapore placed high demands on this wood for charcoal production for cooking. Ridley, thus, allocated *coups* (logging areas) and issued passes at the rate of 27 dollars per man per day to manage the mangrove reserves. After harvesting, each coup was allowed to recover for several years, thus ensuring continued supply into the future. This is probably one of the earliest recorded instances of sustainable harvesting.[29]

The mangrove forest reserves were not the only source of firewood and neither was firewood the only purpose to which mangrove timbers were put. *Bakau* timber was also obtained from areas that were under the control of the Lands Office (that is, crown lands not gazetted as forest reserves). The Lands Office, which issued firewood passes for one dollar per man per day, did not ensure that the harvesting was sustainable, thus undermining the program that Ridley had installed. In one case, Ridley recalls how a boat builder applied for a pass to cut timber. Curious as to the reason that a boat builder would be interested in firewood, Ridley questioned the applicant and determined that *perapat* (*Soneratia* species) was sought after as struts for boat-building. Ridley refused to provide a pass at firewood rates and offered an alternate rate based on his assessment that any single six-foot length of Soneratia would be worth one dollar. The boat builder refused Ridley's offer as he had previously received access to forests by paying the Land Office $1 for a day pass. Subsequently, the responsibility for managing the Crown Forests was moved from the Botanic Gardens to the Collector of Land Revenue and passes to cut firewood throughout the island were issued without supervision or any regard to the sustainability. As such, by the early 20th century, all of the mangrove forests in Singapore had been exploited and only "useless" trees were left.[30]

For the interior reserves, it is evident that the primary forest patches within the catchment area remained unlogged, most likely due to the creation of a Municipal Catchment Reserve around 1900. Other internal reserves (particularly in Bukit Mandai, Sembawang, and Ang Mo Kio), which Ridley reported as containing patches of good forest,[31] were eventually logged sometime in the early 1900s. By the early 1950s, these areas can be seen to be cleared and had apparently been under cultivation for quite some time.[32]

[29] Ibid., p. 191A.
[30] Ibid., p. 190.
[31] *Annual Reports of the Forest Department*, 1889.
[32] National Archives Aerial Photography 1951–1955.

In addition to the Forest Reserves, there were also "private forests," or rather land leased from the government that contained saleable timber. The Land Office administered these lands and whatever private forest remained untouched by gambier and pepper plantations soon succumbed to exploitation due to the lack of appreciation of either the value of timber resources on lands under their care or the need to manage these resources in a sustainable way. Ridley recounts a notable case where the last remains of the valuable *Tampinis* (*Streblus elongates*) forest at Tampines (a locality named after the prominent forest tree growing in the area) were completely harvested after being leased at normal rates by the Land Office.[33] Several years prior to the incident, Ridley requested that this particular patch of forest be added to the Forest Reserves so that the Forest Department could manage it. The government, however, refused his request. Many years later, a group of Malays applied for the land in question for the purpose of growing vegetables—an unlikely purpose due to the location of the land. The Land Office issued the lease, and subsequently the *Tempines* and all other trees of value were harvested and sold for a very large sum of money. The Land Office was paid its dues of a few hundred dollars and the land was promptly abandoned. This scenario was repeated many times over the island resulting in almost complete loss of forest cover except for that which remained within the Municipal Catchment, Bukit Timah Forest Reserve, and some mangrove areas, particularly in the Pandan Forest Reserve.

The deforestation of the island led to several problems, most prominent among them was fire. Large areas of abandoned gambier and pepper plantations overgrown with *lalang* and brushwood often caught fire. Managing these fires became a substantial challenge in the years to come; various issues of *Annual Report of the Forestry Department* are littered with reports of damage. Through experimentation, Ridley showed that species such as *Syzygium grande*—a species often found to dominate coastal edge forests— and *Gluta Rengas*, a dense grained native forest species, were well suited to establishing fire breaks as they grew quickly in the open *lalang* country and produced sufficiently dense crowns so as to shade out the invasive grass. The *lalang* would die under the poorer light conditions within the firebreaks and, as such, uncontrolled fires were less likely to spread into the forest reserves. Today there are substantial amounts of *Syzygium grande* about the edges of the old forest reserves in Singapore; however, little evidence remains of the *Gluta rengas* plantings or their progeny.

---

[33] H.N. Ridley Notebook (HNR-3-2-2), p. 190.

By the late 1800s, the Straits Government was in a dilemma—hundreds of square kilometers of wasteland covered in *lalang* and brushwood with no prospect of any economic return from it. Indeed it had become common knowledge that nothing could be grown on the denuded soils of Singapore Island. Ultimately, the return of these lands to productive agriculture came in two forms; the establishment of tapioca and Liberian coffee as viable crops under the efforts of Leopold Chasseriau; and, the promotion and establishment of para rubber (*Hevia braziliensis*), under the supervision of Ridley, as a viable crop through development of a sustainable latex harvesting technique.

Leopold Chasseriau was originally a successful planter in Province Wellesley, where he managed the Malakoff plantation and made a small fortune through the successful cultivation of sugar cane. He returned to France, where he invested in vineyards only to have crop failures thwart his efforts. In 1872, he returned to Asia and purchased 200 acres of land near Bukit Tinggi (near Swiss Club Road in modern Singapore). Chasseriau declared his intention to take up tapioca farming. As many of the famous early planters of Singapore—ranging from Joseph Balestier and Jose d'Almeida and their sugar plantations to C.H. Prinsep and Thomas Oxley with their nutmeg ventures—had lost fortunes, it is of little surprise that the community did not show much enthusiasm in this project. Nevertheless, the government of the Straits Settlements welcomed Chasseriau, allowing him to directly purchase the land and to cultivate the adjoining lands under a 999-year lease agreement devoid of a quit rent. Conditions addressing the water catchment needs, however, were attached to this lease that addressed the water quality needs of MacRitchie Reservoir. Chasseriau, for example, was not allowed to clear or cultivate land within 50 yards of certain streams. Although the lease failed to protect the streams that were later to feed the Kalang Reservoir (completed in 1911), Chasseriau is known to have magnanimously offered to keep those Kalang basin streams in original vegetated state in return for the grant of a further 41.15 acres of land adjoining his current holdings.[34]

A report in the *Straits Times Overland Journal* in 1879 described the Chasseriau Estate as comprising some 1,200 acres (485 hectares) with a

---

[34] Maxime Pilon and Danièle Weiler, *The French in Singapore: An Illustrated history (1819–Today)* (Singapore: Editions Didier Millet, 2011), pp. 81–3; Minutes of the proceedings of the Municipal Commissioners on 9 Aug. 1881 as reported in the *Daily Times*, 27 Aug. 1881.

substantial surrounding fence and employing up to 450 coolies. Production of tapioca was estimated to be 20,000 pikuls (over 1.2 million kilograms) over the next 18 months. Carts plied the numerous roads on the estate delivering manure and transporting tapioca to a mill. Much of this activity occurred on former gambier and pepper land, and is unlikely to have been due to the clearing of much virgin jungle.[35] Similar developments, in which new plantations developed over the remains of gambier and pepper plantations, played a role in maintaining agricultural productivity until the end of the colonial period. An example of such an area would be another tapioca plantation, the Trafalgar Estate in the area that the Hougang and Serangoon housing estates now cover. The only other substantial crop in the late 19th century was coconut, which proliferated in smaller estates along the coasts.

The development of the Chasseriau Estate became important for the development of the Central Catchment Nature Reserve. The retention of original forest along the streams in this area is likely due to these allowances for stream buffer as well as the fact that previous gambier and pepper planters were unlikely to have impacted the swampy streams. On the other hand, the estates' activities are also responsible for large areas of Resam fern growing on the hill slopes over the extent of the former estate. By 1884, the Chasseriau Land and Planting Company was formed to take over the Chasseriau Estate. Chasseriau was retained as the manager and he proceeded to expand into cultivation of Liberian coffee, although only relatively small areas of the estate were devoted to coffee production. By 1895, the estate had been sold to the Portuguese mission and the Bukit Timah Rubber company, and very little is known of land use within the estate up till the land was acquired for municipal catchment in 1900 and subsequently as a Nature Reserve in 1951.

Due to continued population growth, Singapore has been in the business of reservoir construction more or less continuously since 1867 when the MacRitchie Reservoir was completed. The reservoirs consumed a substantial amount of former agricultural lands as well as secondary forests and primary freshwater swamp forest. From a conservation viewpoint, the reservoirs were both a blessing and a curse. The construction of the inland reservoirs invariably led to the losses of a significant proportion of remaining

---

[35] 1852 map of Singapore Island and its Dependencies; Survey Department Plans showing gambier plantations on lands applied for lease by Leopold Chasseriau in 1872, National Archives of Singapore.

freshwater swamp forest, while on the other hand, lands reserved within their catchment areas have served a dual purpose of maintaining a suitable drinking water supply and as nature conservation zones that serve to protect the small amount of primary dipterocarp forest that exists outside of the Bukit Timah Nature Reserve as well as large tracts of mature secondary forest.

The MacRitchie Reservoir was originally known variously as the Impounding Reservoir or Thomson Reservoir (after John Turnbull Thomson) and was based on an earth embankment with construction completed in 1867. In 1891, the reservoir was extended and in 1907 renamed the Thomson Road Reservoir. Later the reservoir was again renamed "MacRitchie" in honor of James MacRitchie, the original engineer who designed and oversaw its construction. The catchment area for this reservoir was the first area in Singapore to be gazetted as municipal catchment reserve including and protecting some significant amount of primary forest that may now be seen along the MacRitchie Nature Trail. In July 1876, the government proclaimed that all crown land within the present watershed of the Impounding Reservoir as well as that within the Watershed of the Kalang Stream, in the district of Upper Kalang, would be a Government Reserve. This is an interesting proclamation because it included the lands within the Kalang River catchment, which only four years previously the government had leased to Chasseriau for the purpose of tapioca production; it is assumed that land the Chasseriau Estate occupied was not subject to this proclamation.[36]

By 1902, the Municipal Engineer R. Peirce had laid plans for two more reservoirs on the Kalang and Seletar Rivers. In 1907, tenders were called for the construction of the Kalang Reservoir, which included the clearance of swamps and was completed in 1911.[37] A number of farming communities including squatters were resettled at the time construction began. This confirms that there was agricultural activity in the area at that time. Because of delays caused by funding issues, construction of the Sungei Seletar Reservoir did not commence until 1920. The two reservoirs were renamed as "Seletar" (from "Peirce") and "Peirce" (from "Kalang") in 1922 by which time Peirce had left Singapore.

The expansion of the reservoirs often led to the destruction of freshwater swamp forest habitat. This can be seen most clearly in changes to the Sungei Seletar Reservoir since its original construction in 1920,

---

[36] Pitt, "From Plantations to New Town." In this chapter, the author uses the original spelling "Kalang."
[37] Ibid.

particularly following large expansions in 1940 and 1969. E.J.H. Corner—the longtime assistant director of the Singapore Botanic Gardens—investigated the flora of the swamp forest in 1933 at the same time as clearing work had commenced for the first expansion of this reservoir. By 1940, water inundated the plots where Corner conducted the main body of research, leaving only one partially described plot. This final plot remained intact on the north side of the old Mandai Road until the final expansion of the Sungei Seletar Reservoir between 1967 and 1969.[38]

While the reservoirs were responsible for clearing and inundation of former freshwater swamp forest habitat, they were also responsible for the conservation of a large tract of land within the watershed of the streams that feed them. In 1900, the entire catchment for the Kalang and Seletar Rivers above the dam walls became Municipal Catchment. As a result, all of the secondary and primary forest contained within its boundary was effectively protected from further development. At that time the Chan Chu Kang Forest Reserve already enclosed most of the primary forest patches remaining, and a number of streams remained untouched due to the lease conditions of the Chasseriau Estate, which were also included within the catchment reserve. The remainder of the rural areas of Singapore was in the early stages of regeneration from various agricultural activities including tapioca and Liberian coffee. In 1951, the Municipal Catchment was gazetted as a Nature Reserve, and today this area is known as the Central Catchment Nature Reserve. A comparison between 1951/55 aerial photography and current aerial photography shows that some parts of these regenerating forests of the 1900s have since developed into good 100–150-year-old secondary forest while other areas, most likely areas of most recent agricultural activity remain poorly forested and are covered with Resam or Tiup-Tiup forest.[39] It is within these mature secondary, primary, and swampy stream habitats that a

---

[38] E.J.H. Corner, "The Freshwater Swamp-Forest of South Johore and Singapore," *Gardens' Bulletin Supplement, No. 1* (Singapore: Government Printing Office, 1978). The Lower Seletar Reservoir was constructed in 1986, and consumed the mangrove habitat of Sungei Seletar downstream from the Nee Soon Village with no significant loss of freshwater swamp forest habitat.

[39] Tiup-Tiup (*Adinandra dumosa*) is able to survive on denuded soils that will not support other species; Resam fern (*Dicranopteris linearis*) is also able to grow on denuded soils and its thick mat of roots and fallen leaves stops other species from colonizing once it gets a foothold in former agricultural areas. National Archives 1951–1955 aerial photography; National Parks 2002 aerial photography.

number of native forest dependent fauna including small mammals, reptiles, and fish have managed to survive with some species considered to be now expanding their range due to the improving forest habitat.[40]

In June 1877, James Murton (first Superintendant of the Singapore Botanic Gardens) planted 20 seedlings of para rubber (*Hevea brasiliensis*) in the Singapore Botanic Gardens. By 1881, Nathanial Cantley, who had taken over from Murton, reported that the plants had grown to a height of 25 feet (8 meters) and by 1882 had commenced to fruit. Subsequently, Cantley received more seeds from the Ceylon Botanic Gardens. In 1888, Henry Ridley took over from Cantley and the para rubber trees growing in the Botanic Gardens had matured. Ridley then devoted much energy to research toward making the plant economically viable. To this end he developed cultivation methods as well as a tapping method that would not kill the tree, leading to the development of one of the most important economic crops developed in the region, and one that would transform the landscape.[41]

To promote the adoption of rubber throughout the region, Ridley oversaw the establishment of an experimental plantation in Sembawang in 1891 using seeds produced at the economic gardens adjoining the Singapore Botanic Gardens. By 1897, planters were replacing Liberian coffee with para rubber in rural areas of Singapore, and the rise of the motor car as a common means of transport in the early 1900s fuelled demand for the latex that *H. Brasiliensis* produced. Like gambier, rubber was not planted in swampy alluvial basins or mangrove swamps, as it would not thrive in such places. It is clear from topographic maps dating from the early to middle 1900s that rubber was planted on dry land only, leaving strips of unplanted land along the drainage systems where the ground was either swampy and/or subject to frequent flooding. Tracing the lines that demarcate the borders of rubber plantations alongside the streams on old maps indicates where there was swampy ground that would have been unsuitable for planting rubber. There were exceptions though, such as those on the holdings of Chew Boon Lay, a man credited as being a great entrepreneur who drained swampy land in order to cultivate rubber. No matter where it occurred, the conversion of land for rubber was rapid.

---

[40] The banded leaf monkey (*Presbytis femoralis femoralis*) is thought to be expanding its habitat having been restricted to the Nee Soon swamp forest area until a recent study found their number and range to be increasing into the adjacent mature secondary forests.

[41] Also see Nigel P. Taylor's contribution to this volume.

By 1920, two of the largest rubber plantation companies—Bukit Sembawang Rubber Company Ltd and an associated company Singapore United Rubber Plantation Ltd—were responsible for approximately 20,000 acres (8,094 ha or 81 square kilometers) of the covered landscape of Singapore.[42] Lim Nee Soon was employed as a consultant to the Bukit Sembawang Rubber Company in 1908 due to his prior experience with the crop. Lim did not remain for long in their employ, however, and soon set out on his own when he formed Lim Nee Soon & Co, which developed pineapple and rubber plantations. Lim owned plantations in the Nee Soon and Jurong areas and soon established a rubber mill at Nee Soon. Employment opportunities in the area increased and soon the small Seletar village became a significant rural center later being renamed Nee Soon Village. Lim Nee Soon was now a major landholder and community leader in the Seletar district, enjoying some influence with the Municipal government. In 1911, when the increasing population of Singapore was causing shortages of vegetables, it was Lim Nee Soon who suggested that the Crown lands in the area be opened to vegetable farming. These Crown lands were actually parts of the Seletar Forest Reserve, which covered the north and south banks of the Seletar River downstream from the main village area. His recommendation was accepted and the area became a major vegetable growing center in Singapore.[43]

The Great Depression greatly affected the rubber industry in Singapore with prices falling in response to falling demand for the commodity. The situation continued when the International Scheme of Rubber Regulation was introduced in 1934 to impose export limitations. The industry did not recover and even Lim Nee Soon sold off assets including the rubber factory at Nee Soon Village. The land that was not under rubber cultivation also fell under other types of farm production, mostly vegetable farming, or was intermixed with the rubber plantings.[44] The decline of rubber plantations, and the rise in intermixed vegetable farms, were the main characteristics of

---

[42] Anonymous, *Singapore Rubber Centenary 1877–1977* (Singapore: Rubber Centenary Committee, 1977), pp. 51–2.

[43] Pitt, "From Plantations to New Town."

[44] Cantley also made the observation in his Forests Report of 1883 that the alluvial valleys were everywhere squatted upon for the purpose of vegetable production. In later years, there are also records of aquaculture ponds being established in low-lying swampy areas (Lim & Lim, 1987). See Cynthia Chou's contribution to this volume.

the landscape of Singapore through the Japanese occupation. This would rapidly change following the move to independence and self-government in the post-Second World War era.

The region that best characterizes the development of modern Singapore is the Jurong Industrial area and Jurong Port. The construction of vast zone of industrial production, as well as housing estates, in western Singapore was an important part of the package that drew foreign investment to fledgling nation-state, allowing it to develop into the successful manufacturing and commercial center it is today. The land upon which much of this was constructed had previously been rubber estates, including those of Chew Boon Lay, as well as former forest reserve areas, which contained regenerating mangroves following intense logging during the colonial period. Besides the mangrove forest, the Jurong area was also originally rich in freshwater swamp forest habitat. By 1932, Corner noted that the last remaining stand of this habitat made way for pineapple farms.[45] Beyond these mangroves, another noteworthy habitat in western Singapore was at the head of the Jurong River, where low-lying brackish marshlands flooded with brackish water during spring high tides, making it a small ecosystem unique to the island, which would have been very rich in birdlife prior to development. This area was developed into parkland and is today known as Jurong Lake Park, and the Jurong Lake is now filled with fresh water as the Jurong River is dammed further downstream. The first phase of the Jurong Project that launched much of this change began in September 1968, reclaiming some 1,000 acres (400 hectares) of this swampland.[46]

In order to accommodate a population of sufficient size to service the manpower needs of the industrial projects, the Housing and Development Board constructed high-rise housing in New Towns throughout the island. Citizens were relocated from villages and kampungs, which were deemed to be inefficient in terms of the amount of land they occupied, into these high-rise housing estates. Most of these estates involved major earth works to flatten out hills and fill stream basins, replacing their function with concretized drains, known locally as *longkangs*. Over time, some of these *longkangs* have been converted to green natural areas like Bishan Park. Typically, these HDB estates replaced former rubber lands, degraded and

---

[45] Corner enumerated the trees shrubs and epiphytes found in this last remaining patch of freshwater swamp forest near the 15th milestone of the old Jurong Road. Corner, "The Freshwater Swamp-Forests."

[46] "$30 mil Jurong Project to Begin Soon," *The Straits Times*, 4 Sep. 1968, p. 5.

recovering mangrove habitat, and agricultural areas located in the alluvial soils that previously hosted freshwater swamp forest.

Beyond the development of industry and public housing, a significant influence on the natural habitat of Singapore since independence has been the "Garden City" plan. The origins of this program date from 1968 when the intention of the government to make Singapore a Garden City was enshrined in the Environmental Public Health Bill. Later in 1992, the Singapore Green Plan was published and represented a formal approach to balancing environmental and development needs. A comparison between aerial photography from the 1950s and modern satellite imagery covering Singapore reveals the success in implementation of the policy achieved mainly through street planting. In 1963, Prime Minister Lee Kuan Yew launched a concerted government plan, which placed more emphasis on urban areas, with a tree-planting campaign. The trees involved in these projects, which have gone by a variety of names, have mainly been exotics such as the Rain Tree and the Angsana that have been planted along roadsides. In addition, nature parks—such as Bukit Batok Nature Park, Admiralty Park, and Dairy Farm Nature Park—have been added to complement the existing small areas of Nature Reserve. This has resulted in a city that is noticeably greener than it was in the immediate postwar period.[47]

During the early years, very little consideration was given to retention of any remaining natural habitat, no matter if it was secondary forest or regenerating mangrove habitat. Industrial and residential development was considered a "do or die" activity. Today, and owing to the success of the industry of modern Singapore's forefathers, higher standards of living and educational attainment, Singaporeans are more conscious of their natural surroundings and as a result are more vocal and demanding in asking that such areas be conserved. Recent examples of this include Bukit Brown Cemetery, which was completely clear of vegetation in the 1950s only to revert to secondary forest since then. This area became the subject of a spirited debate when a new road was proposed along its perimeter in 2012.[48] Areas

[47] To better understand how the state envisions this process, please see "Singapore: A City in a Garden," which conveys the perspectives of the Ministry of National Development with regard to the modern re-planting of Singapore. Available at http://www.mndlink.sg/2009/2009_May/NParks_article.htm [accessed 10 Jan. 2013].

[48] See Goh Hong Yi's contribution to this volume; Harvey Neo, "Challenging the Developmental State: Nature Conservation in Singapore," *Asia Pacific Viewpoint* 48, 2 (Aug. 2007): 186–99.

such as Bukit Brown, which offer a mixture of cultural and natural heritage, are sites of continued concern and debate, regions that reflect the discussions that exist between the government and citizenry of Singapore, and will most likely continue into the future as the landscape constantly changes.

Conclusion

The early colonial administration of Singapore did little in the area of land management. Failure to assess the value of lands and forests thereon as well as failure to control tenure and uses to which the lands were put resulted in rapid and almost complete destruction of the primary forest habitats within the first century of colonization. By the time the colonial government woke up and began to make an effort to protect Crown forest resources, most of it had already vanished. The mangroves had been logged out, and gambier planters had felled and burned the primary dipterocarp forest while the freshwater swamp forest of the alluvial valleys were cleared and drained for agricultural production. After the gambier wave had passed from southeast to northwest, leaving large areas of *lalang* in its wake, some moderate areas were put under tapioca cultivation—and activity that lasted almost to 1900 with the Chasseriau and Trafalgar Estates. Outside of these estates, however, most of the former gambier lands remained waste while Forest Reserves and catchment reserves preserved some of the natural forests—or promoted their regeneration at least.

The next significant wave of agricultural activity came with the rubber boom. Henry Ridley developed a tapping technique known as the herringbone method, which made collection of latex more efficient and increased the lifespan of the trees. The rubber plantations simply replaced former gambier wastelands and these plantations consumed very little, if any, of the original vegetation—the damage to the natural forests had already been completed during the gambier period. The Forest Reserves remained till 1936 at which time most were rescinded with the exception of Kranji, Bukit Timah, and Pandan Forest Reserves which the Director and Assistant Director of the Singapore Botanic Gardens "rescued;" they remained more or less as nature reserves till the war years. The reservoirs—particularly the interior reservoirs along with their all-encompassing catchment reserve were the beginnings of Singapore's largest nature reserve—the Central Catchment Nature Reserve. The lands the Municipal Catchment enclosed in 1900 included primary forest that the Chan Chu Kang Forest Reserve and the Reservoir Jungle (currently the MacRitchie catchment area) previously encompassed,

Table 1.5 Summary of areas for principle habitats illustrating losses to date[49]

Forest Type	Primeval Area (square kilometers)	Remaining Area (square kilometers)	Percentage remaining
Dryland Primary Forest	410	2.01	0.49
Freshwater Swamp Forest	74	1.33	1.65
Mangrove Forest	87	5.7	6.55

regenerated secondary forest, some swamp forest, and substantial areas of recent agricultural areas from the former Chasseriau Estate.

Due to the increasing population of Singapore, greater pressure is being brought to bear on the existing Nature Reserves. Attempts have been made to mitigate the pressure by opening interim parks about the boundaries of the nature reserves as well as other areas as and when opportunities reveal themselves. Typically, these interim parks contain secondary forest regenerating since kampong or other land uses have expired over the past 50 years. The Sungei Buloh Wetlands Reserve covering part of the former Sungei Buloh Forest Reserve is an example of a former interim park that has been elevated to full Nature Reserve status. This has allowed park management strategies to be based on a longer-term outlook, as interim parks are based on ten-year plans, and hopefully restore the habitat towards the original level of biodiversity it enjoyed prior to colonization.

Today, Nature Reserves in Singapore hold a mere 0.5 percent (see Table 1.5) of the original dryland primary rainforest that originally covered most of the island. This loss is almost totally attributed to gambier plantations. The swamp forests, which account for 200 species of plant thought to be unique to that habitat, are mainly concentrated in a single alluvial valley that has been spared from vegetable farming and reservoir construction. Fragments of the original mangroves, significantly degraded through uncontrolled firewood harvesting during the 19th century and losses due to reclamation

---

[49] Figures obtained from the following sources: 1924 Topographic Maps of Singapore; A.T.K. Yee et al., "The Present Extent of Mangrove Forests in Singapore," *Nature in Singapore* 3 (2010): 139–45; Richard Corlett "Vegetation," in *The Biophysical Environment of Singapore*, ed. Chia Lin Sien, Ausafur Rahman, and Dorothy Tay B.H. (Singapore: Singapore University Press, 1991), pp. 134–54.

for industrial and residential lands in the 20th century, remain spread over a thin margin about the northwestern shores of the island of Singapore with some fragmented clusters at Sungei Buloh, Kathib, and Bongsu, as well as on the surrounding islands. These small fragments of the original vegetation are a most precious and valuable natural asset of the citizens of Singapore and need to be protected from further losses or degradation at all costs.

SOURCE 2

The Tiger Club: Excerpts from Accounts of Tigers in 19th-Century Singapore

We regret to learn that tigers are beginning to infest the vicinity of the town, to such a degree as to require serious attention on part of the local authorities, with regard to their destruction. Not many days ago, the friends of a Chinese woodcutter, who had been missing for some days, discovered the head, and part of one leg of their companion in the thicket not far distant from the rear of the Chinese temple which lays near the road leading to New Harbour, and contiguous to the Sepoy lines. Marks of a tiger's feet were plainly indented in the ground, round about the spot. We have heard that another native has been killed, since, by a tiger, in a different direction.

—*The Singapore Chronicle and Commercial Register*, 8 Sep. 1831, p. 3

We have this week to report three deaths from Tigers, both in the immediate vicinity of cultivated lands. One occurred at Tanling where a Chinaman was the victim—his body was recovered by his friends, and, as usual, buried without any intimation being given to the Police of the cause of his death. It coming to the knowledge of the Deputy Magistrate that a body had been buried under rather suspicious circumstances he caused the Coffin to be dug up and opened when the appearance of the body at once shewed the cause of his death. The Chinese who live in the jungle it is known never think of giving information of the ravages committed by Tigers, so that it is only by enquiry that the facts become known. Their feelings of superstition in regard to Tigers may perhaps be a cause of this—we have been informed that they believe that when a person is killed by a Tiger his *hantu* or ghost becomes a slave to the beast, and attend upon it—that the spirit acts the part of a Jackal as it were and leads the Tiger to his prey—and, so thoroughly subservient does this poor ghost become to his Tigerish master, that he often brings the Tiger to the presence of his wife and children and calmly sees them devoured before his ghostly face. The old pyongs or umbrellas which may often be seen stuck on the tops of newly made graves are intended to mark the spot where a Tiger-slain body is deposited, but from what motive they are placed there we have not been able to learn. That the general belief as to the extent of the deaths caused by Tigers and their prevalence on the Island is not based on false grounds, we can attest, having made considerable enquiry on the subject. We are informed on the best authority that in one district between Bukit Timah and the old Straits, six persons on an average are every month carried off from the Gambier plantations, and that not one of these cases is ever made known to the authorities. Lately in the Kallang district a Cow which was grazing at no great distance from a house on one of the large plantations was attacked by a Tiger who carried it off. On Monday morning the body of a Chinaman was brought to the Police Office having been found at a short distance beyond the Sepoy lines near the road leading to the New Harbour—the body was quite fresh and apparently newly killed—the companion of this man who had gone with him into the jungle has not since appeared so that it may be concluded that the Tiger had also killed him, and carried the body to his lair.

—*The Singapore Free Press and Mercantile Advertiser*, 26 Oct. 1843, p. 2

Tiger's heads were frequently brought into town, and the Chinese were encouraged, by rewards, to catch them in pit falls. When they were successful in securing one, it was declared a general holiday amongst the European residents, who hastened out to see the monster, and be at his death. The pit would be 14 to 15 feet deep, and a strong frame of spars would be seen to have fallen over the mouth. Two fiery globes, the tiger's eyes, would be seen at the bottom of the pit, and an occasional noise would be heard, as of rolling thunder. A long bamboo would be poked at the two globes; it would be responded to by the tiger leaping up to the very top, grasping the spars, and then falling down with a loud, hollow roar. Many bamboos would be torn to pieces in this way. Perhaps a real sportsman being present, he would suggest fair play, and the letting loose of the game; but this would be overruled by the more discreet majority. Tired of teasing the animal, lots would be drawn for their turns of shooting. This ceremony being over, shot one would miss, responded to by a spring to the top; shot two, hits, another spring and a deep bellow; shot three, hits the forehead, this quiets the animal a little; shot four, another hit, and the tiger falls; shot five, he revives and redoubles his strength and ferocity for a moment, and then falls dead at the bottom. Having poked him well with a bamboo, and seeing no stir, the lid is taken off and the animal hauled up by the Chinese. They sell the head to Government for 100 Spanish dollars, and the flesh they sell for as much, for medicine to their countrymen. The skin may be purchased by some gentlemen present. Thus would end a safe system of tiger hunting—the only king that I, being no shot, ever affected to engage in, with but one exception.

—John Turnbull Thomson, *Some Glimpses of Life in the Far East*
(London: Richardson and Company, 1864), pp. 229–30

I was indebted to the kindness of the Messrs. Behu and Meyer for a very interesting excursion into the jungle. The gentlemen, four in number, all well provided with fowling-pieces, having determined to start a tiger, besides which they were obliged to be prepared for bears, wild boars, and large serpents. We drove as far as the river Gallon, where we found two boats in readiness for us, but, before entering them, paid a visit to a sugar-refining establishment situated upon the banks of the river …

We asked the labourers if they could not put us on the track of a tiger; they described to us a part of the wood where one was reported to have taken up his abode a few days previously, and we immediately set off. We had great difficulty in forcing our way through the forest, having, at every instant, to clamber over prostrate trees, creep through brambles or cross over swamps, but we had, at all events, the satisfaction of progressing, which we certainly should not have had in the forests of Brazil, where such an undertaking would have been impracticable …

We beat about the forest for some hours without meeting the game of which we were in search. We once thought that we had found the lair, but we soon found that we were mistaken. One of the gentlemen, too, affirmed that he heard the growl of a bear; it must, however, have been a very gentle growl, as no one else heard it, although we were all close together.

We returned home without any further addition to our stock of game, but highly delighted with our agreeable trip.

Although Singapore is a small island, and all means have been used and rewards offered for the extirpation of the tigers, they have failed. Government gives a premium of a hundred dollars, and the Society of Singapore Merchants a similar sum for every tiger killed. Besides this, the valuable skin belongs to the fortunate hunter, and even the flesh is worth something, as it is eagerly bought by the Chinese for eating. The tigers, however, swim over from the neighbouring peninsula of Malacca, which is only separated from Singapore by a very narrow channel, and hence it will be impossible to eradicate them entirely.

—Ida Pfeiffer, *A Woman's Journey Round the World from Vienna to Brazil, Chili, Tahiti, China, Hindostan, Persia and Asia Minor* (London: Ingram, Cooke, and Co., 1852), pp. 122–4

In the midst of this entomological banquet there is, however, one drawback—a sword suspended by a hair over the head of the unfortunate flycatcher: it is the possibility of being eaten up by a tiger! While watching with eager eyes some lovely insect, the thought will occasionally occur that a hungry tiger may be lurking in that dense jungle immediately behind intent upon catching you. Hundreds of Chinamen are annually devoured. Pitfalls are made for the animals all over the country; and in one of them, within two miles of our house, a tiger was captured a short time before my arrival. Only last night a party of Chinamen, going home to their plantation, turned back afraid, having heard the roaring of a tiger in the path. These are unpleasant reminders of the proximity of a deadly foe; and though perhaps the absolute danger is little enough, as the tiger is a great coward and will not attack unless he can do it unawares, yet it is still better to have the mind quite free from any such apprehensions.

I shall therefore most probably leave here in a month or so for Borneo, before which, however, I hope to make such a collection as to give a tolerably correct idea of the Entomology of Singapore.

—A.R. Wallace, Letter, 9 May 1954

A SCHOOL FOR TIGERS IN THE EAST

The following rather alarming account is taken from a daily Newspaper:—

> Rapid DEPOPULATION OF SINGAPORE BY TIGERS—Two deaths by tigers ever week (says the *Singapore Free Press*) are read of in the papers just about as much a matter of course as the arrival or departure of the P. and O. Company's steamers. It is notorious that during the last fifteen or twenty years many thousands of men have lost their lives from this cause. Yet the only measure adopted by the Government, so far as we know, to prevent this enormous sacrifice of life, have been to dig tiger-pits in various parts of the island (which we are told did little or no good), and to give a reward of 100 Company's rupees for every tiger killed on the island. The reward is, for all practical purposes, ineffective; it ought to be increased to 250 rupees; for the price of procuring the destruction of one tiger in the jungle of Singapore is a hundred dollars, and the thing cannot be done for 110 Company's dollars. Such is the position in which we are now placed.

If the population of Singapore is really being converted into food for tigers, and the inhabitants are departing as regularly as steamers, it is high time that something should be done to save the remnant of the populace. Considering that the tigers have evidently got the upper hand, we think they show a sort of moderation in taking only two inhabitants per week, and there is consequently no hope of any further diminution, for it is clear that the brutes are already on what we may consider a low diet. We cannot be surprised at the anxiety of the Editor of the *Singapore Free Press*, who may any day be selected as a moiety of the weekly allowance of the somewhat abstemious tigers, who appear to be practicing the negative virtue of moderation and regular living. Since the Government will not, or cannot, take the matter up, and put the tigers down, we would advise the population of Singapore to enter into an arrangement with the brute-slayer at the top of the Haymarket, and we have no doubt that Mr. CUMMING would be hailed as the Coming Man, if he were to offer his services.

The Singapore journalist expresses his fear that the 'evil will go on increasing,'— or in other words, that the population will go on diminishing—and we fully sympathise with his editorial fears; for even should he be so lucky as to escape till after every other inhabitant is disposed of, it would be but a sorry consolation to feel oneself constituting the last mouthful at a feast of tigers.

We suspect that our Eastern contemporary is either indulging in a little romance, or is agitated by fears that have grown up under the enervating influence of the climate, for we cannot suppose that the people and the Government are quietly submitting to the gradual consumption of the inhabitants in the manner described, and our friends at Singapore will excuse us, therefore, if we have treated somewhat lightly a subject that we should certainly regard as no joke, if we put faith in the statements on which we have commented.

—*Punch, or the London Charivari*, Volume 29 (17 Oct. 1855): 170

… It is a good many years since the attention of the House of Commons was directed to the mortality reported to be then caused by tigers in Singapore. It was asked, could it be possible in an island of such limited area and with such a numerous population, that men, at the rate of one per diem, were destroyed by these jungle monsters; and inquiries were directed to be made of the Indian authorities. The then Governor, Colonel Butterworth, was written to on the subject, and his answer, I believe, was, that he could not affirm to so extensive a destruction, but that he thought at least 200 lives were each year lost in this way. Since the period that question was put and answered, the evil has been gradually growing worse, till, at the present moment, the mortality stands higher than ever it did before. It becomes, indeed, a serious consideration whether this increase is to go on or not, and the subject, altogether a singular one, must be earnestly taken in hand by the future Government.

—John Cameron, *Our Tropical Possessions in Malayan India* (1865), pp. 106–7

The Singapore residents have devised many amusements for themselves. They have their clubs, their bowling-alleys and fives' courts, and their racecourse. Picnics are numerous, and the frequent gatherings at private houses are pleasantly diversified by performances at the Theatre, and concerts in the Town Hall.

There used also to be a sporting club, and more than once I have been out tiger-hunting with its members, but I never encountered anything more formidable than a deer. Singapore has a great name for tigers; however, I never saw but one in its native jungle, during three years' residence on the island. I have frequently heard them roaring at night round my house at 'Bendulia', a plantation in which I held a share. It may be safely said that tigers do not nowadays destroy a man per diem, as they are reported to have done in former times. Nor is the Singapore tiger an animal at all likely to attack a man face to face. What they usually do is to pounce upon a single unfortunate victim as he bends over his work in some lonely field. The natives say that the tiger almost always attacks from behind, and I once saw the body of a coolie who had come thus to his end. Though only slightly mutilated, it had been thoroughly drained of its blood, and showed deep ragged incisions along the back and behind the head.

—John Thomson, *The Straits of Malacca, Indo-China, and China, or Ten Years' Rravels, Adventures, and Residence Abroad* (1875), pp. 72–3

Tigers

To the Editor of the Daily Times

Sir, —One of the noteworthy characteristics of the Island of Singapore mentioned in the old (and repeated in many modern) books of Travel, is that the place is so infested by 'tigers, that an average of one death *per diem* is caused by them throughout the year.' The lately published Returns of H. M. Coroner for 1879, give two deaths only from this cause for the whole year, and, judging from the report current at the time of the Inquest, there would appear to have been a certain doubt about one, so that as far as Official Records go, the average is reduced to *one per annum*. From the admirable system of Police throughout the Island, and the Reports sent in from villages and plantations whenever a Tiger is heard of &c., I presume H. M. Coroner is always well posted up, and instances of men, women or children being carried off, as in some parts of India, without the circumstance at once being known, would be very rare. I presume I am right therefore in accepting the Official Record as correct. I am sorry to weaken a piece of romance that has been current so long, by dry statistics. That there are still two or three tigers remaining in the Island, is proved, by the loss of an occasional Chinaman's pig, the scarcity of deer in some parts, and the tracks which have been seen by some of my sporting friends; but the number must have lessened a great deal of late years. Like a writer in a late number of the *'Field'* who questions the Reports about the enormous annual death rate from snake bites in India, I query whether Tigers have ever been in such numbers, or had the taste for human beings in Singapore, for which credit has been given them. What I am curious to find out is the actual number, *dead or alive*, that have been *seen* during the last three or four years.

Perhaps some of your readers, planters, sportsmen or residents in country districts could (with your permission) afford the information in the columns of your paper. Any evidence as to a tiger having ever been *seen* to cross from the mainland, might be interesting, as the Straits of Johore, with the exception of one place (Tanjong Boar which is a quarter of a mile wide) have an average width of two miles.

I am,
Your obedient Servant,
"Gun Wad."
Singapore, 19th April, 1880

—*Straits Times Overland Journal*, 20 Apr. 1880, p. 12

CHAPTER 2

Tigers of Colonial Singapore

Timothy P. Barnard and Mark Emmanuel

In 1835, a theodolite—a tool for measuring the angles of horizontal and vertical planes—lay unclaimed on the side of a road under construction some six kilometers outside the main port of Singapore. This particular theodolite was of tremendous value to George David Coleman, the first Government Superintendent of Public Works in Singapore, who needed it to help lay out a smoothly engineered road that would push the limits of habitation beyond the immediate harbor area of the young colony. Coleman and his convict laborers, however, left the device where it lay because of a greater threat. They had fled back to the town after a "huge tiger leaped right into the thick of the party," scattering the group. Once they returned to the town, however, Coleman found it difficult to convince anyone that they had just experienced a close encounter with a ferocious beast. After all, tigers had never been a problem in Singapore up to that point.[1]

The veracity of this story, conveyed 30 years later, is doubtful.[2] Residents of Singapore in 1835 knew that tigers roamed the jungles beyond the harbor area—the first newspaper report was in 1831. It also would

The authors would like to thank Joanna Tan for her help in gathering research materials for this chapter.

[1] John Cameron, *Our Tropical Possessions in Malayan India: Being a Descriptive Account of Singapore, Penang, Province Wellesley, and Malacca; Their Peoples, Products, Commerce, and Government* (London: Smith, Elder, 1865), p. 95.

[2] "The War at Malacca," *The Singapore Chronicle and Commercial Register*, 8 Sep. 1831, p. 3; Charles Burton Buckley, *An Anecdotal History of Old Times in Singapore: From the Foundation of the Settlement under the Honourable East India Company on February 6th, 1819 to the Transfer to the Colonial Office as Part of the Colonial Possessions of the Crown on April 1st, 1867*, vol. 1 (Singapore: Fraser and Neave, 1902), p. 219.

Plate 2.1 *Unterborchene Strassenmessung auf Singapore* (Road Surveying Interrupted in Singapore), by Heinrich Leutemann (c. 1885). Courtesy of the National Museum of Singapore, National Heritage Board.

not have been difficult convincing residents of the port that a work crew beyond the edge of town had fled from a tiger, particular if Coleman, a builder of early Singapore and a well-established figure in society, told the tale. While most likely not true, the story of the abandoned theodolite does reflect a perception that was held as a truth in 19th-century Europe. The British colonial port of Singapore had a reputation as a place under threat from roaming bands of man-eating beasts, which attacked and killed at least one person per day. Tigers threatened the civilizing push of the British Empire. The stories from Singapore became so alarming, and believable, to the British public by the mid-19th century that William Butterworth, the Governor of the Straits Settlements from 1843 to 1855, answered inquiries from the House of Commons in 1850 on the issue of tigers in Singapore. Butterworth claimed that stories of a death per day were an exaggeration. The number—he stated—was more likely around 200 a year, still a shocking sum in a port with some 50,000 people.[3] Singapore was a

[3] Peter Boomgaard, *Frontiers of Fear: Tigers and People in the Malay World, 1600–1950* (New Haven, CT: Yale University Press, 2001), pp. 103, 251; Cameron, *Our Tropical Possessions in Malayan India*, p. 106.

tropical island filled with danger, where wild beasts roamed, at least in the public imagination.

Tigers have long been the focus of lore and history in the region. As settlements on the forest fringe encountered tigers, the animals came to be featured in the mythology and belief systems throughout island Southeast Asia. Tigers became infused into court rituals in Java as well as a belief in the existence of were-tigers, which was particularly strong in Sumatra and the Malay Peninsula, where it was based in shamanistic ritual beliefs, and was often associated with a physically disfigured outsider or newcomer who had supernatural powers.[4] The "mythicized history" of the founding of pre-colonial Singapore even featured a tiger. When Sri Tri Buana, a fleeing 14th-century prince, saw a strange beast when he first arrived on the island and named it "Singapura" (or lion city), he was most likely misidentifying a tiger.[5]

The metaphorical role that tigers have played in understandings of colonial Singapore has been the focus of a number of excellent studies by scholars such as Peter Boomgaard as well as Kevin Chua and Lillian Chee.[6] When Europeans encountered tigers in their newly established colonies, they saw them as a threat to their presence. This interaction, and the perceptions of it, became a cornerstone of literature, art, myth, and even architecture, providing allegorical insight into Western perceptions of their

---

[4] Boomgaard, *Frontiers of Fear*, pp. 145–66, 205–6.

[5] The transfiguring of a tiger for a lion in the tale is understandable, as lions were important figures in the traditional belief systems of the time. The lion had been a symbol of Buddha in Indian art since the time of King Asoka. In addition, the phrase "Singa-pura" appears in the Jataka tales about the previous lives of the Buddha as a name of a place in India, as well as settlements in central Vietnam, Thailand, and Java before the founding of "Temasek." "Mythicized history" is taken from Cheryl-Ann Low Mei Gek, "Singapore from the 14th–19th century," in *Early Singapore 1300s–1819: Evidence in Maps, Texts and Artifacts*, ed. John N. Miksic and Cheryl-Ann Low Mei Gek (Singapore: Singapore History Museum, 2004), pp. 41–54; C.C. Brown, ed., *Malay Annals, translated by C.C. Brown from MS Raffles no. 18* (Kuala Lumpur: MBRAS, 2009), pp. 30–1; we would like to thank John Miksic for his help clarifying some of these issues.

[6] Boomgaard, *Frontiers of Fear*; Kevin Chua, "The Tiger and the Theodolite; George Coleman's Dream of Extinction," *FOCAS: Forum on Contemporary Art and Society* 6 (2007): 124–49; Lillian Chee, "Under the Billiard Table: Animality, Anecdote and the Tiger's Subversive Significance at the Raffles Hotel," *Singapore Journal of Tropical Geography* 32, 3 (2011): 350–64.

efforts in establishing trade ports and control over a vast tropical area; tigers represented a savage Asia that needed to be countered. The tiger, a unique Asian species of cat, became the metaphorical "other" as humans and animals clashed over space. This discourse with regard to tigers in Singapore was rooted in initial conflicts when man first pushed into the forests in the first few decades following the establishment of a British settlement in 1819. In the process, tigers became important historical actors in the history of 19th-century Singapore.

The tiger (*Panthera tigris*) can only be found in Asia, with a range from eastern China to the Indian subcontinent, and is among the largest land carnivores in the world. Although scholars previously classified the subspecies found in the Malay Peninsula as the "Indo-Chinese tiger," in 2004 they established a new classification, *Panthera tigris jacksoni* (to honor Peter Jackson, a conservationist of tigers in the region) for the "Malayan tiger." This new classification is based on slight cranial variances between the feline found in the Malay Peninsula and its Sumatran and Indo-Chinese neighbors, though few people are able to distinguish these morphological differences. To reach Singapore, Malayan tigers swam across the narrow straits separating the Malay Peninsula from the island, which has occurred as recently as 1997, when a tiger reached Pulau Ubin, an island located midway in the straits (an elephant also reached the island in this manner in 1991). Malayan tigers can attain a length of 280 centimeters and a height of 110 centimeters, and can weigh up to 130 kilograms. Two tigers can comfortably live in 100 square kilometers, and in this habitat they stalk and ambush their prey, using the element of surprise. To do so, they attack their prey from behind, usually going for the throat or head; they then drag the victim to a location near water or in the shade, which is one reason it is often difficult to find the tiger and its victim following an attack. Only then do they eat, a process that often takes days.[7]

---

[7] Shu-Jin Luo et al., "Phylogeography and Genetic Ancestry of Tigers (*Panthera tigris*)," *PLoS Biol* 2, 12 (2004): 2275–93; J.H. Mazák and C.P. Groves, "A Taxonomic Revision of the Tigers (Panthera tigris) of Southeast Asia," *Mammalian Biology—Zeitschrift für Säugetierkunde* 71, 5 (2006): 268–87; M.K.M. Khan, "Tigers in Malaysia," *The Journal of Wildlife and Parks* 5 (1986): 1–23; Boomgaard, *Frontiers of Fear*, pp. 12–28; Eric Dinerstein et al., "The Fate of Wild Tigers," *BioScience* 57, 6 (2007): 508–14; H.N. Ridley, "The Mammals of the Malay Peninsula, Part II," *Natural Science* 6, 36 (Feb. 1895): 89; "Pulau Ubin Stories," at http://habitatnews. nus.edu.sg/heritage/ubin/stories/2004/05/ubin-tiger-april-1997.html [accessed 11 Nov. 2012].

The interaction between humans and animals is one of the core elements of environmental history. The focus on the role that animals play in history is a relatively new topic of research, although they have appeared in literature and on the margins of other histories for centuries. The rise in the study of animal-human historical interaction is an offshoot of the larger development of Environmental History since the 1960s. Harriet Ritvo, one of the leading scholars in animal studies, argues that this role has been enhanced as animals intersect a number of research topics ranging from emerging diseases to overexploitation of natural resources.[8] Animals can also provide an understanding into historical events and trends. In Southeast Asian history, scholars such as Robert Cribb and Greg Bankoff have used animals, such as birds of paradise and horses, and their interaction with humans, to provide insight into how societies developed in Southeast Asia over the past few hundred years.[9] In this historical subfield, Boomgaard is also one of the leading researchers. In his wide-ranging book, *Frontiers of Fear*, he surveys human-tiger interaction in the Malay World, including Singapore.

This chapter will explore in detail the threat that tigers represented to Singapore in the 19th century and how their presence exposed the environmental change the island was undergoing. Tigers were among the main characters in early Singaporean history, acting as hindrance for expansion beyond the port. To better understand these forces, the first section will focus on early reports of tiger attacks in Singapore, and how they occurred against a backdrop of agricultural expansion. The second section will focus on how humans responded to this threat, with various methods developed to counter the menace in newly opened agricultural lands, thus providing a narrative of British control over their colonial environment. The final section of this chapter will discuss how tigers eventually became less of

---

[8] Harriet Ritvo, "Animal Planet," *Environmental History* 9, 2 (2004): 204–20.

[9] Robert Cribb, "Birds of Paradise and Environmental Politics in Colonial Indonesia, 1890–1931," in *Paper Landscapes: Explorations in the Environmental History of Indonesia*, ed. Peter Boomgaard, Freek Columbijn, and David Henley (Leiden: KITLV, 1997), pp. 379–408; Greg Bankoff, "Big Men, Small Horses: Ridership, Social Standing and Environmental Adaptation in the Early Modern Philippines," in *The Horse as Cultural Icon: The Real and Symbolic Horse in the Early Modern World*, ed. Peter Edwards, Karl Enenkel, and Elspeth Graham (Leiden: Brill, 2011), pp. 91–120; Greg Bankoff and Sandra Short, eds., *Breeds of Empire: The 'Invention' of the Horse in Southeast Asia and Southern Africa, 1500–1950* (Copenhagen: Nordic Institute of Asian Studies Press, 2007).

a threat, as humans gained supremacy over the natural environment of the island, and how tigers came to represent Singapore in the imagination of the world, and particularly within the British Empire, as a society bordering a dangerous, tropical environment. After all, man-eating tigers could not be allowed to stop the spread of imperial rule.

Tiger Attacks in a Transforming Landscape

The first reported death from a tiger attack in Singapore occurred in September 1831. The victim was a Chinese woodcutter, whose body was found in a thicket behind a Chinese temple that was located near the Sepoy Lines, which at the time was a gambier plantation. Friends of the woodcutter only found his head and a leg.[10] In the same month, another "native" also died following a tiger attack. Two months later, in November 1831, a British couple on a buggy ride outside the "New Harbour" area saw a tiger cross their path. These sightings, and the death of the two workers, were considered exceptional at the time. Few people ventured deep into the thick forest cover on the island of Singapore; most stayed in the town close to the port.[11] It was only when this human habitation pushed outward that attacks would become more frequent.

The first three decades after 1819 was a period of rapid expansion of gambier and pepper plantations in Singapore. While these two products were imported from Java, Riau and Siam, an equally healthy production market developed in Singapore itself, as they were "the only cultivation on the island which has yet assumed any degree of commercial importance."[12] Although William Farquhar and Thomas Stamford Raffles found 20 small farms along the waterfront upon their arrival in 1819, by 1827 these plantations had rapidly expanded, reaching as far as 15 kilometers inland. In 1836, gambier and pepper plantations took up an estimated 2,350 acres (950 hectares) and produced 22,000 pikuls (1.32 million kilograms) of gambier; the land use for gambier and pepper expanded to 4,000–5,000 acres (over 2,000 hectares) by 1840; and, reached more than 24,220 acres (9,700 hectares) by 1850.

---

[10] The Sepoy Lines was a road that was located near modern-day Singapore General Hospital. "War at Malacca;" see also "Singapore Map, 1825" at http://commons.wikimedia.org/wiki/File:Singapore-map-1825.jpg [accessed 28 Oct. 2012].
[11] Buckley, *An Anecdotal History of Old Times in Singapore*, pp. 219–20.
[12] "Gambier and Pepper Plantations," *SFP*, 28 Mar. 1839, p. 3; Buckley, *An Anecdotal History of Singapore*, p. 335; Chua, "The Tiger and the Theodolite," pp. 130–1.

Production also grew, with exports of gambier reaching 80,000 pikuls (4.8 million kilograms) in 1848, with an equally impressive cultivation of 39,000 pikuls (2.3 million kilograms) of pepper.[13]

Gambier—which was an important product for the tanning of hides as well as a component in the betel quid—and black pepper were environmentally symbiotic for the purposes of profitability and labor. The gambier leaf fertilized the pepper plant as well as protected its roots from erosion. The structure of these plantations, known as *bangsal*s, also played a role. There were usually eight workers on each plantation, which averaged 12 hectares (30 acres) in size. According to John Thomson, the Government Surveyor in the 1840s and early 1850s, gambier plantations had "the appearance of brushwood of 3 years growth whose leaves are of a light green colour." Workers collected the leaves three or four times a year, allowing these Chinese agriculturalists to focus on their pepper vines as well as the processing of the two products. The processing of gambier, which involved the boiling of the leaves in pots, and pepper, which was dried in wood-fuelled kilns, also required the cutting of an area equal to the size of the plantation. The need for huge amounts of timber further exacerbated deforestation in mid-19th-century Singapore. This rapid expansion in plantation land—by one estimate, there were least 500 gambier and pepper plantations throughout Singapore in 1841, and over 800 by 1850—led to workers cutting down the forest "a considerable distance" from the town.[14] As agricultural settlements expanded into the hinterland, and engineers, such as Coleman and Thomson, and laborers pushed roads out to serve them, the amount of disturbed forest—the natural habitat of tigers—increased, making encounters between these animals and humans more likely.

---

[13] T. Oxley, "The Botany of Singapore," *Journal of the Indian Archipelago and Eastern Asia* [hereafter *JIAEA*] 4 (1850): 438; James C. Jackson, "Chinese Agricultural Pioneering in Singapore and Johore, 1800–1917," *Journal of the Malayan Branch of the Royal Asiatic Society* 38 (1965): 77–82.

[14] Oxley, "The Botany of Singapore"; J.T. Thomson, "General Report on the Residency of Singapore, Drawn Principally with a View of Illustrating Its Agricultural Statistics," *JIAEA* 4 (1850): 219; Carl Trocki, *Prince of Pirates: The Temenggongs and the Development of Johor and Singapore, 1784–1885* (Singapore: NUS Press, 2007), pp. 104–9; Jackson, "Chinese Agricultural Pioneering in Singapore and Johore;" Richard T. Corlett, "The Ecological Transformation of Singapore, 1819–1990," *Journal of Biogeography* 19 (1992): 413; Buckley, *An Anecdotal History of Singapore*, pp. 346, 352–3; Chua, "The Tiger and the Theodolite," p. 132. Also see Tony O'Dempsey's contribution to this volume.

Tigers were not unknown in Singapore during this period of agricultural expansion, as reports of the time imply. Newspaper accounts convey the
idea that it was simply the proximity of the attacks to the town that caused
concern. For example, in the first newspaper report of a tiger attack in 1831
the author used phrases such as "beginning to infest the vicinity of the town"
and another in 1839 referred to an attack "at a distance scarcely more than
two miles from town." Also signaling that their presence in Singapore was
not surprising, the latter article is titled "More Tigers," and refers to more
than a dozen deaths due to tigers "within the last year or so."[15] The main
focus of these early accounts is that the attacks occurred close to harbor, and
were relatively common—if underreported—thus reflecting the anxiety with
the implications of pushing colonial civilization beyond the town.

Between 1839 and 1844, tigers attacks and deaths occurred on such a
regular basis that William Napier—the editor of *The Singapore Free Press and
Mercantile Advertiser*—proclaimed "it has now become nearly a regular part
of our weekly duty to chronicle these melancholy tragedies." In mid-1839,
there were official reports of at least seven deaths for the first half of the year,
including a woman found dead near Tanjong Rhu, as well as a ten-year-old
child being carried off. Although the body of the child was never found,
during the search the mutilated remains of a Chinese man were encountered
on a plantation "two or three miles from Town." By 1840, the presence of
tigers became so common that there was a report of one near Race Course
Road (at the time "Buffalo Village") "taking his morning *siesta* beneath the
shade of some bushy underwood."[16]

In one week in February 1843, tigers killed at least five men in the
Tanglin area. In July of the same year, workers found the partly devoured
remains of a man behind the Sepoy Lines. The discovery of the body created
further shocks when "at the same place bones and other remains of human
bodies were found, from which it is judged that no less than ten persons
must have been destroyed at this spot by the Tiger."[17] This led to increased
speculation in the number of deaths, and the beginning of estimations on
their numbers. In a newspaper report three months later, Napier stated that

---

[15] "War at Malacca;" "More Tigers," *The Singapore Free Press and Mercantile Advertiser*
[hereafter *SFP*], 20 June 1839, p. 2.
[16] "Miscellaneous," *SFP*, 31 Jan. 1839, p. 7; "Tigers Again," *SFP*, 6 Aug. 1840, p. 3;
"A Singapore Tiger Hunt," *SFP*, 16 Apr. 1840, p. 3; "Tigers," *SFP*, 26 Oct. 1843, p.
2; Buckley, *An Anecdotal History of Singapore*, pp. 338, 342.
[17] "Tigers," *SFP*, 23 Feb. 1843, p. 3; "Tigers," *SFP*, 13 July 1843, p. 3.

it was a commonly held belief that up to six people a month died from tiger attacks "in one district between Bukit Timah and the old Straits" and "not one of these cases is ever made known to the authorities." "The Chinese who live in the jungle," he went on to add, "never think of giving information of the ravages committed by tigers." The same report even describes how a colonial official, upon hearing of a death, forced one victim's friends to disinter the body and remove it from its coffin, so the Magistrate could confirm the cause. Under such circumstances, the number of reported deaths was most likely underreported.[18] Based on the perceptions of the time, there must have been more, although it is difficult to estimate the number. It is doubtful they attained the dizzying heights of one per day.

Many government officials at the time understood that many of these deaths occurred against the backdrop of a rapidly deforested Singapore. As analyzed in the press in 1839, "it is somewhat singular that ... fatal accidents of this kind should happen just as the island begins to be cleared of jungle, and roads to be carried into the interior in various directions."[19] This conclusion reflects what is known about tigers and their habitat, as they are not found in dense, undisturbed forest, where most animal life would be in the canopy and thus limit the number of viable prey. Disturbed forests, such as recently cut plantations, however, are ideal for tigers. These transitional zones allow for sufficient forest cover to hide, are often near a water source, and host much of their ground-dwelling prey of deer, pigs, and other mammals. This is an apt description of Singapore in the mid-19th century. The disturbance to the forest was so widespread at the time that Thomson wrote that "the whole of the interior is occupied by Pepper and Gambier plantations intermixed with Primary Forest." As Chinese migrants were the residents of the *bangsal*s, they were also the primary victims. Thomson also saw this link between Chinese agricultural expansion and tiger attacks when he observed, "the gambier and pepper plantations, with which the island was studded all over, promoted their increase. The gambier plant afforded an excellent cover; and the naked, lusty Chinaman, at work in all directions, provided a food of which the animal was exceedingly fond."[20]

---

[18] "Tigers," *SFP*, 26 Oct. 1843, p. 2; Ridley, "The Mammals of the Malay Peninsula, Part II," p. 90.

[19] "More Tigers," *SFP*, 25 July 1839, p. 3; Boomgaard, *Frontiers of Fear*, pp. 22–6.

[20] Thomson, "General Report on the Residency of Singapore," p. 219; John Turnbull Thomson, *Some Glimpses of Life in the Far East* (London: Richardson and Company, 1864), p. 227.

Colonial officials felt they had little control over, or knowledge of, much of this plantation expansion. In the 1840s, for example, the authorities were surprised to learn that there were extensive gambier plantations along the Seletar River, far from the main settlement in Singapore.[21] Much of the anxiety that resulted was the result of a gap in communication and culture between the British and Chinese communities, as the plantation residents were perceived as living on the edge of civilization. Members of this European elite perceived the Asians who were victims of the tigers as foolish for living in such dangerous conditions. As "a sportsman" proclaimed to the newspaper in 1843, "who but lawless, opium smoking, gambling, and robbing Chinese, would settle and cultivate a country cursed with such scourges."[22] Even when Europeans ventured into these plantations, there was a distance between the two communities. Thomson, who took a canoe up the Kallang River in the 1840s while on a tiger hunt and alighted at one of these plantations, found them to be picturesque, "though of that rude, primitive kind which does more to repel than to charm." He also found the Chinese workers on these plantations to be gracious and friendly although they were "of a rough, independent stamp, which generally does not consort well with the self-importance of the European."[23]

As alarm over the frequency of the attacks rose, there was a growing trend of abandoning farms and plantations. While some of the abandonment was due to fluctuations in the price of gambier, as well as farms reaching their 20-year limit of productivity, blame was placed primarily on the threat tigers represented. Napier described the situation in 1843 as one in which Chinese planters "who make advances as cultivators used to visit the plantations occasionally for the purpose of looking after their interest, but now they shudder at the thought of venturing into the jungle." The value of plantations plunged, with one supposedly going from \$300 to \$25, and plantation owners threatened to move their operation to the tiger-free Riau Islands. Such entreaties became common in the local press and changed little over time. Seven years later, in 1850, Napier noted that the number of residents living on plantations was dropping, due to "several causes" including

---

[21] K.W. Pitt, "From Plantations to New Town: The Story of Nee Soon," in *The Development of the Nee Soon Community*, ed. L.G. Lim How Seng (Singapore: The Grassroots Organisations of Nee Soon Community and National Archives, Oral History Department, 1987), pp. 193–225.

[22] "A Sportsman," "Letter to the Editor," *SFP*, 16 Nov. 1843, p. 3.

[23] Thomson, *Some Glimpses of Life in the Far East*, p. 228.

the exhaustion of the soil, the scarcity of firewood, and "above all the very alarming increase which appears to have taken place in the numbers of those scourges of our jungle population—tigers."[24]

Following this initial period of publicly discussed tiger attacks amidst rapid transformation of the landscape from 1839 to 1844, the presence of tigers was accepted as a norm in Singaporean society for the rest of the 1840s. The few tigers that had created the chaos and destruction seem to have moved on, or been captured and killed. Reports took on the tone of sightings, with little discussion of deaths. For example, Orchard Road near Mt. Elizabeth became "notorious for tigers" in 1846 although there were no reported attacks.[25] In that same year, Indian laborers found two tiger cubs on a coconut plantation, leading Napier to opine:

> It is so long ago since there was any report of a tiger having been observed, that we were in hopes that they had finally quitted the Settlement, disgusted with the rapid opening up of the country and the consequent intrusion upon the privacy of their forest haunts, but the appearance of the cubs ... dispels the too pleasing idea, and bids us to be prepared to hear of future ravages by these deadly enemies of the dwellers of the jungle.[26]

The next year, Napier described the sighting of a tiger as a rare occurrence, as their presence "is now happily as rare as it once was frequent."[27]

In 1849, "ravages" returned to shake the rightful "dwellers of the jungle," when tigers killed six people—two each at Bukit Timah, Tanah Merah, and Tulloh Mata Ikan (Changi). The news was greeted with a government initiative to have convicts "beat the jungle once every month, with tomtoms, horns, &c., which, if they do not lead to the destruction of the tigers, may

---

[24] *SFP*, 4 Jan. 1850, p. 2. Napier also placed some blame on the weather. During one period of increased tiger attacks, he argued that a drought had led to the unfortunate deaths as tigers ventured toward the habited parts of Singapore. "All the pools and small streams in the jungle having been dried up, the Tigers being unable to quench their thirst, are forced to come in to the neighbourhood of cultivated places, and in their fury attack the first living object they see, most generally some unfortunate wood cutter." "Tigers," *SFP*, 23 Feb. 1843, p. 3; "Tigers," *SFP*, 3 Aug. 1843, p. 2; Trocki, *Prince of Pirates*, p. 108; Buckley, *An Anecdotal History of Singapore*, p. 391.

[25] Buckley, *An Anecdotal History of Singapore*, p. 449.

[26] *SFP*, 26 Feb. 1846, p. 2.

[27] *SFP*, 4 Nov. 1847, p. 1.

frighten them away from the island."[28] Such efforts seemed to have worked, as there were very few reports of human deaths for the rest of the year. The devastation tigers wracked upon the animal community, however, was widespread, as livestock often fell prey to the predators. One report in May 1850 best reflects this when—in one paragraph—Napier provides a long list of animals that the "ferocious beasts" had killed in the "Bukit Timah district and along Thomson's road." They included a "goat, which was fastened below the house now building on the top of the hill on Mr Brown's plantation" as well as "a sow from a pigstye on the plantation of a Christian Chinese named Pedro." Tigers also took "two good watchdogs" and a hunting dog, whose cries caused its owner to lose "his presence of mind."[29] By the next year, the number of attacks on humans would also rise.

In 1851, the Serangoon district of Singapore became the sight of a number of attacks that sealed Singapore's reputation as a haunt for tigers. It began in early April when a group of Malay woodcutters collecting rattan and wood encountered a tiger. As they fled, the tiger—"singling out the fattest man in the party"—"sprang upon" the victim and dragged his body into the nearby brush. After gathering their wits, the woodcutters chased the tiger with *parang*s, forcing the animal to drop the man and retreat. "The poor man was found in the agonies of death with his throat and face severely lacerated." That night, the same tiger carried off a Chinese laborer in the same area. His body was found the next day without one of his legs.[30] By late May, Serangoon was the sight of "fearful ravages" in which the tiger killed a number—"as high as 55"—of workers in two months. Chinese workers eventually found the animal causing this destruction on 17 June, "lying in a pepper plantation in a helpless state" as it had been wounded earlier. They killed it. While the menace may have been temporarily stopped, it was reported that "the loss of life by tigers in this district still continues very frightful, there being at least one person taken per day." This estimate, which was developed during these attacks in 1851, came to be repeated continually in the local press. Singapore had become a place where one person per day was dying from tiger attacks—well, at least in April and May of 1851.[31]

---

[28] "Miscellaneous," *SFP*, 17 Aug. 1849, p. 2; Buckley, *An Anecdotal History of Singapore*, p. 501.

[29] "Local," *SFP*, 17 May 1850, p. 2.

[30] "Tigers," *SFP*, 2 May 1851, p. 5.

[31] This is despite Napier commenting that these numbers were probably "an overestimate" in the article published in May. *SFP*, 23 May 1851, p. 2; 1 July 1851, p. 1; 5 Dec. 1851, p. 5.

For the remainder of the 19th century, the estimation of attacks came in bursts. Years would pass without a report, or more usually "only" a few random deaths, such as the Malay bird-catcher who died in Paya Lebar two months after the terror in Serangoon. Relative calm would follow, only to be interrupted by a spasm of violence, which would remind the residents of Singapore that tigers were present in their forests.[32] In 1852, this pattern held true. One man died in each of the first months of the year—in Kranji and Pasir Ris—followed by a report of ten deaths in Kranji over a period of two days during the month of May. For the remainder of the year, there were only four more deaths reported, one being a woman at Sungei Jurong in July, followed by two Chinese workers in "Booko-Kang" (Lim Chu Kang) in August, and a Chinese resident of Pulau Ubin named Kwah Ah Seong in December.[33]

The actual number of deaths due to tiger attacks, however, remained uncertain. Contradictory numbers and data were bandied about throughout the 1840s and 1850s, pointing to both a steady, and alarming large, number of deaths from tiger attacks, and—at the same time—a reduction in their numbers. In a paper Thomas Oxley wrote on animal life in Singapore in 1843, for example, he claimed 300 people died that year from tiger attacks while only seven were reported to the authorities; he also estimated that tigers had killed at least 200 people each of the three previous years. The threat was so great that he claimed, "the jungle, with the exception of its outskirts, is unexplorable without great risk from the number of tigers."[34] In the meantime, newspapers did not report any deaths from tiger attacks in 1846 and 1847, and only two in 1848.[35] While a continued reluctance on behalf of plantation owners to report such cases may have led to the confusing data, reports such as Oxley's and the frenzied reports of 1851 led to Singapore developing a reputation as a haunt for tigers.

---

[32] *SFP*, 22 Aug. 1851, p. 2.

[33] "Tigers," *SFP*, 27 July 1852, p. 4; "Singapore—Local," *The Straits Times*, 17 Aug. 1852, p. 5; "Singapore—Local," *The Straits Times*, 21 Dec. 1852, p. 5; Buckley, *An Anecdotal History of Singapore*, p. 565; Tan Kee Soon, "The Chinese Names of Streets and Places in Singapore," *Journal of the Straits Branch of the Royal Asiatic Society* 46 (1906): 195.

[34] T. Oxley, "The Zoology of Singapore," *JIAEA* 3 (1849): 594; Oxley, "The Botany of Singapore," p. 437.

[35] "Tigers," *SFP*, 29 Mar. 1848, p. 2; 30 Nov. 1848, p. 2. See Tony O'Dempsey's contribution to this volume.

Accounts of these deaths soon reached London. When pressed on these numbers, William Butterworth claimed that 200 people died per year in Singapore from tiger attacks.[36] Other leading figures, of the Singaporean elite, however, doubted these estimates. John Thomson, who described Butterworth as "what was termed in the East a hard-working man; that is, he sat tenaciously in his office-chair from ten to four daily"—viewed the issue with concern but was reluctant to offer easily misconstrued estimates.[37] Doubts over these reports persisted, leading Britons outside of Singapore to offer explanations, including an editor of a Calcutta newspaper who suggested that the deaths were actually the result of Chinese secret societies attempting to cover up their activities. Facing such doubt, after the sighting of several tigers in the Bukit Timah district, *The Singapore Free Press and Mercantile Advertiser* proposed that it would be better to catch them and "send them to London for Prince Alberts projected show of curiosities." The London satirical magazine *Punch* even entered the fray when it mocked Singapore-based Britons—particularly Napier—over the estimated number of deaths, proclaiming that, if they were true, the island would soon be depopulated.[38] The residents of Singapore had to develop ways to eradicate the beasts, no matter what the debatable numbers implied; the presence of tigers could not be allowed to continue.

Tiger Hunting in Singapore

Although tigers had killed residents of Singapore as early as 1831, concentrated efforts to hunt them only began in the late 1830s. The various sources on tigers in 19th-century Singapore provide little insight into how tigers were captured, or handled, during this initial period. Singapore, however, was part of a larger environmental and cultural ecosystem that had to deal with tigers. In the Malay Peninsula, communities had traditionally been hesitant

---

[36] Buckley, *An Anecdotal History of Singapore*, p. 220.

[37] Thomson also claimed that Butterworth had little influence beyond the harbor, and conducted his affairs with a certain "pomposity" and without any knowledge of local languages or cultures. Thomson, *Some Glimpses of Life in the Far East*, pp. 270–1; J. Thomson, *The Straits of Malacca, Indo-China, and China, or Ten Years' Travels, Adventures, and Residence Abroad* (New York: Harper and Brothers, 1875), pp. 72–3.

[38] Buckley, *An Anecdotal History of Singapore*, p. 622; "Correspondence," *SFP*, 21 Dec. 1849, p. 2; "A School for Tigers in the East," *Punch, or the London Charivari* 29 (17 Oct. 1855): 170.

to capture and kill tigers due to traditional beliefs in their link to ancestors and the wrath their destruction could bring on the society. Despite reluctance to approach tigers, when one began attacking humans it had to be stopped. Malay hunters would usually dig pits with stakes in them, or create traps to capture tigers.[39]

In early Singapore, it was up to these same communities, as well as Chinese agricultural pioneers, to capture these beasts. Napier and early leaders of the merchant community proposed that a reward system be developed to "induce the natives to undergo the risk of capturing or killing them" in the late 1830s. The government initially offered a reward of $20, but few took it up, necessitating a rise in value to $50, and ultimately to $100, a considerable amount considering that plantation owners—if they were "frugal, and did not smoke opium or gamble"—could net between $300 and $400 a year, and common laborers of all ethnicities earned approximately three dollars a month in the 1840s.[40]

The reward system for the capture of a tiger seems to have worked. An unnamed Chinese squatter captured at least four in 1841. As *The Singapore Free Press and Mercantile Advertiser* recounted, "whenever one is discovered to be prowling about in search of prey, notice is conveyed to him of his whereabouts; and the Chinaman makes his observations, digs his pits, effects his other arrangements, and on the morrow has his victim all snug!"[41] In total, five tigers were killed in 1841; an additional one had fallen into an old pit near the New Harbour. This "adventurous Son of Han"—as

---

[39] T.J. Newbold, *Political and Statistical Account of the British Settlements in the Straits of Malacca, viz. Pinang, Malacca, and Singapore; with a History of the Malayan States on the Peninsula of Malacca*, vol. 2 (London: John Murray, 1839), pp. 190–3; Peter Boomgaard, "'Primitive' tiger hunting in Indonesia and Malaysia, 1800–1950," in *Wildlife in Asia: Cultural Perspectives*, ed. John Knight (London: RoutledgeCurzon, 2004), pp. 185–206.

[40] In the 1850s, as another comparison, European police officers in Singapore earned $40–$55 a month, making the reward for capturing a tiger a considerable amount. The "dollar" was the Spanish dollar, which was the most commonly traded currency in island Southeast Asia at the time. Buckley, *An Anecdotal History of Singapore*, vol. 1, pp. 220–1, 540; Trocki, *Prince of Pirates*, pp. 108–9; "More Tigers," *SFP*, 20 June 1839, p. 2; Ida Pfeiffer, *A Woman's Journey Round the World from Vienna to Brazil, Chili, Tahiti, China, Hindostan, Persia and Asia Minor* (London: Ingram, Cooke, and Co., 1852), p. 123; Thomas Oxley, "Some Account of the Nutmeg and Its Cultivation," *JIAEA* 2, 10 (1848): 652.

[41] *SFP*, 4 Nov. 1841, p. 3.

the newspaper referred to him—was so effective Napier proposed that the amount of the reward be reduced, with it remaining $100 for the next two captured, followed by a reduction to $75 for the subsequent three or four, and then an eventual reduction to $50. This plan went into effect, and by late 1842, Chinese workers, who captured a tiger in the Tanah Merah area, were given the reduced amount, although they also profited from selling the flesh to Chinese residents.[42] Chinese plantation workers were the main hunters of tigers in the late 1830s and early 1840s in Singapore.

Pits were the most successful method for the capture of a tiger in Singapore in the 19th century. The pits were usually four meters (14–15 feet) deep and about between one and two meters (4–7 feet) square at the mouth, which was covered with dead branches, grass, and ferns. In Singapore it was not the normal practice to place bait near these pits. The construction of these pits was not an easy task, as a "proper" one "fully occupies a man for a month—while the risk of being interrupted in their labours in the jungle by the Tiger … might well daunt the stoutest heart." Convicts dug the earliest pits under the supervision of engineers such as Coleman or Thomson; later, plantation owners forced their coolies to construct them. To fund their construction in the late 1840s, the government offered $300 to encourage people to dig them. Originally a sharp stake was placed in the bottom of the pit. The government forbade these stakes, however, according to Alfred Russel Wallace, because an unfortunate traveler had fallen in a pit and died after becoming impaled on a spike. In 1852, one "gentleman" fell into a pit, but did not die, although he was "much injured." The Police Superintendent issued new regulations with regard to tiger pits, requiring small bamboo markers with white cotton cloth tied at the top of each pole be placed at each corner of a pit to warn those who ventured near one. Once completed, no one kept watch over a pit. Laborers would check on them every second day, and when a tiger was found inside, numerous tree trunks were thrown over the mouth of the pit, and crowds would gather once word got out. The tiger was then killed. In the 1830s and early 1840s, Chinese laborers usually did this with spears; as Europeans got involved, the weapon of choice was a firearm.[43]

---

[42] Ibid.; "Tiger Killed," *SFP*, 13 Oct. 1842, p. 3.

[43] Cameron, *Our Tropical Possessions in Malayan India*, p. 104; "Tigers," *SFP*, 3 Aug. 1843, p. 2; "Correspondence," *SFP*, 23 Nov. 1849, p. 2; Buckley, *An Anecdotal History of Singapore*, p. 221; Alfred Russel Wallace, *The Malay Archipelago: The Land of the Orang-Utan, and the Bird of Paradise. A Narrative of Travel, with Studies of Man and Nature* (New York: Harper and Brothers, 1869), p. 35; Boomgaard, *Frontiers of Fear*, pp. 117–8; *The Straits Times*, 10 Aug. 1852, p. 5.

The firearms hunters originally used were smoothbore, flintlock fire-arms, which shot a ball with limited accuracy and velocity. In the late 1840s, Ida Pfeiffer, one of the first female explorers of Asia to come from an indus-trializing Europe, wrote that she went on a tiger hunt in Singapore with a "fowling piece," an early version of the shotgun for hunting that was a close cousin of the musket or blunderbuss. European armies transitioned from such firearms to more reliable percussion weapons, bolt-action rifles, in the 1840s and 1850s. As weapons technology improved, it filtered into Southeast Asia over the subsequent decades, although at a rather slow pace or in a transitional form of the technology. While elite Europeans in Singapore could have upgraded their weaponry earlier, as hunting guns with bolt-action loading mechanisms were available in Europe in the 1820s, Pfeiffer's account reflects the slow nature of such adoptions. This can also be seen in the case of Alfred Russel Wallace, who used a percussion gun—which was muzzle-loaded with a ball or shot, but used copper percussion caps—while in Southeast Asia in the 1850s and 1860s. The shift in technology throughout the 19th century improved the chances of hunters when they encountered a tiger outside of a pit, although early efforts required a certain faith in the efficacy of single shot weapons.[44] As this technology filtered into Singapore, the hunting of tigers transformed into "sport."

As tigers became a problem in Singapore in the early 1840s after the reward had been reduced following the successful campaign of "the son of Han," the European business elite began advocating a return of the reward to $100 in 1843. They argued that the $50 reward—once divided among the many men were engaged in the capturing and killing of a tiger—amounted to little incentive to take part in the effort. At this time, Chinese plantation owners also approached the government asking for increased support. If gambier and pepper production were to continue as the main crops of Singapore, it was at the behest of the elite of society to take notice. Napier even proposed allowing convicts a reduction on their sentence if they captured a certain number of tigers.[45] As the number of

---

[44] Dutch armies transitioned from such firearms to more reliable percussion weapons, bolt-action rifles, in 1841. The British army first adopted rifles with grooved bores—which provides increased velocity and accuracy—in 1853; the Dutch armies converted to such weapons between 1850 and 1860. Boomgaard, *Frontiers of Fear*, pp. 133–4; Pfeiffer, *A Woman's Journey Round the World*, p. 123. We would like to thank Brian Farrell and John van Wyhe for helping to clarify many of these issues.
[45] "Tigers," *SFP*, 3 Aug. 1843, p. 2.

attacks rose, it was time to form an organization—a club—to eradicate tigers from Singapore.

In late 1843, the Western elite of Singapore formed a "Tiger Club." As part of the battle against tigers, members promised Chinese plantation owners a more generous reward if they told the authorities about any tigers captured on their properties, which members of the club then would be allowed to kill. The Tiger Club also promoted the digging of numerous pits around gambier plantations. One of their first successes occurred in November, when a large tiger fell into a pit "on the left of Bukit Timah Road" about five kilometers from the town. When word of this tiger reached the town, "vehicles of every description were seen conveying Europeans to the place." Eventually about a dozen Europeans gathered over the pit, peering through the "heavy grating of logs" that covered it. The men argued over whom got the first shot. When an agreement was finally reached, they took their turns, eventually firing into the pit "about a dozen" times. When the logs were removed, the tiger roared—"sending the frightened Chinese," who had gathered nearby, "reeling down the hill"—while a few more shots finished the tiger. As one European witness concluded, it was "the triumph of *skill* over brute force."[46]

The "*skill*" of the Tiger Club was in protecting Singapore from vicious beasts in a manner that became an honorable hobby, as "sportsman-like" rules were developed to oversee the procedures for shooting a tiger in a pit. The first arrivals would shoot the tiger several times, and then wait for other members. In the meantime, while they waited, "those present amuse themselves by stirring the brute up with a long pole" to provoke rage and growls. Once this amusement passed, often lasting an hour, the members of the club would fire in the order of their arrival at the tiger through the slats covering the pit. When the tiger finally died, it would be presented to the plantation owner, who received the various rewards. He would present the head to the government, who would then reward him $50 (which quickly went up to $100 by the late 1840s), while the Tiger Club provided an additional $100. A European member of the Tiger Club often bought the skin and—based on market price in 1844—10 to 12 dollars could be obtained selling the tiger flesh in the Singaporean market.[47] The joy that

---

[46] Emphasis in original. "A Sportsman," "Letter to the Editor," *SFP*, 16 Nov. 1843, p. 3; "Turf," "Letter to the Editor," *SFP*, 16 Nov. 1843, p. 3.
[47] "Tiger Caught," *SFP*, 4 Jan. 1844, p. 3; Thomson, *Some Glimpses of Life in the Far East*, pp. 229–30; Pfeiffer, *A Woman's Journey Round the World*, p. 124.

members felt in being members of the Tiger Club, however, quickly waned. By June 1846, no members showed up—"owing to the heavy rain"—when a tiger fell into a pit on a gambier plantation near Bukit Timah Road.[48] The Tiger Club eventually transformed into the "Singapore Sporting Club," one of the first in Singapore. As the Tiger Club grew less popular among the Western elite, the police, under the leadership of the first Commissioner of Police, Thomas Dunman, took on many of the duties of capturing tigers, from investigating sightings to setting rules for pits and traps.

A new brand of hunters, distinguished by their eccentricity, worked alongside the police in Singapore in the 1850s and early 1860s. Armed with bolt-action rifles, they made tiger hunting their business, as the government continued to pay $50 for each tiger killed, and local merchants matched the reward "when the Government certificate is shown." In addition, the "nimrods" who killed tigers could also make $50 selling the "skin, claws, flesh."[49]

Two hunters—one French Canadian, the other Singaporean Eurasian—represented this new phenomenon well. The French Canadian was *"Tiger Hunter* Carrol," who lived in Serangoon and survived on the rewards offered for dead tigers. He was known for his skills as a sharp shooter as well as the golden ring he threaded through his long, grey beard. Carrol spent many nights in the forest, searching for tigers; he also enjoyed shooting and eating monkeys and other animals he encountered. In one of the better-known stories related to Carrol, he heard of a tiger attack at a gambier plantation in Serangoon and rushed to the scene, where he found the body of a Chinese laborer who had been carried off. Carrol shooed away his helpers, built a "stage," and used the dead body as bait. When two tigers approached the body, Carrol shot. Believing that the Canadian had killed the beast, the Chinese workers on the plantation rushed out yelling, and the two tigers made their way back into the jungle. Following the publicity of this incident, Carrol never told the press if he found the two tigers.[50]

The Eurasian tiger hunter was Neil Martin Carnie, who was born in Singapore. Carnie was a clerk for the Municipality, as well as a police inspector, who was trusted enough to negotiate a peace between the ruler

---

[48] *SFP*, 18 June 1846, p. 5.
[49] "Correspondence. Tigers," *The Straits Times*, 20 Feb. 1864, p. 33.
[50] *The Straits Times*, 28 Dec. 1861, p. 1; "News of the Week," *The Straits Times*, 20 Sep. 1862, p. 3; Buckley, *An Anecdotal History of Singapore*, pp. 221–2, 679; Thomson, *Some Glimpses of Life in the Far East*, pp. 227–8.

of the Sumatran sultanate of Siak and rebels that British mercenaries from Singapore assisted over a succession dispute in the 1850s. Carnie soon discovered, however, that the rewards for killing tigers were higher than his civil service salary, and began to roam the jungle at night with a Malay former Sergeant Major from the police force. Carnie's most famous exploit in tiger hunting occurred when a tiger cub was found in a pit in January 1864. When a latter day "Tiger Club" of police officers arrived, Carnie ordered wood be thrown in the pit to antagonize the cub, whose whelps brought the mother. The cub's mother appeared, and sprang at the party, creating chaos and confused shooting, which killed "Police Peon, No. 28, named Sallay" and almost killed the Deputy Commissioner of Police. Carnie, "by slipping a little to one side to get a shot at her shoulders ... planted 2½ oz. of lead into her, on receiving which she gave a grunt of dissatisfaction, raised her head, and shook her tail, and expired."[51]

While pits continued to be used throughout Singapore, traps also grew in popularity as a belief developed among the Western elite in Singapore that pits were not as an effective tool against tigers since there were "no means taken to engage and to oblige the animal to walk exactly over the spot where the pit lay." An unnamed "European" proposed that a series of baited cages be placed systematically around the island in late 1849, and even offered to pay for the entire venture as the government reward for capturing a tiger would easily pay for their construction. Following the attacks on animals near Bukit Timah and along Thomson Road in 1850, the police supported this proposal and recommended the "establishment of a set of tiger traps on the Javanese principle."[52] These traps (known as *bekungkung* in Java) were usually wooden cages, with the bars of the cage driven into the ground for stability. Boomgaard describes them as being open on two sides with—usually, live—bait placed in the middle. When the tiger entered the trap, a mechanism slammed the door shut, capturing the animal. The effectiveness of these traps was limited, however, as tigers quickly learned to avoid them or simply broke free of them.[53] One of the first tigers caught in a Javanese trap in Singapore escaped, although it had bars 45 cm in circumference, which had been driven 75 cm into the ground. The "ferocious animal" simply lifted the

---

[51] "The Tiger," *The Straits Times*, 30 Jan. 1864; "Untitled," 30 Jan. 1864, p. 18; Buckley, *An Anecdotal History of Singapore*, pp. 221–2, 663–4, 709.
[52] "Correspondence," *SFP*, 23 Nov. 1849, p. 2; "Local," *SFP*, 17 May 1850, p. 2.
[53] Boomgaard, *Frontiers of Fear*, pp. 116–8.

cage by pressing its body against the bars, and walked away.[54] While traps would continue to be used, pits remained the main method of capturing a tiger in Singapore.

Beyond the use of pits and traps, there were also attempts to poison tigers in Singapore. These attempts, however, were unsuccessful. Henry Nelson, a leading figure in Madras, suggested such an approach after he found them to be effective in India. Nelson proposed lacing the carcass of a buffalo or other animal with strychnine, and placing it in areas where tigers roamed. This was also a common method in the Malay Peninsula, where local hunters would place animal carcasses next to poisoned waterholes to deal with troublesome predators. Dunman tried a variation on this approach, by shaving the necks of living dogs and cattle and then slathering strychnine on them. The animals were tied to posts. Tigers did approach, but would not fall for the bait. Finally, strychnine was placed on dead human bodies, and left in the jungle. Tigers also passed on this offering.[55] Tigers would be trapped in Singapore.

The hunting, and destruction, of tigers was successful over time. While reports of tiger attacks continued for the next few decades, they grew fewer in number, and even "Mr. Carrol's ardour in the hunt is not what it used to be" by the early 1860s.[56] Some of this success was due to the changing forest cover. Much of the Singaporean landscape had been deforested by the 1860s and 1870s, with only the hilltops being spared, as they were unsuitable for gambier cultivation. The remainder had become a wasteland of brushwood and *lalang* grass. The situation was so serious the government appointed Nathaniel Cantley, the Superintendent of the Singapore Botanic Gardens, to develop a plan to manage the remaining forest reserves.[57] The functional habitat for wild animals had become limited under these circumstances, and this also led to a subsequent shift in the local perception of tigers and the threat they represented to humans. Reports in newspapers began to focus

---

[54] The article went on to add, "the traps require therefore strengthening," which will be achieved by placing a "crossbar under ground." "Local," *SFP*, 26 July 1850, p. 2.

[55] Newbold, *Political and Statistical Account of the British Settlements*, p. 190; Buckley, *An Anecdotal History of Singapore*, p. 710.

[56] "News of the Week," *The Straits Times*, 30 Aug. 1862, p. 3. At times, Carrol's name is spelled with one "r" in the various newspapers.

[57] Nathaniel Cantley, *Report on the Forests of the Straits Settlements* (Singapore: Government Printing Office, 1883); see also Nigel P. Taylor's and Tony O'Dempsey's contributions to this volume.

around sightings or the killing of tigers, and only rarely was a person killed. In 1875, for example, a tiger killed dogs and pigs belonging to Chinese farmers along Bukit Timah Road, some 20 kilometers from the main town, and in all of 1879, only two people died due to tiger attacks in Singapore.[58] As the number of deaths due to tiger attacks dropped, references to the animal in Singapore began to focus on encounters and display, representing a shift in human-animal interactions.

The Decline, and Display, of Tigers in Singapore

Prior to the 1850s, tigers were considered a menace in Singapore, pushing back against the relentless expansion of plantations. Any tiger found was to be destroyed. This attitude began to change, however, as the number of attacks began to dwindle. Tigers now would often be kept for display, or were the focus of European hunters in search of a hobby. The focus on display began as early as 1848, when a living tiger, which had been captured in Melaka, was exported from Singapore to Australia for £45, "a rate of remuneration sufficient to induce the capture of the Tigers which now infest this Island." The next year, John Little purchased from a Malay businessman a live tiger captured in Siak.[59] The display of living tigers also became a point of curiosity in Singapore, "especially to the native portion of the community." By the 1870s, the Singapore Botanic Gardens had a zoo featuring a tiger and leopards. The presence of jungle beasts for show led to new anxieties, as the savage was brought into the civilized areas. Letter writers even expressed concern that it was "possible—if not probable"—that they would escape and wreck havoc on the populace, particularly after "some miscreant forced the locks from off the cages" at the Botanic Gardens in November 1876.[60]

A unique report in *The Straits Times* in December 1883 represents this shift in attitudes with a story of a tiger that had fallen into an 11-foot deep (3.5 meters) pit at the foot of Bukit Timah Hill. Chinese laborers had not dug the pit for the capture of tigers; it was constructed "for the purpose

---

[58] *The Straits Observer*, 15 Feb. 1875, p. 2; "Tigers," *Straits Times Overland Journal* (20 Apr. 1880): 12.

[59] "Colonial," *The Straits Times*, 9 Dec. 1848, p. 2; "Correspondence," *SFP*, 28 Dec. 1849, p. 2.

[60] "The Botanical Gardens," *The Straits Times*, 11 Nov. 1876, p. 4; "The Zoological Gardens," *The Straits Times*, 14 July 1877, p. 4. See also Nigel P. Taylor's contribution to this volume.

of catching the wild pigs that infest" the plantations of the area, further reflecting how the threat from tigers was much reduced by this time. Instead of killing the tiger, the goal of the plantation owner was to keep it alive. Heavy planks were placed over the pit to insure the tiger remained inside. When word got out that a tiger was being held alive in Singapore, crowds rushed the eight miles (13 kilometers) up Bukit Timah Road and gathered around the pit to observe a "large, handsome beast." In the meantime, the Chinese owner of the plantation fed the tiger pork while he negotiated a price for its sale, which took several days. An Indian businessman—"a Kling in Victoria Street, Campong Glam"—"bought the tiger for $125 with the intention of exhibiting it." To raise it out of the pit, three ropes were lowered and placed around its body. With a block and tackle, workers pulled the tiger—which had sustained a broken or sprained leg, most likely when it fell into the pit—to the surface, and "a pig-basket was immediately [placed] over it and securely fastened." The tiger became an attraction in Kampong Glam, and its leg healed. Its period of captivity, however, did not last long. On 16 January 1884, the tiger escaped from its cage "to the great consternation of the natives of the locality, who with their women and children hastened to secure their front and back doors, and the streets were soon deserted." The tiger jumped into the Rochor Canal separating Kampong Glam and Kampong Kapor and swam to the other side, making its way to the swamp and forest behind the Indian settlement.[61]

Tigers in Singapore had now become an attraction for interested residents, not an animal that prohibited movement into the hinterland. As one typical newspaper report in 1884 stated, "Tigers are by no means extinct in Singapore. The tracks of a large one have been seen lately on Trafalgar Estate, Sirangoon, and a few days ago the beast was seen by some coolies but left without attempting to harm them." In 1890, one person died from a tiger attack in Singapore, the same number that died from lightening strikes. There were so few tigers the reward system "lapsed" by 1898. Sightings, reports of missing livestock, or even the concern of a resident when the loud "*woogh*" of tiger awakened him from his bungalow located near MacRitchie Reservoir in 1901, continued, but tigers were no longer feared in Singapore.[62]

---

[61] *The Straits Times*, 6 Dec. 1883, p. 2; 8 Dec. 1883, p. 2; 12 Dec. 1883, p. 2; 17 Jan. 1884, p. 2.
[62] "Summary of the Week," *Straits Times Weekly Issue*, 13 Aug. 1884, p. 1; "Glances at the Blue Book for 1890," *The Straits Times*, 19 Sep. 1891, p. 3; "A Tiger at the Reservoir," *SFP*, 25 Mar. 1901, p. 2.

By the late 19th century, the success of game hunters for sport in Singapore would be limited. As Henry Ridley proclaimed at the time, tigers "were rarely seen and very seldom shot."[63] Tiger hunters began to shift their focus to the Malay Peninsula and Sumatra, which provided a much larger habitat for tigers and were undergoing an opening of its lands to plantation agriculture just as Singapore had a few decades earlier. This was also a period—stretching into the 1930s—in which animal collectors, such as Charles Mayer and Frank Buck, operated in the region. These collectors oversaw a system in which trapped animals such as elephants, *orang utans* and tigers were sent to Singapore before being shipped to ports in Europe or America. The flow of animals, according to Mayer, was a "steady stream," and "almost every boat that came to Singapore from the districts where animals were captured brought specimens."[64] While Buck and Mayer became well known for this system, as they were masters of self-promotion, they also represented a wider economy of capturing animals for Western zoological gardens and circuses that centered on Singapore. The wild animals of the region, such as the tiger, now became a commodity for Western consumers. The "hunting" of tigers also became a commercialized product to sell to tourists and visitors. In the case of Singapore, it shifted to Johor and became so "business-like" that a popular story in the first decade of the 20th century involved a tourist who awoke in Singapore, traveled to Johor, visited a hotel with tigers in cages, paid the owner, promptly shot one behind the ear, and returned to Singapore by nightfall, all in order to become a "blooded shikari" in one day.[65]

By the end of the 19th century, tigers had become an export to the West representing a dangerous Far East to the wider world. They had become a simile and a metaphor, even one of exaggeration, used to suggest larger concerns in the society. "Simon Simple," who wrote a letter to the editor of *The Straits Times* in 1887, reflected this pattern when he proclaimed "the mosquitoes went for me like tigers" following a recent bout of poor weather and flooding that he expected the Municipal Commissioners to

---

[63] Ridley, "The Mammals of the Malay Peninsula, Part II," p. 89.

[64] Charles Mayer, *Trapping Wild Animals in Malay Jungles* (New York: Duffield and Company, 1921), pp. 107, 193; Frank Buck and Edward Anthony, *Bring 'em Back Alive* (New York: Simon and Schuster, 1930); see also Fiona Tan's contribution to this volume.

[65] "A Tiger Shot in Singapore," 28 Oct. 1898, p. 4; *The Straits Times*, 2 Mar. 1904, p. 4.

address and solve.[66] The most famous allegory of a tiger encroaching on civilization involved the Raffles Hotel. According to eyewitness reports from August 1902, a tiger, that "belonged to a native show performing on Beach Road," had escaped captivity when it initially swam in the Singapore River before making its way to the Raffles Hotel, where it avoided notice for at least a day. At closing hour on 13 August, a "boy" working at the hotel saw the tiger "staring through the low verandah railing on the hotel side of the Billiard room," and informed other workers and guests. Charles M. Philips, principal of the Raffles Institution and a member of the "Singapore rifle team," shot the tiger several times with hollow-nosed bullets; it took several people to drag the carcass from beneath the building.[67] The story soon became exaggerated; the tiger became a wild beast—"the sole surviving wild tiger in Singapore"—that had wandered in from the hinterland, scrambled under a billiard table, and even interrupted a game, only to be shot following the quick thinking of the Britons gathered around. This oft-repeated version began in local papers in September 1902, and is the most commonly repeated "true tale" of colonial tigers told in modern Singapore.[68]

Tigers, which were considered a legitimate threat to civilization on the island between the 1830s and 1850s, were now a quirky aspect of the Singaporean past. Tigers became part of the cultural heritage of Singapore, something to be remembered, perhaps not accurately, in a society moving away from the terror and influence they had exerted. This was a process that began, like the tiger threat, in the 1830s and transformed throughout the 19th century as society changed. In the first few decades of colonial rule in Singapore, tigers had been a hindrance to human expansion on the island, and their presence represented the rapid environmental change that pepper and gambier plantations caused. The swift decline in tiger numbers from the mid-19th century onward represented not only a focused effort on eradicating tigers as a menace, but also the deforestation of Singapore at a time that alarmed the authorities into creating forest reserves on the small island. Singapore's reputation as a haunt of tigers, however, had been sealed. When Ong Kim Hong shot the last *Panthera tigris jacksoni* in Singapore

---

[66] "The Weather," *Straits Times Weekly Issue*, 14 Mar. 1887, p. 13.

[67] "A Tiger in Town," *The Straits Times*, 13 Aug. 1902, p. 4; "He Shot a Tiger in Raffles Hotel," *The Straits Times*, 15 Aug. 1955, p. 2.

[68] Chee, "Under the Billiard Table," pp. 350–64; "What Makes the Raffles Hotel Special," Aug. 2012, at http://www.raffles.com [accessed 3 Oct. 2012].

in 1930 in Choa Chu Kang, it was the end of an environmental era that lasted 100 years for an important actor in Singaporean history, the tiger. [69] Two years later, in 1932, when searching for the proper name for Singaporean beer, officials of Fraser and Neave chose the name "Tiger."[70] The wild animal environment of Singapore had been tamed; tigers would now take on a new connotation.

---

[69] "Notes of the Day," *The Straits Times*, 27 Oct. 1930, p. 10. Tigers, however, continued to be present in Singapore. There are reports in 1935 of a tiger living in Mandai, although "it has caused no trouble." Its fate is unknown. "Tiger Your Fate is Sealed," *The Straits Times*, 27 Mar. 1935, p. 11.

[70] Anisha Anne Johnson, "It's (about) Time for a Tiger: A Social History of Malayan Breweries Limited, 1931–1957," unpublished Honours Thesis, Department of History, National University of Singapore, 2010/11, pp. 17–8.

SOURCE 3

Wallace's Singapore:
An Excerpt from *The Malay Archipelago* (1869)[1]

SINGAPORE.
(A SKETCH OF THE TOWN AND ISLAND AS SEEN DURING SEVERAL VISITS FROM 1854
TO 1862.)

Few places are more interesting to a traveller from Europe than the town and island of Singapore, furnishing, as it does, examples of a variety of Eastern races, and of many different religions and modes of life. The government, the garrison, and the chief merchants are English; but the great mass of the population is Chinese, including some of the wealthiest merchants, the agriculturists of the interior, and most of the mechanics and labourers. The native Malays are usually fishermen and boatmen, and they form the main body of the police. The Portuguese of Malacca supply a large number of the clerks and smaller merchants. The Klings of Western India are a numerous body of Mahometans, and, with many Arabs, are petty merchants and shopkeepers. The grooms and washermen are all Bengalees, and there is a small but highly respectable class of Parsee merchants. Besides these, there are numbers of Javanese sailors and domestic servants, as well as traders from Celebes, Bali, and many other islands of the Archipelago. The harbour is crowded with men-of-war and trading vessels of many European nations, and hundreds of Malay praus and Chinese junks, from vessels of several hundred tons burthen down to little fishing boats and passenger sampans; and the town comprises handsome public buildings and churches, Mahometan mosques, Hindoo temples, Chinese joss-houses, good European houses, massive warehouses, queer old Kling and China bazaars, and long suburbs of Chinese and Malay cottages.

By far the most conspicuous of the various kinds of people in Singapore, and those which most attract the stranger's attention, are the Chinese, whose numbers and incessant activity give the place very much the appearance of a town in China.

---

[1] Alfred Russel Wallace, *The Malay Archipelago: The Land of the Orang-Utan, and the Bird of Paradise. A Narrative of Travel, with Studies of Man and Nature*, vol. 1 (London: Macmillan and Co., 1869), Chapter 2.

The Chinese merchant is generally a fat round-faced man with an important and business-like look. He wears the same style of clothing (loose white smock, and blue or black trousers) as the meanest coolie, but of finer materials, and is always clean and neat; and his long tail tipped with red silk hangs down to his heels. He has a handsome warehouse or shop in town and a good house in the country. He keeps a fine horse and gig, and every evening may be seen taking a drive bareheaded to enjoy the cool breeze. He is rich, he owns several retail shops and trading schooners, he lends money at high interest and on good security, he makes hard bargains and gets fatter and richer every year.

In the Chinese bazaar are hundreds of small shops in which a miscellaneous collection of hardware and dry goods are to be found, and where many things are sold wonderfully cheap. You may buy gimlets at a penny each, white cotton thread at four balls for a halfpenny and penknives, corkscrews, gunpowder, writing-paper, and many other articles as cheap or cheaper than you can purchase them in England. The shopkeeper is very good-natured; he will show you everything he has, and does not seem to mind if you buy nothing. He bates a little, but not so much as the Klings, who almost always ask twice what they are willing to take. If you buy a few things of him, he will speak to you afterwards every time you pass his shop, asking you to walk in and sit down, or take a cup of tea, and you wonder how he can get a living where so many sell the same trifling articles. The tailors sit at a table, not on one; and both they and the shoe-makers work well and cheaply. The barbers have plenty to do, shaving heads and cleaning ears; for which latter operation they have a great array of little tweezers, picks, and brushes. In the outskirts of the town are scores of carpenters and blacksmiths. The former seem chiefly to make coffins and highly painted and decorated clothes-boxes. The latter are mostly gun-makers, and bore the barrels of guns by hand, out of solid bars of iron. At this tedious operation they may be seen every day, and they manage to finish off a gun with a flint lock very handsomely. All about the streets are sellers of water, vegetables, fruit, soup, and agar-agar (a jelly made of seaweed), who have many cries as unintelligible as those of London. Others carry a portable cooking-apparatus on a pole balanced by a table at the other end, and serve up a meal of shell-fish, rice, and vegetables for two or three halfpence; while coolies and boatmen waiting to be hired are everywhere to be met with.

In the interior of the island the Chinese cut down forest trees in the jungle, and saw them up into planks; they cultivate vegetables, which they bring to market; and they grow pepper and gambir, which form important articles of export. The French Jesuits have established missions among these inland Chinese, which seem very successful. I lived for several weeks at a time with the missionary at Bukit-tima, about the centre of the island, where a pretty church has been built and there are about 300 converts. While there, I met a missionary who had just arrived from Tonquin, where he had been living for many years. The Jesuits still do their work thoroughly as of old. In Cochin China, Tonquin, and China, where all Christian teachers are obliged to live in secret, and are liable to persecution, expulsion, and sometimes death, every province, even those farthest in the interior, has a permanent Jesuit mission establishment, constantly kept up by fresh aspirants, who are taught the languages of the countries they are going to at Penang or Singapore. In China there are said to be near a million converts; in Tonquin and Cochin China, more than half a million. One secret of the success of these missions is the rigid economy practised in the expenditure of the funds. A missionary is allowed about £30 a year, on which he lives in whatever country he may be. This renders it possible to support a large number of missionaries with very limited means; and the natives, seeing their teachers living in poverty and with none of the luxuries of life, are convinced that they are sincere in what they teach, and have really given up home and friends and ease and safety, for the good of others. No wonder they make converts for it must be a great blessing to the poor people among whom they labour to have a man among them to whom they can go in any trouble or distress, who will comfort and advise them, who visits them in sickness, who relieves them in want, and who they see living from day to day in danger of persecution and death entirely for their sakes.

My friend at Bukit-tima was truly a father to his flock. He preached to them in Chinese every Sunday, and had evenings for discussion and conversation on religion during the week. He had a school to teach their children. His house was open to them day and night. If a man came to him and said, "I have no rice for my family to eat today," he would give him half of what he had in the house, however little that might be. If another said, "I have no money to pay my debt," he would give him half the contents of his purse, were it his last dollar. So, when he was himself in want, he would send to some of the wealthiest among his flock, and say, "I have no rice in the house," or "I have given away my money, and am in want of such and such articles." The result was that his flock trusted and loved him, for they felt sure that he was their true friend, and had no ulterior designs in living among them.

The island of Singapore consists of a multitude of small hills, three or four hundred feet high, the summits of many of which are still covered with virgin forest. The mission-house at Bukit-tima was surrounded by several of these wood-topped hills, which were much frequented by woodcutters and sawyers, and offered me an excellent collecting ground for insects. Here and there, too, were tiger pits, carefully covered over with sticks and leaves, and so well concealed, that in several cases I had a narrow escape from falling into them. They are shaped like an iron furnace, wider at the bottom than the top, and are perhaps fifteen or twenty feet deep, so that it would be almost impossible for a person unassisted to get out of one. Formerly a sharp stake was stuck erect in the bottom; but after an unfortunate traveller had been killed by falling on one, its use was forbidden. There are always a few tigers roaming about Singapore, and they kill on an average a Chinaman every day, principally those who work in the gambir plantations, which are always made in newly-cleared jungle. We heard a tiger roar once or twice in the evening, and it was rather nervous work hunting for insects among the fallen trunks and old sawpits, when one of these savage animals might be lurking close by, waiting an opportunity to spring upon us.

Several hours in the middle of every fine day were spent in these patches of forest, which were delightfully cool and shady by contrast with the bare open country we had to walk over to reach them. The vegetation was most luxuriant, comprising enormous forest trees, as well as a variety of ferns, caladiums, and other undergrowth, and abundance of climbing rattan palms. Insects were exceedingly abundant and very interesting, and every day furnished scores of new and curious forms. In about two months I obtained no less than 700 species of beetles, a large proportion of which were quite new, and among them were 130 distinct kinds of the elegant Longicorns (Cerambycidæ), so much esteemed by collectors. Almost all these were collected in one patch of jungle, not more than a square mile in extent, and in all my subsequent travels in the East I rarely if ever met with so productive a spot. This exceeding productiveness was due in part no doubt to some favourable conditions in the soil, climate, and vegetation, and to the season being very bright and sunny, with sufficient showers to keep everything fresh. But it was also in a great measure dependent, I feel sure, on the labours of the Chinese wood-cutters. They had been at work here for several years, and during all that time had furnished a continual supply of dry and dead and decaying leaves and bark, together with abundance of wood and sawdust, for the nourishment of insects and their larvæ. This had led to the assemblage of a great variety of species in a limited space, and I was the first naturalist who had come to reap the harvest they had prepared. In the same place, and during my walks in other directions, I obtained a fair collection of butterflies and of other orders of insects, so that on the whole I was quite satisfied with these my first attempts to gain a knowledge of the Natural History of the Malay Archipelago.

CHAPTER 3

Wallace in Singapore

John van Wyhe

The great Victorian naturalist Alfred Russel Wallace (1823–1913) spent eight years collecting natural history specimens throughout what are now Malaysia, Singapore, and Indonesia from 1854 until 1862. During this period, he collected 125,660 specimens of insects, birds, mammals, and shells, discovered hundreds of new species—including the world's largest bee and rarest cat—and was the first person to delineate the sharp boundary line separating the Asian and Australian faunas still known as the Wallace Line. And, most famously of all, Wallace independently formulated the theory of evolution by natural selection and published these findings together with Charles Darwin in 1858.

Wallace used Singapore as his base, staying on the island for a total of 228 days when he was in Southeast Asia, and his name is still commemorated in the city-state. In the Bukit Timah Nature Reserve, there is a splendid Wallace Education Centre. One half of the center is devoted to the Wallace Environmental Learning Lab (WELL) and nearby there is a "Wallace Trail" through the forest where he once collected specimens. The Raffles Museum of Biodiversity Research at the National University of Singapore also has a series of "Wallace Lectures," and there are plans to house a permanent Wallace exhibition in the new Natural History Museum on the campus of the National University of Singapore. There is even a street named after him, Wallace Way.

The Singapore that Wallace experienced in the 1850s and 1860s is not a well-remembered period in the island's history, as the national narrative familiar to most people—"The Singapore Story"—emphasizes Raffles arrival, a "colonial" period (usually imagined as the 1890s–1930s), and then the Japanese occupation from 1942 to 1945 before focusing on political independence, merger and then separation from Malaysia in 1965. Within this narrative, all of these events are merely a backdrop for the subsequent unparalleled economic rise of an independent nation-state.

In the 1850s, however, Singapore was a new, and rapidly developing, port. Seemingly, every visitor to Singapore marveled at the speed at which the settlement had expanded from a forested island to a thriving and bustling international entrepôt, a hub of trade and communication ranked as the fourth commercial port in all of Asia.[1] When Wallace arrived in 1854, the population was about 70,000 of which 30,000 were Chinese, 10,000 Malay, as well as 400 Westerners and small numbers of Armenians, Arabs, Jews, Bugis, Javanese, and Indians. There were about 4,700 buildings in the town clustered along the southeast coast, mostly brick covered in whitewashed stucco with red tile roofs. The European houses were typically two stories. The town was laid out on a neat grid, which the Singapore River bisected.[2]

The time Wallace spent in Singapore has not been the focus of much publication or research, mostly because he gave a very thin account of it in his famous travel book, *The Malay Archipelago*. This, he recalled, was "due to my having trusted chiefly to some private letters and a note-book, which were lost."[3] Wallace, however, wrote much more from, and about, the region than that contained in his most famous work. Eight notebooks survive that he seems to have written while in the eastern archipelago.[4] These have not

---

[1] "Annual Report of the Administration of the Straits Settlement 1860–61," *Calcutta Review* (1861): 43.

[2] "Free Trade and Foul Trade," *The Straits Times*, 14 Feb. 1854, p. 7; "Reminisces of Eastern Travel," *Macphail's Edinburgh Ecclesiastical Journal and Literary Review* 19 (June 1855): 261.

[3] Alfred Russel Wallace, *The Malay Archipelago: The Land of the Orang-Utan, and the Bird of Paradise. A Narrative of Travel, with Studies of Man and Nature*, vol. 1 (London: Macmillan and Co., 1869), p. 52. See the reading excerpt provided in this collection. Wallace's complete publications can be found online in John van Wyhe, ed., *Wallace Online*, at http://wallace-online.org/.

[4] The first, *Journal 1*: Linnean Society of London MS178a, commences in June 1856. The gap in coverage from his arrival in April 1854 to March 1855 (when the first existing entries begin) is about the same as covered in the extant notebooks and may have been covered in the notebook Wallace said was lost. A section of *Notebook 4*: Linnean Society of London MS180, contains journal entries from March–June 1855. If the notebooks were all labeled later, this would explain why the notebook Wallace labeled *Journal 1* may actually have been his second.

previously received the scholarly attention and meticulous examination of his other writings, or even the similarly important Darwin *Beagle* and evolution notebooks.[5] Wallace's notebooks are not even very consistently or accurately described. Compared to Darwin's expensive field notebooks, mostly leather bound and with heavy paper, Wallace's notebooks also are decidedly shabby with cheap paper and thin cover material often worn off.[6] They are falling to pieces. It is a telling reminder of the differences, as well as the similarities, between the two men. While one is given the primary credit for developing the theory of evolution, the other—who did very important work in this regard—is largely overlooked.

This chapter will discuss Alfred Russel Wallace as both a naturalist and observer of the Singaporean human and natural environment. Wallace was a British naturalist coming to a port, which was both his base but also a place for research. Through his observations, a picture of Singapore emerges providing both an environmental snapshot of the island, but also of the society, all from the perspective of one of the leading British naturalists of the 19th century. To gain an understanding of this perspective, this chapter will use not only his journals and letters, but also the observations and comments of other Westerners of the period. As his base Singapore would influence his work and findings.

Arrival and Initial Impressions

Wallace was born in 1823, the son of an impoverished English solicitor. Although he received a fine grammar school education, university was not an option. Wallace became an apprentice land surveyor, which meant working in the countryside. This led to his interest in botany and natural history. Eventually, in 1848, Wallace and his friend Henry Walter Bates set out on a privately funded expedition to Brazil as commercial specimen collectors. They sent their birds and insects back to an agent in London for sale. Five years of

---

[5] Charles Darwin, *Charles Darwin's Notebooks, 1836–1844*, ed. Paul H. Barrett et al. (London: British Museum [Natural History], 1987); Charles Darwin, *Charles Darwin's Notebooks from the Voyage of the Beagle*, ed. Gordon Chancellor and John van Wyhe (Cambridge: Cambridge University Press, 2009); David Kohn, "Theories to Work by: Rejected Theories, Reproduction, and Darwin's Path to Natural Selection," *Studies in History of Biology* 4 (1980): 67–170.

[6] See Chancellor and van Wyhe's introduction in *Charles Darwin's Notebooks from the Voyage of the Beagle*.

collecting earned Wallace many times more than surveying ever could. When Wallace was returning home in 1852, however, his private specimen collection was destroyed in a ship fire. Undeterred, he decided to set out on a second expedition. As Bates and other naturalists were busy in the Amazon, Wallace sought a new destination. His agent, Samuel Stevens, had just sold some unusually valuable natural history specimens that the well-known Austrian traveler and authoress Ida Pfeiffer collected in Southeast Asia. This might have confirmed for Wallace to explore the region. Carefully networking in the London scientific community secured him government assistance in the form of a free first-class ticket to Singapore. Wallace arrived on board the P&O steamer *Pottinger* on 18 April 1854 (not 20 April as he recorded). He lost no time in beginning his investigations of Southeast Asia.

Despite its hustle and bustle, Singapore had not been systematically explored and catalogued by naturalists. In the same year Wallace arrived, travel writer Fred Arthur Neale claimed that Singapore "is a wide field yet to be explored by the botanist on the island and on the neighbouring shores, and a still wider one for the geologist and naturalist."[7] *Eliza Cook's Journal*, a wide-ranging, middle-class British periodical of the period, reinforced this notion when it reported—accurately—in the early 1850s that vast flocks of giant fruit bats lived in the mangrove swamps along the northern coast of Singapore. To best understand these bats, however, British terms of reference were required. The fruit bat, it was written:

> breeds in such numbers as to rival the pigeons of North America. Flocks are sometimes seen flying across the Straits of Malacca continuously for several hours. A mangrove creek at the head of the Jahore is their head-quarters, where, during the day, they hang in millions from the branches; but at sunset they begin to move, and fly away to the plantations, and pass the whole night in devouring fruit, of which they are great destroyers, and return to roost as soon as dawn appears. The natives eat the flesh, but it is described as ranker than the rankest fox that ever broke cover in Leicestershire.

These numbers were mentioned not as a natural history curiosity, but as an opportunity for sport. As the description continued, "There is no lack of game at Singapore; the flying squirrel is said to afford good sport in the

---

[7] Fred Arthur Neale, *The Old Arm-Chair: A Retrospective Panorama of Travels by Land and Sea* (London: Society for Promoting Christian Knowledge, 1854), p. 122.

woods; and [the flying foxes]. Another animal curiosity was a wild hog that stood three feet four high in his hoofs, and cleared a six-feet fence at a leap in his visits to a garden where yams and plantains tempted him to stolen enjoyment. He leaped the fence, however, once too often, and got shot for his pains."[8] There was no mention of the tigers that gripped much of the popular imagination of the time.

In contrast, Wallace wrote to the English popular science journal, *The Zoologist*, about his first days in Singapore:

> I examined the suburbs, and soon came to the conclusion that it was impossible to do anything there in the way of insects, for the virgin forests have been entirely cleared away for four or five miles round (scarcely a tree being left), and plantations of nutmeg and Oreca palm have been formed. These are intersected by straight and dusty roads; and waste places are covered with a vegetation of shrubby Melastonias, which do not seem attractive to insects. A few species of Terias, Cethosia, Danais and Euplœa, with some obscure Satyridæ, are the only butterflies seen, while two or three lamellicorn beetles on the Acacia trees were the only Coleoptera that I could meet with.[9]

Wallace predicted that if the forest clearing continued, the result would be that "countless tribes of interesting insects become extinct."[10] As no complete catalogue of species was made until many decades later, it is impossible to know how many have been lost since Wallace's time, or had disappeared prior to his arrival. Biologist Richard Corlett estimates that between 30–50 percent of species have disappeared since the 1850s.[11] The observation that human occupation vastly reduced the biodiversity became a frequent refrain from Wallace in the ensuing years of his travels throughout the archipelago. Today there are no more flying foxes in Singapore.

Singapore's natural environment was already greatly altered by 1854. There were many introduced species, such as the mimosa plants or touch-me-nots, from South America. In the place of the original forest, there were also hundreds of plantations of pepper vines as well as gambier and nutmeg trees. In 1854, a survey found there were more than 400 plantations and a

---

[8] *Eliza Cook's Journal* 9 (May–Oct. 1853): 26.
[9] A.R. Wallace, "Letter Dated 9 May 1854, Singapore," *Zoologist* 12, 142 (1854): 4395.
[10] Wallace, "Letter Dated 9 May 1854, Singapore," pp. 4395–7.
[11] I am grateful to Richard Corlett for this estimate.

half-million gambier trees in cultivation. In the midst of all of this change, rapid deforestation was taking place.[12]

Ida Pfeiffer visited Singapore in 1847 and 1853. She provided an excellent description of the pepper and gambier plantations near Bukit Timah.

> The pepper-tree is a tall, bush-like plant, that, when trained and supported with props, will attain a height varying from fifteen to eighteen feet. The pepper grows in small, grape-like bunches, which are first red, then green, and lastly nearly black. The plant begins to bear in the second year. ...
>
> The greatest height attained by the gambir plant is eight feet. The leaves alone are used in trade: they are first stripped off the stalk, and then boiled down in large coppers. The thick juice is placed in white wooden vessels, and dried in the sun; it is then cut into slips three inches long, and packed up. Gambir is an article that is very useful in dyeing, and hence is very frequently exported to Europe. Pepper plantations are always to be found near a plantation of the gambir plant, as the former are always manured with the boiled leaves of the latter.[13]

These plantations also depleted the soil and went into decline in the decades following Wallace's time in Singapore.[14] While they only lasted a few decades, they were pivotal in transforming the Singaporean landscape. This was the biological environment in which Wallace collected and observed while in Singapore, particularly in the Bukit Timah area.

About a week after Wallace's arrival, he "got permission to stay with a French Roman Catholic missionary who lives about eight miles out of the town and close to the jungle" in the district of Bukit Timah ("tin hill" in Malay), after Singapore's highest point (530 feet) nearby. The forest was being cleared in this region as pepper and gambier plantations spread, first on the western outskirts of the town and proceeding ever deeper into the island's

---

[12] *The Straits Times*, 2 Jan. 1855, p. 5; Hugh T.W. Tan et al., *The Natural Heritage of Singapore* (Singapore: Prentice Hall, 2010), p. 2. See also Tony O'Dempsey's contribution to this volume.

[13] Ida Pfeiffer, *A Woman's Journey Round the World from Vienna to Brazil, Chili, Tahiti, China, Hindostan, Persia and Asia Minor* (London: Ingram, Cooke, and Co., 1852), p. 123.

[14] Richard Corlett "Vegetation," in *The Biophysical Environment of Singapore*, ed. Chia Lin Sien, Ausafur Rahman, and Dorothy Tay B.H. (Singapore: Singapore University Press, 1991), pp. 134–54. In addition, see Tony O'Dempsey's contribution to this volume, as well as the chapter by Timothy P. Barnard and Mark Emmanuel.

interior. On 26 April 1854, Wallace and his teenage English assistant Charles Allen traveled eight miles along the dusty road out of the town, presumably in a hired gig, to St. Joseph's Church, which was built on a low-lying hill to cater to the hundreds of Chinese plantation laborers in the area.

The Rev. Anatole Mauduit founded the mission in 1846 in the then wild interior of the island. Born in Normandy in 1817, Mauduit arrived in Singapore in 1844. For his efforts, he was paid a sum of about £30 per annum. After some successful fundraising, the original thatched wooden church was replaced with a smart, neo-classical church with Palladian portico supported by six Doric columns in 1853. Wallace described it as "a very pretty church."[15] Wallace later praised the proselytizing efforts of the French Catholics, and particularly Mauduit, in comparison to the lethargy of the Church of England. "My friend at Bukit-tima was truly a father to his flock. He preached to them in Chinese every Sunday, and had evenings for discussion and conversation on religion during the week. He had a school to teach their children. His house was open to them day and night."[16] Wallace wrote to his mother a few days later. "The missionary speaks English, Malay and Chinese, as well as French, and is a very pleasant man. He has ... about 300 Chinese converts. ... Charles gets on pretty well in health, and catches a few insects; but he is very untidy."[17] Mauduit died in Singapore in 1858 and was buried in his church. The grave was later moved to the cemetery behind the church where his tombstone, which the roots and vines that have colonized the cemetery tilt to an odd angle, can still be seen today.

Beyond the mission, the Bukit Timah area was a prime collecting ground for Wallace. As he later described, "The mission-house at Bukit-tima was surrounded by several of these wood-topped hills, which were much frequented by woodcutters and sawyers, and offered me an excellent collecting ground for insects."[18] The hilltops remained covered in forest due to difficulties in growing gambier at elevations greater than 100 meters. While Henry Ridley promoted such an ecological explanation in the early

---

[15] Wallace, *The Malay Archipelago*, vol. 1, pp. 34–6; Clement Liew, "The Roman Catholic Church of Singapore, 1819–1910: From Mission to Church," unpublished Honours Thesis, Department of History, National University of Singapore, 1994.

[16] Wallace, *The Malay Archipelago*, vol. 1, pp. 35–6.

[17] Alfred Russel Wallace, "To M.A. Wallace 30 Apr 1854," in *Alfred Russel Wallace Letters and Reminiscences*, vol. 1, ed. James Marchant (London: Cassell, 1916), pp. 47–8.

[18] Wallace, *The Malay Archipelago*, vol. 1, p. 36.

20th century, when Wallace was in Singapore officials attempted to protect the hilltops due to a concern that their deforestation would adversely affect the climate of the island. This in turn was the result of the efforts of the solicitor and journalist James Richardson Logan whose call to protect forests to preserve local rainfall sounds remarkably prescient today: "climate concerns the whole community, and its protection from injury is one of the duties of Government."[19]

From this base camp on the edge of Bukit Timah, Wallace and Allen set out into their first forays to collect specimens in the eastern archipelago. Following the roads and tracks of the woodcutters was essential as the tall lush forests were impenetrably thick and criss-crossed with vines and creepers, many with vicious thorns. A dirt road led to the top of Bukit Timah. The European elite had used this path for jaunts into the country to enjoy the views from the summit. By 1854, it had fallen into disrepair and the jungle was starting to reclaim it. On his first day, Wallace captured 11 species of long-horned beetles called longicorns.[20] It was a good start.

> In about two months I obtained no less than 700 species of beetles, a large proportion of which were quite new, and among them were 130 distinct kinds of the elegant Longicorns (Cerambycidæ), so much esteemed by collectors. Almost all these were collected in one patch of jungle, not more than a square mile in extent, and in all my subsequent travels in the East I rarely if ever met with so productive a spot. This

---

[19] I am grateful to Richard Corlett for informing me of this. See also Tony O'Dempsey's contribution to this volume. Henry N. Ridley, *Spices* (London: Macmillan, 1912), pp. 254–7; J.R. Logan, "The Probable Effects on the Climate of Pinang of the Continued Destruction of Its Hill Jungles," *Journal of the Indian Archipelago and Eastern Asia* 2 (1848): 534–6. As usual, this story seems to be more complicated than usually told. In July 1845, Governor William Butterworth issued an order forbidding the felling of trees on the hilltops, although the level of compliance is uncertain. *The Singapore Free Press and Mercantile Advertiser* [hereafter *SFP*], 3 July 1845, p. 3; "The Weather," *SFP*, 18 Sep. 1845, p. 2. For more detail on colonial governments and proto-conservation, see Richard H. Grove, *Green Imperialism: Colonial Expansion, Tropical Island Edens, and the Origins of Environmentalism, 1600–1860* (Cambridge: Cambridge University Press, 1995); Jeyamalar Kathirithamby-Wells, *Nature and Nation: Forests and Development in Peninsular Malaysia* (Honolulu, HI: University of Hawai'i Press, 2005).

[20] A.R. Wallace, "Notes on the Localities Given in Longicornia Malayana, With an Estimate of the Comparative Value of the Collections Made at Each of Them," *Transactions of the Entomological Society of London* (ser. 3) 3, 7 (1869): 691–6.

exceeding productiveness was due in part no doubt to some favourable conditions in the soil, climate, and vegetation, and to the season being very bright and sunny, with sufficient showers to keep everything fresh. But it was also in a great measure dependent, I feel sure, on the labours of the Chinese wood-cutters. They had been at work here for several years, and during all that time had furnished a continual supply of dry and dead and decaying leaves and bark, together with abundance of wood and sawdust, for the nourishment of insects and their larvæ. This had led to the assemblage of a great variety of species in a limited space, and I was the first naturalist who had come to reap the harvest they had prepared. In the same place, and during my walks in other directions, I obtained a fair collection of butterflies and of other orders of insects, so that on the whole I was quite satisfied with these my first attempts to gain a knowledge of the natural history of the Malay Archipelago.[21]

The woodcutters were making firewood to boil the gambier leaves. So their business led indirectly to Wallace's. In another sense, the planters and Wallace were deriving their income from Singapore's natural environment. Just as the gambier trees grew in the soil and thrived in the tropical sun, watered by the frequent rains, so Wallace derived his income from the birds and insects that the island produced.

In a 28 May 1854 letter to his mother, Wallace described a typical day at Bukit Timah:

Get up at half-past five. Bath and coffee. Sit down to arrange and put away my insects of the day before, and set them safe out to dry. Charles mending nets, filling pincushions, and getting ready for the day. Breakfast at eight. Out to the jungle at nine. We have to walk up a steep hill to get to it, and always arrive dripping with perspiration. Then we wander about till two or three, generally returning with about 50 or 60 beetles, some very rare and beautiful. Bathe, change clothes, and sit down to kill and pin insects. Charles ditto with flies, bugs and wasps; I do not trust him yet with beetles. Dinner at four. Then to work again till six. Coffee. Read. If very numerous, work at insects till eight or nine. Then to bed.[22]

Wallace was enraptured with the spectacular insects, with his focus often returning to the beetles. He was "delighted" with the "hosts of elegantly varied Longicorns."[23] Some he thought of as "my Singapore

[21] Wallace, *The Malay Archipelago*, vol. 1, p. 36.
[22] Alfred Russel Wallace, "To M.A. Wallace 28 May 1854," in *Alfred Russel Wallace Letters and Reminiscences*, ed. Marchant, p. 49.
[23] Alfred R. Wallace, "The Entomology of Malacca," *Zoologist* 13, 149 (1855): 4637.

friends—beautiful longicorns of the genera Astathes, Glenea and Clytus, the elegant Anthribidæ, the pretty little Pericallus and Colliuris."[24] He also observed life in the canopy of the forest. He commented on the graceful flying lemurs gliding from tree to tree as something other than "good sport," and described the Oriental Magpie Robin as having "a very beautiful and varied note; it is the commonest bird in Singapore … it feeds much on the ground, and its rich black and white plumage makes it a pleasing object."[25]

Amidst this cornucopia of exotic insects, Wallace made one of his earliest theoretical observations in Asia, one that marked his path toward a theory of species. He recognized "The Euplœas [a genus of milkweed butterflies] here quite take the place of the Heliconidæ of the Amazons, and exactly resemble

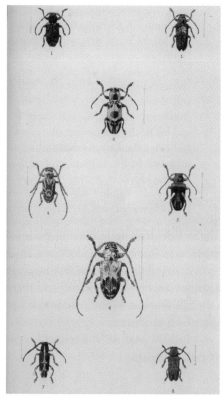

Plate 3.1 An image, taken from plate 8 of "Longicornes Malayana," featuring illustrations of insects Wallace collected in Singapore.[26] Specifically, figures 2, 6 and 7 are from Singapore. The largest, #6, is a *Samia albidorsalis*.

[24] A.R. Wallace, "Letter [dated 8 April 1855, Borneo]," *Zoologist* 13, 154 (1855): 4804.

[25] Alfred R. Wallace, "On the Ornithology of Malacca," *Annals and Magazine of Natural History* (ser. 2) 15, 86 (1855): 97. Now called the Oriental Magpie Robin (*Copsychus saularis*). Richard Corlett informs me that the Magpie Robin was almost extinct in Singapore by the 1980s "but has made a comeback as a result of deliberate releases of imported birds." Personal communication.

[26] Francis P. Pascoe, "Longicornia Malayana; or, a Descriptive Catalogue of the Species of the Three Longicorn Families Lamiidæ, Cerambycidæ and Prionidæ, Collected by Mr. A.R. Wallace in the Malay Archipelago," *Transactions of the Entomological Society of London* 3, 3 (1864): 1–712.

them in their habits."[27] A different and unrelated species filled the same ecological niche on the other side of the world—despite the similarity of climate. This suggested to Wallace that the environment did not just dictate which species existed. He would soon come to believe their history or ancestry was in fact the key.

Singapore, beyond Bukit Timah

During this first period of residence in Singapore, Wallace was absorbed in his forest collecting. This is understandable, considering his interests and purpose for his travels, although he also witnessed numerous important events in the history of Singapore, including a continuation of a series of riots that shook Singapore in the early 1850s. As he recorded later from his perspective at St. Joseph's Church in Bukit Timah, "One morning 600 Chinese passed our house in straggling single file, armed, in the most impromptu manner, with guns, matchlocks, pikes, swords, huge three-pronged fishing-spears, knives, hatchets, and long sharpened stakes of hard wood. They were going to buy rice, they said, but they were stopped on the road by a party of about a dozen Malay police, five of them shot, and the rest turned back. The disturbance lasted a week, and even now men are still occasionally killed, nobody knows why."[28]

Wallace was witnessing the Hokkien-Teochew Riots of May 1854. The conflict was between the immigrant communities of Hokkien and Teochew Chinese from different regions of China (southern region of Fujian Province and the Chaoshan region of eastern Guangdong Province, respectively). The riots were part of a series of conflicts between Chinese communities that wracked the Singaporean countryside during the 1850s. Among the earliest of these confrontations occurred when Chinese secret societies, particularly the Ghee Hin Hoe (which was primarily composed of Cantonese members, although it would become Hokkien-dominated by the 1860s), attacked Catholic converts on gambier and pepper plantations as the agriculturalists were falling outside of their control. These 1851 riots would have placed St. Joseph's Church, a rural mission in the heart of the plantation areas, in the

---

[27] A.R. Wallace, "Letter [dated 9 May 1854, Singapore]," *Zoologist* 12, 142 (1854): 4396.
[28] A.R. Wallace, "Letters from the Eastern Archipelago," *The Literary Gazette, and Journal of the Belles Lettres, Science, and Art* 1961 (1854): 739.

center of the conflict.[29] The events Wallace witnessed began on 5 May 1854 during a quarrel between a Hokkien shopkeeper and a Teochew customer over the price of rice. This soon erupted into large scale and very violent riots between Hokkiens and Teochews and spread over the whole island. Pitched battles took place in the town and across the countryside. Houses were burned, shops looted and hundreds of opponents killed and mutilated. Part of the conflict between the two groups, as was true of the early 1851 riots, was control over the gambier and pepper plantations in the very area where Wallace was collecting.[30] Yet, despite the dramatic events shuddering the island and the smoke of burning houses encircling Bukit Timah, Wallace remained consumed with collecting insects in the forest. This underscores just how peripheral Wallace was at the time, an unknown European busy with an unusual occupation.

Wallace's main focus was in his natural history endeavors while seeking out new areas for exploration. Among the places he visited was Pulau Ubin. He noted that the tiny island in the straits separating Singapore from the Malay Peninsula was known for its granite quarry. Although he did not reap a good harvest on the island, nor did he record specimens from Pulau Ubin separately from Singapore, it may have been where he observed "a wild pig swimming across the arm of the sea that separates Singapore from the Peninsula of Malacca."[31]

At the end of May, Wallace took his first consignment of 1,087 beetles to Hamilton, Gray & Co. on the south side of the Singapore River to be shipped care of "Mr. J. Deal Jun. Custom House Agent High Street

---

[29] Charles Burton Buckley, *An Anecdotal History of Old Times in Singapore: From the Foundation of the Settlement under the Honourable East India Company on February 6th, 1819 to the Transfer to the Colonial Office as Part of the Colonial Possessions of the Crown on April 1st, 1867*, vol. 1 (Singapore: Fraser and Neave, 1902), pp. 542–6; Irene Lim, *Secret Societies in Singapore* (Singapore: National Heritage Board, Singapore History Museum, 1999).

[30] *The Straits Times*, 9 May 1854, p. 4; "The Riots," 16 May 1854, p. 4; "The Singapore Riots," *The Straits Times*, 30 May 1854, p. 4.

[31] Wallace, *The Malay Archipelago*, vol. 2, p. 141; Letter to Norton Shaw 1 Nov. 1854: Royal Geographical Society Letter book 1854 (JMS 8/17); A.R. Wallace, "Introduction," in "A Catalogue of the Aculeate Hymenoptera and Icheumonidae of India and the Eastern Archipelago," *Journal of the Linnean Society, Zoology* 11 (1873): 285; Wallace, "Notes on the Localities Given in Longicornia Malayana," p. 691.

Southampton *with great care*" to his agent Samuel Stevens in London.[32] Stevens, in turn, sold Wallace's specimens to museums and private collectors. Wallace's consignments consisted of items for sale and others that were "private" for his personal collection. He noted on 8 July that he had collected 4,380 insects in Singapore in nine weeks. Wallace later wrote "Even the best collections I have been able to make can only be looked upon as samples of the productions of these luxuriant regions."[33]

In search of richer fields for collecting, Wallace and Allen sailed north to Malacca, probably on 13 July, in the schooner, *Kim Soon Hin*, "with about fifty Chinese, Hindoos and Portuguese passengers," returning to Singapore at the end of September 1854, presumably on the bark *John Bibby*.[34] Wallace and Allen apparently stayed again with Rev. Mauduit at Bukit Timah. Perhaps, having met naturalists in Malacca, Wallace realized that to find novel specimens he would have to travel further east or north. At first he planned to go to Cambodia with one of the French missionaries. They told him it would make excellent collecting ground. The missionary's trip to Cambodia, however, was several months away. Wallace needed to collect and generate revenue continuously. It was at this time that he turned his sights on a newly acquired territory, under the control of a charismatic—and controversial—English adventurer, Sir James Brooke.

On 3 September 1854, Sir James arrived from Sarawak on the brig HMS *Lily* to attend a Commission examining accusations against his conduct in Borneo. The case was widely discussed in the Singapore newspapers at the time. In January 1851, a letter signed by 53 merchants and inhabitants of Singapore "relative to the massacre of the Dyaks, off the Coast of Borneo, in July 1849" was sent to Joseph Hume, a Member of Parliament, in London.[35] Hume brought the questions before Parliament on 10 July 1851.

---

[32] Alfred Russel Wallace, "Autograph Note, Directions for Collecting in the Tropics ... for Mr. H. Squires 1858 Oct 05," at http://wallace-online.org/content/record?itemID=CUL-DAR270.1.2.

[33] *Notebook 1*, p. 130 (Linnean Society of London MS179); Wallace, "Introduction," p. 288.

[34] "Departures," *The Straits Times*, 26 Sep. 1854, p. 8; Alfred Russel Wallace, *My Life: A Record of Events and Opinions*, vol. 1 (London: Chapman and Hall, 1905), p. 338.

[35] A letter to Mr Hume in Jan. 1851: "Letter from Certain Merchants and Inhabitants of Singapore, to Joseph Hume, Esquire, M.P., Relative to the Massacre of the Dyaks, Off the Coast of Borneo, in July 1849." Given as an appendix to anon., 1854.

The result was the institution of a Commission that met three years later. In the interim, and in response to the accusations, a friend published some of Brooke's letters to help clarify his intentions or rather to put a positive shine on his motives and actions in Sarawak and Borneo to the British public.[36]

The proceedings began on Monday, 11 September 1854, at the Singapore Court House at the southern end of the Esplanade. The main issues to be examined were whether it was appropriate for a British subject and the British Consul and Commissioner of Trade to Borneo to be a head of state and to examine reports that Brooke had committed atrocities against purported pirates. The Commission continued to meet almost daily until mid-November before its members returned to Calcutta aboard the steamer *Shanghai* on 20 November. The next month, a book in support of Sir James was published in Singapore detailing the case.[37] No charges were brought against Sir James and he was effectively exonerated. Although the ongoing Commission distracted Brooke, it provided an opportunity for him to meet Wallace. According to Wallace, Sir James "most kindly offered me every assistance in exploring the territories under his rule." Sir James supplied a letter to his nephew and heir-apparent Captain John Brooke "to make [Wallace] at home till he arrives, which may be a month, perhaps."[38]

Wallace was preparing for his future travels. In addition to Sarawak, he was interested in visiting other areas of the vast archipelago. He forwarded his letter from the Dutch government to Batavia (Jakarta) the capital of the Dutch East Indies. He received a civil reply informing him that "I should meet with no obstructions in visiting any of their eastern possessions."[39]

In the midst of these arrangements, Wallace spent most of his time "packing up, arranging & cataloguing all my collection: about 6000 specimens of insects, birds, quadrupeds & shells" he had collected mostly in Singapore. Wallace was, after all, a commercial collector. As he replied rather sharply to his boyhood friend George Silk: "[The botanist] Sir W. Hooker's remarks are

---

[36] John C. Templer, ed., *Private Letters of Sir James Brooke, K.C.B., Rajah of Sarawak, Narrating the Events of His Life, from 1838 to the Present Time*, 3 vols. (London: Bentley, 1853).

[37] *The Straits Times*, 21 Nov. 1854, p. 6; [A. Simonides], *The Borneo Question; Or, The Evidence Produced at Singapore, Before the Commissioners Charged With the Enquiry into the Facts Relating to Sir James Brooke, K.C.B. &c. Compiled from the 'Singapore Free Press,' and other sources* (Singapore: Alfred Simonides, 1854).

[38] To George Silk 15 Oct. 1854. NHM WP1/3/33.

[39] To Norton Shaw 1 Nov. 1854. RGS Letter book 1854 (JMS 8/17).

encouraging, but I cannot afford to collect plants. I have to work for a living, and plants would not pay unless I collect nothing else, which I cannot do, being too much interested in zoology."[40] Wallace recorded in his *Notebook 1* "2nd small Box overland, sent Oct. 16th. 1854."[41] He eventually earned £20 from the consignment. He sent his third consignment to Stevens on the sailing ship *Royal Alice*, which left Singapore on 24 October.[42]

When in town, Wallace used the Singapore Library, which was located in the grounds of the Singapore Institution. The beginning of his *Notebook 1* is filled with early reading notes. Wallace's interest in the origins of species, apart from an oft-quoted 1845 letter about reading the evolutionary *Vestiges of the Natural History of Creation* (1844), now becomes evident for the first time. He took notes on the geologist Joseph Jukes' *A Sketch of the Physical Structure of Australia* (1850). Wallace noted the apparent age of Australia and that the "fossils agree with present fauna & flora" that is that the same unique types (marsupials) were present in its ancient past as now. Given a history of the world then universally accepted, in which parts of continents rise and sink beneath the sea, islands were created where the species remained stranded but hence related on nearby islands: "Thus *species* of the different colonies differ; [but their] *genera* the same."[43]

Wallace also took notes on an article on the relationship between the Edentata (anteaters, armadillos and sloths) and reptiles.

> Edentata allied by internal structure to birds and *reptiles*—but more nearly to reptiles—Reptile Birds also allied to reptiles
> ? Mammalia and birds have both branched out of reptiles, not from *the other*.[44]

---

[40] To George Silk 15 Oct. 1854. NHM WP1/3/33.

[41] On that date, however, the P&O ships only carried the "overland" route and none of their ships sailed. The P&O steamer *Cadiz* departed on the 19 October. "Homeward Mails," *The Straits Times*, 17 Oct. 1854, p. 4; Daniel B. Baker, "Alfred Russel Wallace's Record of his Consignments to Samuel Stevens, 1854–1861," *Zoologische Mededeelingen* 75, 16–25 (2001): 260; *Notebook 1*: Linnean Society of London MS179.

[42] Baker, "Alfred Russel Wallace's Record of his consignments," pp. 254–341.

[43] *Notebook 1*: Linnean Society of London MS179, p. 3. J. Beete Jukes, *A Sketch of the Physical Structure of Australia, So Far as It is at Present Known* (London: T. and W. Boone, 1850).

[44] *Notebook 1*: Linnean Society of London MS179, p. 5. Edward Fry, "On the Relation of the Edentata to the Reptiles, Especially of the Armadillos to the Tortoises," *Annals and Magazine of Natural History* 18 (1846): 278–80.

These notes are a tantalizing beginning. Wallace was interested in the relationships between the major living groups of animals as part of the history of life. Terms such as "branching out" seem to indicate actual genealogical descent. The language of the time, however, could be ambiguous so we cannot be sure, because Wallace later believed in branching descent, that this is what he meant in these early notes. The article he was reading ended with an unattributed quotation: "The true affinities of organic structures branch out irregularly in all directions."[45] This was from naturalist Hugh Edwin Strickland who proposed "branching" relationships between different groups of animals, but did not mean an evolutionary family tree. Strickland proposed categorizing animals according to close similarities rather than superficial resemblances. Before Strickland, branching was used in yet another non-evolutionary sense in Georges Cuvier's famous "radically distinct branches in the animal kingdom."[46] Indeed as far as the surviving evidence reveals, all of Wallace's evolutionary theorizing occurred in the Eastern Archipelago—starting from his stay in Singapore. It was now time to proceed deeper into this archipelago. On 17 October 1854, Wallace and Allen sailed on the brig *Weraff* for the Sarawak River on the island of Borneo, 800 kilometers to the east of Singapore.[47]

Singapore as a Base for Travels

Wallace spent more time on Borneo than any other island in the archipelago. He returned to Singapore without Allen, who stayed in Sarawak, on 17 February 1856. Wallace, however, brought with him a new Malay assistant, Ali, who was a young lad of about 13 or 14 and remained with Wallace for the rest of his voyage. They stayed in town rather than with the missionaries at Bukit Timah. Wallace wrote to his brother-in-law, the London photographer Thomas Sims:

> I quite enjoy being a few days at Singapore now. The scene is at once so familiar and strange. The half-naked Chinese coolies, the neat

---

[45] Fry, "On the Relation of the Edentata to the Reptiles;" H.E. Strickland, "Description of a Chart of the Natural Affinities of the Insessorial Order of Birds," *Report of the Thirteenth Meeting of the British Association for the Advancement of Science Held at Cork in August 1843, Notices and Abstracts of Communications* 13 (1844): 69.

[46] Martin J.S. Rudwick, *The Meaning of Fossils: Episodes in the History of Palaeontology* (Chicago, IL: University of Chicago Press, 1985), p. 153.

[47] "Departures," *The Straits Times*, 24 Oct. 1854, p. 8.

shopkeepers, the clean, fat, old, long-tailed merchants, all as busy and full of business as any Londoners. Then the handsome Klings, who always ask double what they take, and with whom it is most amusing to bargain. The crowd of boatmen at the ferry, a dozen begging and disputing for a farthing fare, the Americans, the Malays, and the Portuguese make up a scene doubly interesting to me now that I know something about them and can talk to them in the general language of the place. The streets of Singapore on a fine day are as crowded and busy as Tottenham Court Road, and from the variety of nations and occupations far more interesting. I am more convinced than ever that no one can appreciate a new country in a short visit. After two years in the country I only now begin to understand Singapore and to marvel at the life and bustle, the varied occupations, and strange population, on a spot which so short a time ago was an uninhabited jungle. A volume may be written on Singapore without exhausting its singularities. 'The Roving Englishman's' is the pen that should do it.[48]

"The Roving Englishman" was the pen name of travel writer George Sala who wrote for Dickens's magazine, *Household Words*, available in the Singapore Library.

Staying in the town gave Wallace the opportunity to use the Library again. He made notes about the construction, by Chinese laborers, of a "Singapore lighthouse," which Wallace and Ali passed on their return from Sarawak.

> At Singapore lighthouse.
> Stones of 660 lbs. carried by 4 chinamen up an inclination of 15° to height of 20 feet = 165 per man.
> largest stone carried by 4 men 990 lbs = 247 lbs per man.
> 4 men raised 3918 lbs 20 feet in 4 hours = 326 lbs raised 1 foot per minute for each man, & working 9 hours a day.
>
> ——
>
> A European can do nearly double, but these chinamen were working by *day* & not by *contract work*.
> —J.G. Thompson. Government Surveyor *at Singapore*.[49]

Wallace got the name slightly wrong. The Government surveyor of Singapore from 1841 to 1853 was John Turnbull Thomson. He was one of the most influential Europeans in early history of Singapore as he helped create

---

[48] To Sims [20 Feb. 1856]. Presumably enclosed with the letter to F. Sims 20 Feb. 1856. NHM WP1/3/37.

[49] *Notebook 4*: Linnean Society of London MS180, p. 56.

and expand the town beyond the harbor area. Much of this involved the laying of roads into the hinterland, such as Bukit Timah Road, and the appropriately named Thomson Road. In addition, he was the architect of important structures such as the spire on St. Andrew's Cathedral, as well as several lighthouses. Beginning in 1850, he turned his focus to the Horsburgh Lighthouse, which was named after a Scottish hydrographer for the East India Company who surveyed the waters of the area. The lighthouse was built on a rocky islet known as Pedra Branca, 24 miles east of Singapore in the South China Sea. The islet received its Portuguese appellation "white rock" in reference to its original whitish appearance that the accumulated guano of the black-naped tern gave the site. The lighthouse is still in use today.[50]

At the end of March 1856, Wallace returned to stay at the French mission at Bukit Timah. He spent seven weeks there "going daily into the jungle," where he found "many pretty new things showing that Singapore is far from exhausted yet, & will furnish hosts of novelties to a resident collector."[51] Wallace recorded in his notebook:

> March. 1856. Singapore. Bee Eater (*Merops*)
> This like a swallow but slower, very graceful circles round & settles on sticks & twigs & posts. Seizes insects on the wing
> & rests to swallow them cleans its bill against the perch. Chirps or twitters during flight.
> At Singapore & Malacca migratory—appears in November, leaves in March–April.[52]

This was apparently the Blue-Throated Bee Eater (*Merops viridis*), which is one of the most colorful and striking birds in Singapore with deep chestnut-colored head, nape, and upper back, its lower back and tail glistening pale blue, pale green wings, and pastel green breast. On 4 April, he made notes on a long-tailed macaque.[53] He also saw the "Galeopithecus, or flying lemur" gliding between forest trees.[54]

---

[50] John Turnbull Thomson, *Account of the Horsburgh Light-House, Erected on Pedra Branca, Near Singapore* (Singapore: G.M. Fredrick, 1852); *Some Glimpses of Life in the Far East* (London: Richardson and Company, 1864); John Hall-Jones and Christopher Hooi, *An Early Surveyor in Singapore: John Turnbull Thomson in Singapore, 1841–1853* (Singapore: National Museum, 1979); S. Jayakumar and Tommy Koh, *Pedra Branca: The Road to the World Court* (Singapore: NUS Press, 2009).

[51] Wallace to Stevens, 12 May 1856. CUL Add. 7339/233.

[52] *Notebook 4*, p. 55.

[53] *Notebook 1*, p. 18.

[54] Wallace, *The Malay Archipelago*, vol. 1, p. 210.

Also during this stay, Wallace met a friend he had made in Malacca, George Rappa, Jr. Wallace wrote to his agent Stevens with a request to help selling two boxes of books for Rappa. "He is the son of the collector who lived many years at Malacca, but has quarrelled with his father & is very badly off."[55] Wallace's assistance may have helped because in 1859, Rappa became a partner of Philip Robinson, founder of Robinson and Co., one of the oldest department stores in Singapore.

Wallace did not stay long in Singapore, and would only return six years later. On 23 May 1856, Wallace, Ali, and a Portuguese shooter sailed from Singapore with the bark *Kembang Djepoon* ("Japanese Blossom" in Malay) into the Dutch East Indies.[56] Wallace thus reached Bali and Lombok and had his first ideas that would later mature into the Wallace Line. Further expeditions took him throughout the eastern islands and eventually to his fateful stay in Ternate and discovery of the principle of natural selection.[57] At the end of his voyage, in 1861, he began to return toward Singapore, collecting in Java and Sumatra. On 18 January 1862, the Dutch mail steamer *Macassar* arrived at Singapore bearing Wallace and Ali from Sumatra.[58] Where Wallace stayed in Singapore went unrecorded, perhaps at a hotel, or with his friend the mining engineer Frederick Geach, or another resident named John Fisher. According to a 1904 obituary, "Wallace was for some time the guest of Mr Fisher in Singapore, and received much substantial assistance from him at a difficult period in his residence in the East."[59]

The connection to these friends in Singapore was important for Wallace's first assistant in the Malay Archipelago, Charles Allen, as he later worked for John Fisher. Allen would finish collecting shortly after Wallace's departure for England in 1862. Allen drifted into several jobs, particularly related to mining in the region before settling in Singapore. He eventually married and raised a large family and became the manager of Fisher's Perseverance Estate located in the Geylang district. The estate grew and processed lemon grass to make citronella oil, which was used in soaps and insect repellent. In 1887, he became the owner of the estate. The

---

[55] Wallace to Stevens 12 May 1856. CUL Add. 7339/233.

[56] "Departures," *The Straits Times*, 27 May 1856, p. 8.

[57] John van Wyhe and Kees Rookmaaker, "A New Theory to Explain the Receipt of Wallace's Ternate Essay by Darwin in 1858," *Biological Journal of the Linnean Society* 105, 1 (2012): 249–52.

[58] "Singapore Shipping," *The Straits Times*, 25 Jan. 1862, p. 3.

[59] "The Late John Fisher," *SFP*, 19 July 1904, p. 3.

poor London boy finally made his fortune in the East. A 1906 article on Wallace (actually a mistaken obituary!) stated: "The late Mr Charles Allen, whose many friends yet in Singapore will remember, used often to speak of his friend Wallace, of whom Mr Allen's family hold some interesting reminiscences, connected with his residence in Singapore." His daughters married well, one even to the architect of Singapore's famous Raffles Hotel. Allen died in 1892, and his descendants lived in Singapore until the Japanese invasion in 1942. His great-granddaughter still lives in Fremantle, Western Australia.[60]

During this time, Wallace made his final arrangements to leave the East. Wallace had photographs taken of himself with Geach and one of Ali who, for the first time, adopted European dress. Presumably this had to do with his final payment and gifts from Wallace. "On parting, besides a present in money, I gave him my two double-barrelled guns and whatever ammunition I had, with a lot of surplus stores, tools, and sundries, which made him quite rich. He here, for the first time, adopted European clothes, which did not suit him nearly so well as his native dress, and thus clad a friend took a very good photograph of him."[61] Which of his friends might have been a photographer is unknown. There were, of course, commercial photographers in Singapore such as Mr T. Heritage from London whose shop on Queen Street had been open for six months.[62] During this period, Wallace also arranged for the shipment to London of a *siamang* (gibbon) he had brought from Sumatra. It was a big hit in Singapore where such a creature was unknown. It was sent on a sailing ship via the Cape route, possibly on the German barque *Henry & Oscar* bound for Falmouth on 23 January, but did not survive the journey.[63]

Singapore had one last profitable collection for Wallace—and it was the most valuable he found in the archipelago—two live birds of paradise. He had been offered a free passage home if he could bring living examples

---

[60] "The Late Alfred Russel Wallace," *SFP*, 2 Apr. 1906, p. 5; Kees Rookmaaker and John van Wyhe, "In Wallace's Shadow: The Forgotten Assistant of Alfred Russel Wallace, Charles Allen," *Journal of the Malaysian Branch of the Royal Asiatic Society* 85, 2 (2012): 17–54.

[61] Wallace, *My Life*, vol. 1, p. 383.

[62] "Advertisements," *The Straits Times*, 18 May 1861, p. 4.

[63] "Singapore Shipping," *The Straits Times*, 25 Jan. 1862, p. 3. Yet, as Raby pointed out, in MA, Wallace stated that the *siamang* "died just before he started." Peter Raby, *Alfred Russel Wallace: A Life* (Princeton, NJ: Princeton University Press, 2001), p. 161.

Plate 3.2 Photograph of Geach and Wallace. The originals survive in the Natural History Museum Wallace collection. A version of the Wallace photograph, with Geach removed, was later published in Marchant 1916.

Plate 3.3 "My faithful boy—Ali." From Wallace, *My Life*, vol. 1, p. 383.

of these extraordinary birds back to Britain. On 6 February, Wallace paid $400 to the commission agents Mark Moss and William Waterworth on Serangoon Road and received a receipt for two live "Paradize Birds."[64] That evening, the P&O steamer *Emeu* arrived bringing the Hong Kong mails of 1 February. The next day, Wallace wrote to Philip Lutley Sclater, the secretary of the Zoological Society of London: "They were in the hands of a European

---

[64] Note kept with the letter to Sclater of 7 Feb. 1862. Zoological Society of London, GB 0814 BADW. The account in Raby 2001 on the acquisition, sale, and display of the birds of paradise in London is excellent. See also Fiona Tan's contribution to this volume.

merchant who was well aware of their value & asked an exorbitant price. As however they seemed in excellent health, had been in Singapore 3 months & in possession of a Bugis trader a year before that, I determined if possible to obtain them. After protracted negotiations I have purchased them."[65]

Wallace checked with the P&O office to see if they had received word that he and the birds should receive free passage to London. He was "much surprised & disappointed to find that no order for a free passage had been sent out, but merely instructions to take care of the birds if sent on board." So Wallace was forced to buy a first-class ticket to Southampton for $552, plus $33 passage through Egypt.[66] He would later claim the cost of his journey from the Zoological Society, which, including the $400 for the birds of paradise, made a whopping $1,000 for the Zoological Society to bear. On 8 February, Wallace's boxes and birdcage were weighed on the wharf. Presumably, Geach, Fisher, Rappa, and Ali were there to send him off as he was rowed out in a small sampan to the giant P&O steamer, *Emeu*, never to return. Many years later, he would look back on this time as "the best part of my life."[67]

Conclusions

Wallace's commercial collections of natural history specimens were sold to institutions such as the British Museum, the Derby Museum, the Berlin Museum, and the University Museum, Oxford. Individual collectors who purchased Wallace specimens included Francis Walker, Frederick Smith, J.B. Davis, Edwin Brown, E.W. Janson, F.P. Pascoe, and even French collectors, Abbe Marseul and Count Minszech. According to Daniel B. Baker, "The British Museum purchased a total of 7,758 insects of all orders, a substantial number but still an insignificant portion, 7%, of the whole." Whereas Wallace's much smaller collection of mammals and reptiles "purchased by the British Museum was, apparently, less than 150."[68]

---

[65] To P.L. Sclater 7 Feb. 1862. Zoological Society of London, GB 0814 BADW; "Shipping in Singapore Harbour," *The Straits Times*, 8 Feb. 1862, p. 3.
[66] "Notice," *The Straits Times*, 15 Feb. 1862, p. 4. The ticket for Marseilles was $528 which is where he eventually alighted, but not according to his original plan.
[67] James Marchant, "A Man of the Time: Dr. Alfred Russel Wallace and His Coming Autobiography," *Book Monthly* 2, 8 (1905): 545–9.
[68] Baker, "Alfred Russel Wallace's Record of His Consignments," pp. 255, 257.

Wallace had an impressive number of specimens, and almost every writer on Wallace cites the total of 125,660 specimens collected.[69] Wallace gave a breakdown: 310 mammals, 100 reptiles, 8,050 birds, 7,500 shells, 13,100 Lepidoptera (moths and butterflies), 83,200 Coleoptera (beetles), and 13,400 other insects. The collection was remarkable; it included at least 212 new species of birds. Wallace also bagged 200 new species of ants and a staggering 900 new species of beetles.[70]

It is a mistake, repeated by virtually every writer however, to imply that Wallace collected 125,660 specimens himself. He employed full-time collecting assistants throughout his voyage. His records do not allow us to see exactly how many specimens his assistants collected. Charles Allen alone collected at least 40,000.[71] There was (not counting boat crews, porters, and cooks) a long list of collecting assistants that included not just Ali. There was a Portuguese shooter in Malacca; Fernandez in Bali and Lombok; in Macassar, there was Baderoon, Baso, and two others. In New Guinea, it was Lahagi, Lahi, and Jumaat; servants at Menado included Thomas and Cornelius; Wallace employed two hunters at Lotta, a man at Langowan, and two boys with blowpipes at Panghu. At Lempias, there were two men, while Petrus Rehatta, Headonus, Mesach, and Theodorus Matakena assisted Wallace at Amboyna. On Ceram, there was a lad from Awaiya and two hunters, at Bouru another hunter, and in Sumatra Wallace employed a hunter and even Geach to add to the collection.[72] Specimens were also purchased from local peoples like the Dyaks in Borneo, the bird of paradise hunters on Bessir and dealers and colonials like Willem Mesman and Captain Brooke. Working for Wallace was dangerous too. Ali was struck by fever, two were stranded on a deserted island, possibly to die, one became a slave at Aru, and another died in New Guinea. Wallace's collecting total was so high not because he was a superhuman collector but because he paid a small army of assistants to maximize specimen production.

---

[69] Wallace, *The Malay Archipelago*, p. xiv.

[70] Wilma George, "Alfred Wallace, the Gentle Trader: Collecting in Amazonia and the Malay Archipelago 1848–1862," *Journal of the Society for the Bibliography of Natural History* 9, 4 (1979): 503–14.

[71] Kees Rookmaaker and John van Wyhe, "In Wallace's Shadow: The Forgotten Assistant of Alfred Russel Wallace, Charles Allen," *Journal of the Malaysian Branch of the Royal Asiatic Society* 85, 2 (2012): 17–54.

[72] *Notebook 4*, p. 63b; Wallace, *The Malay Archipelago*, p. 476; Apr.–Oct. 1862 *Notebook 5*: Natural History Museum (London) Z MSS 89 O WAL. Raby, *Alfred Russel Wallace*.

The description of Wallace's collections was mainly the work of other naturalists. The *Wallace Online* project at the National University of Singapore has identified more than 130 publications that described Wallace specimens from the Eastern Archipelago. This is about the same number of publications on Darwin's *Beagle* specimens identified by the *Darwin Online* project.[73] Darwin tried to place his collections by group with specialists and sent his specimens to national collections, whereas most of Wallace's collections were dispersed amongst the cabinets of individual collectors.

Wallace was far from the only naturalist in the archipelago, though the others are seldom mentioned. He is much to blame for this tradition since he often claimed it was a region "which hardly any naturalist had then properly explored."[74] But there were other naturalists who studied the region like Rosenberg, Mohnike, Doleschall, Motley, Zollinger, Huguenin, von Richthofen, Bernstein, Cantor, and Collingwood. Not to mention the Dutch Scientific Commission and scores of lesser-known figures. Wallace soon had serious competitors on his heels, such as the American naturalist Albert Bickmore and the French entomologist P.J.M. Lorquin.[75] Many others followed. So to fully restore Wallace to his original context reveals him to be not a lone discoverer or "heroic pioneer" in the scientific exploration of Southeast Asia but one of a community of investigators—who has only subsequently became so much more famous as to outshine, and render invisible, the others. It is rather ironic, since Wallace has been called "Darwin's moon," that Wallace has so many moons.

[73] John van Wyhe, ed., *The Complete Work of Charles Darwin Online*, at http://darwin-online.org.uk/specimens.html.
[74] Marchant, "A Man of the Time," p. 545.
[75] I am grateful to Anna Mayer for informing me of Lorquin.

Visiting the Botanical Gardens:
Excerpts from Fox's *Guide to the Botanic Gardens* (1889)[1]

By-Laws

1. The Botanical Gardens shall be open to the public daily from sunrise to sunset and, on nights when the Band plays, to 11 P. M.

2. Carriages of all kinds are admitted, but it is forbidden to feed the horses in the Gardens. A halt can only be made at the side of the walks and where sufficient room can be left for other carriages to pass. No gharries or jinrickshas are allowed to ply for hire in the Gardens.

3. Driving or riding over the lawns is strictly prohibited.

4. Walking or playing over the flower beds is prohibited.

5. It is forbidden to touch the plants or flowers, and the cutting or removal from the Gardens of any plant, flower, or seed, or anything appertaining to the Gardens, will render those so doing liable to expulsion and prosecution.

6. Fishing or bathing in the lakes is prohibited.

7. Dogs are not admitted, unless led by a short string or chain.

8. It is forbidden to enter or leave the Gardens except by the proper entrances and exits.

9. All animals found straying in the Gardens will be impounded and destroyed.

10. Shooting in the Gardens is prohibited.

January, 1889

....

---

[1] Walter Fox, *Guide to the Botanical Gardens* (Singapore: Government Printing Office, 1889), inside cover, pp. 7–19.

THE GARDENS

The Botanical Gardens, Singapore, situated in the district of Tanglin, are about three miles from the town. The Gardens proper cover an area of about 66 acres, of which about 10 acres are original jungle.

With one or two exceptions, this is the only piece of original jungle left on the Island. Although it necessarily gives a very poor impression of the dense jungles in the interior of the Malay Peninsula, it does give a visitor some idea of the wonderful richness of tropical vegetation. Special notice should be taken of the banks of ferns, which bound this piece of jungle on the side next to Garden Road.

These ferns are locally known by the Natives as *Resam* and botanically as *Gleichenia dichotoma*.

CLIMATE

Situated nearly on the Equator, in Latitude 1° 17" N., Singapore possesses a very equable climate. The mean monthly temperature ranges between 78° and 82° Fahr., the highest and lowest temperature in the shade, during last year, being 91° 8' Fahr. and 68° 6' Fahr. No very distinct dry or wet seasons exist. A fortnight without rain would be considered a long drought.

As might be expected, it sometimes rains very heavily; as much as six inches falling in twenty-four hours. In 1887, the rainfall reached 112.97 inches. During these heavy rains, tender annuals, planted in the open ground, are more or less spoiled, hence the paucity of flowers, which is frequently remarked by visitors.

ROUTE

Route suggested to be taken by any one who has only a limited time in which to see the Gardens

...

On referring to the plan, this route (marked with a dotted line) will be seen to start from the entrance gates of the Gardens, and to proceed to the various lawns, where objects of interest are situated.

The lawns are marked alphabetically, and in the Appendix, lists are given of the principal trees and shrubs to be found on each lawn.

Starting from the entrance gates, on the right hand of the road, is lawn *A*. The plants on this lawn are mostly of an ornamental character; a list of these plants is given in Appendix *A*.

With this list, and the assistance of the labels attached to the plants, visitors should have no difficulty in identifying the various species.

On the left of the road, on the lawn marked *L*, a fine drooping tree is to be noticed. This is the gum copal (*Hymenaea verrucosa*) affording a copal used in varnish.

It is a native of Madagascar, and attains to a great size. Here are several plants of the Traveller's tree (*Ravenala speciosa*), so called from the water contained in the sheathing leaf stalks, which are hollow. If these leaves are pierced with a spear or knife, a considerable amount of palatable water can be obtained from them. These trees are natives of Madagascar. The following passage occurs in ELLIS'S "Madagascar":—"This tree has been most celebrated for containing during the most arid season a large quantity of pure fresh water, supplying to the traveller the place of wells in the desert. Having formerly been somewhat sceptical on the point, I determined to examine some of the trees, and during my journey this morning, we stopped near a clump of the trees. One of my bearers struck a spear four or five inches deep into the thick firm end of the stalk of the leaf, about six inches above its junction with its trunk, and on drawing it back a stream of pure clear water gushed out, about a quart of which we caught in a pitcher, and all drank of it on the spot. It was cool, clear, and perfectly sweet."

A little further along the drive, looking still to the left, will be seen a fine clump of sago palm (*Sagus laevis*) from which is obtained the sago of commerce. Sago is also produced in small quantities from several other plants, such as Cycas. It is prepared from the soft inner portion of the trunk, which is scooped out, and pounded in water until the starchy matter separates, when it is drained off with the water and allowed to settle. It is in this stage known as sago meal.

Close to these palms is the Nymphoea pond. The best time to see this pond is in the early morning. There, are to be seen the fine plants of the Victoria water lily (*Victoria regia*) presented to the Botanical Gardens by the representatives of the late Mr. WHAMPOA, whose gardens in Singapore have long been noted for them. This lily is a native of the tributaries of the Amazon, and was first brought into public notice by R.H. SCHOMBURGHK, who in 1837 discovered it on the Berbice River, in British Guiana. It was not, however, successfully introduced into cultivation until 1849. The seeds are edible, and the farina is said to be as good as the flour of the finest wheat.

At the far end of the pond, will be found the Sacred lotus (*Nelumbium speciosum*), regarded by the early Egyptians and Buddhists as an emblem of peculiar sanctity. The seeds and stem contain a quantity of starch and are used as food.

On the triangular plot marked *M* are several very showy flowering trees and shrubs. Of the former, the *Spathodea campanulata*, and the beautiful *Amherstia nobilis*, named after Countess AMHERST, wife of a Viceroy of India, are the most conspicuous. Of the shrubs, the best is the beautiful golden flowered Allamanda—*A. Cathartica*.

Further on to the left is the main lake, which covers an area of two acres. It has a small island in the middle, and is of varying depth, from three to nine feet.

Striking off to the right, and taking the small path which leads to the aviaries, a clump of trees will be seen on the left, among them are some Tembusee (*Fagraea peregrine [peregrine]*), one of the most graceful and beautiful indigenous trees. On the same lawn *B*, but more in the centre, are also several very fine specimens of it. The wood is very hard and durable. Another tree in the clump worth notice is the scandent one, with large bright green leaves and yellow flowers (*Wormia suffruticosa*).

On the small triangular plot of grass to the right of the path is a tree of Champaca (*Michelia champaca*). Its flowers are most exquisitely scented. There are two varieties—a yellow one with a powerful odour, and the white one with a delicate one. This is the white variety. It belongs to the Magnolia family.

After crossing the inner drive, the path leads to the aviaries. Here will be found a fairly representative collection of our native birds, together with specimens from Australia, New Guinea, Japan, etc. On leaving the aviaries on the opposite side, a tall Norfolk Island pine (*Araucaria excelsa*) immediately arrests one's attention. This pine attains in its own country a height of 200 feet. Here it is much subject to the attack of the white ants, which have carried of 7 or 8 during the last five years. The building seen on the right is the gardens office, library, and herbarium.

The lawn marked *D* is entirely devoted to palms. Here will be seen several very fine young specimens. Amongst them, at the point of the walk were it joins the drive, is a specimen of the Date palm (*Phoenix dactylifera*). It does not seem to be happy removed from its beloved desert, and has as yet shown no signs of flowering. Before crossing the road, notice on the left hand, bordering the inner drive, several trees of *Amherstia nobilis*. Should they happen to be in flower, they are worthy of close inspection. Resuming the route, on the point of the lawn *E*, is a specimen tree of the Funeral Cypress (*Cupressus funebris*), somewhat analogous in its weird aspect, and use, to our yew trees at home. On the right hand, a little further along the drive, is the beautiful red-stemmed palm (*Cyrtostachys rendah [renda]*) which is peculiar to the Straits, and is, from its high colouring, quite unique even among its own princely relations. To the left is the old rosery. The Queen of flowers, as she appears in Singapore, is no doubt a little disappointing. It is not, however, to be wondered at, considering the nature of the Singapore climate.

At the bottom of the steps leading to the terrace is a magnificent specimen of the *Bougainvillea speciosa*. At the top of the steps is the lower terrace, which nearly encircles the band-stand. Here is an attempt at tropical flower gardening with fairly good success.

On turning to the left, the beds, which fringe the walks, will be seen to contain different plants of vivid colours. From this walk are steps leading to the band-stand. This is the highest point in the Gardens, and from it several fine views are to be seen. On the north-east side the wall of creepers composed of *Thunbergia Chamberlainiana* is very noticeable. The band-stand drive is surrounded by several fine trees. In particular two *Adenantheras*, the one on the south side, bearing on its trunk several very large plants of the Elk's horn fern (*Platycerium biforme*).

Taking the small walk, at the opposite side, which leads past the bulb garden, the chief plant-house is reached. This house was erected in 1884 at a cost of $6,000. Here, from time to time, Flower Shows are held, for which purpose the house is admirably adapted. As the contents are constantly changing, it is impossible to give anything but a general reference to the plants. By looking at the plan, it will be easy to find where plants such as crotons, begonias, orchids and ferns are placed. The object aimed at is to keep in the house standard collections, of the more beautiful flowering and ornamental foliage plants, ferns, palms, and orchids. A feature is also made of the creepers. The house contains about 3,000 plants.

Leaving the plant-house, and passing through the plant-sheds (where there are plants in various stages of growth, the larger ones intended for the chief plant-house, the smaller ones as stock plants for exchange and sale), the Fern Rockery is reached. The Rockery, which was made in 1884, contains a good collection of our indigenous ferns, conspicuous amongst them are the large plants of *Angiopteris evecta*, the *paka gadjah*, or elephant fern, of the Malays.

On emerging from the fernery, two routes are open—the one leading to the jungle (*see* Plan), the other direct to the Palmetum. If the jungle route is preferred, a detour can be made, which leads back along the jungle road to the starting point. Wild monkeys are sometimes seen in the jungle.

The road now to be taken is that which leads towards the Palmetum. On the right, it will pass through the upper part of the economic, and medicinal gardens. (Visitors wishing to visit the "Experimental Gardens," on the Cluny Road some quarter of a mile away, should leave the gardens at this point, and take the Cluny Road, following it, until they come to the entrance which is notified by a sign-board—"Experimental Forest Nursery.") The groups of medicinal economic plants are still in the course of formation, and a great number have yet to be planted. Amongst those already here, are the following (*See* Appendix *B*).

The Palmetum follows next in order. In it will be found a very fair collection arranged in their proper genera. (*See* Appendix *C*).

Close to the Palmetum is the Herbaceous grounds, where all the smaller indigenous plants are arranged in their natural families.

The course will now be across, to the small walks leading to the lake, which will bring the visitor back to the main entrance from which he started.

In Appendix *D*, will be found a list of the principal fruits, growing in the experimental nursery, and in the Appendices *E* and *F*, respectively, lists of the principal plants producing India rubber, gums and resins, and of the plants producing oils and dyes.

CHAPTER 4

The Environmental Relevance of the Singapore Botanic Gardens

Nigel P. Taylor

The Singapore Botanic Gardens is the most intact historical designed landscape of any size in Singapore. Although it is an institution that has been present in Singapore for over 150 years, it remains one of the most popular attractions in the city-state. Between April 2012 and March 2013, the Gardens received 4 million visits, making it the most visited botanical gardens in the world.[1] As a major tourist attraction, as well as a feature of Singapore, the Botanic Gardens has become part of the everyday social and natural environment of the city-state.

The Singapore Botanic Gardens has made four major contributions to the island's environment. The first, and most enduring, is that it remains the premier outdoor, green, landscaped space for public relaxation and enjoyment; second, the 19th-century Superintendents and Directors of the Singapore Botanic Gardens were charged with gazetting, managing, and re-planting Straits Settlements forest reserves;[2] third, the Gardens was responsible for large scale environmental and economic change through the introduction of new crops and ornamental species; and, fourth, it was the center from which the early stages of the modern "greening" of Singapore as an island city-state was carried out. These, then, are the principal foci of this chapter, but they will be described as part of the broader history of the Singapore

---

[1] Visitor entry and exit is measured by means of infra-red beams at its various public gates and via car park entry and exit data.

[2] Please see Tony O'Dempsey's contribution to this volume for further details on this aspect of Singaporean environmental history.

Botanic Gardens, in order to set the four elements in context. The stories of these four elements, however, intertwine. As each Director added—and subtracted—from the Garden, it developed into a key center for both the study of the Singaporean environment as well as the greening of an island.

Developing a Garden, Aesthetically and Economically

Singapore's environment had already undergone significant change when the Singapore Botanic Gardens was founded in 1859. Indeed, its foundation was in part a consequence of such change. Although Sir Stamford Raffles established botanical and experimental gardens beside his residence on Government Hill (now Fort Canning) soon after his arrival in 1819, they initially existed only for spice cultivation. By 1823, these gardens had expanded to cover 19 hectares and were focused on the cultivation of nutmeg, cloves, and cocoa, in effect founding a spice industry that would benefit the island for over the next 40 years. In 1829, however, Raffles' gardens were abandoned for lack of resources—he had left the island in June 1823, never to return, and in his absence no one was interested in their upkeep. Briefly, in 1836, the Agri-Horticultural Society revived 2.8 hectares of the abandoned area for what they hoped would be a lucrative nutmeg plantation. A decade later, this plantation was also abandoned after the price of the commodity crashed, although nutmeg remained a viable crop in Singapore for another decade until it was subject to a devastating blight, which between 1857 and 1860 brought the industry to a virtual close. This loss followed the earlier decline of gambier and pepper plantations and the natural forest their production consumed, leaving the colonial government presiding over large swaths of abandoned land that covered the island in secondary vegetation.[3]

In the late 1850s, the influential Chinese businessman, Hoo Ah Kay, better known as "Whampoa" (from Huangpo, his place of origin in China),

---

[3] J.W. Purseglove, "History and Functions of Botanic Gardens with Special Reference to Singapore," *Gardens Bulletin, Singapore* 17 (1959): 168; Bonnie Tinsley, *Gardens of Perpetual Summer: The Singapore Botanic Gardens* (Singapore: National Parks Board, Singapore Botanic Gardens, 2009), pp. 21–7; G.M. Reith, *Handbook to Singapore: With Map and Plans of the Botanic Gardens* (Singapore: The Singapore and Straits Printing Office, 1892), p. 17; Mark Ravinder Frost and Yu-Mei Balasingamchow, *Singapore: A Biography* (Singapore: Editions Didier Millet, 2009), pp. 99–100; I.H. Burkill, "The Establishment of the Botanic Gardens, Singapore," *Gardens' Bulletin, Straits Settlements* 2 (1918): 55.

began negotiating a deal with the government that would soon surpass these earlier efforts at developing experimental gardens. Whampoa offered his no longer productive nutmeg plantation at Tanglin (located between Tanglin and Napier Roads and the present-day Dempsey Village) as a site for the army to establish its main barracks. In exchange, the government would facilitate the acquisition of the land adjacent to the north, which was a former gambier plantation, for the Gardens of the Agri-Horticultural Society, of which Whampoa was a leading member.[4] The Society's land, thus, was bounded to the south by Napier (now Holland) Road, to the east and north by Cluny Road, and to the west by an estate belonging to the Temenggong, who eventually became the Sultan of Johor.

The Agri-Horticultural Society's acquisition amounted to 23 hectares and included, in addition to secondary vegetation called *"belukar,"* some freshwater swamp forest and, at its northern extent, six hectares of virgin jungle, claimed by some to be the haunt of tigers.[5] This rainforest remnant survives today and, though relatively small, is an important resource for plant conservation activities. Having secured this land, in 1860 the Society appointed Lawrence (or Laurence) Niven, the manager of a local nutmeg plantation and descendent of a well-known Scottish family of gardeners, to develop it as a garden.[6] Given the contemporary decline of the nutmeg business, it is understandable that Niven was interested in this supplementary employment, which, based on the favorable acknowledgments for his work repeated in the Society's Annual Reports over the next 14 years together with increases in his salary, he seems to have performed with considerable ability.[7]

Niven displayed particular skill in understanding the "capabilities" of the Gardens' rolling landscape, which he developed in a style similar to the English Landscape Movement that "Capability" (Lancelot) Brown made so famous in the previous century. Within a year, Niven had opened on the highest point of the site the Bandstand, a leveled parade area for military bands to play music, especially on moonlit evenings. Soon thereafter, the colonial government began providing convict labor for Niven to manage and

---

[4] Tinsley, *Gardens of Perpetual Summer*, p. 28.

[5] Ibid.

[6] Other 19th-century members of the Niven family were Curators or Head Gardeners at the botanic gardens of Glasnevin (Dublin, Ireland) and Hull (England). This information is courtesy of Bonnie Tinsley, via email, 4 Apr. 2012.

[7] Burkill, "The Establishment of the Botanic Gardens," pp. 58, 65, 68, 70–1.

even began contributing to his salary from 1866. With such help, he cleared the site of *belukar*; besides the rainforest tract, he also seems to have spared some of the existing trees, amongst which *tembusu* (*Cyrtophyllum fragrans*, near Lawn E, which also appears on the Singaporean five-dollar note), *Penaga laut* (*Calophyllum inophyllum*, Botany Centre), *Pulai basong* (*Alstonia pneumatophora*, Lawn H), and sago palm (*Metroxylon sagu*, Lawn A near Tanglin Gate) are thought to be survivors.[8] By 1864, a system of curving roads and footpaths was in place and the initial access gate to the site off Cluny Road, the Office Gate, had been replaced with the Main Gate at the junction of Cluny and Napier Roads. Flowerbeds were provided from which blooms could be cut to supply the Society's members, a right they exercised in return for the subscriptions they gave for the Gardens' upkeep. Access to the Singapore Botanic Gardens was in theory restricted to members, at least on some days of the week, and carriages and horse riding through the Gardens were allowed.[9]

In 1866, the Society's finances permitted the expansion of the site to the northwest and, together with another boundary adjustment connected to the construction of Gardens Road to the west (subsequently called Tyersall Avenue), the Gardens' area grew by more than ten hectares. The adjustment for the road was to avoid a patch of swamp, which was utilized for the excavation and landscaping of Swan Lake in the same year. This appears to be Singapore's oldest ornamental water body and, like the other lakes in the Gardens, remains a source of irrigation water. The road from the Main Gate now ran along the eastern margin of the lake, whilst on the northwest extension a residence for Niven was built. The Society paid for the house, first contracted in 1867 with a Chinese builder, with borrowed funds. This colonial style bungalow still exists today as Burkill Hall. Until 1969, it was the official residence of Gardens' Superintendents and Directors and sits in a commanding position at the highest point overlooking most of the site. It was extensively restored prior to the 1995 opening of the National

---

[8] The *Pulai basong* is endemic to freshwater swamp forest and is proof that such vegetation previously existed in the Gardens. It has been designated a Heritage Tree, and is one of only some 17 specimens known to remain in Singapore, most of the others being found in the Nee Soon swamp. It is assumed that trees not listed in the "Lawns" appendix to Walter Fox's *Guide to the Gardens* (Singapore: Singapore Botanic Gardens, 1889) were not planted but already extant in 1859. The sago palms are remarked upon by Burkill, "The Establishment of the Botanic Gardens," p. 98.

[9] Burkill, "The Establishment of the Botanic Gardens," pp. 56–8.

Orchid Garden, which now surrounds it. Its first occupant, Lawrence Niven, after more than a decade of loyal service, went on home leave in 1875 and promptly died in his native Scotland.[10]

At the close of 1874, the Agri-Horticultural Society, following some years of obsolescence, was found to be in serious financial debt, largely as a consequence of having built the Superintendent's house, and so it appealed to the colonial government to formally take charge of the Gardens. Although the legal details of this transfer were not completed until some years later, the government agreed. Soon thereafter, an oversight committee, with the assistance of the Director of the Royal Botanic Gardens at Kew, England, sought a botanically qualified Gardens Superintendent. Kew was the hub of the British Empire's gardens and its Director, Joseph Hooker, recommended a young gardener-botanist named James Murton, who took up his appointment in 1875, stopping *en route* to gain three months of tropical experience at Peradeniya Botanical Gardens (Sri Lanka), whence he brought a number of new plant introductions to the Singapore Botanic Gardens. Subsequently, and at the request of the authorities, he traveled in the Malay Peninsula collecting material for the Gardens, soon establishing an herbarium and botanical library, the first in the Straits Settlements, and turning the Gardens into a typical colonial botanic garden with a focus on plants of economic interest.[11]

Murton filled the Gardens with new plants, many of which would become important to the local economy and the interests of the larger British Empire. An early plant he introduced, for example, was the African oil palm (*Elaeis guineensis*), which was to have a major impact in the next century. In addition to the oil palm, Murton experimented with a wide range of crops, with applications for food, latex, medicines, as well as timber, including various kinds of coffee, tea, cacao, sugar cane, avocado, cardamom, gutta-percha, and cinchona.[12] To accommodate these efforts, Murton began

---

[10] Frances Burford (née Taylor), the author's sister, who lives in Scotland, has located Niven's grave (email, 11 June 2012).

[11] Peter Crane, "Botanic Gardens for the 21st century," *Gardenwise: The Newsletter of the Singapore Botanic Gardens* 16 (Jan. 2001): 4–8; Ray Desmond and F. Nigel Hepper, *A Century of Kew Plantsmen. A Celebration of the Kew Guild* (Richmond: Royal Botanic Gardens, Kew, 1993), pp. 79–84.

[12] I.H. Burkill, "The Second Phase in the History of the Botanic Gardens, Singapore," *Gardens' Bulletin, Straits Settlements* 2 (1918): 100; Purseglove, "History and Functions of Botanic Gardens," p. 170.

an economic garden in 1877 in the otherwise little developed northwest extension, and in the same year, 22 Brazilian Pará rubber seedlings (*Hevea brasiliensis*) arrived from Kew, 12 being retained at the Singapore Botanic Gardens and planted the following year. Murton filled the Gardens with so many new plantings that space soon became limited. To address this issue, the government granted a major land extension in 1879 between Bukit Timah Road and Cluny Road, where the latter had previously delimited the northern boundary of the site. These 41 hectares had been designated as "Military Reserve" and continued to be physically separated from the earlier acquired land by Cluny Road, but now became the new Economic Gardens, an area of major importance for the next four decades.[13] In addition to his vital role in introducing new species to the region, in 1879 Murton also oversaw construction of the Garden's most spectacular landscape element—Palm Valley. This gently northward-sloping depression is sandwiched between the hill upon which Burkill Hall stands and the elevation from which the towering trees of the rainforest, or Gardens' Jungle, soar.[14]

Beyond construction of such new features, as well as the development of economically related research, another matter frequently distracted Murton. The colonial governor, when agreeing to take responsibility for the Gardens, had made a number of recommendations, one being the establishment of a zoological collection. Animals of all kinds were soon being donated and whilst these must have greatly increased the site's appeal to visitors, it resulted in many challenges for the Superintendent, especially since some of the larger creatures required elaborate accommodation, though

---

[13] Ray Desmond, *Kew* (Richmond: Royal Botanic Gardens, Kew, 1995), p. 257, claims that an earlier consignment of rubber seedlings sent in 1876 had failed to survive. Also in 1878 (*Singapore Botanic Gardens' Annual Report*, 1878), a planting of palms was made near Office Gate (Cluny Road) and a probable survivor from this time is the elderly clump of Nibung palm (*Oncosperma tigillarium*), currently at the junction between Office Gate and Herbarium Ring Roads. Over more than a century, the clump has expanded outward in a circle of stems, the oldest part at the centre now a hollow space in which a number of people can stand.

[14] Hereafter (and until 1974) many details of the Gardens' development, where not referenced, are extracted from *Singapore Botanic Gardens' Annual Reports*, issued by the Government Printing Office, Singapore. The valley continues to display some 220 species of palms and is at times the site of the spectacular flowering and subsequent demise of giant talipot palms (*Corypha umbraculifera*), which most recently occurred in 2004/05; Ohn Set, "Beginning of the End," *Gardenwise* 24 (2005): 22–3 and front cover.

they invariably did not live very long; the skeletons of some of the deceased were donated to the Raffles Museum.[15] Only smaller animals were retained after 1878 and the zoo collection was formally terminated around 1904. Nevertheless, the early development of the zoo in the Singapore Botanic Gardens merits mention, since it left its mark on the landscape: for example, the Marsh Garden developed in 1969 to the southeast of Swan Lake, along the Gardens' southern border (Lawn A), is in fact the remains of a wallow dug for a short-lived rhinoceros, which died in 1877. Such features, however, remained secondary to most visitors. The indefatigable Victorian botanical artist, Marianne North, was an early visitor to the Gardens in 1876, and her diary does not remark on the developing zoo. Rather she notes: "The Botanical Garden at Singapore was beautiful. Behind it was a jungle of real untouched forest, which added much to its charm. In the jungle I found real pitcher-plants (*Nepenthes*) winding themselves amongst the tropical bracken. It was the first time I had seen them growing wild, and I screamed with delight."[16]

Poor financial accounting caused Murton to be relieved of his duties in 1880. His replacement was another Kew-trained Superintendent, Nathaniel Cantley, who came to Singapore from Mauritius, where he had been the second-in-charge of its historic botanical gardens, Pamplemousses. In Singapore, Cantley focused on labeling the living collections and rationalizing the buildings, removing the random assortment constructed during Murton's time and grouping all the workers' accommodation in the southern end of the Economic Gardens, which he was busy filling up with Malaysian timber and latex-producing trees, including rubber. In 1882, Cantley built a herbarium and library—now called Ridley Hall—as well as the Plant House, a structure roofed in 1885 and used to display plants requiring of protection, as well as being a venue for public flower shows and plant sales in support of the Gardens' finances. Cantley's last conspicuous achievement at the Gardens was the construction of the Main (Tanglin) Gate pillars, completed in 1886—the modern pillars are at the same spacing as Cantley's, though not in exactly the same location.

Beyond construction of buildings in the Singapore Botanic Gardens, Cantley also made significant contributions to the plant life found through-out Singapore. Cantley became unwell soon after his appointment, and left

---

[15] See Timothy P. Barnard's contribution to this volume.
[16] Marianne North, *A Vision of Eden: The Life and Work of Marianne North* (Richmond: Royal Botanic Gardens, Kew, 1993), p. 94.

on extended sick leave to England in March 1881, taking with him many dried voucher specimens from the Garden's collections and Rainforest for identification at Kew. He returned later that year, bringing back more than 260 living specimens from Kew and British nurseries to augment the Garden's displays. Another role Cantley took on was the propagation of trees for planting in Singapore's streets and parks, for which nurseries were established in the Singapore Botanic Gardens—the Potting Yard beside Cluny Road is one that survives today.[17] A classic street tree introduced at this time was the tropical American Rain Tree (*Samanea saman*), raised from seed in the Gardens in 1882 and now found along many roads on the island. Its spreading habit, rough bark and hinged leaflets, which fold down as rain approaches, make it an ideal perch for epiphytes, especially ferns and orchids, lending much to the tropical luxuriance that typifies the island's roads and parks today. In 1885, Cantley also received four plants of Ipecacuanha (*Carapichea ipecacuanha*), the standard drug for dysentery, for trial cultivation. Trials had previously failed in India, but success was immediate at the Singapore Botanic Gardens, and within two years the first commercial consignment appeared on the London market.[18]

In 1887, Cantley fell ill again and went on sick leave to Australia, where he later died. That he achieved so much in the seven years he oversaw the Singapore Botanic Gardens is the more remarkable in view of his "other job," which was the survey and designation of forest reserves in the Straits Settlements, which the government realized were in decline. This was particularly true during 1883–84 when he was Superintendent of the newly established Forest Department.[19] These early years of the Singapore Botanic Gardens were important in establishing the area as one in which plants could be developed for study, as well as the aesthetic pleasure of a garden. Beyond the gardens, it was the beginning of programs that distributed plants throughout the island, as well as larger Malaya, which changed the economics as well as the appearance of the region. For example, much of the surviving stands of primary forest vegetation in Singapore owe their existence to Cantley and his successor, Henry Ridley.

---

[17] Tinsley, *Gardens of Perpetual Summer*, p. 36.

[18] Desmond, *Kew*, p. 253.

[19] Nathaniel Cantley, *Report on the Forests of the Straits Settlements* (Singapore: Government Printing Office, 1883); see also Tony O'Dempsey's contribution to this volume.

Rubber, Palms, and Orchids: Colonial Botanic Gardens

With the arrival of Ridley in 1888 as the first "Director," the Singapore Botanic Gardens entered a new era, becoming a regional center for understanding the flora of Southeast Asia, for forestry and for economic botany and plantation agriculture. By any measure, Ridley must rank amongst the greatest botanists and plantsmen in history and a biography of this remarkable man is long overdue. In a sense, success in the world of botanic gardens could be said to have been in his genes, since he was the great-great grandson of John Stuart, 3rd Earl of Bute, who was the botanical and garden adviser to Princess Augusta, the mother of King George III and the Princess of Wales who founded the botanic gardens at Kew in 1759.[20] Ridley's interests were wide-ranging, encompassing zoology, geology, and botany, especially orchids. He came to Singapore from the Natural History Museum in London, but it is certain that officials at Kew recommended his appointment. Ridley had gained field experience in Brazil, visiting the archipelago of Fernando de Noronha, and soon took a deep interest in the Malaysian flora. He was a prolific writer, publishing a range of materials including an annotated checklist of the native plants of Singapore and the monumental five-volume *Malayan Flora*, which he completed following his retirement while living at Kew.[21] In addition, Ridley launched the first scientific agricultural journal in the Malay Peninsula in 1891—*Agricultural Bulletin of the Malay Peninsula*—which he filled with useful information.[22]

Under Ridley's direction, the Gardens' collections grew apace and the Economic Gardens even more so. Ridley was exceptionally focused on practical applications, inventing new methods for tapping and curing rubber, perfecting its cultivation and that of oil palm, whilst publishing his results and advice all the while. At the time of his arrival, coffee was the main

---

[20] Christian Lamb, *This Infant Adventure: Offspring of the Royal Gardens at Kew* (London: Bene Factum Publishing, 2010), p. 61; Desmond, *Kew*, p. 31.

[21] H.N. Ridley, "Flora of Singapore," *Journal of the Straits Branch of the Royal Asiatic Society* 33 (1900): 27–196; *The Flora of the Malay Peninsula*, 5 vols. (London: L. Reeve & Co., 1925); Timothy P. Barnard, "Noting Occurrences of Every Day Daily": H.N. Ridley, "Book of Travels," in *Fiction and Faction in the Malay World*, ed. Mohamad Rashidi Pakri and Arndt Graf (Newcastle upon Tyne: Cambridge Scholars Publishing, 2012), pp. 1–25.

[22] In 1901, the journal appeared under a new name, *Agricultural Bulletin, Straits and Federated Malay States*.

plantation crop in the region. His predecessors at the Singapore Botanic Gardens had collected, grown, and displayed examples of different coffee varieties in an attempt to introduce it to Singapore and the Peninsula. The crop, however, was suffering from *Hemileia vastatrix*, a devastating rust. It was at this time that Ridley began focusing on rubber.

While J. Purseglove claims that 1,000 mature (i.e. seed-producing) rubber trees were growing in the Economic Gardens when Ridley arrived in 1888, the plantation was not well-maintained, being half hidden in secondary forest.[23] Ridley soon turned the rubber gardens around and they were producing plenty of seed. He adopted the practice of filling his jacket pockets with fresh seed when visiting plantation managers in the Straits Settlements, in the hope that they would consider planting the crop he believed was a valuable new investment. They stubbornly ignored his recommendations until Tan Chay Yan, a tapioca estate owner from Malacca, agreed to plant a modest 16 hectares with rubber at Bukit Lintang in 1895. By 1901, Tan expanded the area under rubber cultivation to 1,200 hectares and was encouraging others to do likewise, including estate owners in Singapore, where today rubber remains relatively abundant as a naturalized and at times invasive plant in much of the island's forests.[24]

The rubber boom began, out of necessity, by the reality that Brazilians, who had cornered the market, produced coffee more competitively. There is a deep irony here in that Brazil has sometimes claimed the British stole rubber from their territory for imperial gain, but seems to forget that they in turn did much the same with African coffee! Indeed, rubber might not have succeeded when it did in Malaya were it not for the Brazilian acquisition of coffee (of course tires for Henry Ford's assembly line motorcars was soon after the principal economic driver). By 1917, it was calculated, the Singapore Botanic Gardens had supplied and sold seven million rubber seeds from its Economic Gardens, an income that supported much of the Gardens' work. By 1920, Malaya was supplying half of the world's demand for rubber, much of it being exported from the port of Singapore.[25]

---

[23] Purseglove, "History and Functions of Botanic Gardens," p. 173; Lamb, *This Infant Adventure*, pp. 67–8.

[24] Some references give 1896 as the year of the first rubber plantation. Kamala Devi Dhoraisingam and D.S. Samuel, *Tan Tock Seng; Pioneer; His Life, Times, Contributions and Legacy* (Kota Kinabalu: Natural History Publications, Borneo, 2003), p. 85.

[25] Tinsley, *Gardens of Perpetual Summer*, p. 42.

Rubber was not the only plantation crop that Ridley promoted. African oil palms had been growing at the Singapore Botanic Gardens since Murton's tenure, but appear to have been regarded as a mainly ornamental species, supplies of their oil being sourced directly from Africa. Ridley, in a seminal paper published in 1907, states that Murton's oldest plantings of this species had reached 40 feet (c. 13 meters) in height after some 30 years.[26] In this paper, Ridley extolled the economic potential of the palm and described how it should be propagated and planted. This evidently created a demand for seed, and from 1917, commercial plantations were being established in the Malay Peninsula (first at the Tennamaram Estate at Kuala Selangor).[27] Though no oil plantations of any size developed in Singapore, the business grew steadily in the Peninsula and Borneo before expanding exponentially from the 1960s, resulting in the destruction of much of the remaining primary forest in Southeast Asia as a whole. In Singapore, the species is widespread in many natural and managed environments, roadsides and gardens, self-propagating readily and believed to be a favorite food of wild boar, whose increase is suspected by some to be linked in part to the availability of the palm's highly nutritious seeds.[28] The Singapore Botanic Gardens has seven elderly oil palm specimens located in the southern part of the former Economic Gardens and from their size and bald trunks likely the remains of the plantation that was being planned in 1920, as E. Mathieu reported.[29]

Another experimental crop was the latex-producing gutta trees of the genus *Palaquium*, which Ridley planted on the west-facing slope in the southern part of the Economic Gardens between 1897 and 1903, where a fine specimen of white gutta (*P. obovatum*) survives to this day. Sugar and

---

[26] H.N. Ridley, "The Oil Palm," *Agricultural Bulletin of the Straits and Federated Malay States* 6, 2 (1907): 37–40.

[27] B. Bunting, C.D.V. Georgi, and J.N. Milsum, *The Oil Palm in Malaya* (Kuala Lumpur: Department of Agriculture, Straits Settlements and Federated Malay States, 1934), p. 2; Mark Wong, "Oil Palm: The Imported Wonder," at http://www.a2o.com.sg/a2o/public/html/etc/Oil_Palm.htm [accessed 1 July 2012].

[28] Kalan Ickes, "Hyper-Abundance of Native Wild Pigs (*Sus scrofa*) in a Lowland Dipterocarp Rain Forest of Peninsular Malaysia," *Biotropica* 33, 4 (2001): 682–90; Junichi Fujinuma and Rhett D. Harrison, "Wild Pigs (*Sus scrofa*) Mediate Large-Scale Edge Effects in a Lowland Tropical Rainforest in Peninsular Malaysia," *PLoS ONE* 7, 5 (2012): e37321.

[29] *Gardens' Bulletin, Straits Settlements* 2 (1920): 217. This plantation is clearly visible in a 1950 aerial photograph.

starch producing crops were also cultivated in the Gardens. The sugar palm, *Arenga pinnata*, and the widely used Southeast Asian sago palm also had devoted areas, as did pineapples, for a time a popular crop in the Straits and one which is marked as occupying a large area around the Southern Ridges (Kent Ridge to Mount Faber) on the 1892 visitor handbook map.[30]

These economic botany duties, however, did not deflect Ridley from the development of the Singapore Botanic Gardens and its diverse collections. His floristic studies and field expeditions in Southeast Asia were swelling the Herbarium's holdings—a new building to house these began construction in 1903. He also employed botanical artists, the brothers James and Charles de Alwis, to make more than 260 paintings of the Gardens' specimens as they flowered, and built artist's accommodation in the Economic Gardens in 1890. The first *Guide to the Gardens*, written by Head Gardener Walter Fox prior to Ridley's arrival, was published in 1889 and records what was planted by 1888 on the "Lawns" A–M, as they have since been known (Lawns N–Z were designated at a later date). Subsequent to this is recorded a series of Gardens' developments and plantings that were made during Ridley's tenure.[31] On Lawn F, located to the west of Swan Lake, a collection of leguminous trees and shrubs was planted in 1889, of which the Heritage Millettia tree (*Callerya atropurpurea*) is presumed to be a survivor, whilst others potentially of this age include *Caesalpinia coriaria* and *Baikiaea insignis*. The same year, an extension to Cantley's Plant House was built for orchids—now occupied by the Fernery. In 1891, a second lake ("Cluny Lake") was excavated from part of a swamp in the 1866 northwest extension; over subsequent years, this grew and shrank in size, finally being reinstituted

---

[30] Reith, *Handbook to Singapore*. Ridley's agricultural responsibilities went beyond the testing and introduction of new crops to include the monitoring and control of pests and diseases in the Straits Settlements. An example of such work are the steps he took in attempting to limit the rhinoceros beetle that in 1890 was causing much concern for its attacks on coconut palms, of which there were extensive plantations in Singapore toward the close of the 19th century; for "The Coconut Trees Preservation Ordinance," see Purseglove, "History and Functions of Botanic Gardens," p. 171. Responsibility for the Straits' forest reserves and their reinforcement with native species also took up a significant part of Ridley's time until the authorities relieved him of this remit in 1895; for further information, see Tony O'Dempsey's contribution to this volume.

[31] Burkill, "The Second Phase in the History of the Botanic Gardens, Singapore," pp. 105–8; *Singapore Botanic Gardens' Annual Reports*, 1889–1911.

in 1974 as the modern Symphony Lake. Meanwhile, the island in Swan Lake was replanted with pandans and palms, where the fine old Nibung palm seen there today is presumed to date from this time (1891). The following year, a crocodile became an undesirable occupant of the lake. When it attacked a Gardens' worker, the lake was drained, so the victim's colleagues could deal with the beast.[32]

In the early 1890s, Miss Agnes Joachim contacted Ridley about an interesting and beautiful orchid hybrid that had appeared in her Tanjong Pagar garden. In 1893, Ridley named this flower *Vanda* "Miss Joaquim," suggesting that its parentage was *Vanda hookeriana* × *V. teres*, following the botanical tradition of the first-name being the supposed mother or seed parent, the latter the pollen parent.[33] This fine climbing orchid became Singapore's national flower in 1981, and an extensive planting comprising some 20,000 individuals densely arranged on wooden posts below the west side of the Bandstand represent this national icon at the Singapore Botanic Gardens today. Another plant that later became a key part of the Gardens' brand was the sealing wax palm (*Cyrtostachys renda*) of which an avenue was planted in 1905, and replanted in 1936. It can be seen today along the Lower Ring Road between the Bonsai collection and the Swiss Granite Fountain. This red-stemmed palm is a fresh water swamp forest species and is a reminder that such vegetation existed in the Gardens until 1915, when almost the final remnant was filled in as Cluny Lake was enlarged.[34] There is still a tiny fragment of this swamp surviving near Palm Valley Gate, inside the fence around the northern, low-lying end of the nursery serving the National Orchid Garden. In this little patch of swampy ground can be seen a fine old common Pulai (*Alstonia angustiloba*), one of the species often found in or at the margins of swamp forest and a strong candidate for being part of the original native vegetation.

---

[32] "The Gardens Crocodile," *The Straits Times*, 23 Jan. 1892, p. 2; "The Hunting of the Crocodile," *The Straits Times*, 27 Jan. 1892, p. 3.

[33] H.N. Ridley, "Vanda Miss Joaquim," *The Gardener's Chronical* 13 (1893): 740; Modern molecular-based research conducted at the Singapore Botanic Gardens confirms this parentage, although *V. teres* was the seed parent. Gillian Su-Wen Khew and Tet Fatt Chia, "Parentage Determination of *Vanda* Miss Joaquim (Orchidaceae) through two chloroplast genes *rbcL* and *matK*," *AoB PLANTS*: 10.1093/aobpla/plr018 (2011). Available at www.aobplants.oxfordjournals.org.

[34] Ruth Kiew, "The Vanished Forests of Singapore Recaptured," *Gardenwise* 24 (2005): 28.

Ridley left Singapore in January 1912, aged 56 (he would live to be 100). Isaac Henry Burkill—another outstanding scientist and, as it turned out, the last to preside over the Singapore Botanic Gardens as a typical colonial garden—succeeded Ridley. Burkill reinforced the scientific team at the Gardens, renamed Ridley's *Agricultural Bulletin* as *Gardens' Bulletin, Straits Settlements* in reflection of its now more varied content, and, in 1918, published the first history of the Gardens.[35]

Burkill oversaw the Singapore Botanic Gardens when the colonial authorities sought to reassign much of the land of the Economic Gardens to other uses. The Singapore Housing Commission first showed interest, but eventually the Raffles College, Singapore's first higher education institution (later as the University of Malaya, then the University of Singapore and now in part the Ministry of Education's sports complex) annexed the site. The level grounds that were not built upon were earmarked for the College's sports fields and the once extensive plantations of rubber and sago were clear felled. In anticipation of this loss from 1918 onward, some of the presumably younger plantings of trees were rescued and transferred to the pre-1879 part of the Singapore Botanic Gardens, specifically to Lawn Z, which is nowadays the orchid nursery behind the National Orchid Garden. Thus, the old specimens of American and African mahoganies (*Swietenia*, *Khaya*), durian and tamarind in and around the nursery appear to be survivors from this rescue operation. Propagations of two of the highest yielding second generation clones of rubber were also made and one of these survived near Botany Centre until 2013, as well as third-generation saplings planted nearby on the occasion of the Gardens' sesquicentennial.[36] Fortunately, not all of the land of the Economic Gardens was lost to the College grounds, since the Singapore Botanic Gardens retained the steeply sloping ground of the southernmost section, including the newly constructed Field Assistant's house (1919), other employee accommodations and oil palm, gutta, and timber specimens.[37]

---

[35] Burkill, "The Second Phase in the History of the Botanic Gardens, Singapore," pp. 93–108; K.M. Wong, "A Hundred Years of the *Gardens' Bulletin*, Singapore," *Gardens' Bulletin Singapore* 64, 1 (2012): 1–32.

[36] H.M. Burkill, "Gardens' Trust," *Straights Times Annual 1971*, pp. 101–7; Terri Oh, "Celebrating 150 Magical Years of the Gardens," *Gardenwise* 33 (2009): 2–3.

[37] The Field Assistant was the day-to-day manager of the crops and plantation workers, but no sooner had his residence been built than the plantations had gone!

Eric Holttum succeeded Burkill as Director in 1925, and a new era began for the Singapore Botanic Gardens. Holttum was a scientist, like his predecessor, but soon developed an emphasis on horticulture.[38] His botanical interests were varied, but orchids became a focus and in 1928 he set up an *in vitro* propagation unit for these plants on the upper floor of a two-story building completed in 1921 and now named Holttum Hall. Orchids can readily be hybridized to produce exciting new varieties and this was an active program at the Singapore Botanic Gardens from 1930, but their specialized life cycle made the raising of the hybrid seed a very hit-and-miss process.[39] Orchid seeds are produced in huge numbers, but are minute and lack any food resource, being essentially just a tiny embryo. To germinate and develop, they need the presence of a symbiotic fungus or, alternatively, a special growing medium adjusted to deliver the same resources. Whilst Holttum did not invent the *in vitro* technique (the American Lewis Knudson did), he saw its merits and was able to demonstrate them in his lab, permitting hybrids to be raised with confidence and in greater quantity, the first being *Spathoglottis* "Primrose" in 1932.[40] Over subsequent decades, the technique was perfected and soon led to a new industry in Singapore and eventually in various other Southeast Asian countries.

Orchid breeding at the Singapore Botanic Gardens soon became an important activity and resulted in 1956 in an established yet unique program of "VIP Orchid Namings," the first being *Aranthera* "Anne Black," after Lady Black, the colonial governor's wife.[41] More than 190 VIP orchid namings later, visitors to the Gardens can see elements of this laboratory-based propagation technique through a series of windows on the ground floor of Botany Centre, where glass flasks gyrate on shaker tables tended by staff in white lab coats (the technical nurses looking after so many test-tube babies), as well as at the National Orchid Garden. Orchid breeding and the exhibition of new varieties in shows the Malayan Orchid Society and its successor, the Orchid Society of South-East Asia (OSSEA) organized, are activities that have been closely associated with the Gardens from the start.

---

[38] R.E. Holttum, "The Society's Early Days," *Malayan Orchid Review* 22 (1988): 22–6.

[39] *Singapore Botanic Gardens Annual Report* (1948), p. 4.

[40] Tinsley, *Gardens of Perpetual Summer*, p. 50.

[41] *Singapore Botanic Gardens Annual Report* (1956), p. 9, plate 5.

One of Holttum's successors, J.W. Purseglove, further recognized the importance of orchid breeding to horticulture and the Gardens' visitors by creating in 1955 an Orchid Enclosure, where the plants could be featured (it was sited where the Ginger Garden now stands). The growth of orchids in the Gardens became globally known; the Malayan Orchid Society even received a gold medal for its exhibit at the Chelsea Flower Show in London in 1960.[42] The president of the society was Tan Hoon Siang, the son of Tan Chay Yan—the first large-scale planter of rubber in Malaya. The younger Tan was a famous orchid grower, and created an award winning orchid hybrid, which the Gardens raised and was named *Vanda* "Tan Chay Yan" in his father's honor, thereby neatly connecting the two plant groups that more than any others symbolize the Singapore Botanic Gardens—rubber and orchids. Today orchid specialists at the Gardens make on average 1,000 new hybridizations each year. These are raised from seed to flowering, a process averaging five or more years, using the *in vitro* method, with the very best being retained, named, and employed in the breeding of further new varieties.

Holttum's contribution to the Singaporean environment was not limited to orchids. Ferns, bamboo, and gingers were his other interests and he is credited with popularizing two of the most commonly seen plants in Singapore's parks, gardens, and road bridges, namely the frangipani (various *Plumeria* species) and *Bougainvillea*. Both have spectacular large-scale plantings in the Singapore Botanic Gardens, but arguably it is their pervasive presence throughout Singapore that is more significant. An early innovation to the Gardens' landscape that both he and Mrs Holttum contributed also deserves mention, although with a caveat. In 1929, Holttum laid out a Sundial Garden where, it is thought, Cantley had planted roses on a terrace in 1882. This rectangular garden feature was formal in character with a sundial at its centre designed by Ursula, the Director's wife, and cast in concrete (still a novel material in those days). At a later date, around 1970, four lily ponds were added and Grecian statues at each corner. Attractive as this feature is, it is starkly out-of-character with the historic, but post-formal, Capability Brown-like English Landscape that Niven designed and suggests Holttum failed to see that these two themes were difficult to integrate and, especially, since there have been no subsequent formal designs proposed, leaving his as the exception. The following year (1930), the previously open

[42] Dhoraisingam and Samuel, *Tan Tock Seng*, p. 93.

band parade area was augmented with the formal bandstand structure that exists today, providing shelter for the musicians during inclement weather and a centerpiece for Niven's earliest landscape element (1860–61).[43] The audience sat around the periphery on the lawn, but nowadays there is a shrubbery around the Bandstand's base and the bands, or rather orchestras, play on the Shaw Symphony Stage. Thus, the Gardens have provided a green venue for Singaporeans and visitors to enjoy music for more than 150 years. Other lasting additions to the Gardens' landscape during Holttum's tenure included the water lily tanks at the base of the steps down to the Plant House (1932) and a pergola connecting the Upper and Lower Ring Roads to the southwest of the Bandstand (1935).

Holttum and his Assistant Director, E.J.H. Corner (appointed 1929), remained in the Gardens during the Japanese occupation of the Second World War. The British Governor, Sir Shenton Thomas, had managed to persuade the commander of the Japanese forces that the Gardens and Raffles Museum collections should be preserved. Although the two countries remained at war, the Gardens' senior scientists were allowed to continue their work under the direction of an imposed but benevolent Japanese botanist, Kwan Koriba. Events during the Japanese occupation at the Singapore Botanic Gardens are not well-recorded beyond the statements in Corner's *The Marquis* and the briefest of postwar Director's annual reports (1947). In a letter written late in his life, Holttum remarked that he did not agree with all that Corner had recorded and at least the latter's statement regarding irreparable damage to the Gardens' Rainforest from shelling and storms seems dubious or exaggerated when postwar aerial photography showed little if any signs of destruction and an intact canopy.[44]

One interesting development during the Japanese occupation, that has gone unrecorded until quite recently, is the construction of two flights of brick steps leading down from the Lower Ring Road to the Plant House. Pim Sanderson, at one time a consultant working for Singapore Botanic Gardens, recalls a visit to the Gardens in August 1995 of eight elderly Australian ex-prisoners-of-war, who requested to be taken to the Plant

---

[43] Thereis Choo, "Uncovering the History of the Bandstand," *Gardenwise* 39 (2012): 7–8.

[44] E.J.H. Corner, *The Marquis. A Tale of Syonan-to* (Singapore: Heinemann Asia, 1981), p. 77; R.E. Holttum to Mrs Mary Kogan, 12 May 1989 ("1090"), in reply to hers dated 9 May 1989—copies of this correspondence supplied by Ali Ibrahim (NParks).

House. There they became excited as they pointed out the steps and the bricks from which they are made, explaining that they had been required to construct both during the occupation. The bricks, at least many of them, bear the tell-tale arrow marks that are associated with being "government property," meaning, in the modern sense, those detained by the authorities (in this case in the Salarang Barracks near Changi gaol).[45] This recently transmitted record of the visit on the 50th anniversary of the cessation of hostilities is the only thing that will ensure that the flights of steps are not renewed, because the bricks are not of the quality that is otherwise expected of the Singapore Botanic Gardens' hard landscape, no doubt due to the difficult conditions prevailing at the time they were made.

Following the war, the Singapore Botanic Gardens struggled, as many of its best gardeners had died building the Burma-Siam railway under Japanese enslavement, whilst subsequent "Malayanization" also limited efforts to recruit talent as British colonial rule came to an end. Amongst the few developments in the Gardens that are recorded is an avenue of royal palms (*Roystonea regia*), planted along Office Gate Road in 1950 and now towering above a modern pergola over which a climber with long hair-like aerial roots has been trained (*Cissus sicyoides*). The "Nature Reserves Ordinance" of 1951 placed some 8,000 acres under the charge of Singapore Botanic Gardens to "set aside for the purpose of the propagation, protection and preservation of the indigenous fauna and flora of the Colony." This included the Bukit Timah Reserve, which currently the National Parks Board administers as a Nature Reserve.

After various changes of director, Humphrey Burkill, son of I.H. Burkill and born onsite in Burkill Hall, was appointed to succeed Purseglove in 1957. The water feature in the center of the Plant House quadrangle was begun in that year and over the following decades the Herbarium buildings were renewed and enlarged and a large tea kiosk built on Lawn H, but little else of note appears to have happened to the Gardens' physical structure that has not already been mentioned until the "greening" of Singapore kicked off in the 1960s. However, there were some large public events held on site in 1959, the year of the Singapore Botanic Gardens' 100th anniversary, not least a series of concerts and shows the Ministry of Culture organized and Prime Minister Lee Kuan Yew opened in front of an audience of 22,000. A later

---

[45] Nigel Taylor, "Singapore Botanic Gardens: A Living and Growing Heritage," *BeMUSE* 5, 3 (2012): 29; Pim Sanderson, mss dated & signed 19 Mar. 2012.

concert in the series, which included experimental night lighting, drew an audience of 30,000, the largest gathering ever held in the Gardens.[46]

The Singapore Botanic Gardens and the "Garden City"

In June 1963, PM Lee Kuan Yew launched a tree-planting campaign, followed in 1967 by his "Garden City" vision, which the newly established Parks and Trees Unit within the Public Works Department oversaw. As an institution with more than 100 years of experience in science and horticulture, the Singapore Botanic Gardens soon became a key player in carrying this vision forward—in a sense a repeat of Cantley's remit in the 1880s.[47] In support of this, the new second lake area subsequently grew into a large nursery ground, producing stock for planting along public roads and traffic islands throughout Singapore.[48] Such large-scale production of trees and shrubs in support of the planting campaign necessitated an expansion of nursery facilities beyond the Gardens' boundaries at various sites, the first at Ulu Pandan, as well as the establishment of sales outlets along Dunearn Road's "Floral Mile" to stimulate public interest and encourage private endeavor. Inside the Gardens, Burkill Hall, vacated by Humphrey Burkill upon his retirement in 1969, was utilized as the venue for a new diploma qualification in "Ornamental Horticulture and Landscape Design," including both theory and practical elements.[49] This was the first of its kind in Southeast Asia and was modeled on the Diploma in Horticulture established at the Royal Botanic Gardens, Kew in 1963. The greening of Singapore was not just about trees. It also coincided with an expansion of orchid breeding and commercial production. Once again a Kew-trained chief administrator, Arthur George Alphonso, led the Singapore Botanic Gardens, and during his tenure (1970–76) the *in vitro* laboratory facilities were augmented and moved from the upper floor of Holttum Hall. His influence continued after

---

[46] There were fewer trees occupying the Lawns in those days. "30,000 at Festival of Music and Fun in Gardens," *The Straits Times*, 16 Sep. 1959, p. 4; UK National Archives, British Empire Collection of Photographs, INF 10/322/17 (photograph no. K 26179).

[47] Purseglove, "History and Functions of Botanic Gardens," p. 186.

[48] Ng Siew Yin (former Botanist and Chief Administrator, SBG), pers. comm., 8 Aug. 2012.

[49] Foong Thai Wu et al., "Roadmap of the School of Horticulture: 1972–1999," *Gardenwise* 13 (1999): 12–3.

retirement when he was re-employed for two years as "Senior Curator" in charge of orchid breeding.

In the 1970s, the Singapore Botanic Gardens' public facilities and landscape were also upgraded as it assumed the role of a public park. The second lake, re-excavated in 1974 where Cluny Lake had previously been sited, later became the Symphony Lake, and various new garden features were installed including a Japanese Garden, plant houses for cacti, succulents and temperate species (in a cooled glasshouse), and a miniature waterfall. Although these changes were all swept away with major redevelopments in the Gardens since 1990, it reflects the ever-changing nature of a garden.

When the Singapore Botanic Gardens began providing support for the "Garden City" concept in the 1960s, government officials advised that regional and international work in taxonomic research cease.[50] While research in these areas was suspended, new threads of inquiry were introduced, often related to the greening of the nation, particularly after the Singapore Botanic Gardens became the Parks and Recreation Department of the Ministry of National Development in 1976. From that point, its success was measured in terms of its advancement of horticulture in Singapore. Particular effort was put into behind-the-scenes enhancements to science and horticultural capabilities, including the expansion of plant entomology, pathology, and nursery facilities, especially in support of a unit charged with the search for, experimentation with, and introduction of new plants to Singapore's parks and gardens. For example, in the fiscal year 1979/80, it was responsible for planting 56,000 ornamental trees, 10,000 fruit trees, and 400,000 shrubs, a performance that was maintained over a decade until a ministry reorganization parceled out some of these activities to other new branches supplementary to the Singapore Botanic Gardens.[51] Through these efforts, the greening of the island through the Garden City vision was substantially realized.

In 1983, some 60 years after the annexation of the major part of the Economic Gardens, 17 hectares of that land was returned to the Singapore Botanic Gardens and the development commenced of what would later

---

[50] Ng Siew Yin, pers. comm., 8 Aug. 2012. A similar mandate with regard to fauna was also given to the natural history collection employees of the soon to be defunct Raffles Museum a few years after this. See Timothy P. Barnard's contribution to this volume.

[51] Tinsley, *Gardens of Perpetual Summer*, p. 67. See Timothy P. Barnard and Corinne Heng's contribution to this volume.

be called the Bukit Timah Core. This re-expansion soon included a large pond, a new arboretum, footpaths, rest areas, and a modern innovation—the provision of jogging tracks for the benefit of office-bound Singaporeans in need of physical exercise. In the historic southern end of the Singapore Botanic Gardens, a Rose Garden was installed in May 1985 between the Bandstand and the Sundial Garden, near to where Cantley had planted roses a hundred years before.[52] The Rose Garden employed a hydroponic system under shelter, but roses grown in Singapore's perhumid tropical climate tend to suffer from many pests and diseases, requiring much staff time for their maintenance, so this garden feature did not survive later redevelopments. While orchid breeding continued, the Gardens also hosted orchid shows for OSSEA and thereby gained awards for its own hybrids, such as *Dendrobium* "Margaret Thatcher" (1987). However, by this time an architect of major change was on board and the Gardens entered its modern phase.

Tan Wee Kiat joined the Singapore Botanic Gardens' senior staff in 1983 from the Marie Selby Botanical Gardens in Florida, where he was an accomplished orchid specialist and director of the museum of botany and the arts. He began with an overhaul of the orchid breeding program, focusing on high quality orchid hybrids with commercial value. In 1988, Tan became the Director of the Singapore Botanic Gardens, and the following year was given funds to develop a master plan—along with Chief Landscape Architect, Junichi Inada—that took the Gardens into the 21st century.[53] After 130 years of somewhat ad hoc development, Tan and Inada—along with subsequent Director Chin See Chung—rationalized an overall plan that replaced most of the additions from the 1950s to the 1980s, whilst the surviving heritage landscapes of Niven and Murton were carefully preserved and historic buildings refurbished. Equally significant, botanical science and the conservation of biological diversity were to be properly resourced, representing activities as fundamental to the Gardens as its role in attracting and engaging the visitor by offering better amenities and innovative horticultural displays.

Many of these changes began with the return of part of the former Economic Gardens' land in 1983. The Singapore Botanic Gardens had

---

[52] Tay Eng Pin et al., *A Pictorial Guide to the Singapore Botanic Gardens* (Singapore: Singapore Botanic Gardens, 1989), p. 34.
[53] Bonnie Tinsley, *Visions of Delight: The Singapore Botanic Gardens Through the Ages* (Singapore: Singapore Botanic Gardens, 1989).

become a long, and in places rather narrow, site stretched out over 1.7 kilometers north to south. In a subsequent 1991 revision of the master plan, this lent to the recognition of three core areas, the Tanglin (Heritage), Central, and Bukit Timah Cores. Developments in each core proceeded in tandem, but were divided into three overlapping phases of public funding, the first running from 1988 until 1998.[54] Eventually, by the first decade of the 21st century, the Singapore Botanic Gardens' overall area returned to the maximum it attained in 1879, at c.75 hectares. This was achieved following a grant of a piece of adjacent land formerly belonging to the Sultan of Johor, to the west of Tyersall Avenue along the new western boundary of the Gardens. This area will become the Tyersall Learning Forest, an area of some 10 hectares of secondary forest including a number of rare species and a few trees of upwards of 100 years' growth. While over the past three decades the Singapore Botanic Gardens has expanded to reach its greatest geographic extent, it has also helped maintain a number of endangered species while also reinforcing the greening of the "Garden City."

One success story on these lines, which is perhaps the best example of the Gardens' modern relevance to Singapore's environment, is the program Tim Yam has led since 1999 of orchid reintroduction.[55] To date, some 15 species of rare, endangered, and locally extinct orchids have been re-established all over the island, in gardens, parks, Nature Reserves, and even on roadside trees, both in the city and along the island's main highways. The majority of these 5,000-plus reintroductions are growing well, flowering, and producing seeds, demonstrating that the pollinators of these species are still present and functional. This is the conservation role that many botanic gardens around the world aspire to, but at the Singapore Botanic Gardens it has become a reality and is something that Singaporeans can be proud of. This reintroduction work is also a good example of the beneficial fusion of science and horticulture, since the orchids are propagated initially in the laboratory by science teams, then "weaned" from their life in aseptic media and grown on in more conventional horticultural nursery conditions, before being lifted by man and crane, fixed into their new epiphytic habitat, and

---

[54] While government backed most of this redevelopment, funds, and in-kind support were also forthcoming from the Gardens' dedicated individual supporters, some of whom served on the newly created National Parks Board set up in 1990; Nura Abdul Karim, "The Passing of Lady Yuen-Peng McNeice," *Gardenwise* 39 (2012): 2–5.

[55] An early success from this program is reported in *Gardenwise* 23 (2004): 8.

monitored for years thereafter. Their new habitats, as already indicated, are subject to differing degrees of human impact and local climatic effects, so these are being studied and compared by means of environmental monitoring kits placed up in the trees, from which data are regularly downloaded. So when a pedestrian happens to see an orchid in bloom by the roadside or in a park, in some cases he may also observe a small-scale weather station attached to the tree. These data are being compared with the success rates of the reintroduced orchid species in order to understand their preferences, but it is already clear that some man-made habitats, such as tree-lined expressways, are far from being unsatisfactory and that nature can still thrive where trucks and motorcars rush by.

The Singapore Botanic Gardens has been a place whose history and relevance to Singapore and beyond is understood and valued, and hopefully will continue to do so. It has been vital in the introduction of important economic species, and in the greening of the nation. Beyond these scientific and economic contributions, it is a garden, a park. In this regard, however, it is very much more than a pretty park. Its role in the social history of Singapore cannot be underestimated, for it is clear that there are many Singaporeans whose lives are connected with its enduring landscape, whether through their parents or grandparents having first met within its green expanse (in the days of arranged marriages, it was seen as the appropriate "neutral" territory upon which to meet), or by it being a place of lifelong pilgrimage for relaxation, exercise, and education. It is deeply rooted in the memories of many Singaporeans and tourists and it is a place for young and old alike and, through its expanding educational programs, has the potential to help us mitigate the dangers of man's divorce from nature that is inherent in our modern urban lifestyle.

Regulating the Wildlife Trade: Excerpts from *Report of the Wild Animals and Wild Birds Committee, Singapore, 1933*[1]

INSPECTION OF BIRD SHOPS

On July 25, 1933, the Chairman and Vice-Chairman visited all the licensed premises for the housing of wild animals and a note of this visit was prepared as follows:—

General Remarks

"The licences, except in one case (60 Rochore Road) do not differentiate between the classes of animals and birds, and it is reasonable to presume that premises, ordinarily used only for domestic birds might, under these licences, be used for the housing of wild animals and wild birds were, in our opinion, unsuitable beyond the general suitability expressed above.

"We found binturong (bear-cat) in several shops, alleged to have come from Sumatra. Subsequent information pointed to the fact that these animals were used for food or medicine, but we have no direct proof of this. It was, however, significant that there were quite a large number of these rare and harmless animals in these shops, which indicates a demand for them, but what that demand is due to we cannot definitely state. We also saw musangs (civet cats) in several of the shops, and cannot believe that these would be sold as pets.

Notes on the Shops Visited

"54, 58, 59 and 61 Rochore Road. We found that the small wild birds seemed to be in fair condition and had reasonable cages. Monkeys and binturong were housed in unsuitable cages and in uncongenial surroundings. At No. 61, Rochore Road we found one tenggliing (scaly ant-eater) said to have been imported from Sumatra by a steamer which had arrived from Siak on the 23rd July. This importation was illegal.

---

[1] *Report of the Wild Animals and Wild Birds Committee, Singapore, 1933* (Singapore: Government Printing Office, 1934), pp. 12–19.

60 Rochore Road. Licensed only for ducks and fowls.

62 Rochore Road. Only ducks and fowls.

62-1, and 67 Rochore Road. Only ducks and fowls. Quite unsuitable as licensed premises for wild animals and birds.

58 and 69 Rochore Road. Ducks and Fowls only.

532 North Bridge Road. A well kept bird shop, but animals not suitably caged. Monkeys should not be kept in cages with slatted bottoms for birds.

50 Desker Road. Private house, with cages in back premises. (believed to be an overflow from 61 Rochore Road.)

7A Prinsep Street. Deserted, nothing there.

60 Japan Street. Nothing there. Premises quite unsuitable and should not be licensed.

239 New Bridge Road. Large numbers of small tortoises only.

15 Club Street. Dogs Only. Quite unsuitable for wild animals and should not be licensed.

32 Mosque Street. An unsuitable place. Bad and gloomy. Should not be licensed.

The Great World Zoo. Only birds, which were adequately and reasonably caged.

"As mentioned above some of these premises, although suitably licensed for animals and birds, were undoubtedly in now suitable for the carrying on of a trade in wild animals and wild birds. Such premises only contained fowls or ducks, but legally the licensee could have housed an elephant.

"We arrived at the conclusion that the small birds were generally confined in cages which were not unsuitable and which did not inflict cruelty on them provided that they were not kept in such confinement for any length of time—say a week—, but the housing of animals such as monkeys, binturong, etc. was not satisfactory.

"One fact was clear, and it applied to practically all the shops; the cages were used indiscriminately for any sort of large bird or animal. For instance the cages used for domestic fowls, such cages having slatted bottoms, were used for monkeys, whose habits cannot be considered as similar to those of domestic fowls.

"We found small honey bears in dark and restricted quarters, binturong, animals found only in primeval jungle, confined in small and dark cages, cut off from everything, except food, that they would now as "life". Slow loris and civet cats, whose ultimate fate we recoil from contemplating, were to be found in these premises.

"We unhesitatingly came to the conclusion that whatever might be our recommendations regarding the small birds, the trading of wild animals in such places must be stopped.

"Two days after our visit Mr. ELPHICK made an independent inspection by himself, and his conclusions were the same as ours, Mr FORBES, who constantly in the execution of his duties, visits these places, holds the same opinions. The Hon'ble Mr. TAN CHENG LOCK, who had made an earlier inspection supports our views."

Representation to Owners

At a later date the Chairman, the Vice-Chairman and Mr. ELPHICK visited the two largest shops to question the licensees regarding what they could or would do in certain eventualities.

The first shop visited was 532 North Bridge Road. The licensee was interviewed and after having been informed who we were told that we should probably recommend that no mammals could be kept in these shop houses but that possibly a small bird trade might be allowed. The licensee immediately stated that his business would close if he could not deal in animals, because the rent of his shop-house was high—about $80 a month—and that the profit in the small bird trade was so little that he would be unable to carry on.

He was told that under those circumstances the only thing for him to do was to close down, but that as we did not want to destroy his business altogether, what was his opinion of the idea of a central market where all the "bird shop traders" could be located and although no large animals could be sold in such a place possibly small ones might be dealt with.

This licensee was an old man and he disliked the idea of having to move at all; he reiterated the statement that it would be very difficult for him to alter his business methods at his time of life—a perfectly reasonable view from his angle. But he gave no cogent reasons why the trade should not be concentrated in a market.

No. 61 Rochore Road was also visited, and after a discussion similar to the above, the proprietors or licensees of that business welcomed the idea of a central market.

Subsequently the Chairman received a letter signed by four of the Proprietors of certain shops complaining of the hardship if they were made to move. The Proprietor of 61 Rochore Road had changed his views!

The letter is reproduced herewith:

Singapore, 3rd August 1933.

T. R. HUBBACK, Esq.
    Chairman of Committee
        of Wild Animals and Wild Birds,
            SINGAPORE

Dear Sir,

We understand that Government intends building a new market for the sole purpose of selling wild animals and wild birds. It is intended that all dealers in this line should sell their wild animals and birds in this new building.

We, the undersigned, would kindly entreat you not to adopt such a measure at present owing to the prevailing bad state of business and also to the fact that our premises are opened daily from 6 A.M. right up to 9 P.M.

We would state that many species of birds, such as the canary, cannot withstand the breeze and as a result their feathers wither and they soon collapse.

We hope you will be kind enough to give due consideration to our entreaty.

We remain, dear Sir,
Yours faithfully,
- (1) CHOP JOO SOON HIN,
  532 North Bridge Road
- (2) CHOP KIAN HUAT & CO.
  59 Rochore Road.
- (3) CHOP GUAN KEE,
  61 Rochore Road
- (4) CHOP CHENG KEE,
  239 New Bridge Road."

Although concern is shown for the semi-domestic canaries, which one would imagine could easily be protected from the wind, little consideration has been shown for the unfortunate animals whose world has been the jungle but whose gaol has subsequently been a small unsavoury cage in a noisome corner of a shop house. Mr. ELPHICK, a Member of the Committee has pointed out that he keeps canaries in open cages on his verandah where they are liable to just as much wind as they would be likely to experience in a market. He has not noticed any serious effect from this exposure. The fact must not be lost sight of that shop house where these wild creatures are confined are also dwelling places, and those portions of these premises which are used for domestic occupation are not open to or available for inspection.

RECOMMENDATIONS

The members of the Committee are unanimous in agreeing that there is only one solution to the problem of retaining a retail trade in wild animals and wild birds in Singapore and that is by the erection of a Central Market where such a trade could be exercised. By such an arrangement adequate and efficient supervision of this trade could be possible. Under the present arrangement it is impossible.

With this idea in view the reclamation at Teluk Ayer was visited and it was seen that at a locality marked D on the attached plan—which is not drawn to scale— there was in our opinion sufficient space on which to erect a suitable building as a market for this purpose. The land belongs to the Harbour Board and we conclude that arrangements could be made with that body to obtain the land for these requirements.

Formal meetings of the Committee were held in Mr. ELPHICK's office in Ocean Building on the 1st August and 25th November, 1933. At the former meeting Mr. CHASEN was absent having been empanelled to serve on a Jury in the Supreme Court;

at the meeting on the 25th November, the Hon'ble Mr. TAN CHENG LOCK, who was absent from Singapore, was not present.

After lengthy discussions of all the points raised under our terms of reference, we unanimously agreed to pass certain resolutions on which we base our recommendations.

Resolutions

(a)   That the shop houses in Rochore Road, North Bridge Road, and other places in the City area are not suitable places for housing of wild animals and wild birds.

(b)   That some of the premises inspected might be considered as suitable for a small trade in small birds, but on inquiry we found that the rents of the shop houses was too high to permit a restricted trade in small birds only, and by prohibiting the trade in wild animals the mixed trade as now carried on would cease and hardship on these traders would be the result.

(c)   That the housing of monkeys in cages which had been constructed and used for fowls, which we found in several shops, was wrong and should not be allowed.

(d)   That we recognize that the profit on the occasional sale of large animals is much greater than that on a large number of birds, and although we are agreed that the sale of certain animals might be permitted to retail dealers under strict control, it should not be allowed in the present premises beyond the periods indicated in recommendations (1) and (1) (a).

Recommendations

(1)   We recommend that any future licensing of premises where wild animals and wild birds are exposed for sale in Rochore Road, North Bridge Road, and other localities within the Municipal limits should cease, provided the Government will undertake the construction of a suitable market on the lines recommended in this report and provided further that at least six months notice shall be given to the present licensees that their licences will not be renewed. These notices will be invalid if suitable premises in the form of a market are not available at the end of the six months period. Further short period licences should then be issued until suitable premises are available, but not beyond the 1st July, 1935.

(1)   (a) In event of no action being taken to provide a market we feel bound to recommend that the retail trade in wild animals and wild birds as at present conducted in Singapore should cease and be made illegal as from 1st July, 1935.

(2)   It is obvious that unless it is desired to destroy the trade altogether, some constructive policy to deal with the housing of wild animals and wild birds must be put forward. We do not recommend that the trade be destroyed entirely, but that it should come under strict control.

(3)   We recommend that the retail trade should be controlled by only licencing premises in a properly constructed market, and that steps be taken to acquire a site for a market of 120 feet long and 40 feet wide, which would be large enough to meet all the requirements of the retail trade for many years.

(4)   We recommend that the cost of the erection of the market and the acquisition of the site should be borne by the Government of the Straits Settlements, because the Municipal Commissioners appear to be debarred by their Ordinance from using their funds for such a purpose.

(5)   We recommend that the capital cost of the market should not exceed $10,000, that it should be of the dimensions stated above, be built with reinforced concrete pillars, tiled roof on wooden trusses, with a jack rook and long overhanging eaves to protect the inside of the building from rain storms, with a cement floor properly drained. Shutters could be fitted to the sides and ends of the building if it was thought necessary.

The stalls should consist of spaces of 15 feet by 10 feet, on which could be erected suitable cages with the backs to the outer sides of the building.

The annual license for a stall should be $2 for birds and $4 for mammals, and the annual rent for a stall should be $48, including water, light and cages.

(6)   We recommend that no cages are allowed within one foot of the floor; that no licenses are issued for animals other than certain types of monkeys, squirrels, rabbits and guinea-pigs; and that no animals which are obtained for purposes other than those of utility or as pets should be allowed in the market.

[*Editor's Note: Recommendations 7–8, which extensively quotes the 1931 Report of the Wild Life Commission of Malaya, on the subject of professional oversight of bird shops and zoological gardens, is not included in this excerpt.*]

....

CONTROL OF ZOOLOGICAL GARDENS

We have not, so far, mentioned the control of Zoological Gardens, such as the one at Ponggol, which is outside the Municipal limits. In our opinion this Zoo is, at the present time, well managed and carefully looked after, but should come under the provisions stated above as being included in the draft Enactment referred to. But we recommend that the licensing fees for such places should be greater than those proposed for the retail dealers, and suggest that any place exhibiting not more than 50 animals should pay an annual fee of $25, or if more than 50 animals an annual fee of $50. The licence to cover an undefined number of birds, but no licence to be less than $25 even if there are no animals displayed at all.

GENERAL CONCLUSIONS

There is little doubt but that there is considerable smuggling of wild animals and birds into Singapore. Now that there is a long list of animals and birds that are not allowed to be brought into Singapore except under permit from the Colonial Secretary (see Gazette Notification No. 1432, dated July 21, 1933), the necessity to prevent smuggling is more imperative than ever. It does not appear, however, under the present law (Ordinance No. 88 of 18th November 1904, as amended by Ordinance No. 2 of 1930) to be unlawful to be in possession of an animal or bird which is prohibited from import unless proof of the illegal importation is forthcoming—except when such animal or bird can be proved to have been taken during the close season.

For instance it is now illegal to import into Singapore a pelandok or a kijang unless accompanied by a permit. But no action can be taken against any person fond in possession of such animals unless it can be proved that they were taken during a close season.

It is necessary that a provision should be made to make it an offence to be in possession of an illegally obtained or illegally imported wild animals or wild bird and we recommend that the provisions shewn in the draft Enactment in the Report of the Wild Life Commission should be included in any future legislation which may be contemplated. Those provisions as drafted make it an offence to be found in possession of any wild animal or wild bird which has been taken or is held in possession contrary to the provisions of the Enactment and the burden of proof would be on the defendant to show that the charge was unfounded.

Such legislative action would prevent animals and birds, prohibited from import, being sold in Singapore, which can be done at present. The possession or otherwise of a permit would readily show whether the animal or bird about which some suspicion had been aroused was legally held in possession.

Another provision which we think is desirable is one providing that a fee be charged for licences which may be issued for the importation of wild life into Singapore. It is dealt with in the Wild Life Commission Report and a form of licence is shown on page 123 of Volume II. The fee suggested in the Report is one of $1 for ten head, or less. It is not desirable that licences should be issued for numbers smaller than ten head, and the licence only refers to animals and birds that are prohibited from import by an order to that effect.

SUMMARY OF RECOMMENDATIONS

To sum up our recommendations:—

1. The construction of a Market to deal with the retail trade in certain Wild Animals and Wild Birds.
2. The trade in Wild Animals and Wild Birds to be controlled by a qualified organization as suggested in the Report of the Wild Life Commission of Malaya, if such an organization is established, otherwise to remain under the present arrangements of supervision.
3. The provision of fees for licenses allowing importations into Singapore of Wild Animals and Wild Birds otherwise prohibited from such importation.

CHAPTER 5

The Beastly Business of Regulating the Wildlife Trade in Colonial Singapore

Fiona L.P. Tan

In 1993, Robert Kwan, chairman of the National Council on the Environment, characterized the illegal trade in wildlife as a "blot on Singapore's record." This "blot" remains into the new millennium. As recent as 2005, according to reports, Singapore continued to be a "hub for illegal wildlife trade." Singapore's reputation as a key destination and trans-shipment port for the trade in wild and exotic animals is not a recent development, however, as the British colonial administration also struggled with this "scandalous" trade. In 1934, a letter written to *The Straits Times* described the practice as a "blot on the landscape" of Singapore. These "blots" have marred the glorified image of Singapore's development from the colonial "second doorway of the wide world's trade" between "East and West"—as Kipling depicted in his poem "The Song of the Cities"—to the entrepôt of today; it was a trade that both the colonial and independent national governments could not "loose or bar."[1]

The trade in Singapore of wildlife from other regions of Southeast Asia has drawn little interest from historians and economists, and this is indicative

---

[1] "Illegal Trade in Wildlife 'A Blot on Singapore's Record'," *The Straits Times* [hereafter *ST*], 21 May 1993, p. 32; Jasmine Yin, "S'pore Labelled 'A Hub for Illegal Wildlife Trade'; Strategic Position May Be Attracting Organised Crime, says AVA," *Today*, 28 Jan. 2005; "A Blot on the Landscape," *ST*, 22 Aug. 1934, p. 5; Kipling's poem can be found in Far Eastern Tourist Agency, *Information for Travellers Landing at Singapore* (Singapore: The Far East Tourist Agency, 1911), p. 5.

of broader historiographical trends.[2] While animals have always been included in historical narratives as characters in the margins, new approaches toward the study of animals in the past few decades has resulted in their inclusion as legitimate and mainstream subjects of historical inquiry. Harriet Ritvo, a historian of British cultural attitudes toward animals, attributes this shift to the growth of environmental history and a "democratizing tendency" amongst historians generally.[3] Despite a growing interest in environmental histories of Southeast Asia, there are few such studies focused on Singapore, and none on the topic of wildlife trade, which may be due to its size or the perceived lack of unique species as compared to other states in Southeast Asia.[4] Moreover, as the sources delineating general attitudes toward animals and nature are more readily available than those specifically about wildlife trade, none of these environmental histories addresses the issue of such trade in the region, much less in Singapore. The sketchy statistical record on wildlife trade, fundamental to a history of any trade good, also compounds the difficulty of constructing a complete statistical history of the subject.

Out of the sketchy statistical record and sporadic mentions in memoirs and newspapers, a single document—the *Report of the Wild Animals and Wild Birds Committee* prepared in 1933, henceforth referred to as the *1933 Report*—stands out. The Committee, appointed in July 1933, in a climate

---

[2] Discussions of wildlife trade in Singapore tend to either consider it generally as a trans-shipment point for the region without any attempts to delve into historical details, or limit it to the discussion of independent Singapore's late entry into the Convention on International Trade in Endangered Species of Wild Fauna and Flora (CITES). Lesley Layton, *Songbirds in Singapore* (Singapore: Oxford University Press, 1991); D. G. Donovan, "Cultural Underpinnings of the Wildlife Trade in Southeast Asia," in *Wildlife in Asia: Cultural Perspectives*, ed. John Knight (London: Routledge, 2004), p. 92; Lye Lin Heng, "Wildlife Protection Laws in Singapore," *Singapore Journal of Legal Studies* 288 (1991): 287–319; see also Goh Hong Yi's contribution to this volume.

[3] Harriet Ritvo, "Animal Planet," *Environmental History* 9, 2 (2004): 205.

[4] Historians, prior to this current work, have not written any of the existing studies of wildlife trade in Singapore, or even other environmental issues. Heng's "Wildlife Protection Laws in Singapore" is a legal history of Singaporean wildlife protection laws. For instances of ecological histories by scientists, see H.M. Burkill, "Protection of Wild Life on Singapore Island," in *Nature Conservation in Western Malaysia*, ed. J. Wyatt-Smith and P.R. Wycherley (Kuala Lumpur: Malayan Nature Society, 1961), pp. 152–64; and Richard T. Corlett, "The Ecological Transformation of Singapore, 1819–1990," *Journal of Biogeography* 19, 4 (July 1992): 411–20.

of growing concern for animal welfare and wildlife preservation from both public and official quarters, published its findings in 1934. Despite being one of the most articulate attempts in detailing the wildlife trade in Singapore, it has not surfaced in any historical accounts of Singapore or Malaya.

Using this document as a starting point, this chapter will sketch a chronological account of wildlife trade in colonial Singapore, with special emphasis on the 1930s. First, I will begin with a brief historical background of wildlife trade in colonial Singapore, before tracing the convergence of the animal welfare and wildlife protection movements in the 1930s, which culminated in the formation of the Wild Animals and Wild Birds Committee in 1933. A final section will examine the possible reasons why the *1933 Report* did not effect any tangible changes, demonstrating the complex workings of colonial government and difficulties of enforcement in 1930s Singapore, as well as a general apathy toward considering animals and their treatment as worthy of increased governmental intervention.

History of the Wildlife Trade, and External Influences, in Singapore

The wildlife trade in island Southeast Asia existed long before colonial times.[5] With the entry of colonial rule, such trade became more visible in Singapore, due to the development of the colonial settlement as a key trading port in the region, and the availability of sources, such as travelogues and memoirs, which highlight the existence of such trade. Local pet-keeping habits in Singapore, which appeared well-established by the late 19th century, if not earlier, also supported the trade in wild animals. For instance, Isabella Bird commented in her travels in Southeast Asia in 1877 that Malays were "passionately fond of pets" and had "much skill in taming birds."[6] Chinese and Indians immigrants also had a similar fondness for pet birds that at times was connected to customs such as the Buddhist belief of *fong sang*,

---

[5] Elephants were imported and traded in the region before colonial rule, from places as near as Java and Melaka to places as far as India. See Peter Boomgaard, "Hunting and Trapping in the Indonesian Archipelago, 1500–1950," in *Paper Landscapes: Explorations in the Environmental History of Indonesia*, ed. Peter Boomgaard, Freek Colombijn, and David Henley (Leiden: KITLV Press, 1997), p. 195; Barbara Watson Andaya, *Perak, the Abode of Grace: A Study of an Eighteenth-Century Malay State* (Kuala Lumpur: Oxford University Press, 1979), pp. 77–8.

[6] Isabella Bird, *The Golden Chersonese and the Way Thither* (New York: G.P. Putnam's Sons, 1884), p. 381.

which required Chinese devotees to purchase and release caged pigeons to accumulate merit. The rise of the animal shows, circuses, zoological gardens, and pet shops in Europe and America in the 19th century further encouraged an international trade in live animals. In such circumstances, colonial Singapore developed into one of the most important centers of the international wildlife trade.[7]

Malays dominated the wildlife trade in early colonial Singapore. Roland Braddell, a prominent lawyer and amateur historian, traced the history of Singapore's wildlife trade to Haji Marap in 1880; other accounts suggests that Singapore had been a thriving port for wildlife trade much earlier. For example, Thomas Newbold described Malays as "admirable snarers of birds and wild animals," while an article in the *Illustrated London News* in 1872 described Singapore as "one of the best places for buying birds," with the ubiquitous presence of Malay bird sellers, especially when a P. and O. steamer arrived. Moreover, the same article also invoked the stereotype of young Malay adults being temperamentally suited for the nature-oriented job, as "it was common for a [Malay] boy, when he has finished his career as a diver, to make a new start, and become a birdseller."[8] During his visit to Southeast Asia in 1878, American zoologist William Hornaday remarked, "had I been a showman or collector of live animals, I could have gathered quite a harvest of wild beasts in Singapore." From tigers, rhinoceroses and *orang utans* costing above $100 to tapirs and slow lemurs costing $2, the trade in wild animals ranged from the large and exotic to the small and common.[9]

While indigenous animal catchers and middlemen remained important participants in this trade, Europeans and Americans began to dominate

---

[7] Layton, *Songbirds in Singapore*, pp. 1–5; I.H. Burkill lists the different birds Malays and Chinese kept as pets in *A Dictionary of the Economic Products of the Malay Peninsula*, vol. 1 (London: Governments of the Straits Settlements and Federated Malay States, 1935), pp. 328–9.

[8] Roland Braddell, *The Lights of Singapore* (London: Methuen & Co., 1934), p. 135; T.J. Newbold, *Political and Statistical Account of the British Settlements in the Straits of Malacca, viz. Pinang, Malacca, and Singapore; With a History of the Malayan States on the Peninsula of Malacca*, vol. 2 (London: John Murray, 1839), p. 190; D.J.M. Tate, *Straits Affairs: The Malay World and Singapore, Being Glimpses of the Straits Settlements and the Malay Peninsula in the Nineteenth Century as Seen Through the Illustrated London News and Other Contemporary Sources* (Hong Kong: John Nicholson Ltd., 1989), p. 23.

[9] William T. Hornaday, *The Experiences of a Hunter and Naturalist in the Malay Peninsula and Borneo* (Kuala Lumpur: Oxford University Press, 1993), p. 8.

the process during the late 19th century, mirroring the development Nigel Rothfels has observed in animal collection in colonial Africa.[10] For instance, in his memoirs, American animal collector Charles Mayer, described how—by going directly to Palembang to collect animals—he successfully broke Mohammed Ariff's monopoly on animal trade in Singapore, which were stored in a house in Orchard Road before being shipped to American circuses or Australian zoos in the late 19th century.[11] Frank Buck, of *Bring 'Em Back Alive* fame, had a similar system in place during the interwar years, maintaining a compound in Katong while he traveled to Borneo, Malaya, and the East Indies to collect wild animals. Despite the entrance of these foreign animal dealers, local animal traders remained important. In fact, there was often a symbiotic relationship between foreign animal dealers and local animal traders, as reflected in Buck's accounts of his dealings with Chop Joo Soon, a Chinese bird trader in Rochore Road, who supplied him with birds and even information.[12] However, unlike the charismatic foreign animal dealers such as Mayer and Buck, these local traders left few archival traces.

It is difficult to reconstruct a comprehensive statistical history of wildlife trade in colonial Singapore. While colonial records did contain statistics on the import and export of "Animals Living not for Food," the exact nature of what was included in this category is not clear. This category was further sub-divided into three groups, "Birds," "Horses and Ponies," and "Other Animals." The wildlife trade probably straddled two of the three sub-categories under this broad label: "Birds" and "Other Animals." Moreover, import and export statistics detailing the various foreign trade partners were only available for British Malaya as a whole, without differentiating between its constituent states. Furthermore, most of the trade was undocumented due to its illicit nature and insignificant position on the list of British economic priorities.

Despite these limitations, some useful inferences can be made from the sketchy statistical record. First, Singapore was a center for the import and

---

[10] Nigel Rothfels, *Savages and Beasts: The Birth of the Modern Zoo* (Baltimore, MD: Johns Hopkins University Press, 2002), p. 52.

[11] Charles Mayer, *Trapping Wild Animals in Malay Jungles* (London: T. Fisher Unwin, 1922), pp. 25–30.

[12] Ilsa Sharp, *The First 21 Years: The Singapore Zoological Gardens Story* (Singapore: Singapore Zoological Gardens, 1994), p. 22; Frank Buck and Edward Anthony, *Bring 'Em Back Alive* (New York: Simon and Schuster, 1930). Chop Joo Soon, the Chinese bird trader, is described as an "old friend" and informant on p. 28, and occasional dealer in wild animals such as *orang utans* on p. 120.

export of "Animals Living not for Food" and responsible for a significant majority of imports and exports of birds and other animals in British Malaya. A state-based breakdown of the total imports and exports for birds and other animals in Malaya in 1933 reveals that Singapore was the center of this trade, making up almost all the exports for birds and other animals and importing at least 59.88 percent of them (see Table 5.1). Second, the statistics highlight the international nature of the trade during the period, with exports to Europe and North America, reflecting how Singapore's wildlife trade was plugged into the international demand for exotic animals.[13]

Attitudes toward this significant wildlife trade were linked to the attitudes toward animals in general, which were reflected in the development of animal welfare movements during the colonial period. The history of the institutions involved in protecting animal welfare in Singapore is a convoluted one. The concern for animal welfare in the Colony was raised in the English-language press as early as 1876, in the form of a letter from D.F.A. Hervey, a Malayan Civil Service official, who commented on the need for a Society for the Prevention of Cruelty to Animals.[14] Formed shortly thereafter, the Society was dissolved and absorbed into the Municipal Council as the Prevention of Cruelty to Animals (PCA) Department in 1901 to facilitate more efficient prosecution and enforcement of laws against cruelty toward animals.[15] The understaffed PCA Department, however, came under constant criticism about its inability to deal with the rampant ill-treatment of animals. For instance, *The Malaya Tribune* editor described the staff of PCA Department as "ludicrous, ineffectual half-amateurs," with only "two minor officials and two peons to deal with an evil that is spattered right through the town." In response to the inadequacies of the PCA, a new Society for the Prevention of Cruelty to Animals (SPCA) was formed in 1927.[16]

---

[13] While Table 6.1 only cites statistics in 1933, the patterns of percentages were similar in the 1920s and 1930s. These are produced for reference to emphasize the role that Singapore played in Malaya and the region with regard to the animal trade at the point in time when the *1933 Report* was produced.

[14] D.F.A. Hervey, "Cruelty to Animals," *Straits Times Overland Journal*, 9 Mar. 1876, p. 4.

[15] Administration Report of the Singapore Municipality 1901, p. 22.

[16] "Are You Esteemed?," *The Malaya Tribune*, 1 Oct. 1924, p. 6. A kinder assessment of the PCA's efforts as a "halfhearted dealing with ill-treatment of animals," is found in "SPCA," *The Singapore Free Press and Mercantile Advertiser* [hereafter *SFP*], 21 May 1927, p. 10.

Table 5.1 Comparison of Singapore's imports and exports of birds and other animals with other entities in British Malaya (1933)

IMPORTS

	Singapore		Straits Settlements		Singapore's Percentage of Straits Settlements Imports (%)		British Malaya		Singapore's Percentage of British Malaya Imports (%)	
	Quantity (Nos.)	Value	Quantity (Nos.)	Value	By Quantity	By Value	Quantity (Nos.)	Value	By Quantity	By Value
Birds	7,626	2,443	12,619	3,228	60.43	75.68	12,735	3,942	59.88	61.97
Other Animals	1,890	19,354	1,896	19,819	99.68	97.65	1,930	21,557	97.93	89.78

EXPORTS

	Singapore		Straits Settlements		Singapore's Percentage of Straits Settlements Imports (%)		British Malaya		Singapore's Percentage of British Malaya Imports (%)	
	Quantity (Nos.)	Value	Quantity (Nos.)	Value	By Quantity	By Value	Quantity (Nos.)	Value	By Quantity	By Value
Birds	13,596	7,309	13,596	7,309	100	100	13,596	7,309	100	100
Other Animals	16,788	17,526	16,788	17,526	100	100	16,807	17,675	99.89	99.16

Source: Malaya Foreign Imports and Exports during the Year 1933, CO740/11, pp. 1260–1 and 1298–9.

Some of the strongest critics of the wildlife trade were also champions of animal welfare, and among the most prominent members of society. Likening the "cruel commercial exploitation of wild life" in Singapore to a "slave trade" in these "poor denizens of the forest," Tan Cheng Lock, a vocal member of the Straits Settlements Legislative Council, was not alone in expressing his disdain for the trade on the basis of the cruelty involved.[17] Apart from the re-emergence of the SPCA in Singapore, the heightened interest in animal welfare issues during the interwar period was also evident from persistence of interest in Legislative Council Proceedings from the late 1920s and well into the 1930s. In 1927, a committee of five was appointed to investigate into the alleged prevalence of cruelty to animals. They produced a short four-page report that detailed the situation at bird shops, abattoirs and ports and concluded that there was "not a prevalence of cruelty" except for "accidents" caused by "carelessness." Not everyone agreed, as Tan Cheng Lock later spoke up on the subject of "humane slaughtering" in response to that report in 1928. In 1929, Tan and H.H. Abdoolcader advocated an update of the Ordinance on Cruelty to Animals, which resulted in a new Prevention of Cruelty to Animals Bill presented to the Legislative Council in 1930.[18]

The issue of animal welfare during the early 1930s also received public attention. In 1931, an anonymous writer who identified himself as "For the Utterly Helpless" wrote to *The Singapore Free Press* condemning the "cruelties of the bird trade" in Singapore, considering it "disgraceful." The editorial in the same paper eight days later echoed the same sentiment, but in a more tempered manner, concluding that "the mere existence of the trade [was] a depressing comment upon modern civilization, but if we [were] to permit the enslavement of the Wild we might at least have sufficient regard for our own self-respect to make it as bearable as possible," presumably via regulation.[19] These non-exhaustive instances of commentaries on the much-

---

[17] Proceedings of Straits Settlements Legislative Council, 6 Mar. 1933, CO275/133, p. B43.

[18] "Cruelty to Animals: Government Ask for Facts," *SFP*, 13 Oct. 1926, p. 9; Proceedings of Straits Settlements Legislative Council, 7 Oct. 1929, CO275/122, pp. B125–7; Proceedings of Straits Settlements Legislative Council, 31 Oct. 1927, CO275/116, pp. C206–7; 27 Aug. 1928, CO275/120, pp. B93–4; 12 May 1930, CO275/125, p. B32.

[19] "Cruelties of the Bird Trade: Why is Nothing Ever Done?" *SFP*, 20 Oct. 1931, p. 8; "A Plea for the Wild," *SFP*, 28 Oct. 1931, p. 8.

labored topic of cruelty to animals in 1931 came only months after Governor Cecil Clementi passed the Animal and Bird-Shop By-Laws in July, which promoted "humane" slaughtering of stray dogs and improved educational programs encouraging kindness toward animals in schools, reflecting the public's perception of its inadequacies.[20]

The animal welfare movement in Singapore traces its history back to similar movements in the British metropole. As the first nation to pass an enduring law to protect animals against cruelty in 1822, and to form a Society for the Prevention of Cruelty to Animals in 1824, Britain had established a strong animal welfare movement by the mid-19th century.[21] This animal welfare movement was, however, not simply altruistic. At the first meeting of the British animal protection society, the chairman bluntly explained that its objective was not only "to prevent cruelty toward animals," "but to spread amongst the lower orders of the people ... a degree of moral feeling which would compel them to think and act like those of a superior class."[22] As a "mark of civilization" that also differentiated the English from others, such as the Spanish who condoned bullfighting, the animal welfare movement was used to define the English bourgeoisie against other classes and nationalities.[23]

These civilizational discourses accompanying the animal welfare movement in Britain trickled down to colonial Singapore. Convinced of the need to civilize the "Natives of the East," Hervey expressed the hope that via the SPCA, Singaporeans would be "open to impression by such influences," tempered with a succeeding clause that such influences would be "in a less[er] degree perhaps."[24] Such attitudes persisted into the 1920s and 1930s. In 1924, a letter to *The Straits Times* editor commented condescendingly on the "mental attitude of the Asiatics," who allegedly ignored the misery of a

---

[20] "By-Laws for Birdshop Control. Animal welfare," *SFP*, 26 Mar. 1931, p. 12.

[21] Jerrold Tannebaum, "Animals and the Law," in *Animals and the Law: Property, Cruelty, Rights*, ed. Arien Mack (Columbus, OH: Ohio State University Press, 1999), p. 151. The French Société Protectrice des Animaux was founded in 1845 and the American SPCA in 1866. See Kathleen Kete, "Animals and Ideology: The Politics of Animal Protection in Europe," in *Representing Animals*, ed. Nigel Rothfels (Bloomington, IN: Indiana University Press, 2002), p. 25.

[22] As quoted in Harriet Ritvo, *The Animal Estate: The English and Other Creatures in the Victorian Age* (Cambridge: Harvard University Press, 1987), p. 135.

[23] Kete, "Animals and Ideology," p. 26.

[24] Hervey, "Cruelty to Animals."

crippled dog.[25] Even though Europeans and Americans were also involved in the creation of the demand for wildlife trade, the voices disparaging the trade in animals tended to blame it on non-Europeans, commenting that the "disgraceful cruelty" was perpetuated just to "fill the pockets of those, most of whom (perhaps all), are not even British subjects."[26] Beneath his comments on the "scandalous" state of affairs in Singapore, despite the presence of a "sizeable European community," the editor of *The Singapore Free Press* harbored an unspoken assumption that Europeans ought to know better and promote better treatment of animals. The countless reports of Asians being fined for cruelty toward animals also reflect the widespread visibility of the stereotype of the callous Asian vis-à-vis the enlightened British.[27]

Admittedly, not all the reported cases of cruelty were fabricated. The torturous death inflicted on an iguana by imprisonment in an empty pint bottle or confining 296 Java sparrows in a cage constructed to hold only 50 were undeniably cruel.[28] The pertinent point, however, is not whether these reports were factually accurate, but that such stereotypes existed and that Europeans, especially the British, used them to differentiate themselves from the barbarian "Other." The silence on the involvement of Europeans and Americans in the trade also reveals the civilizational biases that pinned blame solely on Asians.

The history of wildlife trade in colonial Singapore was also intertwined with that of wildlife protection. After all, one of the key concerns of the wildlife protection movement was the uncontrolled wildlife trade that threatened the survival of some species. Legislation to protect wildlife in the Straits Settlements dated to 1884, when the Wild Birds Protection Ordinance was passed. The Wild Animals and Birds Protection Ordinance in 1904, which now included animals and allowed for the Governor to

---

[25] "Humanity in the East," *ST*, 20 Aug. 1924, p. 10.

[26] "Cruelties of the Bird Trade: Why is Nothing Ever Done?," *SFP*, 20 Oct. 1931, p. 8.

[27] "A Plea for the Wild," *SFP*, 28 Oct. 1931, p. 8. Further instances of such reports in the 1930s include: "A Callous Chinese: Exemplary Sentence for Cruelty to Ducklings," *ST*, 26 Apr. 1930, p. 12; "Cruelty to Animals: Indian Menagerie Owner Fined," *ST*, 27 Nov. 1930, p. 12; "Cruelty to Birds: Two Chinese Fined for Overcrowding," *ST*, 15 June 1933, p. 16; "Smile Disappeared: Chinese Fined for Cruelty to Birds," *SFP*, 13 Jan. 1934, p. 6.

[28] "Exhausted Lizard: Chinese Fined for Cruelty," *SFP*, 28 Oct. 1933, p. 5; "296 Instead of 50: Overcrowding Even in a Bird Cage," *SFP*, 24 Aug. 1933, p. 7.

declare closed seasons for certain wildlife, eventually superseded the 1884 legislation. These laws, however, only prohibited the hunting of wildlife found in Singapore and did not address the problems related to the trade in wildlife not indigenous to Singapore. Only after pressures from officials in the Netherlands Indies and London did the Straits Settlements implement legislation protecting non-native species.

Pressure from the Netherlands Indies greatly influenced British considerations, especially for the prohibition of imports of non-native species in the 1930s, as the wildlife trade in Singapore was a significant concern to conservationists of the time. Between 1918 and 1925, practically all the wild animals exported from the Netherlands Indies, excluding cattle, poultry, and domesticated animals, went to Singapore. In addition to wild animals, Singapore was also the principal port of destination for products derived from wild animals, such as rhinoceros horns, ivory, and animal skins. In 1928, K.W. Dammerman, the Director of the Buitenzorg Museum and Chairman of the Netherlands Indies Society for the Protection of Nature, wrote to Cecil Boden Kloss, Director of the Raffles Museum, to enquire if the latter could help to "stop the [illegal] importation [of *orang utans*] in Singapore." Willem Daniels, Consul-General for the Netherlands, followed with a more official request in 1929, when he revisited the issue by requesting that Singapore "consider the desirability of legislative action prohibiting the importation into the Colony of orang-utans."[29]

While British reaction to the initial pleas of Dammerman to legislate for the protection of non-native species was lukewarm in 1928, they took swift action after the memorandum from Consul-General Daniels in August 1929. The Executive Council amended the existing Wild Animals and Birds Ordinance in 1930, following the Legislative Council's recommendations. During the first reading of the proposed Bill to prohibit the unlicensed importation of *orang utans* in the Legislative Council meeting on 24 March 1930, the Attorney-General, W.C. Huggard, explicitly stated that the "object of this amending Bill ... is to enable this Government to co-operate with the

---

[29] The percentage of wildlife exported to Singapore from Netherlands Indies between 1918 and 1925 was never below 80 percent. Dammerman, *Preservation of Wildlife and Nature Reserves in the Netherlands Indies*, pp. 17, 34. K. Dammerman to C. Kloss, 11 Sep. 1928, MSA 1139/10, C.S.O. Museums 8366/1928, National Archives of Singapore [henceforth NAS]; W. Daniels to Colonial Secretary of Straits Settlements, 16 Aug. 1929, MSA 1139/10, C.S.O. Museums 8366/1928, NAS.

Table 5.2 Export of wild animals and their products from the Netherlands Indies to Singapore, 1918–25

	1918		1919		1920		1921		1922		1923		1924		1925	
	Quan-tity	% of total	Quan-tity	% of total	Quan-tity	% of total	Quan-tity	% of total	Quan-tity	% of total	Quan-tity	% of total	Quan-tity	% of total	Quan-tity	% of total
Living animals (pieces)	69211	99.9	7805	99.49	4080	99.44	68322	86.37	126071	80.38	188095	85.7	260472	99.01	346516	94.2
Skins (kilos)	142817	66.85	122901	32.68	83719	33.02	98227	49.2	126598	52.15	127681	42	117370	35.4	107839	31.61
Deer Skins (pieces)	55059	32.97	45698	20.27	39172	31.48	20139	28.38	38244	50.69	53103	29.66	23428	14.77	23817	30.61
Deer antlers (kilos)	6412	17.65	4379	3.42	7665	9.95	4446	6.89	5406	7.13	2010	2.11	2415	2.61	2755	4.79
Ivory (raw) (kilos)			164	45.94	106	40.3	65	23.55	95	21.84			242	52.95		
Rhinocerous horns (kilos)			31	63.27	65	92.86	38	100	59	86.76	24	61.54	13	54.17	6	37.5
Bird-skins (pieces)	18546	30.32	32041	26.33	271	0.44	376	0.38					114	0.19	38	0.13
Feathers (kilos)																
Birds-nests (edible) (kilos)	64054	96.74	59680	81.88	107611	94.67	151421	98.26	84656	95.74	75995	96.63	64464	84.75	64632	88.05
Varanus skins																
Tortoise-shell (raw) (kilos)	1038	15.09	5925	36.38	4557	29.06	2610	9.87	1838	25.33	7198	31.89	3728	18.71	11932	55.29

Source: Dammerman, *Preservation of Wildlife and Nature Reserves in the Netherlands Indies*, pp. 88–91.

Government of the Netherlands East Indies."[30] Nor was frustration over this "monkey business" restricted to *orang utans*, as the memorandum also pointed out that protected bird species like crown pigeons and birds of paradise were "still smuggled in large quantities into Singapore." By 1933, the prohibited list of animals and birds for importation from the Netherlands Indies was increased to 28 species.[31] Dutch pressure clearly had a great impact on encouraging the British colonial administration to improve upon legislation protecting wildlife, even if they were not indigenous to Malaya.

Metropolitan developments in the conservation movement also affected legislation on wildlife in Singapore. For instance, the revision of the 1884 Ordinance to include wild animals in 1904 came after the institutionalization of preservationist movements to protect colonial fauna in London, with the formation of the Society for the Preservation of the Fauna of the Empire (SPFE) in 1900. In 1916, a Plumage Ordinance, which prohibited the importation and exportation of plumage, was passed to protect non-native birds such as the colorful and endangered birds of paradise in the Netherlands Indies. This Plumage Ordinance was also partly a result of pressures the London-based Society for the Protection of Birds had placed on British officials since the late 19th century, efforts which slowly trickled down to the colonies.[32]

---

[30] For the discussion of course of action to Netherlands Indies' official request, see Orang-Utan: Prohibition of importation into S.S. and F.M.S., 1930, CO717/72, No. 72378/1930; for the amendment of Ordinance 88, see Straits Settlements Government Gazette Notification [henceforth SSGGN] 1685, 22 Aug. 1930; Proceedings of Straits Settlements Legislative Council, 24 Mar. 1930, CO275/125, p. B19.

[31] Memorial Concerning the Exportation of Orang Utans from the Netherlands Indies and the Importation and Transit at Singapore, 1930, CO717/72, No. 72378/1930; SSGGN 1283, 30 June 1933.

[32] John MacKenzie, *The Empire of Nature: Hunting, Conservation and British Imperialism* (Manchester: Manchester University Press, 1988), pp. 201–2; for a history of wildlife protection legislations in Singapore, see Heng's "Wildlife Protection Laws in Singapore," pp. 292–4; due to the popularity of feathers in women's hats during the period and the resulting entrenched commercial interests, the campaign for a ban on plumage trade was slow. The trickle-down effect to the colonies was thus also slow, with India passing an ordinance against exports in 1902, followed by a similar ordinance in Australia in 1912. See R.J. Moore-Colyer, "Feathered Women and the Persecuted Birds: The Struggle Against the Plumage Trade, c.1860–1922," *Rural History* 11, 1 (2000): 65. MacKenzie points out that the SPFE did not take much interest in Asia until the 1930s, concentrating on its African colonies in the early years of its conception due to the background of its founding members. MacKenzie, *The Empire of Nature*, p. 262.

While the SPFE and other metropolitan movements actively cam-
paigned to protect wildlife in London, in Malaya the task mainly fell to
Theodore Hubback, a Pahang planter and big-game hunter who became
an "indefatigable champion of Malayan wildlife."[33] Throughout the 1920s,
Hubback made overtures to the British Parliament through the SPFE,
which eventually earned him the appointment as the Chairman of the Wild
Life Commission of Malaya in 1930. From August 1930 to March 1931,
Hubback conducted a total of 64 interviews throughout the various states in
British Malaya, gathering evidence and sentiments from Europeans, Malays,
as well as elite Chinese and Indian residents on wildlife issues. Described
as an exhaustive enquiry prepared with "extraordinary thoroughness" which
reached "somewhat forbidding proportions," the three-volume *tour d'force*
contained a general survey of the status of wildlife in Malaya, lists of wildlife
enactments in other countries and in Malaya, and a comprehensive draft
Enactment for the Preservation of Wild Life.[34]

The Wild Life Commission's evidence gathering sessions in Singapore
yielded a unanimous view on the need for regulating and licensing of wild
animal and bird shops. In February 1931, Hubback accompanied Colina
Hussey, Vice-President of the SPCA, on a visit of the bird shops along
Rochor Road and North Bridge Road. He concluded that there was "serious
overcrowding" as well as the presence of birds, such as the crowned pigeon,
prohibited for export from the Netherlands Indies. Although Section 64
of the draft Enactment for the Preservation of Wild Life published in the
Report of the Wild Life Commission of Malaya briefly addressed the issue of
wildlife trade, the scale of the problem in Singapore necessitated a separate
investigation.[35]

The Wild Animals and Bird Committee, and their Report

With the growing interest in the animal welfare and the protection of wildlife
movements, the formation of a Committee to inquire and report on the
wildlife trade in Singapore, announced on 21 July 1933, was hardly surprising.

---

[33] Kathirithamby-Wells, *Nature and Nation*, pp. 198–9.
[34] *Report of the Wild Life Commission*, I (Singapore: Government Printing Office,
1932), p. 12; "The Wild Life Report," *ST*, 15 Aug. 1932, p. 10.
[35] *Report of the Wild Life Commission*, I, pp. 47–57; *Report of the Wild Life Commission*,
II, p. 46; *Report of the Wild Animals and Wild Birds Committee* (Singapore:
Government Printing Office, 1934) [henceforth cited as the *1933 Report*], p. 17.

Governor Cecil Clementi appointed a committee of five to inquire and make recommendations on "(a) The import and export trade in Wild Animals and Wild Birds in Singapore ... [and] (b) The suitability or otherwise of the methods adopted in Singapore ... for the transport, housing and care of Wild Animals and Wild Birds ... so as to ensure humane treatment [of them]."[36] The members of the Committee were Theodore Rathborne Hubback, Frederick Nutter Chasen, Tan Cheng Lock, Harry Elphick, and James Thompson Forbes. The 21-page report was completed on 22 December 1933 and presented before the Legislative Council on 16 April 1934.[37]

The Chairman of the Wild Animals and Wild Birds Committee was Theodore Hubback. Born in Liverpool in 1872, he came to British Malaya in 1895 and worked in the Public Works Department for a short while before becoming a planter in Negri Sembilan. As an avid hunter of big game, Hubback published two influential texts on the subject, and his hunting abilities were so well-known that natural history museums in London and New York commissioned him to secure specimens of a rare Alaskan sheep, *Ovis dalli*, in 1919. The next year, he settled in Pahang as a planter and later took up the unsalaried position of Game Warden of Pahang in 1921, embarking on a lifelong mission of campaigning for better protection of wildlife in Malaya. In 1930, the Secretary of State for the Colonies, Lord Sidney Passfield, appointed Hubback as the Chairman of a Wild Life Commission to investigate and recommend ways and means of protecting wildlife in Malaya.[38] His expert knowledge of Malaya's flora and fauna, and prior experience with the Wild Life Commission of Malaya, made him a suitable candidate to lead this 1933 Committee to inquire into the wildlife trade in Singapore, an issue that surfaced in the Wild Life Commission's investigations in 1932.

The Vice-Chairman of the Committee was Frederick Chasen, Director of the Raffles Museum. Born in Norfolk in 1896, Chasen was appointed Assistant Curator of the Raffles Museum in 1921, and assumed

---

[36] SSGGN 1412, 21 July 1933.

[37] Proceedings of Straits Settlements Legislative Council, 16 Apr. 1934, CO275/135, p. B32.

[38] Theodore Hubback, *Elephant and Seladang Hunting in the Federated Malay States* (London: R. Ward, 1905); *Three Months in Pahang in Search of Big Game: A Reminiscence of Malaya* (Singapore: Kelly and Walsh, 1907); John Gullick and Gerald Hawkins, *Malayan Pioneers* (Singapore: Eastern Universities Press, 1958), pp. 78–85; Kathirithamby-Wells, *Nature and Nation*, pp. 198–208.

the Directorship in 1932 when Cecil B. Kloss retired. Although he did not have a university degree or other formal qualifications, by the time of his appointment as Director of the Raffles Museum in 1932, he was known as the "most reliable and accurate authority on far-eastern birds and mammals in the region," taking over the task of completing the late H.C. Robinson's encyclopedic *The Birds of the Malay Peninsula* in the 1930s.[39] As birds made up a significant portion of the wildlife trade, the appointment of someone with a scientific expertise in such animals in the region was useful for the Committee inquiring into the trade.

As Director of the Raffles Museum, Chasen was part of a larger scientific and animal collecting network in the region.[40] Although he did not necessarily have much contact with wildlife traders because the museum generally preferred dead specimens to living ones, letters exchanged between Chasen and William Basapa, the owner of the Punggol Zoo, suggest that Chasen used his position to facilitate some wildlife trade. For instance, on 21 January 1937, Basapa wrote to Chasen to seek the latter's aid in securing permits from the Dutch Government for a consignment that Basapa undertook for the Director of the Paris Zoo.[41] Although the letters were written in the late 1930s, Chasen would have established these networks with wildlife traders long before, given that he had been working at the Raffles Museum since 1921. Such networks came in especially useful for his fact-finding mission to Palembang and Siak, an important section of the *1933 Report*.

The third member of the Committee was Tan Cheng Lock, Unofficial Member of the Straits Settlements Legislative Council and the Executive Council as of 1933. Born in Malacca in 1883, Tan was part of a wealthy Straits Chinese family that owned rubber estates. In 1902, he had a short

---

[39] Robinson, Curator of the Selangor Museum, published Volumes 1 and 2 in 1927 and 1928, while he was still alive. After his death in 1928, Chasen continued the series with Robinson's notes. Michael Tweedie, "Obituary: Frederick Nutter Chasen," *Ibis* 88, 4 (Oct. 1946): 527–8.

[40] For a discussion of the social nature of collecting in the Raffles Museum and the importance of networks which Chasen cultivated, see Brendan Luyt, "Collectors and Collecting for the Raffles Museum in Singapore: 1920 to 1940," *Library and Information History* 26, 3 (Sep. 2010): 183–95. See also Timothy P. Barnard's contribution to this volume.

[41] W. Basapa to F. Chasen, 21 Jan. 1937; F. Chasen to W. Basapa, 18 July 1939; F. Chasen to W. Basapa, 7 Oct. 1939, MSA1140/131, NAS.

stint as a schoolmaster at the Raffles Institution in Singapore before joining the rubber industry in 1909. Tan is, however, best known for his public life, assuming political positions such as Municipal Commissioner of Malacca in 1912 and entering the Straits Settlements Legislative Council in 1923, where he championed issues such as the removal of the Colour Bar and his advocacy for Malayan, rather than Malay, nationalism.[42]

Tan's advocacy for animal issues is less well known. In the late 1920s, he spoke up several times in the Legislative Council on issues regarding animal welfare, humane slaughtering, and the need to revise outdated legislation regarding animals.[43] Undeterred by then Colonial Secretary John Scott's thinly-veiled rebuke in 1929 that topics such as the revision of Ordinances dealing with cruelty to animals should be left to the SPCA to negotiate with the government, Tan demonstrated that his passion for animal welfare was not easily brushed aside. He continued to raise these issues. In 1932, Tan even mentioned that he "happen[ed] to be the President of one of these Societies [for the prevention of cruelty to animals] in Malacca" to support a point he was making in the Legislative Council.[44] In March 1933, he also questioned the intentions of the Straits Settlements Government with regard to the Wild Life Commission's recommendations. In that same meeting, he condemned the wildlife trade in Singapore as a "slave trade in these poor denizens of the forest" and urged the Government to "end the cruel commercial exploitation of wild life in this country."[45] With Tan's track record as a Legislative Council member who expressed concern for animal issues in the Straits Settlements, his appointment as a member of the Wild Animals and Wild Birds Committee was hardly surprising.

---

[42] Most accounts of Tan's public life focus on his progressive ideas for a multi-ethnic Malaya. For instance, see K.G. Tregonning, "Tan Cheng Lock: A Malayan Nationalist," *Journal of Southeast Asian Studies* 10, 1 (Mar. 1979): 25–76; P. Lim Pui Huen, *Tan Cheng Lock Papers: A Descriptive List* (Singapore: Institute of Southeast Asian Studies, 1989), pp. xv–xvii.

[43] Proceedings of Straits Settlements Legislative Council, 27 Aug. 1928, CO275/120, pp. B93–4; Proceedings of Straits Settlements Legislative Council, 7 Oct. 1929, CO275/122, pp. B125–7.

[44] Proceedings of Straits Settlements Legislative Council, 7 Oct. 1929, CO275/122, p. B129; Proceedings of Straits Settlements Legislative Council, 30 May 1932, CO275/130, p. B67.

[45] Proceedings of Straits Settlements Legislative Council, 6 Mar. 1933, CO275/133, pp. B27–8, B43.

Not much is known about the other two members of the Committee. Harry Elphick joined his father in Singapore in 1887, when he was still a boy. In 1897, Elphick joined the trading firm Guthrie and Co., and was involved in its expansion into Kuala Lumpur and Klang. Posted to Guthrie's London office prior to the First World War, Elphick joined the military in 1917 and returned to Singapore in 1919, when he left Guthrie and Co. for its rival William Jacks and Co. Apart from his business career, Elphick was also involved in public service as an active member of the Straits Settlements Association, the Chamber of Commerce and committees of the Municipal Commissioners. Of particular interest in this regard is his involvement in a Government appointed Committee to investigate the alleged prevalence of cruelty to animals in 1927. In addition to his prior experience with the investigation of animal and bird shops, Elphick also hosted the meetings of the Wild Animals and Wild Birds Committee at his office in Ocean Building.[46]

Even less is known about James Forbes, apart from his career as the Municipal Veterinary Surgeon beginning in August 1928. In addition to his duties of managing the Animal Infirmary and the PCA Department, which included inspections of animal and bird shops, the Municipal Veterinary Surgeon was tasked with the annual issuing of licenses for the sale of animals, under the Animal and Bird Shop By-Laws passed in 1931.[47] One of the key recommendations of the Wild Animals and Wild Birds Committee was the construction of a Central Market for bird and small mammal trade, a suggestion that Forbes had previously raised in 1930 upon his pessimistic assessment that although the PCA Department had done "everything possible," he could not "imagine an improvement under existing conditions."[48] This suggestion of the construction of a Central Market elicited a letter of objection from the Chinese animal and bird traders, a rare display of their voices, which will be examined in greater detail later in this section.

The *1933 Report* was addressed to the Governor of the Straits Settlements, Cecil Clementi, who appointed these five people with an interest in the issue of wildlife trade. On page 7 of the *1933 Report* are the terms of the reference for the Committee's investigations, which were set as inquiring

---

[46] "Harry Elphick: Forty Years Spent in Malaya," *ST*, 19 Nov. 1927, p. 12; Proceedings of Straits Settlements Legislative Council, 31 Oct. 1927, CO275/116, pp. C206–7; *1933 Report*, p. 13.
[47] "Untitled notification," *SFP*, 3 Aug. 1928, p. 8; SSGGN 859, 24 Apr. 1931.
[48] J. Forbes to Municipal Office, 24 Oct. 1930, SIT902/30, HDB1023, NAS.

and reporting on the retail trade in wild animals and wild birds, "with special reference to the control and supervision desirable so as to ensure humane treatment for them." These instructions intersect with the growing interest in animal welfare issues from public interest groups such as the SPCA and some concerned Legislative Council members in the late 1920s. The scope of the Committee's investigations was thus understandably limited to shops, such as the infamous Rochor Road shops, which had been the subject of "much adverse criticism ... in the local press." Zoos, such as those owned by Herbert de Souza in East Coast Road and William Basapa in Punggol, were mentioned, although they were considered "beyond the scope of small retail traders."[49]

The focus on the Rochor Road animal dealers and the conspicuous absence of foreign animal dealers mirrored the government's largely discriminatory attitudes toward non-Europeans involved in this business. Not all non-Europeans involved in the wildlife trade were treated equally though, as the influential scientific networks in which some of them were participated, as demonstrated by the close relationship between Basapa and Chasen, may have deterred the Committee from scrutinizing them. The *1933 Report* quoted the opinions of Government Veterinary Surgeon, George Rocker, that "the *bona fide* agent and dealer in wild animals for zoological gardens and collectors usually carrie[d] on his business in a satisfactory manner ... [because] the high monetary value of his stock for an animal kept under unfavorable conditions rapidly depreciates in marketable worth." Unlike Rochor Road animal traders, the Committee's belief that zoo proprietors, such as Basapa and foreign animal dealers such as Buck, did not ill-treat their animals, excluded them from specific scrutiny.[50]

This assumed distinction between bona fide agents and unscrupulous shopkeepers reflected the Committee's personal biases rather than how the trade actually operated. One of the shops the Committee took to task was Chop Joo Soon Hin, operating out of 532 North Bridge Road, which was also frequently mentioned in Frank Buck's *Bring 'Em Back Alive* as a key local animal shop that American dealers frequented.[51] Chop Joo Soon Hin, however, dealt with internationally renowned animal dealers from America and was certainly a bona fide agent, aware of the value of his animals and did not treat it as merely a side business. Moreover, developments in the

---

[49] *1933 Report*, pp. 7–8.
[50] Ibid., p. 11.
[51] Ibid., pp. 14–5; see note 13.

Table 5.3 List of known animal and bird traders in the 1930s

Name of proprietor	Location	Remarks
Unnamed	239 New Bridge Road (Chop Cheng Kee)	One of the signatories of the letter protesting the Central Market suggestion
Lim Lie Ee	532 North Bridge Road (Chop Joo Soon) Swatow Street	Space inadequate for number of animal kept Swatow Street store is a death trap Rent of shop-house was high ($80 per month) and had to deal in animals because profit in small bird trade is insufficient One of the signatories of the letter protesting the Central Market suggestion
Lim Tay	54 Rochor Road	Overcrowded
Kah Tong	55 Rochor Road	Greatly overcrowded and filthy
Lim Cheng Teow	56 Rochor Road	Unfit
Ah Yew	58 Rochor Road	Only slight improvement at present Ducks and fowls only
Unnamed	59 Rochor Road (Chop Kian Huat & co)	One of the signatories of the letter protesting the Central Market suggestion
Unnamed	60 Rochor Road	Licensed only for ducks and fowls
Toh Ah Ban	61 Rochor Road (Chop Guan Kee) 50 Desker Road	Filthy condition; no proper ventilation and animals badly overcrowded Found to have illegally imported a *tenggiling* (scaly ant-eater) from Sumatra by a steamer which had arrived from Siak on 23 July Desker Road private house with cages in back premise believed to be overflow from shop One of the signatories of the letter protesting the Central Market suggestion
Unnamed	62 Rochor Road	Only for ducks and fowls
Wee Seng Soo	62-1 Rochor Road	Totally unfit Only ducks and fowls Unsuitable as licensed premises for wild animals and birds

Table 5.3 (continued)

Name of proprietor	Location	Remarks
Unnamed	63 Rochor Road	Slight improvement as far as premises permit
Lim Beng Hin	64 Rochor Road	Filthy condition; no proper ventilation and animals badly overcrowded
Teo Hock Leong	67 Rochor Road	Filthy premises Only ducks and fowls Unsuitable as licensed premises for wild animals and birds
Unnamed	68 Rochor Road	Ducks and fowls only
Unnamed	532 North Bridge Road	Well kept bird shop but animals not suitably caged. For example, monkeys kept in cages with slated bottoms meant for birds
Unnamed	7A Prinsep Street	Deserted, nothing there
Unnamed	60 Japan Street	Nothing there Premises quite unsuitable and should not be licensed
Unnamed	239 North Bridge Road	Large number of small tortoises only
Unnamed	15 Club Street	Dogs only. Premises quite unsuitable for wild animals and should not be licensed
Unnamed	32 Mosque Street	An unsuitable place. Bad and gloomy. Should not be licensed
Unnamed	The Great World Zoo	Only birds, which were adequately and reasonably caged
Herbert de Souza	East Coast Road, Mavfields Kennels	Little stock seen in 1933
William Basapa	Punggol Zoo	Well managed and carefully looked after

Note: All remarks are quoted from Municipal Veterinary Surgeon in 1930 and the Wild Animals and Wild Birds Committee Report. It is not clear whether things were indeed that dire but this is to provide a sample of the kinds of comments and attitudes expressed toward local animal traders.

Source: J. Forbes to Municipal Office, 24 Oct. 1930, SIT902/30, HDB1023, NAS; *Report of the Wild Animals and Wild Birds Committee 1933.*

late 1930s revealed that zoological gardens were not above ill treatment of animals. For instance, in 1938, the Singapore Rural Board commented on the "appalling stench" from the poorly ventilated cages in the Punggol Zoo.[52] Although this was five years after the Committee conducted its investigations, it nevertheless cautions against the generalizations on which the Committee worked. This limited scope was hardly justifiable simply on rationalized economic grounds, as the Committee explained, but more likely a reflection of the personal biases they had against local animal traders who did not participate in colonial scientific networks.

The Wild Animals and Wild Birds Committee expanded its scope beyond Singapore's territorial boundaries and also investigated the smuggling of animals from the Netherlands Indies. Assisted by letters of introduction from the Consul-General for Netherlands Indies in Singapore and his networks from his position as Director of the Raffles Museum, Chasen traveled to Palembang and Siak from August to September 1933 to "ascertain at first-hand how the animals and birds that reach Singapore leave Sumatra."[53] Given that pressures from the Netherlands Indies shaped some of the legislations passed in the 1930s on the import of protected species, it is not surprising that the Committee was interested in investigating this underground trade that so frustrated Dutch scientists and officials.

In addition to direct overtures from the Netherlands Indies government, there were also comparisons of the state of affairs in both colonies that inspired one to emulate or even outdo the other at the time. For instance, a feature article on the animal welfare groups in Netherlands Indies that appeared in *The Straits Times* painted Dutch efforts as an inspiration to Malaya. As an "account of a very valuable work which is being carried on quite unobtrusively in Netherlands India," the article hoped to "enhance" and encourage more "interested persons" to join the "earnest efforts of a few enthusiasts" in improving the "deplorable condition of animals and birds in many parts of Malaya."[54]

Like *The Straits Times* article, the Committee also shared the sentiment that the Netherlands Indies was a model for legislation with regard to animals. While the *1933 Report* was vague about what could be learned from the Dutch model, with only a general comment that "much of the

---

[52] "'Appalling Stench' in Punggol Zoo Cages," *SFP*, 11 Nov. 1938, p. 3.
[53] *1933 Report*, p. 8.
[54] "Alleviating Suffering among Animals: Work Which is Being Done in Netherlands India," *ST*, 3 Feb. 1934, p. 18.

information gained [was] not strictly germane to the present report" but still useful "to suggest hints for future administration of the trade in British Malaya," a letter Chasen wrote to Hubback suggested that he had gained great insights from the visit.[55] In addition to describing how animals might be smuggled from Sumatra into Singapore, Chasen was full of praise for Dutch officials. He commented that "the Dutch customs are extremely efficient. Their officers know the law, are zealous in its administration and remarkably vigilant. They cannot do more to stop the export of protected species than they do."[56] In other words, the onus was now on the Straits Settlements government to stop the import of protected species. He also noted that in Palembang, "restrictions now in force have almost killed the [large mammal] trade which [was] no longer worth following seriously." The same applied to Siak, where "only a shadow of the former considerable trade in animals and birds" existed.[57] Chasen was clearly impressed with the effects of the Dutch legislation, and hoped that it would inspire similar developments in British Malaya.

Beyond reports from Dutch colonies and lists of animal traders in Singapore, the *1933 Report* also contained an evidence section consisting of information quoted from prior investigations into the wildlife trade and the inquiries of the Committee. Instances of the former include the professional opinions of both the Municipal and Government Veterinary Surgeons recommending the construction of a Central Market, as well as Hubback's findings as printed in the *Report of the Wild Life Commission of Malaya*. Pages 12 to 14 of the *1933 Report* contained the findings of the Committee's first-hand inspections of bird shops. While they did not differ much from the opinions of their predecessors, the use of direct quotations rather than usual prose indicated the Committee's desire to distinguish themselves from previous critics. Acknowledging their debt to indignant and concerned letter-writers, the *1933 Report* commented on the history of "adverse criticism of [the] trade in the local press," mild words used to describe the critical opinions expressed in newspapers.[58] Though the Committee never commented on cruelty directly, they included extracts from previous reports and their notes which described the "dark and unsavoury" places, "utterly miserable agony of their [the animals] captivity" and whose "ultimate fate

---

[55] *1933 Report*, p. 8; F. Chasen to T. Hubback, 3 Oct. 1933, MSA 1139/19, NAS.
[56] Ibid.
[57] Ibid.
[58] *1933 Report*, p. 8.

we [Hubback and Chasen] recoil from contemplating."[59] Framing these comments in the form of cited evidence from their investigations distanced their objective recommendations from the more visceral and judgmental descriptions found in opinionated and often emotional letters to editors.

Another unique aspect of the *1933 Report* was the inclusion of a letter from four local animal traders, Chop Joo Soon Hin, Chop Kian Huat and Co., Chop Guan Kee, and Chop Cheng Kee, objecting to the Committee's suggestion of a Central Market. As a rare expression of these local animal traders' perspective, albeit one the Committee mediated, the letter provided a brief glimpse into how they dealt with the hostile attitudes of the English-speaking public in Singapore that reiterated the civilizational discourse of the English bourgeoisie. The civilizational nature of the animal welfare movement and their exclusion from colonial scientific networks had disadvantaged these Rochor Road animal traders, who were subject to much closer scrutiny than foreign animal dealers and other non-European animal dealers who were part of colonial scientific networks.

The letter of objection quoted in the *1933 Report*, however, revealed that local animal traders were capable of utilizing these discriminatory discourses against the Committee. In addition to their practical concerns regarding the "prevailing bad state of business" and the necessary readjustment of operating hours, one of their moral justifications for the rejection of a Central Market was that "many species of birds, such as the canary, [could not] withstand the breeze and as a result their feathers [would] wither and they [would] soon collapse." The Committee easily picked apart this argument by pointing out that the shopkeepers neglected the welfare of other animals in their—perhaps—misplaced concern for the canaries, which, after all, did not seem to experience any severe effects from exposure to strong winds.[60] While this could be interpreted on one level as an internalization of the dominant discourses, it is more likely an act of defiance by appealing to the same moral grounds the Committee held dear. The positioning of the welfare of birds as a central argument, albeit one as flimsy as the canary the four proprietors claimed to protect, was a creative, but unsuccessful, attempt at appropriating discourses that traditionally discriminated against them in order to subvert the Committee.

The *1933 Report* ends with recommendations of how the government can regulate the wildlife trade. These recommendations can be broadly

---

[59] Ibid., pp. 11–3.
[60] Ibid., pp. 14–5. See the letter in the excerpt of the *1933 Report* in this collection.

categorized into the construction of a Central Market; restructuring the system of authority overseeing the wildlife trade by placing it under the governance of a central Malaya-wide body; refining legislation to prosecute smuggling; and, issuance of licenses for the importation of protected species of wildlife as well as the operation of private zoos in Singapore.[61] While the first two required substantial degrees of restructuring, the latter were a matter of refining existent legislation.

The recommendation for the construction of a Central Market was not unique, as the Committee acknowledged, with both the Government and Municipal Veterinary Surgeons suggesting in 1930 that one be built. The Committee did, however, take the initiative to provide very detailed specifics on this particular recommendation, complete with a suggested location, estimated cost of construction, annual license fees and rents, and size of stalls.[62] Much effort and thought was put into it, as they felt it was the easiest of the four recommendations to achieve, with only Municipal Council's cooperation to be secured. Other recommendations in the *1933 Report* were lifted entirely from pages of the draft Enactment for the Preservation of Wild Life as published the previous year in the *Report of the Wild Life Commission of Malaya*, such as the recommendation to place the control of the wildlife trade throughout Malaya under a single Wild Life Commission and to license importation of wildlife into Singapore at the suggested fee of $1 for ten head or less.[63] The former instance was a problematic legacy that the Committee had inherited from the Wild Life Commission.

The Committee also had original recommendations, such as the suggestion of a permit to indicate legal possession of protected species in order to overcome loopholes in existing legislation, which failed to prosecute until proof of illegal importation was secured. The brief mention of the need to control zoological gardens is also surprising, given the Committee's initial reluctance to expand the scope beyond Rochor Road wildlife dealers. However, as Section 64 of the draft Enactment for the Preservation of Wild Life specifically included zoological gardens, the necessity of ensuring a consistent adoption of recommendations from the *Report of the Wild Life Commission of Malaya* of 1932 would have outweighed the initial preference to exclude zoo proprietors.[64] The report, and any actions to be

---

[61] Ibid., pp. 15–20.
[62] Ibid., pp. 16–7.
[63] Ibid., pp. 17–9.
[64] *Report of the Wild Life Commission*, II, p. 83.

taken, was now the prerogative of various Municipal Commissioners and the Legislative Council.

A Reluctance of Public Bodies

Despite favorable public opinion lauding the formation of the Wild Animals and Wild Birds Committee as a "welcome announcement" and a "step in the right direction," the *1933 Report* did not effect any tangible change. After it was tabled on 16 April 1934, there were no subsequent discussions in the Legislative Council on the issue. The Municipal Commissioners discussed the Committee's recommendations in a meeting on 4 May 1934, but concluded that "expenditure from the Municipal Fund for the establishment of a market for the purposes proposed [that is, the sale of birds and small mammals not for food] would be illegal."[65] None of the recommendations of the Report were subsequently implemented.

Letters commenting on the "scandalous state of affairs," the "evil smelling birdshops of Singapore," the "filthy emporiums" of "squalor and sordidness," and "appalling conditions" of the wildlife trade continued to be published in the latter half of 1934.[66] Articles lamenting the lack of action continued the next year when two articles appeared in *The Straits Times* in September 1935. One article had the self-explanatory title "Has Bird Market Been Forgotten: Singapore Conditions Can be Improved" while the other was an editorial pointedly describing the 1933 Committee's recommendations as "lost en route to the last resting place of so many [other] Good Ideas" in the bureaucratic system.[67] In 1939, the Singapore Municipal Commissioner still described the conditions of the wildlife trade as a "disgrace to Singapore." From the aforementioned criticisms, it is clear that although the recommendations of the Committee were not adopted, they remained relevant as the need to regulate the wildlife trade persisted.

---

[65] Minutes of Meeting of Committee No. 2 of the Municipal Council, Minutes of the Proceedings of the Municipal Commissioners, 4 May 1934, p. 178; "Week-End Comment," *SFP*, 24 July 1933, p. 8; Proceedings of Straits Settlements Legislative Council, 16 Apr. 1934, CO275/135, p. B32.
[66] "A Blot on the Landscape," *ST*, 22 Aug. 1934, p. 5; "Cruelty to Animals," *ST*, 14 Sep. 1934, p. 10; "Bring 'Em Back Alive," *ST*, 6 Sep. 1934, p. 6; "Bring 'Em back Alive," *ST*, 18 Aug. 1934, p. 13; "More Blots on the Landscape," *ST*, 31 Aug. 1934, p. 18.
[67] "Has Bird Market Been Forgotten: Singapore Conditions Can be Improved," *ST*, 3 Sep. 1935, p. 12; "Lost, Stolen or Strayed," *ST*, 13 Sep. 1935, p. 10.

While the *1933 Report* failed to effect tangible policy changes, an examination of the possible reasons for its failure highlights the complex workings of colonial government and society. There were three factors that led to the (lack of) results: the laissez-faire attitudes of the British colonial government; the personality clashes between the government and the Committee; and the difficulty of regulating an illicit trade along a border which has historically been difficult to police.

One of the first reasons suggested for the inaction that followed the *1933 Report* was the mutual reluctance of both levels of Government, comprising the Legislative and Executive Councils, and the local Municipality Commissioners, in taking responsibility for the recommendations. As *The Straits Times* editor commented:

> The report followed years of agitation in the Press ... against a very disgraced state of affairs. There had been almost complete unanimity in urging that something should be done ... But the optimists failed to make allowance for the reluctance of public bodies to undertake anything which they might conveniently push on to someone else. Apparently the ball of responsibility was tossed to and fro between the Government and the Municipality until public interest in the question became dim.[68]

The tendency for one public institution to push the responsibility to another as a delaying tactic was attempted in 1929, when John Scott, the Colonial Secretary, deflected Tan Cheng Lock's and H.H. Abdoolcader's suggestions for updating the Ordinance for the Prevention of Cruelty to Animals by urging them to join the SPCA, which would then "make representations to Government" that would be "considered very fully and sympathetically."[69] The Municipal Commissioners in 1933 employed a similar delaying tactic by shirking their responsibility by emphasizing that they "cannot admit any financial responsibility ... [as it] is more a matter for private enterprise."[70]

Avoiding responsibility with regard to animal-related issues was common in the Straits Settlements. Discussing Dammerman's plea for the Straits Settlements to ban the import of *orang utans* in 1928, W. Bartley,

---

[68] "Lost, Stolen or Strayed," *ST*, 13 Sep. 1935, p. 10.
[69] Proceedings of Straits Settlements Legislative Council, 7 Oct. 1929, CO275/122, pp. B129–30.
[70] Minutes of Meeting of Committee No. 2 of the Municipal Council, 4 May 1934, p. 178.

acting Under Secretary of the Straits Settlements, was against passing "possibly doubtful legislation simply because the Govt. of N.E.I. are unable to enforce their laws," especially because *orang utans* were not indigenous to the Straits Settlements and thus could not be protected through the relevant wildlife legislation.[71] Formal action was only considered after the Dutch Consul-General officially approached the British authorities alongside pressures from the animal welfare and wildlife preservation movements.

Beyond institutional and bureaucratic inertia, this laissez-faire attitude also reflected the priorities of the British colonial government. Wildlife and its associated products were never economically significant to Singapore. For instance, the value of import of "Animals not living for food" was $172,377 and the value of export $31,935 in 1933. This amounted to only about 0.05 percent of the total value of imports into the Colony and 0.009 percent of total exports. This was miniscule compared to key trade products like rubber and gutta percha, which made up about six percent of total imports and 21 percent of total exports.[72] Compared with other morally ambiguous and licensed items of trade, such as opium, the revenue from licensing wildlife trade was negligible. For instance, the revenue brought in for licensing shops selling wild animals and birds in 1933 was about $78, an inconsequential amount when compared to the revenue from licensing the sale of opium, which was $4,291,693.26 in 1933.[73] Since there was little to be gained from regulating an economically insignificant trade, the government was understandably reluctant to bother with the issue until confronted with mounting local, regional, and metropolitan pressures.

In addition to its laissez-faire policy, Theodore Hubback, who chaired the Committee, did not give the government much incentive to explore the issue any further. With his track record as the "indefatigable champion of Malayan wildlife" and his previous experience with the Wild

[71] Minute by W. Bartley, 17 Sep. 1928, MSA 1139/10, C. S. O. Museums 8366/1928, NAS.

[72] Percentage calculated based on total imports of $330,661,128 and total exports of $346,471,451. Imports of raw rubber and gutta percha estimated at 22,251,167 and total exports estimated 73,726,509. "The Foreign Trade of Malaya," CO275/134, pp. 700, 702–3.

[73] The sum of $78.00 was based on the $1 annual license fee according to the Animal and Bird Shop By-Laws and the PCA Department Annual Report figure of 78 shops being licensed in 1933. The revenue from opium licensing is taken from Straits Settlements Blue Book 1933, CO277/85, p. 85.

Life Commission in 1932, Hubback was both the best and worst possible candidate to lead the 1933 Committee. Some of the recommendations in the *1933 Report* were already raised in the 1932 *Report of the Wild Life Commission of Malaya*. In particular, the recommendation for a central agency to oversee wildlife trade in the whole of Malaya possibly deterred the government from taking the *1933 Report* seriously, especially in the light of the decentralization policy that regained momentum under Clementi beginning in 1930.[74] While the Colonial Office was appreciative of Hubback's "full and valuable appreciation of the whole problem" of wildlife preservation in Malaya, the decentralization principle held precedent. To officials such as Edward Gent, Assistant Under-Secretary of the Indian Round Table Conference, wildlife preservation policies "must be framed in accord with that [decentralization] policy." The *1933 Report* was thus another instance of Hubback "kick[ing] against the bricks" of decentralization and was not to be taken too seriously.[75] The proposal to centralize the regulatory personnel of the wildlife trade throughout Malaya was also questioned beyond official circles. In response to the recommendations of the Wild Life Commission in 1932, an editorial in *The Straits Times* commented that a municipal authority could more easily controlled the wildlife trade in Singapore than a central authority based in the Federated Malay States.[76] Clearly, there is some truth in the characterization of Hubback's intransigent position as the *1933 Report* ignored these voices of opposition and never suggested possible reconciliatory solutions to the strong opposition to the suggestion of a centralized authority.

Besides the contentious nature of the recommendations that ran contrary to the Colonial Office's overall thrust of decentralization, Hubback's personality and methods also did not win him many allies. Many civil servants, such as John Kempe of the Malayan Civil Service, respected Hubback's views "while deploring his lack of balance, misdirected enthusiasm and inability to give a true value to the real facts." By 1936, even representatives from the SPFE, expected allies of a spokesman for conservation in Malaya, commented that Hubback was "like a red rag to a bull to nearly everyone" and that "saying the word 'Game' [to Hubback had] ... the same effect as

---

[74] Simon Smith, *British Relations with the Malay Rulers from Decentralization to Malayan Independence 1930–1957* (Oxford: Oxford University Press, 1995), pp. 22–3.
[75] Note by E. Gent, 16 Jan. 1934, CO717/96, No. 13329/1933.
[76] "The Wild Life Report," *SFP*, 18 Aug. 1932, p. 8.

saying 'rats' to a terrier."[77] Corresponding directly with Ministers of Parliament in England, rather than following official protocol of prior discussion with the Governor/High Commissioner in Malaya, created further tensions, thus influencing his relationship with Governor Cecil Clementi, who presided over the formation of both the Wild Life Commission and the Wild Animals and Wild Birds Committee.[78] H.R. Cowell of the Colonial Office, observed that the poor working relationship between Hubback and Clementi was undesirable for wildlife protection, as he noted:

> [T]heir mutual reactions complicate an issue already sufficiently involved. Sir C. Clementi is probably fully aware that Mr Hubback is intriguing behind his back; Mr Hubback does not cease to boast of the victories over the F.M.S. Govt. which he has secured in the past by interviews and persistence; and Sir C. Clementi is no doubt hoping to spike Mr Hubback's guns by adopting the recommendations of the Retrenchment Commission first and considering the Wild Life Report afterwards.[79]

It is difficult to determine the exact degree to which Hubback's behavior might have prejudiced the Governor's attitudes toward his suggestions. The *1933 Report* did not generate as much official attention as the *Report of the Wild Life Commission*, making it much harder to find sources discussing the impact of Hubback's personality on the implementation of his suggestions for the former. In addition to contemporary criticisms of his personality and methods, however, retrospective assessments of Hubback suggest that his personality was one of the reasons for the lack of comparable official support for nature conservation in British Malaya, unlike the spirit of cooperation between the government and the interest groups in the Netherlands Indies.[80]

Beyond the difficulties that Hubback presented to civil servants, as well as legislative changes in the 1930s to prevent importation of protected species from Netherlands Indies, problems still existed due to loopholes in trade and customs. Although it was illegal to import protected animals from the Netherlands Indies, the inability to prosecute the possession of such animals unless proof of illegal importation was secured meant that many

---

[77] Letter from Kempe to Colonial Office, 29 Apr. 1934, CO717/104, No. 33359/1934; D. Ornsby-Gore to W. Onslow, 10 July 1936, CO717/116, No. 51514/1936; T. Comyn-Platt to D. Ornsby-Gore, 8 July 1936, CO717/116, No. 51514/1936.

[78] T. Hubback to C. Clementi, 14 July 1931, CO717/78, No. 82352/1931; T. Hubback to G. Penny, 15 July 1931, CO717/78, No. 82352/1931.

[79] Note by H.R. Cowell, 22 Feb. 1933, CO717/96, No. 13329/1933.

[80] Kathirithamby-Wells, *Nature and Nation*, p. 205.

smugglers went scot-free.[81] It was, however, difficult to overcome these loopholes. Although the Committee's suggestions to license and tighten existing legislation were never implemented, it is not difficult to imagine that it would only drive the trade into the black market, just as the ban on imports and exports did not stamp out the flow of crowned pigeons and other protected species into Singapore. Though not included in the *1933 Report*, Chasen realized the impossibility of completely eradicating the issue of smuggling, when he noted that the Dutch customs officers, for whom he was full of praise, "admit that their great weakness is the long coast line."[82]

Although Eric Tagliacozzo ends his innovative study on smuggling along the Anglo-Dutch frontier in Southeast Asia in 1915, many of his observations on the difficulties of enforcing a colonial boundary arguably still applied to Singapore two decades later. According to Tagliacozzo, undertrading, which refers to "the passage of goods ... at the legal and geographic interstices of the majority of items being traded in this arena," occurred most frequently at borders and peripheries, natural choke points and in urban confusion.[83] Wildlife trade fits into this category of "undertrading" as its legal status was never determined ontologically, but was based on particular historical circumstances, which have been examined in the previous sections, leading to some cases to be considered illegal at particular historical moments.

Located along the long border of the Melaka Straits and at choke point of the narrow waterway between the British-influenced Malay Peninsula and Dutch-influenced Sumatra, Singapore remained an ideal place for such activities even in the 1930s. Though the various "administrative strengthenings" by 1915 logically implied that both the British and Dutch had better enforcement capabilities to police the border, Singapore's geographic position and the evolution of smuggling techniques worked against the colonial powers. This was not limited to wildlife trade. For instance, tobacco smuggling continued to be an issue for both governments despite the numerous attempts at regulation and legislation, with 144 smugglers convicted in the year 1932.[84]

---

[81] *1933 Report*, p. 19.

[82] F. Chasen to T. Hubback, 3 Oct. 1933, MSA 1139/19, NAS.

[83] Eric Tagliacozzo, *Secret Trades, Porous Borders: Smuggling and States along a Southeast Asian Frontier, 1865–1915* (New Haven, CT: Yale University Press, 2005), p. 5.

[84] Ibid., p. 18; "Smuggling Rife in Singapore: Tobacco Worth $17,000 and 42 Cars Confiscated," *SFP*, 26 Sep. 1932, p. 7.

For all the constructive and unique suggestions the Committee put forth to regulate the trade, they never addressed the issue of demand. The Committee observed that despite previous legislation aimed at reducing the import of protected species from the Netherlands Indies, the fact that they still turned up in shops along Rochor Road suggested that the smuggling was—to put it mildly—"considerable."[85] The Committee, however, did not question why people would continue breaking the law. While it is not possible to calculate the profit margins for the smuggler, as no records of the prices exist, the margins must have been high enough for them to risk the fines of up to $100.[86] Live exotic wild animals were not an affordable commodity, with each participant in this transaction chain taking profits. Records that Chasen left behind reflect this as he was frequently on the receiving end of this chain of compounded price mark-ups. For example, when he purchased a pair of pheasants, *Lophura* of unknown genus, from the Bandung Zoo for $40 in the late 1930s, Chasen lamented that he could have obtained more specimens but he could not afford any more at that price.[87] As Chasen has noted, the wildlife trade favored the middleman and smuggler, who had the freedom to offer the animal to the highest bidder in Singapore. This system gave the original vendor, and often also the catcher, little say in the price. If Chasen observed that sellers in Palembang quoted him a price of five guilders for a gibbon, or that a slow loris only cost the middleman 30 cents, the profit margin for a smuggler who sold his goods to Singaporean traders was clearly significant.[88]

The demand for animals in Singapore also contributed to the persistence of smuggling. As mentioned earlier, the international trade in live animals was linked to the international growth of zoological gardens in places such as America, Europe, and Australia. In the 1930s, the popularity of the jungle film genre fuelled an even greater demand. Some of these films were set in Singapore, such as Ward Wing's *Out of the Sea*, which featured lovers "temporarily marooned amid the menace of wild life" along the coasts of Katong, or represented the combination of both animal collectors and film. Frank Buck, producer and star of *Bring 'Em Back Alive* and *Wild Cargo*, used Singapore as the location for some of the shots in his popular jungle

---

[85] *1933 Report*, p. 19.
[86] See Section 7 of Ordinance 88 in *The Laws of the Straits Settlements: Vol II, 1901–1907* (London: Waterlow & Sons Ltd, 1920), p. 136.
[87] F. Chasen to E. Jacobson, 28 Sep. 1937, MSA 1140/169, NAS.
[88] F. Chasen to T. Hubback, 3 Oct. 1933, MSA 1139/19, NAS.

movies. Buck even admitted that many of the close-ups of wild animals had to be taken in Singapore rather than in the dense Malayan jungle due to logistical constraints.[89] In 1938, William Basapa, proprietor of the Punggol Zoo, wrote to Chasen regarding a disagreement over remuneration he had with a wildlife film producer and anthropologist Paul Fejos, who failed to ensure the safety of tigers rented from Basapa's zoo.[90] Another example involves the New York World's Fair in 1939, which featured as the promised highlight of the Malay Village Frank Buck's "Jungle Show" with live wild animals shipped from Singapore.[91] The international demand for wildlife, from zoological gardens, wildlife filmmakers and exhibitions did not help abate the demand in Singapore, the port city from which these animals, or films of them, reached other continents.

Conclusion

The attempt in 1933 to tame the wildlife trade that existed in colonial Singapore was one fraught with difficulties. In addition to the laissez-faire attitudes of government institutions, personal conflicts between the Chairman of the Committee and the Governor also did not help to expedite matters. Finally, the demand for wildlife and the strategic position of Singapore meant that even if the Straits Settlements Government was willing to act against its preferences and stepped in to regulate the trade, the high demand and difficulty of addressing smuggling might have thwarted attempts at regulation. Involving issues that seem intractable and others that reflect the multi-layered and nuanced workings of colonial governance, the *1933 Report* and its subsequent failure to initiate significant changes reflected the complex nature of the question of wildlife trade.

As Erica Fudge, a scholar specializing in animal studies in Renaissance Europe, points out, the "'human' always relies upon 'animal' for its meaning"

---

[89] "Out of the Sea Off Singapore: New Jungle Film," *ST*, 9 Oct. 1932, p. 9; "Adventures with Wild Animals: Interesting Talk at Rotary Tiffin," *ST*, 6 Aug. 1931, p. 12.

[90] W. Basapa to F. Chasen, 13 Jan. 1937, MSA1140/131, NAS. Fejos had considerable problems in Southeast Asia. For an account of his troubles when visiting Komodo island during this same period, see Timothy P. Barnard, "Protecting the Dragon: Dutch Attempts to Limit Access to Komodo Lizards in the 1920s and 1930s," *Indonesia* 92 (2011): 122.

[91] "Malay Village at World Fair," *ST*, 18 Dec. 1938, p. 17.

and the two cannot be separated as the "history of animals cannot just tell us what has been … it must intervene, make us think again about our past and, more importantly, about ourselves."[92] Similarly, this chapter is not simply a history of the beastly business of the wildlife trade; it goes beyond animals to reflect on the interactions between human communities and governments in colonial Singapore. Moving beyond existing uncritical historical narratives of the existence of such a trade, the *1933 Report* reflects the attitudes of the British colonial government, the Dutch authorities and the English-speaking public opinion toward the wildlife trade in colonial Singapore, and the underlying cultural assumptions that this attempt to regulate the trade in 1933 magnified. Perceived to be the domain of less civilized non-Europeans and a reflection of the inadequacies of the laissez-faire Straits Settlements Government, the trade in wildlife was not simply about animals, but also about how different communities viewed one another.

---

[92] Erica Fudge, "A Left-Handed Blow: Writing the History of Animals," in *Representing Animals*, ed. Nigel Rothfels, p. 15.

SOURCE 6

A Whale's Tale: Excerpts from *The Annual Reports of the Raffles Museum and Library*, Newspaper Accounts and Visitors' Memories

Correspondence

Mr. Justice Wood, Mr. Harwood, the Acting Attorney-General and Mr. Rodesse returned by the *Sea Belle* from Malacca yesterday.

A large whale, some 35 feet long, was seen by the *Bengkalis* on their last trip to Muar, the animal having been stranded on the beach near the Kesang River, nine miles to the north of Muar. Hearing that there was a strange animal spouting water a little distance away, Capt. Angus went out in a boat and examined the monster, apparently a male, which had been dead some few days, and was even then in a highly savoury condition. The whale was stranded some eight days ago, and took about four days time in which to make up its mind and draw its last breath. Its presence caused no little consternation amongst the natives, who dreaded to approach it.

—*The Singapore Free Press and Mercantile Advertiser*, 25 June 1892, p. 2

Muar News
(From our Correspondent)
25th June, 1892

Boatmen from Malacca brought word the other day that fish of monstrous size (*ikan besar skali*) had been stranded upon the shore on the coast a little to the northward of the Kessang river; the exaggerated descriptions excited a deal of curiosity sufficient to induce people to go in a steam launch in quest of this monster of the deep. Accordingly, on Friday afternoon, a party left Muar including the Resident, Ungku Suleiman, and other chiefs of the place. On nearing the spot, somewhere about Sebatu in Malacca the carcase came in sight at a distance. The party found much difficulty in getting near it owing to the depth of mud around. They found that it was the carcase of a whale. It's extreme length was 44 feet, unfortunately it was on it back and the upper surface of the head was imbedded in the soft mud so that no observations could be made as the existence of a dorsal fin &c.—it bulked largely being about 9 feet high—at its greatest girth. The carcase was rather offensive and swollen with gases from decomposition, so that the notes taken by those who came near enough were rather hurriedly made. It is said that some of the Malacca officials had been to inspect it before, so that fuller details may be unavailable. It is hoped that the steps will be taken for the securing the skeleton for the Raffles's Museum. None of the Malays call to mind ever having seen such a creature before.

—*The Straits Times Weekly*, 29 June 1892, p. 9

The skull of the whale (Megaptera boops?) in the Museum collection had so far been with only scanty information as to its origin, and as through the kindness of Mr. M. HELLIER, Acting Sub-Inspector of Schools, Malacca, I have succeeded in obtaining some interesting details, it is as well to put them on record. Mr. HELLIER who got his information from the Pengulu of Sa' Batu partly orally and partly from the man's diary, writes:—"The whale was left stranded at a place called Sa'Batu about eighteen miles to the south of Malacca town on 19th June, 1892. A 'pagar' was built round it to prevent it getting back to sea at high tide. The diary give the dimensions as about seven 'depas' long and one 'depa' wide (1 depa = 6 feet). The whale took a week to die making a great noise for about three days. Nothing was done with the blubber. Mr. HERVEY, the Resident, gave a 'hadiah' to the Penghulu and others and took the skeleton." The rest of the skeleton, although not quite complete, is still in the Museum and will be mounted as soon as space is available.

—R. Hanitsch, *Annual Report on the Raffles Library and Museum for the Year 1905*
(Singapore: Government Printing Office, 1906), pp. 3–4.

MUSEUM

7.   The removal of the zoological collection building, begun at the end of November 1906, was continued during the first few weeks of the year, and on Chinese New Year's day, February 13th, the new gallery was opened to the public. Within a few minutes of throwing open of the doors both the new and the old galleries were filled to over-flowing by dense masses of Chinese holiday makers, and the interest in the Museum of at least the native population of Singapore shown at that day has well been kept up throughout the year.

8.   *Zoology*—The greater portion of the zoological exhibits was housed in twenty new cases, the Mammals and Birds receiving nine each, the Reptiles two. The cases are constructed of polished teak and plate glass and were supplied by Messrs. John Little & Co. Sixteen of them are of uniform size, 14 feet by 9 feet by 2 feet 6 inches, with four doors each, the dimensions having been taken from standard cases in the British Museum, Natural History. For the man-like Apes a specially large case was constructed, measuring 22 feet by 10 feet by 2 feet 6

inches, with five doors. Most of the Fishes and Invertebrates were left in their old cases: only the Crustacea received two new wall cases, and the Shells and Insects several new table cases.

9.   Mammals—On June 19, 1892, a whale was left stranded at a place called Sa'Batu about 18 miles to the South of Malacca town. A pagar was built round it to prevent it getting back to the sea at high tide, and when the animal was dead—it took a week to die—the Hon'ble Mr. D.F.A. HERVEY, the then Resident-Councillor of Malacca, caused the skeleton to be prepared and to be conveyed to Singapore. Owing to the lack of space it has only now—after a lapse of fifteen years—been possible to mount it. Many bones were found missing and had to be modelled out of wood and plaster of Paris, as a scapula, the hands, several vertebrae and a number of ribs. The skeleton when completed was suspended by steel ropes from the ceiling and forms now certainly the most striking exhibit in the Zoological gallery. It is forty-three feet in length. It was a serious piece of work for the small Museum staff, and great credit is due to Mr. V. KNIGHT who accomplished it, assisted by Mr. DE FONTAINE.

I am indebted to Mr. J. HEWITT, of the Sarawak Museum, and to Mr. EDGAR THURSTON, of the Madras Museum, for measurements and drawings of the whale skeletons in their charge, which were of much help in modelling the missing bones, and enabled me to identify the Malacca specimen as *Balaenoptera indica*, the same species as the one exhibited in the Madras Museum.

Several valuable donations were received. Dr. LIM BOON KENG and SEAH ENG TIONG presented, on behalf of the Singapore Planting Company, a huge domestic boar, English breed, which has been skeletonized. Mr M. LOEBELL gave, amongst other things, an Anoa, from Celebes, which has been skeletonized too, as the Museum already possesses two stuffed specimens, one of them previously presented by Mr. LOEBELL. Dr. ABBOTT gave a *Semnopthiecus sumatranus*, from Sungei Mandau, Sumatra, and Mr. R.A. Campbell a Dugong skull. The most interesting specimen purchased was a *Hemigalia hardwickii*, from Pahang.

—R. Hanitsch, *Annual Report on the Raffles Library and Museum for the Year 1907* (Singapore: Government Printing Office, 1908), pp. 4–5.

The Collections

...

Formerly, one of the most popular exhibits in the Museum was the skeleton of the Indian whale (Balaentptera indica) stranded at Malacca in 1892.

During structural alterations to the Museum in 1924 this skeleton was removed from the public gallery, but in the year under review it was rearticulated and bleached and finally suspended from the ceiling above the staircase.

All the store-cabinets containing the reference collection of mammals were numbered, their contents listed and plotted on a detailed plan to facilitate working in the future. That such action was necessary indicates the large size and rapid growth of the collection.

—C. Boden Kloss, *Annual Report on the Raffles Museum and Library for the Year 1928* (Singapore: Government Printing Office, 1929), p. 3.

....

"Museums in London? Obviously my ... mother must have dragged me to museums but I don't remember it. [Q: What about in Singapore?] Yes. [I was] fairly familiar with the Raffles Museum and the big whale... above the staircase there. Everybody of my age group who goes to the museum can remember that whale ... Stuffed animals. Poor stuffed animals which migrated out to Sentosa. Where are they now? Are they back? Still in Sentosa? You know, the tiger that was shot by some gung ho white hunter and mounted."

—Stella Kon
(National Archives [Singapore] Oral History Centre, 00296, Reel 11)

"Oh, I remember visiting the museum with my best friend. There wasn't much to do after school, and so we'd walk over [from CHIJ]. There was a big spiral staircase with a huge whale hanging over it. Really long. We never went up the stairs because it was supposed to be haunted up there. But, I would stare at the whale and try and count all the bones. Every time. Then we would go and look at all the coins and weaving ... But, I always liked the stuffed animals. There wasn't a zoo then, so it was the only place where you could go to see animals. Whatever happened to all those stuffed animals? Are they still there?"

—Maureen Danker (Interview with Editor, 26 October 2012)

....

Workers at the National Museum in Stamford Road are getting ready a whale of a gift from Singapore to Malaysia ... The Singapore Science Centre has presented the skeleton, an exhibit at the museum since 1907, to the National Museum in Kuala Lumpur. In return, the Malaysians will train Singapore museum technicians on the finer points of modelling and casting exhibition specimens. The specimen was dismantled into three pieces and sent by truck to Kuala Lumpur ...

— "A Whale of a Gift for Malaysian National Museum,"
The Straits Times, 6 May 1974, p. 8.

Let me express my indignation at the presentation of the National Museum's blue whale to the museum in Kuala Lumpur. It is like a personal loss to me. For as a child I never failed to look at it whenever I visited the museum. I have seen children looking at the vast structure with awe. It was one of the museum's finest and most impressive exhibits. What a shame that it was given in return for training offered to our museum technicians. Is the museum so short of funds that it has to trade in exhibits for training of its staff?

—Letter to Editor, "Whale of a Loss," *The Straits Times*, 9 May 1974, p. 10.

Just for the record, the skeleton of the blue whale which was exhibited in the National Museum was given away to Muzium Negara in Kuala Lumpur by the Science Centre and not by the National Museum. The skeleton of the blue whale, together with all other zoological or life-science exhibits in the National Museum became property of the Science Centre when the Centre was established on April 1, 1972. Your report on May 6, 1974 that the skeleton of the blue whale was given away by the Science Centre for the training of National Museum technicians is also not correct.

—Jimmy Lee, for Director, National Museum
Letter to Editor, "Untitled," *The Straits Times*, 23 May 1974, p. 10.

CHAPTER 6

The Raffles Museum and the Fate of Natural History in Singapore

Timothy P. Barnard

Natural history museums are often quite perplexing. They come from a different era, with their glass cases of stuffed animals and pinned insects that obsessively explain taxonomic classifications. These classic institutions, through their display of unique plant and animal life and placing it within a classification system that brings order to our surroundings, played a key role in influencing how we understand and organize the environment. Natural history museums placed us in a world of nature that was comprehensible and controlled. Today these institutions are not solely about identifying new species; they play an important role in providing insight into areas such as biodiversity, evolution and population genetics, thus reflecting changes in how the study of biology and ecology have shifted over time.[1] In Singapore, the Raffles Museum—the precursor to the National Museum—was one of the finest natural history collections in the British Empire, and its transition from the former to the later type of natural history museum was one embedded in a variety of forces reflecting a shifting understanding of nature and the environment in Singapore.

The influence and reputation of the Raffles Museum reached far beyond the shores of Singapore. In July 1971, a small note attached to a

---

[1] Narisara Murray, "From Birds of Paradise to Drosophila: The Changing Roles of Scientific Specimens to 1920," *A Cultural History of Animals in the Age of Empire*, ed. Kathleen Kete (Oxford: Oxford University Press, 2007), pp. 113–34; Paolo Viscardi, "Natural History Collections—Why are They Relevant?," *The Guardian*, 12 Apr. 2011, at http://www.guardian.co.uk/science/punctuated-equilibrium/2011/apr/12/2 [accessed 12 Sep. 2012].

report from Singapore created a tremendous amount of interest in the halls of the Natural History Museum in London. The note explained that there were plans to convert the National Museum of Singapore into a "cultural museum," which would entail the removal of "the natural history section with no clear idea what is to become of it."[2] This short explanation led the keepers of various departments in the London museum to exchange notes and memos speculating on what was to become of the specimens, and how they might be able to obtain the entire collection, or at least parts of it. In the conversion of the Raffles Museum to the National Museum of Singapore, the fate of its natural history collection—one of the cornerstones of a colonial era institution, as well as a legacy of nature and science in Singapore—seemed to be up in the air.

Originally developed as a museum based on a European model, the natural history collection of the Raffles Museum contained hundreds of thousands of specimens, reflecting the diversity and richness of the Southeast Asian environment that the British colonial government had come to rule. As scientific approaches, and support for environmental study, shifted, however, the importance and relevance of the collection came into question. The fate of the specimens mentioned in correspondence between Singapore and London in 1971, therefore, was not simply a discussion of what to do with some dried or pickled animal hides. It was part of a larger dialogue involving issues such as science, the environment, cultural outlooks and worldviews, in addition to decolonization. At that moment, beyond any scientific issues, it represented how a modernizing, decolonizing government viewed the fauna of not only Singapore, but also the region.

This chapter will examine the role that natural history collectors have played in influencing our understanding of animals in the region, and the fate of the institutions they created when national priorities related to science and nature shifted following independence. Before such an examination can take place, however, an understanding of the role that the Raffles Museum and its natural history collection played in colonial society, and consciousness, will be explored. Only then will the letters of 1971, as well as other correspondence, help uncover how a large collection of long dead animals that fell into increasingly tightened storage provide insight into the shifting approaches and mindsets of Singaporean leaders with regard to the environment and nature.

---

[2] Note to J. Pope from E.C. Dixon, 9 July 1971, DF206/137, Museum of Natural History Archives, London.

The Raffles Museum

The Raffles Library and Museum was one of the most important colonial institutions in Singapore. With its iconic and imposing building along Stamford Road, it represented the glory of colonial knowledge and presentation. Originally conceived in 1823 as the library of the Singapore Institution (later the Raffles Institution), before transforming into a public library in 1844, by the end of the 1840s it also included a small museum. In 1874, the government assumed control over the Singapore Library, renamed it the Raffles Library and Museum, and housed it in the Town Hall. By 1878, the government also took control over the Botanic Gardens, placing both institutions under the control of a committee that the Governor appointed. The impetus for this change lay in dispatches from London urging officials to collect "not only commercial products, but objects of interest of whatever kind, illustrating the ethnology, antiquities, natural history and physical character of the country."[3] The Singapore Botanic Gardens would fulfill this directive with regard to flora, while the Raffles Museum focused on fauna in the study of "natural history." Governor F.A. Weld opened the new Library and Museum building at the base of Fort Canning Hill in October 1887. The physical building of the Library and Museum expanded over the next 20 years, and in 1908 the institution changed its name to the Raffles Museum and Library. While it functioned as the only library and museum in the city-port for a century, and its zoological collection became the focus of the public displays for visitors, it was also the main center in the Straits Settlements for scientific research of the surrounding region.[4]

The combination of public display and research was a cornerstone of colonial-era natural history museums, and the Raffles Museum was firmly situated in the context of an imperial interest in science and nature, which often manifested itself in the development of such institutions in the 19th century. Early natural history collections grew out of a fascination with exotica stretching back to ancient Greek states. The desire to possess strange wonders from afar grew further with the era of exploration, beginning with the voyages of Christopher Columbus and Vasco Da Gama in the late 15th century. Abnormal, bizarre, and even imaginary objects that sailors brought back to Europe became prize possessions, and were soon displayed

[3] R. Hanitsch, "Raffles Library and Museum, Singapore," in *One Hundred Years of Singapore*, Vol. 1, ed. Walter Makepeace, Gilbert E. Brooke, and Roland St. J. Braddell (London: John Murray, 1921), p. 542.
[4] Hanitsch, "Raffles Library and Museum, Singapore," pp. 519–58.

in "cabinets of curiosities," in which the principle of organization was left to the discretion of the owner of the object, and often followed principles of smallest to largest or by color. To deal with the resulting visual and organizational uncertainty, scholars in Europe soon began to impose order by classifying the objects based on newly developed schemata that promoted a deeper understanding of nature and its connections. A key figure in these events was Carl Linnaeus, who developed the modern system of binomial nomenclature, in which any plant or animal is given a name with two parts representing its genus, and then the species within that genus, thus linking them to the larger plant and animal kingdoms.[5]

The most influential natural history museum in the world for the powerful in the British colony of the Straits Settlements was the British Museum, which began when Hans Sloane sold his private cabinet of curiosities—as well as his library—to the government in 1753. By the mid-19th century, incompetence and discontent among the staff led to its decline, and calls for its purpose and presentation to be reconsidered. As the center of a mighty empire, many within the British government believed that a new institution in London needed to reflect the breadth and extent of its power and knowledge over the natural world. Based on these ideals, Richard Owen proposed the reorganization of the natural history collection into its own museum, the British Museum (Natural History), which was finally completed in 1883.[6]

The new Natural History Museum in London revolutionized the role such institutions played in society. The director that followed Owen, William Henry Flower, promoted the museum as having two purposes: research and education. While previous museums had displayed every specimen, leading to a mishmash of objects that often confused visitors, Flower promoted a reduction in the number of displays, while nearby storage drawers and

---

[5] Susan Sheets-Pyenson, *Cathedrals of Science: The Development of Colonial Natural History Museums during the Late Nineteenth Century* (Montreal: McGill-Queen's University Press, 1988), pp. 3–5; Lisbet Koerner, "Carl Linnaeus in His Time and Place," in *Cultures of Natural History*, ed. N. Jardine, J.A. Secord, and E.C. Spary (Cambridge: Cambridge University Press, 1996), pp. 145–62; Philipp Blom, *To Have and to Hold: An Intimate History of Collectors and Collecting* (New York: The Overlook Press, 2002), pp. 13–74; Stephen T. Asma, *Stuffed Animals and Pickled Heads: The Culture and Evolution of Natural History Museums* (Oxford: Oxford University Press, 2001), pp. 114–20.
[6] Blom, *To Have and to Hold*, pp. 78–91; Asma, *Stuffed Animals and Pickled Heads*, pp. 168–70, 194–6.

cabinets would help preserve specimens from dust, pests, light, and—in Singapore—humidity. For research, more specimens and other research materials could be kept in nearby rooms where scholars conducted their studies. In the meantime, the public displays would provide the general public with a greater understanding of nature by illustrating a particular principle or taxonomic category. By 1900, this format of instructive displays with the inventory of specimens preserved for scientific research stored in other rooms became the norm for natural history museums throughout the world, including the Raffles Museum.[7]

While the Raffles Museum contained a variety of objects, from displays of local weaponry to ancient coins, the zoological collection was its centerpiece, and it fascinated visitors. The collection began when Straits Settlements Governor Andrew Clarke presented a large female rhinoceros skeleton to the Botanic Gardens in 1875. After two years, the members of the Gardens Committee were unsure what to do with the gift, so they passed it to the Museum. The collection expanded beyond this lone rhinoceros in 1883, when T.I. Rowell, a prominent figure in the Singaporean Municipal Government, prepared over 200 specimens for the museum, a taxidermic task that Valentine Knight continued for the remainder of the 19th century. The collection grew as more colonial officials ventured into Malaya and Borneo, often returning with the skeletons or carcasses of animals they had encountered, which the employees of the museum would identify, classify and—at times—name. The most famous of these specimens was a 13-meter (42-foot) blue whale that washed ashore near Melaka in 1892. D.F.A. Hervey, the Resident Councillor of Malacca, prepared and shipped it to Singapore, where it was finally exhibited following an expansion of space in the Museum in 1907.[8]

Specimens began to flow into the Raffles Museum, and their display and organization fell under the purview of a series of Directors who oversaw an ordering of the natural world of Singapore, the Straits Settlements and larger Malaya. Karl Richard Hanitsch, the Curator (and later Director)

---

[7] Murray, "From Birds of Paradise to Drosophila"; Sheets-Pyenson, *Cathedrals of Science*, pp. 6–8.

[8] Megan S. Osborne, "Early Collectors and Their Impact on the Raffles Museum and Library," *The Heritage Journal* 3 (2008): 1–15; Jeyamalar Kathirithamby-Wells, "Peninsular Malaysia in the Context of Natural History and Colonial Science," *New Zealand Journal of Asian Studies* 11, 1 (2009): 337–74; Hanitsch, "Raffles Library and Museum, Singapore," pp. 552–62.

of the Museum from 1895 to 1918, set the initial tone. An entomologist by training, he masterminded the expansion of the Museum and Library space as well as the cataloguing of the materials. Hanitsch, with the help of assistants such as Kong Tian Chen, documented the growing collection, placed particular emphasis on birds. In 1919, over 1,300 birds—representing 680 species—were on display, thus reflecting a lag in the adoption of a Flower-influenced approach to displays and research at the Raffles Museum. During that centenary year, the Museum also had exhibits featuring proboscis monkeys, reptiles (with a particularly impressive 4.5-meter [15.5-foot] crocodile), and fish.[9]

These collections improved over time, and much pride was taken in the ability of the workers to stuff the animals and paint them in their natural colors. These exhibits displayed the vast diversity of animals that British scientists and collectors could gather from throughout British territories in Southeast Asia, and eventually included thousands of insects, particularly moths and butterflies, as well as marine fauna such as mollusks and coral. Following Hanitsch, a series of scientists—such as C. Boden Kloss and F.N. Chasen—took up the position of Director of the Museum and continued to collect fauna from throughout the Malay Peninsula and wider Southeast Asia. Kloss also reorganized the Raffles Museum in 1924, resulting in displays that informed the public without overwhelming them, finalizing a process Hanitsch had first started moving toward in 1906, when a new wing of the Museum was opened, and thus adopting the approach Flower developed several decades earlier in London.[10]

Beyond their role in developing the Museum displays, each of the Directors was a dedicated scientist who, along with a team of taxidermists, assistants, and collectors, conducted research on the fauna of the region. Each Director of the museum had a speciality, and the focus of the collections often reflected this. Both Kloss and Chasen had a particular interest in birds and mammals, resulting in these two classes of animals taking up some

---

[9] R. Hanitsch, *Guide to the Zoological Collections of the Raffles Museum, Singapore* (Singapore: Straits Times Press, 1908); R. Hanitsch, *List of the Birds, Reptiles and Amphibians in the Raffles Museum, Singapore* (Singapore: Straits Settlements Government Printing House, 1912); Hanitsch, "Raffles Library and Museum, Singapore," pp. 562–3.

[10] R. Hanitsch, *Annual Report on the Raffles Library and Museum for the Year 1905* (Singapore: Government Printing Office, 1906), p. 3; C. Boden Kloss, *Annual Report on the Raffles Museum and Library for the Year 1928* (Singapore: Government Printing Office, 1929), p. 3.

three-fourths of the storage space by the mid-1930s. While some of this was due to the size of the animals under consideration, Michael Tweedie, who joined the Museum in 1932, and was its Director from 1946 until 1971, tempered this emphasis on birds and mammals with his academic interest in crustaceans, fish, and reptiles.[11]

Officials from the Museum often went on "excursions," followed by painstaking research in the lab to better understand the species that were uncovered. The animals collected were usually from Singapore, Malaya, and nearby islands. An example of one of these expeditions is a trip that Kloss took with the Straits Settlements Governor, Laurence Guillemard, along the east coast of the Malay Peninsula in 1926. During the "cruise," Kloss found a new subspecies of coconut squirrel on Tenggol Island.[12] Local guides and assistants also were vital parts of this collecting process. During expeditions to Sarawak, for example, Tweedie recalled that the Iban assistants were "intelligent, energetic men and born naturalists. They and I would go together, sometimes on day excursions, sometimes camping for a week or more, and they were soon far more adept at finding centipedes, scorpions and the like than I was."[13]

While officials from the Raffles Museum collected many of the specimens, a considerable number were also the result of requests, gifts or purchases that could be used to not only fill holes in the collection, but point toward the interests of the Directors. An example of this approach appears in a letter Chasen wrote to Carl Gibson-Hill in 1939 while the latter was collecting on Christmas Island, in which he requests "a series of authenticated eggs of the various indigenous species."[14] Files from the Raffles Museum also contain a considerable amount of correspondence that deals

---

[11] Eric R. Alfred, "The Zoological Collections of the National Museum 1957–1974," in *Our Heritage: Zoological Reference Collection: Official Opening Souvenir Brochure, 31 October 1988* (Singapore: National University of Singapore, Zoological Reference Collection, 1988), p. 5.

[12] C. Boden Kloss, *Annual Report on the Raffles Museum and Library for the year 1926* (Singapore: Government Printing Office, 1927), p. 3.

[13] M.W.F. Tweedie, "Zoology in the Raffles Museum, 1932–1957," in *Our Heritage: Zoological Reference Collection: Official Opening Souvenir Brochure, 31 October 1988* (Singapore: National University of Singapore, Zoological Reference Collection, 1988), p. 2.

[14] "Letter from F.N. Chasen to C. Gibson-Hill," 18 Nov. 1939, Chasen Files, Asian Civilisations Museum, Singapore. I would like to thank Fiona Tan for directing me to this resource.

Plate 6.1 A fraction of the bird collection of the Raffles Museum of Biodiversity Research. Courtesy of the Raffles Museum of Biodiversity Research, National University
of Singapore.

with financial transactions with organizations willing to sell specimens. For
example, in 1940 Chasen purchased 90 Malayan bird skins from W.F.H.
Rosenberg—"Naturalist and Importer of Exotic Zoological Collections"—in
England. The extensive list Rosenberg provided of birds available even has
Chasen's notes accounting for this purchase as well as his desire to also find
an *Ardeola grayi* (Indian Pond Heron) specimen.[15] Through such efforts, a
constant stream of natural history specimens flowed into Singapore during
the colonial era.

Upon arrival at the Raffles Museum, the collected, donated, or purchased specimens entered a series of cabinets and jars. For mammals and
birds, curators placed the skins in glass-topped boxes inside the drawers of
wooden cabinets. The skins and skeletons of larger animals were stored in
"wooden (coffin-like) boxes," which were then placed in "the Skin Room or
the bottom of display cases in the Zoological Galleries" at the Museum. The
remaining collection—mostly reptiles, amphibians, fish, and crustaceans—

---

[15] "Letter from F.N. Chasen to W.F.H. Rosenberg," 12 Mar. 1940, Chasen Files,
Asian Civilisations Museum, Singapore.

were "wet specimens" stored in the "Spirit Room" in jars with a mixture of water and either 10 percent formalin or 70 percent alcohol.[16]

Once the specimens had been preserved, the various scholars working at the Raffles Museum would sort them into categories and search through relevant journals and guides to classify the specimen. Labels were then put on the jars, or attached to the skin, to identify the animal, and the specimen entered the extensive catalogue to the collection.[17] As the collection grew, the material found its way into the larger academic world through journal articles—often in the *Bulletin of the Raffles Museum*—or books such as *The Birds of Singapore Island*.[18] When particularly unique specimens were found, the Director or other officials would contact a taxonomic specialist and inquire whether they would be interested in using these specimens for their studies. Using such an approach, the specimens from the Raffles Museum became vital for the study of tropical fauna throughout the world, appearing in journals and other publications in Europe and North America as well as in their own bulletin. Through this process, the number of new species that specialists working at the Raffles Museum found was startling. For example, in 1937 Tweedie sent a collection of 36 Malayan centipedes to Germany, where K.W. Verhoff identified 28 previously unknown species as well as three new genera. As Tweedie summarized, "the lesson to be learned is how very meagre our knowledge was, and still is, of the less studied fauna of the tropical forest."[19]

Just as the Botanic Gardens at the other end of Orchard Road expanded their research program under Kew-trained scientists in the late 19th century to fulfill needs related to economic botany, the Raffles Museum played a role in research that reflected colonial desires and pursuits.[20] While they never identified an economic valuable animal that could match the development of rubber or palm oil, as scientists in the Botanic Gardens did, the work of researchers and administrators in the natural history collection of the Raffles Museum created a symbolic mastery over the environment. Within this context, the rise in interest in natural history coincided with

---

[16] Alfred, "The Zoological Collections of the National Museum 1957–1974," p. 5.

[17] John van Wyhe and Kees Rookmaaker, "Wallace's Mystery Flycatcher," unpublished manuscript, forthcoming.

[18] John A.S. Bucknill and F.N. Chasen, *The Birds of Singapore Island* (Singapore: Government Printing Office, 1927).

[19] Tweedie, "Zoology in the Raffles Museum, 1932–1957," p. 3.

[20] See Nigel P. Taylor's contribution to this volume.

the spread of colonialism as it emphasized controlling and identifying the environment while often exploring it for economic potential. The men, and invariably they were men, at the Raffles Museum brought order to the natural world of the Straits Settlements and Malaya.[21]

The Raffles Museum and Library thus fit firmly within the realms of colonial knowledge; it was where the desire, and need, to catalogue and categorize different aspects of the British imperial world were put on display. This is reflected in not only the voluminous output of scholars associated with the Museum in scientific journals, but also correspondence and lectures as well as their status as respected members of colonial society. The pages of the *Annual Reports on the Raffles Museum and Library* as well as the *Journal of the Straits Branch of the Royal Asiatic Society* (after 1923 named the "Malayan Branch") documented this process through a statistical accounting of the constant inflow of specimens, and their handling. The scientists associated with the institution, over time, compiled and produced massive amounts of information that became one of the definitive collections of knowledge of the region's environment.[22] Prior to the Japanese occupation, the Raffles

---

[21] Kathirithamby-Wells, "'Peninsular Malaysia in the Context of Natural History and Colonial Science;" Daniel Headrick, *The Tools of Empire: Technology and European Imperialism in the Nineteenth Century* (New York: Oxford University Press, 1981); Bernard Cohn, *Colonialism and Its Forms of Knowledge: The British in India* (Princeton, NJ: Princeton University Press, 1996); Sheets-Pyenson, *Cathedrals of Science*, pp. 12–4. I would like to thank Justin Ng and Fiona Tan for help in gathering many of these materials.

[22] In addition, the scientific journals of the Museum produced a considerable amount of research, with more than 2,000 papers and books. While it was less than the research coming out of the Dutch East Indies, where there was a specific focus on making it a centre of science in the tropics, it was still an important outpost for English-language understandings of the tropical world. Andrew Goss, "Decent Colonialism? Pure Science and Colonial Ideology in the Netherlands East Indies, 1910–1929," *Journal of Southeast Asian Studies* 40, 1 (2009): 187–214; Michael Adas, *Machines as a Measure of Men: Science, Technology and Ideologies of Western Dominance* (Ithaca, NY: Cornell University Press, 1989). Other works that have focused on the role of science in the Dutch East Indies, and its relationship to the colonial state, include Peter Boomgaard, "The Making and Unmaking of Tropical Science: Dutch Research on Indonesia, 1600–2000," *BKI* 162, 2–3 (2006): 191–217; Suzanne Moon, *Technology and Ethical Idealism: A History of Development in the Netherlands East Indies* (Leiden: CNWS, 2007); Lewis Pyenson, *Empire of Reason: Exact Sciences in Indonesia, 1840–1940* (Leiden: E.J. Brill, 1989).

Plate 6.2 A mounted tiger on display. Courtesy of the Raffles Museum of Biodiversity Research, National University of Singapore.

Museum was clearly one of the great symbols of British colonial rule in Singapore and the Straits Settlements, and it was based in collection and classification of the natural world. The work that took place at the Raffles Library and Museum—along with the Botanic Gardens—set the standard for scientific research in Singapore for over a century, and played a vital role in British understandings of the tropics, informing their view of the region.

In this pursuit of knowledge, the Raffles Museum and Library was not only a scientific institution; it was also a cultural institution. The Museum commemorated the natural environment of Singapore and the region, allowing everyone to see it on display, reflecting the glory of knowledge and empire. It was held in high esteem throughout colonial society, creating a unity of the Straits Settlements and Malaya, making the borders of interest and control correspond to areas of British power. Visitors could observe a variety of animals and displays reflecting the rich fauna of the surrounding tropical forests and seas that plantations and development were in the process of taming. This made it immensely popular. While membership in the Library was by subscription, admittance to the Museum was free, making it a premier attraction for locals and visitors.[23]

Natural history, however, was changing. Beginning in the 1930s, research began to shift from collection and taxonomic classification to a focus on nature and environment as a complete ecosystem. Proponents of such an approach would come to see the collection of the Raffles Museum as an antiquated legacy of a colonial past. The study of nature would now shift from identification to preservation, as scientists and government officials promoted the study of the ecosystem, which following decolonization would diminish the boundaries that Singaporean officials oversaw.[24] Popular perceptions of the institution were also beginning to shift.

From Museum to Science Centre

In a period of rapidly shifting political transition and upheaval, when labor issues, *merdeka* (independence), and merger were at the forefront of most minds, the Raffles Museum and Library had become a symbol of an earlier period, one in which most Singaporeans had little time or interest. By 1960, the library collection of the museum became the National Library, housed in a newly constructed building nearby. The museum, with its mix of ethnographic and natural history displays, continued to be housed in the main building, with visitor numbers dropping each year. It was, according to one letter to *The Straits Times* in 1965, "dead." The writer of the letter went on to describe the institution as "an example of what an inadequate museum looked like in 1935."[25]

---

[23] When Singapore's population was only around 450,000 in 1927, for example, the Museum had 298,546 visitors with 29,562 coming over the Chinese New Year holiday. These numbers were consistent throughout the 1920s and 1930s. In 1937, for example, over 250,000 people visited the Museum. I would like to thank Fiona Tan for helping me with this information. C. Boden Kloss, *Annual Report on the Raffles Museum and Library for the year 1927* (Singapore: Government Printing Office, 1928), p. 1; M.W.F. Tweedie, *Annual Report of the Raffles Museum and Library for the Year 1937* (Singapore: Government Printing Office, 1938), p. 2.

[24] Kathirithamby-Wells, "Peninsular Malaysia in the Context of Natural History and Colonial Science," p. 372; Richard Seah, "Saved from the Dustbin," *The Straits Times Annual 1980* (Singapore: Times Periodicals, 1980), pp. 80–9.

[25] "Doing More for the National Museum," *The Straits Times* [hereafter *ST*], 3 July 1965, p. 8.

In 1968, the government began to address complaints related to the Raffles Museum. Toh Chin Chye, as the Minister of Science and Technology, announced that a change was necessary as the museum had become "'junk shop' containing a hodge-podge of exhibits. A new policy was needed."[26] As visitors had proclaimed their preference for exhibits focusing on nature ("flora and fauna"), Toh decided to convert it into a natural history museum at a cost of $245,000 following the advice of the Science Council of Singapore. In addition, the Raffles Museum would be renamed the National Museum, and a government-appointed board would oversee its operation. Among the members of the newly formed Museum Board, tasked with overseeing this conversion, were prominent scientists at the University of Singapore and Nanyang University, including Chan Kai Lok, Chen Ti Wen, Chew Wee-Lek, and Chuang Shou-Hwa. Chew was even appointed as the deputy chairman of the board.[27] Singapore's National Museum was to be a natural history museum.

In early 1970, James Gardner, a consulting designer from UNESCO, presented a report to the National Museum Board on the plans to convert the National Museum into an institution promoting natural history and science. Gardner recommended that the museum focus on a "thematic treatment" in which the exhibits would reflect "live science," which would entail presenting the stuffed animals in their natural habitat as opposed to simply displaying them in a "glass cage." This would transform it from "an institution associated with musty exhibits of a forgotten past" to one in which research into science and the environment would take precedent. The museum would now focus on "themes and ecological aspects rather than taxological (by classification)." It was now to become a "Museum of Natural Science."[28]

Change in the focus and direction of Singaporean museums, however, was only beginning. While the National Museum was to focus on flora and fauna, Toh announced plans in mid-1970 to develop a Science Centre,

---

[26] "A Change for the National Museum," *ST*, 14 Dec. 1968, p. 7.

[27] Ibid.; "Museum Board officials," *ST*, 18 Feb. 1969, p. 4; "Museum Chiefs," *ST*, 12 Oct. 1969, p. 9; Leo W.H. Tan, "In Transit ... National Museum ... Science Centre ... National University ... Stop!," in *Our Heritage: Zoological Reference Collection: Official Opening Souvenir Brochure, 31 October 1988* (Singapore: National University of Singapore, Zoological Reference Collection, 1988), p. 7.

[28] Chia Poteik, "$2 million Plan to Turn the Museum into Exciting 'Living' Display," *ST*, 15 Feb. 1970, p. 7; "A Make Believe Thunderfall for Science Museum," *ST*, 27 Mar. 1970, p. 15; "Plan to Give Museum a New 'live' Look," *ST*, 16 Sep. 1970, p. 5.

which would be separate from the National Museum. The responsibility for the creation of this new institution was in the hands of a Science Centre Board, which was to replace the National Museum Board. Officials quickly accepted these plans, which called for the construction of the Science Centre elsewhere in Singapore at an estimated cost of $5.2 million. By December 1970, the Science Centre Board announced that the new museum was to be built beside Jurong Lake for an even higher amount, $9.5 million.[29]

Plans for the Science Centre were rapidly changing, and expanding. In line with the emphasis on economic development and industrialization at the time, there would now be a wing featuring technology "to highlight man's achievements in industries, communications and science."[30] The focus on technology at the new Science Centre represented a shift in priorities, as it would provide highlight "projects of national interest," such as "industrial technology," communications and transport with special galleries on land reclamation and the mass transit system. Natural history, however, was not to be lost. Gardner's vision of "live science" would find a home in the second wing, which would feature "natural history specimens … to illustrate the 'mechanisms of life' and the evolution of balanced ecological patterns," with a focus on how these principles can be coordinated with science and technology. The first planned exhibit for this second division was to be a replica of a rainforest. An anonymous Museum spokesman best articulated these ideas when he told *The Straits Times*, "Despite the disappearing countryside, future generations of Singaporeans need not lose touch" with "tropical rainforests." In addition, there was to be a "continuity of life gallery," which would focus on the different stages of life in animals, plants, and humans. In the meantime, the anthropological exhibits left over from the National Museum were to be merged with works of art for a proposed Singapore Art Gallery. At this time, officials announced that the ambitious plans for the development of the Science Centre would take four years, hoping to open this new museum in 1974.[31]

---

[29] "Science Centre at Jurong," *ST*, 3 Dec. 1970, p. 22; Chia, "$2 million Plan;" "Plan to Give Museum a New 'Live' Look;" "Science Centre May Attract 340,000 Visitors Each Year," *ST*, 23 July 1970, p. 11; "Plan for Two Divisions at $5.2 million Science Centre," *ST*, 8 July 1970, p. 8.

[30] "Wee to Head Science Centre Board for Three Years," *ST*, 30 Nov. 1970, p. 21; "Language No Barrier in Parliament House," *ST*, 26 Mar. 1971, p. 10.

[31] "Replica of a Rain Forest to be Set Up in Museum," *ST*, 5 May 1971, p. 23; "$650,000 Art Gallery will be in Museum," *ST*, 18 Oct. 1971, p. 10.

The development of these new institutions also led to changes in natural history programs for the public. Following the Second World War, employees of the Raffles Museum had conducted a taxidermy program for students preparing for their "A-Level" examinations in zoology. With the help of a museum employee, the students would learn how to preserve an animal, often a bird or a squirrel. One participant remembers an employee shooting a yellow-vented bulbul bird on Ft. Canning Hill for her, and then learning how to mount it in the Raffles Museum research laboratories in the early 1960s.[32] Such outreach programs for teachers and students, however, were coming under pressure in a rapidly urbanizing society in which there would be an emphasis on tours and nature walks to help introduce Singaporean children to the natural environment. The taxidermy program, which harked back to an earlier focus on natural history collecting, would have to be jettisoned. During the school break in late 1970, the National Museum organized practical courses on taxidermy of birds for secondary school teachers. This program, however, encountered controversy when a passer-by witnessed the teachers, and museum staff, shooting birds and squirrels at Peirce Reservoir in late November of that year. Chew Kai Seng, writing for the director of the National Museum, denied these accusations, although he also claimed that, if it had occurred, no laws had been broken as the Museum "possesses permits to collect specimens there when necessary for the purpose of display and study."[33] The public taxidermy program soon came to an end.

The presence of a large natural history collection, as well as potentially controversial public taxidermy programs, led to a conundrum for the development of the Science Centre in Jurong. The new institution was to feature technology and "living exhibits" that mainly emphasized ecological themes. For animals, the construction of the Singapore Zoo was taking place—it would open in 1973—while a bird park had already been operating since 1971. In March 1972, much of the uncertainty over the National Museum and its exhibits became clearer. As the Ministry of Science and Technology oversaw the National Museum—which would now be the home for anthropological and art displays—it was transferred to the Ministry

---

[32] Interview with Maureen Danker, 26 Oct. 2012.

[33] Ibid.; "Taxidermy Courses for Teachers," *ST*, 2 Oct. 1970, p. 7; Albert Ong, "Stop This Killing of Animals in the Reserve," *ST*, 28 Nov. 1970, p. 9; Chew Kai Seng, "Letter to Editor," *ST*, 19 Jan. 1971, p. 19; "Garden Ecology," *ST*, 18 Aug. 1972, p. 12.

of Culture. The National Museum would no longer be a natural history museum. The National Museum would temporarily house the natural history and sciences exhibits at the building on Stamford Road until the Science Centre was completed in Jurong. In addition, due to a "lack of student and public interest," the Art Museum at the University of Singapore was closed. Owing to earlier relations and agreements, a quarter of the art collection went to the University of Malaya in Kuala Lumpur, while the remaining pieces were transferred to the National Museum, which had plenty of space due to "the removal of the zoological exhibits from the National Museum."[34] In the meantime, the Science Centre, scheduled to open in 1974, was delayed until December 1977.[35] Amidst all of the construction of a modern, economically and technologically advanced Singapore that was no longer connected to a larger Malaya in a worldview of nature and environment, what was to be done with these various stuffed, pickled and pricked animals that represented colonial-era attempts to better understand the nature and environment of the region? As Eric R. Alfred, the Director of the National Museum from 1967 to 1972, argued, "... no zoologist would suggest throwing away the only mounted fish skins of extinct freshwater fishes of Singapore."[36] This was, however, becoming a possibility.

The Fate of the Specimens

In May 1974, workers dismantled the blue whale skeleton that had been displayed in the Raffles Museum since 1907. An iconic presence in the institution—the whale was one of the "finest and most impressive exhibits" at the museum, as one visitor described it. The Science Centre transferred the skeleton to the National Museum in Kuala Lumpur in exchange for training for its staff "on the finer points of modelling and casting of exhibition specimens." Museum officials in Malaysia hoped it would become a "main attraction" for visitors, and it eventually became a centerpiece of the Labuan

---

[34] "Culture Ministry will Take Over Museum," *ST*, 31 Mar. 1972, p. 12; "Lack of Interest so Varsity to Close Its Art Museum," *ST*, 31 Oct. 1972, p. 11; "Interest was Lacking," *ST*, 5 Nov. 1972, p. 10.

[35] Ilsa Sharp, *The First 21 Years: The Singapore Zoological Gardens Story* (Singapore: Singapore Zoological Gardens, 1994), pp. 3–27; "The Men behind the Project," *ST*, 29 Jan. 1973, p. 14; Seah, "Saved from the Dustbin."

[36] Alfred, "The Zoological Collections of the National Museum 1957–1974," p. 6.

Marine Museum when it opened in 2003.[37] The transfers of materials had been occurring for several years prior to the departure of the blue whale skeleton, and reflect the position that natural history had in Singapore during the 1970s. This position was perilous, and it is through the efforts of a few staff and interested zoologists that most of it would be preserved, and used for Life Science education. As it occurred, however, it would expose the various levels of environmental commitment on behalf of individuals as well as the government.

While the blue whale skeleton was the most famous item in the natural history collection of the National Museum, it was the last—and largest—piece to be transferred as the focus of the museum shifted to ethnological and historical exhibits. The blue whale skeleton was only one in a million—or, to be more accurate, one in 126,000—specimens that had to be either stored or disposed. Although it had inherited the entire natural history collection, as well as all of the reference books and storage containers of the most extensive natural history collection in Southeast Asia, the mandate of the new Science Centre did not focus on taxonomic collection and identification.[38] In addition, the new Life Science Gallery, as it soon came to be known, at the Science Centre would feature only a limited number of specimens from the thousands that the Raffles Museum had collected. The members of the advisory board for the Science Centre began searching for a solution to the difficulty of storing such a large number of specimens, as well as remains—such as the blue whale skeleton—which were found to be too large to accommodate. It was a period in which "the Collection was not only exposed to the risk of considerable material loss or damage but was itself, in danger of being disposed of and relegated to other institutions."[39] It was at the beginning of this process that the letters and inquiries passed over the desk of scientists in the Natural History Museum in London in 1971.

---

[37] "A Whale of a Gift for Malaysian National Museum," *ST*, 6 May 1974, p. 8; "Whale of a Loss," *ST*, 9 May 1974, p. 10; "Labuan's Century-Old Whale," *Daily Express Sabah*, 20 Jan. 2007.

[38] A similar mandate with regard to flora was also given to the Botanic Gardens during this period. See Nigel P. Taylor's contribution to this volume.

[39] Roland E. Sharma, "The Zoological Reference Collection. The Interim Years 1972–1980," in *Our Heritage: Zoological Reference Collection: Official Opening Souvenir Brochure, 31 October 1988* (Singapore: National University of Singapore, Zoological Reference Collection, 1988), p. 10; Tan, "In transit," p. 7.

Officials from London soon contacted Michael Tweedie, who had recently retired from the National Museum, to enquire about the collection and its availability. While Tweedie informed them that no type specimens (the first of a species to be described and named) were available, A.P. Coleman of the Natural History Museum in London asked the heads of various departments if they were "aware of important material which this Museum would wish to obtain." J.P. Harding, the Keeper of Zoology, quickly replied, expressing an interest in knowing what material would be available. Much of the concern seemed to be coming from Eric Alfred, who was ending his tenure as the Director of the Museum. In discussions with visitors, Alfred was pessimistic about the future of the collection, describing it as "an uphill struggle to persuade official circles in Singapore that such 'old' stuff can be of unique and irreplaceable value to thoroughly modern science."[40] Soon thereafter, Alfred transferred to the Maritime Museum.

By October 1971, a letter from Kuala Lumpur clarified the issue. Anthony Berry, of the School of Biological Sciences at the University of Malaya, informed Lord Cranbrook, a well-known naturalist of Southeast Asia, that the collection was not "going begging." The natural history collection was to be presented to the University of Singapore, where it would be the centerpiece of a research collection, and funds would be available for handling it properly. Duplicates of specimens, however, would be made available to outside parties, and Berry planned a trip in November to peruse the collection.[41]

Following his visit to the collection, Berry wrote an assessment in an aerogram he sent to "Gathorne"—Lord Cranbrook—in April 1972. As he saw the situation:

> I went to S'pore recently and worked a lot in the museum. It is really folding up very soon. Exhibits (old or replacements) are to be put up at the grand new Science Centre out at Jurong (close to the bird park and more industrial splendours of S'pore). The reference materials are to go to U. of S'pore where, really, nobody wants them particularly. Some staff there look forward to augmenting their teaching collections; Nan Elliot at Nanyang tried to persuade Chuang at S'pore U to 'share the loot'

---

[40] Medway to Chuang, 28 Apr. 1972; Note from Coleman to "All Keepers," 12 Aug. 1971; Note from Harding, 17 Aug. 1971, DF206/137, Museum of Natural History Archives, London.

[41] Berry to Lord Cranbrook, 22 Oct. 1971, DF206/137, Museum of Natural History Archives, London.

between the Universities. There seems to have been sufficient alarm and concern from all sides, however, to make them realise at least that lots of people are watching and that they should do their best to look after the stuff. Now they have advertised for a curator to work at the University (one only). Also it is clear that no one in Singapore (University, Alfred, Govt.) will contemplate letting the material disperse (except for minor lootings that are best left unspecified).

My assessment is that (a) international alarm has awakened basically uninterested people in S'pore to the value, even world-scale obligation, involved in the materials … (c) the best hope for the collections is for all interested parties to offer support (moral and material) to Chuang S.H. (Head and Prof of Zool.) in his efforts to maintain the collections as they merit; and to seek assurances that the material will continue to be available internationally as in the past and as with other museum collections. The more of this sort of pressure cum 'support', the more they will be forced to treat it as a real set of collections. Otherwise, I'm afraid that with one poor curator and many predatory teachers, the specimens will gradually disappear.[42]

The same month, Lord Cranbrook wrote to Chuang with the hope that he would "keep the collections separate from run-of-the-mill teaching materials," and offering support "in any battles you may be forced to fight."[43]

Chuang and Elliot came to an agreement to house the Zoological Reference Collection (or Raffles Collection), as it quickly came to be known, at the University of Singapore. In August 1972, C.M. Yang, who would quickly become a key figure in this tale, joined the Zoology Department at the University of Singapore; her first assignment was to help with the transfer of materials from the National Museum. When she first visited the National Museum, she found "thousands and thousands of preserved reference specimens of bird skins, mammal skins, skulls, fishes, snakes, crustaceans, insects and shells stored in big wooden cabinets, huge wooden crates or boxes, different sizes of glass jars and other containers" stored in the rooms behind the display galleries at the National Museum.[44] She

---

[42] Berry to Gathorne, 22 Apr. 1972, DF206/137, Museum of Natural History Archives, London.

[43] Medway to Chuang, 28 Apr. 1972, DF206/137, Museum of Natural History Archives, London.

[44] C.M. Yang, "The Reunion of the Zoological Reference Collection," in *Our Heritage: Zoological Reference Collection: Official Opening Souvenir Brochure, 31 October 1988* (Singapore: National University of Singapore, Zoological Reference Collection, 1988), p. 12.

had to move all of this material to the University; the campus on Bukit Timah Road, however, had no space for the vast collection. Along with two laboratory technicians, two laboratory attendants and a clerk, Yang packed, shifted, unpacked, sorted, rearranged, labeled and set up the Zoological Reference Collection in five Romney huts along Ayer Rajah Road. For the next five years, it remained in these huts, and the staff developed a kindred spirit of responsibility in preserving a unique zoological collection. As Yang recalled, staff members became "deeply involved in the special care needed for the delicate, fragile and rare specimens."[45]

The age of the collection, its transfer, and storage in less than ideal conditions did take a toll, despite the best efforts of the staff. Beginning in 1976, Yang, who was now the Scientific Officer for the Collection, began corresponding with I.C.J. Galbraith, of the Ornithology Department at the Museum of Natural History in London, seeking advice on the best steel cabinets to use for storage, as the wooden, non-air-tight ones that had been used resulted in mold for some of the bird specimens, which had to be treated with fungicide. The result was a series of letters discussing the merits of dichlorvos and naphthalene insecticides and their effect on colors, as well as humidity and temperature ideals for storage, which reflect the larger stresses that the Zoological Reference Collection was experiencing during this period of turmoil. In their correspondence, Yang expresses hope that a permanent home for the collection would soon become a reality in late 1976. These hopes were dashed quickly. Yang informed her correspondent early the next year that "due to certain circumstances, the planned building of our collection has been turned down. Therefore, we will now have to look for a new place to house our collection in the near future."[46]

The research value of the Zoological Reference Collection, amid building and storage woes, had now come under question. Yang again wrote to her pen pal Galbraith asking for help in assessing the "scientific value of our collection in this region or in other parts of the world." This was necessary as the curators of the Zoological Reference Collection had to assess "the value (in terms of money) of our collection for our record purposes and possible for insurance coverage." She also emphasized that this exercise needed to be done in terms that would provide a value that would "stress the scientific and

---

[45] Ibid.
[46] Yang to Galbraith, 25 Aug. 1977; Yang to Curator, 14 Aug. 1976; Galbraith to Yang, 2 Sep. 1976; Yang to Galbraith, 10 Dec. 1976; Galbraith to Yang, 24 Jan. 1977, DF206/137, Museum of Natural History Archives, London.

monetary value of our reference collection to the non-zoologists."[47] Galbraith responded quickly. While he apologized for having to make "broadly-based assessments," and bringing up the point that "the monetary value of scientific specimens is a difficult one, since there is fortunately no organized trade in them" and "prices seldom represent more than a fraction of the actual cost of acquiring the specimens," Galbraith estimated that "quite ordinary bird skins—not taking into account the special importance of much of the Raffles material—cannot be less than £10 each."[48]

The request from Yang in 1977 led to a series of memos and notes being sent among the staff of the Natural History Museum in London to provide an estimate of the monetary value of the Raffles Collection. Most of the respondents felt it was absurd to consider such a historic collection in such a manner. In the end, however, most offered advice with regard to its value for the areas that were in their purview. For example, R.W. Sims of the Annelida ("ringed worms") Section wrote that the earthworms (Oligochaeta) in the Raffles Collection were important due to the variety of specimens, some of which G.E. Gates collected in Burma prior to 1942, and represented the only existing examples. Sims, however, could not estimate the monetary value of these worms as "the only yardstick would be the price paid for any other collection, and I have no knowledge of such collections being offered for sale."[49] In addition, as K.H. Hyatt—a specialist in spiders, millipedes, and centipedes (myriapods)—argued, "they almost certainly have materials collected in areas of Malaysia on which little has been published and much has happened in recent years to alter the terrain, e.g. deforestation and war."[50] Specialists in London, in the same series of notes, remark that "the mammalian collections are an unequalled source in Malaysian mammalogy and it "would be financially impossible to replace

---

[47] Yang to Galbraith, 31 Aug. 1977, DF206/137, Museum of Natural History Archives, London.

[48] Galbraith to Yang, 26 Sep. 1977, DF206/137, Museum of Natural History Archives, London. In response to the question about insurance, Yang's British counterpart could not answer as the British Treasury covered any losses of the Museum. Galbraith to Yang, 20 Oct. 1977, DF206/137, Museum of Natural History Archives, London.

[49] Sims to Galbraith, 28 Oct. 1977, DF206/137, Museum of Natural History Archives, London; G.E. Gates, *The Earthworms of Burma* (Cambridge, MA: Harvard University Press, 1934).

[50] Hyatt to Galbraith, 3 Nov. 1977, DF206/137, Museum of Natural History Archives, London.

the collection."[51] Reflecting a more political—and cheeky—solution to the issue, Peter J.P. Whitehead, an ichthyologist, proposed that the Singaporean government be informed that the School of Biological Sciences at Universiti Sains Malaysia in Penang would be interested in the collection, hoping this might persuade officials to "keep and look after it" in the name of national pride and regional competition.[52]

Yang also began receiving letters from other parts of the world at this time, as the curators of natural history museums wanted to offer support and advice. Among the correspondents was Lester L. Short, Curator, the American Museum of Natural History in New York City, who provided the following guidelines:

(i)   type specimens: US$500.00–$1000.00 a piece
(ii)   unique specimens of historical-archival importance: US$100.00 a piece
(iii) for data-bearing specimens from areas in which one cannot obtain replacements: US$50.00 each
(iv)   other specimens bearing data: US$10.00 each
(v)   specimens with little or no data: US$5.00 each

These prices excited Yang as it meant that "based on the above guidelines our bird collection (about 30,000 skins)" was "worth about US$2 million!"[53] Beyond a discussion of monetary value, these exchanges reflected the difficulties biologists and curators faced in Singapore in the 1970s; they were torn between the government's insistence on pragmatism and future economic development and the "responsibility and privilege" of overseeing "important research collections" that many officials saw as having little importance in a future Singapore, or its environment.[54]

Although interested biologists at the two universities in Singapore took responsibility for the collection, it—once again—suffered from the

[51] Hill to Galbraith, 28 Oct. 1977, DF206/137, Museum of Natural History Archives, London.
[52] Whitehead to Galbraith, 25 Oct. 1977, DF206/137, Museum of Natural History Archives, London.
[53] Yang to Galbraith, 11 Nov. 1977, DF206/137, Museum of Natural History Archives, London. The next month, Galbraith wrote that he found Short's guidelines "reasonable." Galbraith to Yang, 7 Dec. 1977, DF206/137, Museum of Natural History Archives, London.
[54] Sharma, "The Zoological Reference Collection," pp. 10–1; Galbraith to Yang, 7 Dec. 1977.

Plate 6.3 "White coffins" used to store specimens on the cramped campus of the University of Singapore during the 1970s. Courtesy of the Raffles Museum of Biodiversity Research, National University of Singapore.

rapid construction and deconstruction of institutions in the modernizing city-state. The area along Ayer Rajah Road, where Yang and her colleagues stored the Zoological Reference Collection for several years, was to be the site of the new campus of the soon to be opened National University of Singapore. When construction began on that campus in 1977, the collection was moved to the Bukit Timah campus, which at that time the University of Singapore and Nanyang University shared (in 1980 the universities would be combined to form the National University of Singapore – NUS). The size of the collection was so large that it took 40 lorries to transfer the contents between Ayer Rajah Road and Bukit Timah. Space limitations on the Bukit Timah campus ultimately meant that the collection was split into three. The mammals, birds, and insects found a home at the University Mess on Dalvey Road; fish were kept in the University Language Centre basement; and, reptiles, amphibians and insects stored in the Menasseh Building.[55]

---

[55] Seah, "Saved from the Dustbin;" Yang to Galbraith, 11 Nov. 1977.

Space considerations continued to haunt the collection for years. By July 1979, the lack of sufficient classrooms at the Bukit Timah campus reached crisis proportions, and university officials pushed each department to justify its use of the facilities. Classes would have priority. In addition, on the newly constructed Kent Ridge campus, there was a continuing problem with space. Although a museum to house the Zoological Reference Collection had been planned, it tumbled down the priority list. Yang felt constantly under pressure, and there were whispers that it would have to be thrown out. A solution was achieved in mid-1979 when Roland Sharma, the head of the Department of Zoology, arranged for most of the collection to be transferred to the Library Building of Nanyang University, which was located in Jurong. The entire Zoological Reference Collection, except for the fish collection, which remained in the Zoology Department on the Bukit Timah campus, moved in 1980 to the top floor of the Nanyang University Library, where Yang and her staff of two technicians found "more reasonable working conditions for the storage of specimens."[56] Despite the uncertainty

Plate 6.4 Squirrel specimens from the Zoological Reference Collection after transfer to Nanyang University in 1980. Courtesy of the Raffles Museum of Biodiversity Research, National University of Singapore.

---

[56] Sharma, "The Zoological Reference Collection," p. 11; Seah, "Saved from the Dustbin."

Plate 6.5 Storage cabinets for the Zoological Reference Collection in the 1980s. Courtesy of the Raffles Museum of Biodiversity Research, National University of Singapore.

throughout this period, the staff continued to catalogue and process research material for scientists. The Zoological Reference Collection also remained mostly intact, containing 127,000 stored specimens, including 4,700 type specimens, although some of the specimens, particularly among mammals, birds and reptiles, were lost or damaged beyond repair.[57]

A profile of the Raffles Museum's natural history collection in 1980 characterized its role in the society as "very Singaporean." "It was born in

---

[57] Over the past 30 years, the Zoological Reference Collection has grown to over 500,000 specimens. Some of the growth was due to new specimens being added. In addition, Yang faced the task of cataloguing some materials left over from the Raffles Museum, as well as differentiating some specimens—such as five separate fish in a jar—as either five specimens or one; Sharma, "The Zoological Reference Collection," p. 11; Tan, "In Transit," p. 7; http://rmbr.nus.edu.sg/collections/index.html [accessed 15 Sep. 2012]. I would like to thank Peter Ng for helping clarify this issue.

Singapore, had 'lived' in Singapore for over 100 years, and is totally different from other Zoological collections in the world. It has become a part of Singapore history and the heritage of Singaporeans."[58] Other scholars connected to the collection echoed these sentiments. It was a collection that deserved "the universal recognition of its scientific and historical value," and "its disposal would incur the loss of an academic heritage closely associated with Singapore and held in trust for the future."[59] It had, however, faced the pressure of constant movement, questions over its worth, and its role in the society. It had gone from a premier colonial display to fodder for storage facilities around the island.

Conclusion

In October 1988, officials at NUS opened a new home for the Zoological Reference Collection. The descendant of the Raffles Museum, the collection consisted of approximately 160,000 specimens, representing more than 7,600 species, mainly originating from Malaysia and Singapore with the rest coming from mainland and island Southeast Asia. Instead of being housed in a magnificent building near the government's seat of power, it was now held in a corner of a vast university campus. Its role in society had changed. As T.J. Lam, the Head of the Department of Zoology at NUS, stated in a brochure printed for the opening ceremony, it was "well placed as a centre of study for the taxonomy and systematics of the fauna in this region and as a depository of specimens as well." Scientists still came from around the world to consult the collection, and it still had an important role to play in research as the premier collection of Southeast Asian, and particularly Malayan, fauna.[60] While school groups could still access it, the Zoological Reference Collection of the new Raffles Museum of Biodiversity Research was not a premier attraction representing the society's connection to the surrounding

---

[58] Seah, "Saved from the Dustbin," p. 87.
[59] Sharma, "The Zoological Reference Collection," p. 11.
[60] T.J. Lam, "Foreword," in *Our Heritage: Zoological Reference Collection: Official Opening Souvenir Brochure, 31 October 1988* (Singapore: National University of Singapore, Zoological Reference Collection, 1988), p. 1. The specimens consisted of 15,000 mammals, 31,000 birds, 6,000 reptiles and amphibians, 30,000 fish, 21,000 mollusks, 25,000 crabs, 10,000 prawns, 10,000 insects, 2,000 corals, and 10,000 other invertebrates.

environment; it was for research, not display. Much like the larger society, it had made a troubled transition to its new position. Visitor numbers, while steady, could never reach the levels of the pre-War period. Natural history in Singapore had shifted once again. The Raffles Museum of Biodiversity Research featured all of the specimens, and more collected since then, from the original Raffles Museum and was the focus of scientific research, while the Singapore Science Centre in Jurong featured displays on issues such as genomics, climate change, and larger ecosystems. These new displays and their functions were a result of the politics, economics, and understandings of the environment—as well as shifts in scientific approaches—amidst the modernization of Singapore.

The transition in importance that the Raffles Museum and its natural history collection has experienced reflects a changing view of Singapore as an important port city of a corner of a colonial British Empire that included the Straits Settlements and Malaya, and later a small nation-state. When the borders of this world became more restricted following political independence for Singapore, the views of the environment also contracted. Priorities changed; the authorities began to focus on larger ecosystems beyond the individual specimen, while also promoting an industrialized vision of a "city as a garden" that viewed the world through lenses of economic pragmatism. This new Garden City was without bothersome animals; nor did it involve the rich fauna of the region. This left the curators of the vast natural history collection in a difficult position. Housing an aging collection of stuffed and pickled animals, they had to search for space, maintain the collection and even expand it, while also justifying its existence. Its continued presence as a research collection for two decades on the National University of Singapore campus is remarkable, and it continues to hold an important role in environmental education and research in Singapore today.

The ideological descendants of C.M. Yang, particularly Peter Ng and Leo Tan, will soon oversee the move of the Zoological Reference Collection into the new Lee Kong Chian Natural History Museum on the campus of the National University of Singapore. While the collection began with the gift of a rhinoceros from the Straits Settlements Governor in 1875, and came to reflect the richness of Malayan fauna, this new institution will have a centerpiece exhibit that suggests a globalized Singapore of the 21st century. Instead of a blue whale stranded near Melaka, visitors will be able to see the skeletons of three diplodocid sauropod dinosaurs, dug up from the western United States, as well as some 500,000 Southeast

Asian specimens.[61] While the purchase of these dinosaurs harks back to early "collecting" practices at the colonial Raffles Museum, and also has led to some controversy, the maintenance of the collection for education and research in Singapore is a legacy of the continuing attempts of residents of Singapore to better understand and contextualize the fauna that makes up part of the natural world of the island and its surrounding region, and even the wider world.[62]

[61] "First Natural History Museum in Singapore Unveiled!" at http://rafflesmuseum. wordpress.com/2012/06/06/first-natural-history-museum-in-singapore-unveiled/ [accessed 28 Sep. 2012].

[62] Ong Sor Fern, "What Have Dinosaurs Got to Do with S'pore," *ST*, 16 July 2011, p. A2; Rudolf Maier, Peter Ng, and Leo Tan, "Dinosaurs Part of S'pore's 'Deep' History," *ST*, 19 July 2011, p. A22.

SOURCE 7

Agricultural Production in Singapore: Excerpts from *Annual Reports of the Primary Production Department*, Ministry of National Development from the 1970s and 1980s[1]

PPD Annual Report (1970), p. 1

The year 1970 saw steady progress and expansion in all fields of activity of the Primary Production Department.

Efforts were channelled to further increase the efficiency of animal production in the Republic and maintain the status of self-sufficiency in pigs, poultry and eggs. Studies on various aspects of intensive forms of animal production were also carried out. The Meat Technology Unit was established with UNDP assistance at Jurong and the staff moved in the Laboratory in August 1970.

In the field of fisheries, the number of fishing vessels calling at the Jurong Fishing Port continued to increase. Landings at the Jurong Auction Market also increased. Four factories were in operation during the year and several applications were received for sites at the Fishing Port for the establishment of processing plants and other shore installations. The ornamental fish export trade in 1970 was valued at $6.2 million, compared to $5.1 million in 1969.

In view of competing uses for limited land resources, efforts were directed towards assisting Singapore farmers to increase productivity and reduce production costs. At the same time development projects were planned with the objective of developing the agricultural sector into a more viable component of the national economy.

The pattern of Agriculture remained very much the same as for 1969 with accent on intensive market gardening and cut flowers. Initial experiments showed that leafy vegetables and sweet pepper could successfully and economically be grown under

---

[1] These excerpts appeared as the introductions to the *Annual Report of the Primary Production Department*, which appeared yearly as a chapter in the Ministry of National Development *Annual Report*. Thanks to Puah You Kai for finding these materials.

hydroponic conditions. Export of cut orchid blooms continued to rise during the year and the value of exported flowers topped the million dollar mark for the first time.

The Rural Development Division formed a vital link between the Department and the farming community by making available to farmers and fishermen scientific and up to date information on agriculture, animal husbandry and fisheries.

About 175,400 people (9 per cent of the total population) were actively engaged in agricultural activities or were indirectly dependent on farming and fishing for a livelihood. The Republic has since 1964 been self sufficient in poultry, eggs and livestock and presently 50 per cent of our vegetable needs and 30 per cent of our fish requirements are produced locally. With greater effort and improved productive capacity, the agricultural sector could provide a significant contribution towards greater economic prosperity.

* * *

MND Annual Report (1976), p. 16

To assist farmers to maximise returns from the limited agricultural land, the Primary Production Department renders technical advice and disseminates its research findings on ways of increasing or improving food production. These efforts have paid off as Singapore is self-sufficient in pork, poultry, meat and eggs although the number of farms licensed in 1976 was 15,022, a decrease of 594 farms from 1975 and the total farm holdings area reduced from 10,588 hectares to 10,370 hectares.

With the exception of fish, Singapore's primary production in 1976 increased over that of the previous year. Pig production increased by 180,000 heads (16.8%), chicken by 2,042,000 birds (7.9%), ducks by 873,000 birds (28.8%) and hen eggs by 42,888,000 pieces (9.2%). Dried tobacco leaves production increased substantially by 96 tonnes or 30.9% while the export value of ornamental fish, aquatic plants, orchid flowers and day-old chicks reached $34 million, a 13% increase. Vegetable, quail egg and crocodile production increased marginally. Fish production dropped by 1,131 tonnes (–6.4%).

However, the value of last year's production is only $474 million, a 3.5% drop over 1975's figure of $491 million. This is due to the lower production value of pigs which fell by $42.4 million because of the drastic drop in prices brought about by a glut during the year. The annual average price of high grade porkers dropped to $215.92 per 100 kg from the previous year's $295.60 per 100 kg.

* * *

MND Annual Report (1980), p. 21

The Primary Production Department is responsible for the implementation of Government policies on agricultural and fisheries development in Singapore. Its major functions are to plan, develop and manage farm estates, conduct research on intensive farming methods, animal nutrition and disease control, and provide extension services to farmers and fishermen.

The Department is headed by Director, Dr. Siew Teck Woh. He is assisted by two Deputy Directors.

GENERAL

Land is a scarce and precious resource in Singapore with many competing demands. A committee was appointed by the Minister of National Development in March 1979 to review and recommend measures to maximise and improve the use of land allocated for farming. Based on the committee's recommendations, the Ministry of National Development adopted in 1980, an agricultural policy under which farming will be placed on an unsubsidised and fully commercial footing. Approximately 3,300 hectares of land in several localities were identified for long-term agricultural use. To optimise usage, the land will be developed into farming estates and subdivided into viable lots. These agricultural land will be leased for a minimum period of 10 years at economic rentals, the rates of which will vary according to the type of farming practised.

For pig farming, land rental will be 6% of the market value of the land. For poultry farming, it will be 4% of market value in the first two years, rising by 1% a year to 6% by the sixth year. Lessees will be required to meet production targets set by the Department.

Two commercial farming schemes were introduced several years ago, namely: intensive pig farming at Punggol and hydroponic farming at Khatib. Following the adoption of the new agricultural policy, four new schemes were introduced at Jalan Kayu during the year. They are for food fish farming, aquarium fish export centre, mushroom cultivation and orchid/flower nurseries.

In recognition of the need to adequately compensate farmers, a new compensation scheme was implemented to pay additional resettlement compensation to farmers affected by clearance a second or subsequent time. This additional compensation varies with the number of years the farmer has stayed on the land, and ranges from 30% to 100%. Affected farmers also qualify for an additional $5000 cash grant.

At the end of 1980, there were 11,604 licensed farms occupying an area of 8,093 hectares compared to 12,446 farms on 8,970 hectares of land in 1979. The trend towards more intensive farming continued. The number of farms keeping more than 1,000 pigs each increased from 132 to 176 and that of farms keeping over 10,000 chickens rose from 210 to 258.

Within the water catchment areas and Kallang Basin, the number of pig farms declined to 1,667 and the pig population dropped to 148,000. This compares with 3,259 farms keeping 330,000 pigs in September 1979 when the programme to phase out pig farming from the catchment areas was launched. By September 1981, pig farming will be completely phased out of the catchment areas of the Kallang Basin.

To abate pollution in the pig farming areas, a pollution levy of $10 was imposed for every pig slaughtered at the abattoirs with effect from 1 January 1980. Funds collected will be used for the development of pig waste treatment facilities.

During the year, the primary production sector produced $605 million worth of farm products at ex-farm prices compared to $561 million the previous year. Local farms produced 1.19 million pigs, 32 million chickens, 553 million hen eggs, 35,000 tonnes of vegetables and 16,000 tonnes of food fish. Thus Singapore continued to be fully self-sufficient in pork and hen eggs and 78% self-sufficient in poultry.

* * *

MND Annual Report (1989), p. 38

The Primary Production Department (PPD) of the Ministry is entrusted with the responsibility of ensuring the adequate supply of wholesome meats, eggs, fish and vegetables to meet the needs of Singapore consumers. The PPD also develops and manages agrotechnology parks, and promotes commercial, high-tech farming and agrotechnology. The Department carries out research and development, and provides regulatory, developmental and advisory services to primary producers and traders.

The continued clearance of farmland for new developments has resulted in a further decrease in the number of farms from 2,075 in 1988 to 1,187 in 1989. The total farm holding area decreased to 1,196 ha, a fall of 41.3% over 1988. Nevertheless, the farming sector still produced $312 million worth of produce comprising 441,123 pigs, 4.3 million chickens, 5.3 million ducks, 323.4 million hen's eggs, 30.4 million quail's eggs and 6,400 tonnes of vegetables. 2,100 tonnes of food fish were produced by local fish farms.

Domestic exports of farm produce came to $89.7 million, consisting of $59.9 million of aquarium fish, $9.6 million of aquatic plants and $20.2 million of flowers (mainly cut orchids) and foliage plants.

Since 1985, the Government has been phasing out pig farming in stages. The farms on temporary leases, in Sembawang, Punggol, Tampines, Changi and Pulau Ubin were phased out by September 1989. The final stage of the programme will involve the remaining 22 commercial farms in Punggol with nearly 300,000 pigs.

CHAPTER 7

Agriculture and the End of Farming in Singapore

Cynthia Chou

The principal aim of the British venturing into Singapore in 1819 was to set up a trading post for the English East India Company. The island was regarded as possessing few natural resources and no products worthy of export. The larger geographic features of the island, however, were appealing. Its natural sheltered harbor, strategic maritime location at the gateway to the Straits of Malacca, and placement at the confluence of the trading route between China and the eastern archipelago persuaded British administrators that it suited their purposes. Discussions in standard textbooks and monographs on Singaporean history, by scholars such as Edwin Lee and Mary Turnbull, have thus focused on how the "artificial creation," a term Turnbull uses, entailed the British establishment of entrepôt trade on the island that is often presented as one that is uncontested and unproblematic.[1]

These prevailing narratives fundamentally obscure alternative understandings of the histories of Singapore by overlooking interpretations that are not rooted in the city's urban economic and political landscape. Among the host of alternative perspectives of the Singaporean past, for example, is one that takes into consideration the rural sectors on the island. Such a history would emphasize the presence of some 20 to 30 Chinese gambier

---

[1] C.M. Turnbull, *The Straits Settlements 1826–67: Indian Presidency to Crown Colony* (London: Athlone Press, 1972), p. 190; Edwin Lee, *Singapore: The Unexpected Nation* (Singapore: Institute of Southeast Asian Studies, 2008), p. 273; Nicole Tarulevicz, "History Making in Singapore: Who is Producing the Knowledge?" *New Zealand Journal of Asian Studies* 11, 1 (2009): 402–25.

plantations operating on the island prior to the arrival of the East India Company in 1819.[2] Following the establishment of a European presence, there was a period of rapid plantation growth, mainly for gambier and black pepper, when capitalist agricultural enterprises led to a clearing of the natural vegetation that reflected attempts to dominate nature and the environment beyond the harbor. The English administrators, and Chinese agriculturalists, looked beyond the port and its trade, seeing an environment that could be shaped for profits. In addition to export crops, such as gambier and pepper, these rural sectors—beyond the Municipality—provided food and sustenance to the colony, and even allowed for self-sufficient food production of pork and eggs as recently as the 1980s.[3] Fundamentally, approaches rooted solely in a consideration of economic and political functioning of a port have limited our understanding of the Singaporean past as well as how humans have interacted with and understood their environment in which they lived on the island.

To understand the development of agriculture and the rural sector in Singapore requires "relational thinking," which will allow for an understanding of people and the environment.[4] This complementary perspective replaces the rigid dichotomy of nature and culture in order to regain a proper understanding of their reciprocal relations. People inhabit what Richard Schweder calls "intentional worlds," in which human beings are "environmentally situated agents" who are at once both "organisms within systems of ecological relations, and as persons within systems of social

---

[2] Wee Yeow Chin and Richard Corlett, *The City and the Forest: Plant Life in Urban Singapore* (Singapore: Singapore University Press, 1986), p. 1.

[3] C.M. Turnbull, *A History of Singapore, 1819–1988* (Singapore: Oxford University Press, 1989); Lee, *Singapore*, p. 8. In a recent study on the history of pig farming in Singapore, Puah You Kai presents a survey of the historiographical oversights in existing scholarship for failing to recognize the fact that a rural sector, which actually played an important role in the country's economy, once existed in Singapore. Puah You Kai, "Pig Farming and the State: Re-Thinking Rural Development in Post-Independent Singapore (1965–1990)," unpublished B.A. (Honours) thesis, Department of History, National University of Singapore, 2012. A number of different sources discuss the achievement of food self-sufficiency in Singapore. Please see the excerpts from the Primary Production Department included in this volume.

[4] Tim Ingold, *The Perception of the Environment: Essays in Livelihood, Dwelling and Skill* (London: Routledge, 2000), p. 5.

relations."[5] Environments are filled with forces of agency and intentionality and thus brim with life. They are not simply physical surfaces upon which human history is scrawled. Rather, as Tim Ingold argues, "history is the process wherein both people and their environments are continually bringing each other into being."[6] This is an observation resonating Karl Marx's earlier assertion that "history itself is a real part of natural history—of nature developing into man."[7] Therefore, they constitute a whole: not as a bounded entity but "a *process* in real time: a process, that is, of growth or development."[8] Environments are themselves essentially history because they are constantly formed and shaped in the course of our lives—in that human beings shape them as much as they shape human beings. "Environment" is therefore a relative and relational term—that is, shaped and defined by the being whose environment it is. While there can be no environment without organisms, what must not be overlooked too is that there can also be no organism without an environment.[9] Starting from this premise of interagentivity, this ethno-historical account of the agencies and intentionalities of agriculture and farming in Singapore demonstrates what happens when the two are brought into juxtaposition, such that imaginations and social relations are mapped onto spatial relations.

This chapter provides an ethno-historical account of agriculture and farming in Singapore, with a focus on food production. Implicitly, it reverses much received wisdom about their absence and non-existence in the island's post-independence push toward industrialization and urbanization, as well as claims of land scarcity. This will be done by chronicling and analyzing the

[5] Ibid., p. 3; Richard Shweder, "Cultural Psychology—What is It?" in *Cultural Psychology: Essays on Comparative Human Development*, ed. James W. Stigler, Richard A. Shweder, and Gilbert Herdt (Cambridge: Cambridge University Press, 1990), p. 2.

[6] Ibid., p. 87; Adrian Tanner, *Bringing Home Animals: Religious Ideology and Mode of Production of the Mistassini Cree Hunters* (New York: St. Martin's Press, 1979), pp. 137–8; Stephen Gudeman, *Economics as Culture: Models and Metaphors as Livelihood* (London: Routledge and Kegan Paul, 1986), pp. 148–9.

[7] Karl Marx, *Pre-Capitalist Economic Formations*, trans. J. Cohen, ed. E.J. Hobsbawm (London: Lawrence and Wishart, 1964), p. 143.

[8] Ingold, *The Perception of the Environment*, p. 20.

[9] Ibid.; James Jerome Gibson, *The Ecological Approach to Visual Perception* (Boston: Houghton Mifflin, 1979), p. 8; Richard Charles Lewotin, "Organism and Environment," in *Learning, Development and Culture*, ed. Henry C. Plotkin (Chichester: Wiley, 1982), p. 160.

reasons for the following developments in the island's agricultural landscape: first, the role that food cultivation played during the colonial history of Singapore; second, the importance of local family farms in helping the nation achieve food security until their sudden curtailment in the late 1980s; and, finally, the promotion of industrial agrotechnological farms that generated little interest among potential investors. A study of these different phases will provide insights into Singaporean society to reveal how shifts and changes to the environment over time were intertwined with larger ideological and political orientations that influenced how people interacted with and understood their environment and vice versa.

The Rise of Capitalist Agricultural Enterprises and Plantations

From 1819 until 1945, agricultural cultivation in Singapore became locked into a system that British colonialists and worldwide centers of distribution dominated economically cum politically. Although many of the farms were Chinese-owned, and the workers were Chinese, they fed into larger British and Western economic and political systems. As a result, there came an influx of traders and settlers seeking opportunities in this British emporium of the East. Domestic demand for food thus rose. Hence, small-scale local families also increased agricultural output to meet the escalating domestic food needs of the people, alongside the larger plantations producing cash crops, such as gambier, for export.[10]

Interest grew in plantation agriculture for a variety of reasons. First, the profuse natural vegetation led the settlers to believe that the soil was rich enough for the successful cultivation of tropical crops. Second, Singapore's free port status and deep-water harbor were conducive to agricultural trade. The English East India Company encouraged cultivation of export crops, especially spices, to pay for Singapore's administration and protection, as well as to undermine the Dutch monopoly on the spice trade throughout the vast Indonesian Archipelago. After 1834, the withdrawal of the East India Company's trade monopoly in the Straits region also led some of the Company's employees to cultivate export crops as a subsidiary activity. This resulted in many people taking up plantation agriculture as a means of

---

[10] Turnbull, *A History of Singapore*, p. 12; Isher Singh Sekhon, "Agriculture in Singapore (1819–1959)," unpublished academic exercise, Department of Geography, University of Malaya, Singapore, 1961, p. 4.

making money.[11] Within this larger capitalist, export-oriented system, the owners of large plantations were in a better position in comparison to small-scale family farms. This was because the family farmers could not afford to initiate agricultural innovations, which was the purview of wealthy plantation owners, known as "gentleman farmers," who cultivated export crops and were able to maximize their profits. This was a factor that contributed to their enterprise acquiring a strongly capitalistic character.[12]

Chinese businessmen supplied the capitalist plantations with much needed cheap labor via a "Credit Ticket System" of labor recruitment. Under this system, passage for Chinese immigrants was arranged and paid for by agencies that passed on the cost to the employers. The new arrival, or *sinkheh* (Hokkien for "new guest"), paid the debt of his passage expense by working for at least a year at reduced wages. The *sinkheh* also came under a "truck system" whereby "a large portion of their wages took the form of food, clothes and opium."[13] This mode of cheap labor enabled the plantation owners to extend their agricultural activities into the unexploited interior of the island with the result that their presence opened up new lands upon which they laid the necessary infrastructure for the arrival of other groups. While the "environment" occasionally pushed back, such as with tiger attacks in the mid-19th century, the expansion continued and reflected an understanding that nature and the environment could be dominated to achieve their ends. The plantation owners also received more support from the colonial government to expand their investments than did the family farms. The latter were in no position to compete for land at this time. It is noteworthy that the political and economic forces behind the establishment of plantations that brought about an increase in indentured labor also led to other societal spatial rearrangements that reflected societal social relations of the time. For residential purposes, British colonialists put different ethnic groups into specified areas under the control of their own headman. The purpose was to establish law and order in an environment that the British considered as a new frontier.[14]

---

[11] Sekhon, "Agriculture in Singapore," p. 14; Wee and Corlett, *The City and the Forest*, p. 2.

[12] Sekhon, "Agriculture in Singapore."

[13] James C. Jackson, *Planters and Speculators: Chinese and European Agricultural Enterprise in Malaya, 1786–1921* (Singapore: University of Malaya Press, 1968), p. 4.

[14] Turnbull, *A History of Singapore*, p. 12; see also Timothy P. Barnard and Mark Emmanuel's contribution to this volume.

Although plantation agriculture had a promising start, it eventually declined. According to James Jackson, English planters transported their concept of plantation agriculture partly from their traditional European attitude toward landed estates and partly from the experience of European planters with tropical crops from other parts of the British Empire.[15] Hence, they concentrated on crops with long maturation periods although this tied up their capital and land for lengthy periods of time. Their high overheads and organizational rigidity made it difficult for them to change the cultivation of their crops quickly enough in an essentially speculative market. The English planters did not realize until later in the 19th century that the island's lush tropical rainforest was a poor indicator of the quality of the soil. Once the soils had been exhausted, in the mid-19th century, secondary natural vegetation consisting mainly of *lalang* (Malay for *Imperata cylindrica*) came to dominate huge swaths of the island. The coarse *lalang* proved difficult to remove, as its roots are deeply lodged in the soil beyond the reach of fire or other efforts to eliminate them. This in turn made it difficult for other seed types to germinate. Even when the forest could be cleared, plant nutrients rapidly disappeared in the exposed soil. This made the cultivation of long-term crops impractical.[16]

A quick look at the agricultural scene from 1819 to 1945 explains why quick changes in the cultivation of crop type, and market pressures, influenced any agricultural enterprise. The cultivation of nutmeg in the 1830s provides an example. Raffles sent the first nutmeg "plants" to Singapore from Bencoolen in late 1819; they were planted at the base of Government Hill (now Fort Canning Hill). The offspring of these plants soon were established beyond the harbor area, often on the site of former pepper and gambier plantations, by the late 1830s with the main motivation being high prices in international markets. Continuous cultivation of nutmeg, however, taxed the soil, which gambier had already exhausted, too heavily. Followed by a drop in the price of the spice, a massive outbreak of disease—which destroyed most of the trees—and the mistake of planting the trees in the wet season, nutmeg never reached its optimal potential in Singapore. Although nutmeg cultivation continued well into the 19th century, "gentlemen farmers" made a

---

[15] Jackson, *Planters and Speculators*, p. xv.
[16] Ooi Jin Bee, "Agriculture Change in Singapore," *Asian Profile* 1, 2 (1973): 366–7; See Tony O'Dempsey's contribution to this volume.

hurried shift back to gambier cultivation as the international market demand for it grew.[17]

Sugar cane was also an early agricultural product in Singapore, with cultivation beginning in 1823. Failure followed too, however, because of a lack of suitable coastal alluvial soils, higher labor costs as compared to the West Indies an important sugar producer, a limit imposed against Straits Settlement sugar imports into Great Britain, and the exposure of the sugar plantations to attacks from robbers due to their distance from the town center. The plantation agriculturalists also tried cultivating cotton, coffee, cocoa, and pineapple on a commercial basis. Without exception, all failed. In the 1870s, there was a revival of pepper and gambier plantations due to increase demand from Europe and the supply of a bigger immigrant labor force to Singapore. By the late 19th century, even pepper and gambier plantations—the early dominant export crops in Singapore—went into decline due to falling prices, deterioration of soil fertility and the exhaustion of accessible forests.[18] Pineapple, coconut, and rubber would now dominate agriculture in Singapore until 1945.

The first coconut plantations were established in the 1830s. They were a success because of their coastal location, appropriate soils, and good local and export markets. Yet, attacks by the red beetle led to a decline in the number of these plantations beginning in 1881, and many were switched to rubber between 1911 and 1926. A revival in coconut plantations took place in 1931 because of the increased demand for coconut oil and fresh coconut. After 1945, urban encroachment on coconut plantations resulted in the land being converted to other purposes.[19]

By 1910 pineapple plantations also ceased due to overproduction and marketing difficulties. The seasonal ripening of pineapples led to production

---

[17] Thomas Oxley, "Some Account of the Nutmeg and Its Cultivation," *Journal of the Indian Archipelago and Eastern Asia* 2, 10 (1848): 641–60; Wee and Corlett, *The City and the Forest*, pp. 2–8; Sekhon, "Agriculture in Singapore," p. 16; Paul Wheatley, "Land Use in the Vicinity of Singapore in the Eighteen-Thirties," *Malayan Journal of Tropical Geography* 2 (1954): 66. See also Tony O'Dempsey's contribution to this volume.

[18] By 1897, an overproduction of pepper also led to a drastic fall in its international market price. *Agricultural Bulletin Straits and Federated Malay States* (Singapore: Government Printing Press, 1905), p. 304; Sekhon, "Agriculture in Singapore," pp. 20–5.

[19] Sekhon, "Agriculture in Singapore," pp. 20–38; *Annual Report of the Agricultural Department, 1947* (Singapore: Government Printing Office, 1948), p. 3.

in large quantities that required immediate disposal. Prices fell to as low as one cent per fruit. Due to inadequate capital and credit obligations arising from loans taken before the sale of the fruits, the pineapple canners could not wait for more favorable market situations in London and Liverpool and huge losses were incurred. The second revival of plantation pineapple cultivation started after 1926 with the rapid growth of the canning industry. When the world depression hit Singapore in the early 1930s though, canned pineapples, which were a luxury product, declined in demand. Prices fell again and pineapple cultivation—which also faced fierce competition from Hawaii, which produced a better quality fruit—became unprofitable. During the war, exports of pineapple to the United Kingdom—the main consumer—stopped; plantations and canneries fell into neglect and were abandoned, their machinery stripped and converted to other uses.[20]

While coconut and pineapple plantations were present in late colonial Singapore, rubber was the king. Huge swaths of the Malay Peninsula came under rubber cultivation, and in Singapore rubber trees took over large portions of the rural sector. The growth of the motorcar industry fuelled much of this boom. In 1910, the price of rubber was over 12 shillings per pound, giving stimulus for plantations to venture into rubber cultivation. At this point, Chinese planters joined the scene to take advantage of the Agricultural Department's policy of distributing the supply of rubber seeds. Post-First World War economic problems, and rubber price fluctuations that began in 1920, as well as the economic depression of the 1930s, however, created further difficulties. Combined with decreased soil fertility and the International Rubber Regulation Agreement in 1934, which prohibited the planning of additional areas of rubber, there was ultimately a decline in its cultivation.[21]

Family farms that focused on the production of a variety of crops—including sweet potatoes, plantains, corn, yams, *kaladie* (a yam), cabbages, and other local vegetables—for sale to local markets had existed alongside large capitalist plantations since the early colonial period. They rarely appeared in the historical record. By 1848, however, there were at least 378 acres of small-scale family-run vegetable farms clustered mainly around the Braddell Road area, and this would continue to expand over the next century due to an increasing population, and their food needs. In 1931, in spite of the limited land available, family farmers produced nearly self-sufficient

[20] Wee and Corlett, *The City and the Forest*, p. 8; Ooi, "Agriculture Change in Singapore," pp. 367–8.
[21] Ibid.; Sekhon, "Agriculture in Singapore," pp. 36–7.

quantities of vegetables for the population. The vegetables grown included "lettuce, cabbage, onions, parsley, celery, spinach, mint, cucumber, cow peas, radish, loofah, lady's finger, brinjal, french beans, bitter gourd, yam, bean, sweet potato, tapioca, groundnut and soya bean."[22]

The Chinese agriculturalists who oversaw these family farms were able to prosper in difficult economic times due to their flexibility. They grew different types of crops, which reflected how they perceived and interacted with their environment and, hence, their different motivations and goals. For example, many of these Chinese planters overcame the problem of soil erosion through shifting cultivation. After exhausting the soil fertility, they left devastated lands of *lalang* and *belukar* (Malay for "secondary forest"). As Ooi Jin Bee argued in an influential article in the 1970s, "a raw, pioneering laissez-faire atmosphere and a sparsely populated country with seemingly endless miles of jungle-covered potential agricultural land for the taking" motivated their actions.[23] They spurned any enterprise that did not offer quick returns on small capital investments. They thus cultivated short-term crops such as tapioca, which required simpler and less expensive equipment. Plantation agriculture was organized on a high overhead and rigid organizational structure that made it unable to adjust rapidly enough to the price fluctuations of crops. Subsequently, this led to the financial downfall of many plantations. Throughout this period, some plantations also grew tapioca, coffee, indigo, and lemongrass. However, unlike small-scale family farms, these plantations failed due to difficulty in reaping profits out of these crops on the scale in which they were grown. Less capital outlay was required and they could respond faster to changing market conditions.[24]

The Japanese occupation of Singapore also played an important role in the shift from cash crop plantations to food production on small farms. Just before the Japanese invasion in 1941, the colonial government began a campaign promoting "grow your own vegetables," which emphasized food and fruit cultivation. These efforts gained momentum during the Japanese occupation as acute food shortages induced many farmers to undertake vegetable cultivation, leading to the conversion of many of the remaining plantations to food cultivation. By 1945, family farms had become the most important agricultural activity, and the shift from pre-war production was

[22] Sekhon, "Agriculture in Singapore," pp. 23–40.
[23] Ooi, "Agriculture Change in Singapore," p. 366.
[24] Jackson, *Planters and Speculators*, pp. xv, 5.

startling. "Vegetable production had quadrupled to 55 tons a day over pre-war production," according to one report. The acreage under cultivation had also risen from 3,000 in 1939 to 9,400 in 1946. Family farmers increased from 6,356 in 1931 to 18,746 in 1947. Plantations, which had dominated the agricultural sector for more than a century, had given way to cost-effective family farms. In addition, as the plantations gradually disappeared, more land became available to family farmers.[25]

"Farms," "Farmers," Family Farms, and Self-Sufficiency

After 1945, family farms continued to concentrate on the production of food crops and livestock. Even when the acreage available to agriculture declined as more land was taken up for housing needs, family farms survived. They were more flexible, due to their relatively smaller size compared to plantations, which allowed the family farm to meet demand fluctuations in crop type in a capitalistic market economy. The intensive farming methods were producing as much as 12 to 13 crops per year of cabbages, lettuce, radishes, watercress, and herbs. In fact, as land for agriculture decreased, vegetable yields increased due to the intensive methods of cultivation that involved using large quantities of indigenous fertilizers, such as river sludge, burned soil, prawn dust, and coconut-based compost. Family farmers also practiced integrated farming or mixed farming. Many Chinese family farmers, for instance, kept pigs, whose droppings formed good manure for vegetables. The "vegetable-pig combination" was ideal for maintaining soil fertility. The pigs fed on discarded vegetables, sweet potato stems, and water hyacinth, and in return, they provided nearly all the manure needed for the vegetable beds. Family farmers also cultivated a large variety of fruit trees. Chinese family farmers who reared pigs especially favored bananas, as the stem could be boiled and used to supplement the commercially prepared fodder. The symbiosis between pig farming and vegetable growing was ecologically sound.[26]

In many respects, the use of terms such a "farmer" or "family farm" reflects the various attitudes of those in power. By the early 20th century, the "agriculturalists" on large-scale plantations transformed into "market

---

[25] Ibid., pp. 40–2; *Singapore Annual Report* (Singapore: Government Printing Office, 1946).

[26] Sekhon, "Agriculture in Singapore," pp. 45–7.

gardeners," based on terms British colonial administers developed to describe their activities. In 1959, following the establishment of "self-governance," the Primary Production Department was formed through the merger of five government agencies: the Agriculture Division, the Veterinary Division, the Co-operative Division, the Fisheries Division, and the Rural Division. Initially, its mission was to coordinate the development and regulation of local farming and fishery industries. Officials of the Primary Production Department continued to use the phrase "market gardeners" to describe those engaged in agriculture in the early 1960s. The label "farmer" was used for the first time in 1968 after a change in the governmental administration of agriculture in Singapore.[27]

The change to the label "farmer" came about when the island gained independence in 1965, and it reflected a changing understanding of their position in the society. A statistician at the Department of Statistics, National Development Board explained that when this change took place, "farmer" was defined as "more for those people commonly found in Lim Chu Kang and Choa Chu Kang." According to officials at the Primary Production Department, these were areas in Singapore that were associated with family farms which produced vegetables, eggs, pigs, chickens, orchids, home plants, freshwater and marine fish, aquarium fish and plants, ducks, and other items.[28] In this new conceptualization, the term "farmer" became associated with a rural, backward peasantry that was traditional, and lacked education, organization, and structure. A farmer was thought of as a person with low status due to "lack of skill" and who is "not productive enough" because of his lack of formal education. In 1968, the Republic began licensing all farms engaged in market gardening, animal husbandry, and mixed farming, thus transforming how they would be understood and regulated. A total of 20,254 farms were licensed in the month-long campaign.[29] The change in terminology was as explained by Choo L.W., a Primary Production official in charge of the licensing of farms:

> In the past, during the period when Singapore was considered Malaya, we don't call people who are cultivating the food crops etc. farmers. We

---

[27] *Primary Production Department Annual Report* (Singapore: Government Printing Office, 1968).

[28] The Department has since taken on new functions such as overseeing food safety testing and to facilitating agri-trade for the nation (http://www.ava.gov.sg/AboutAVA/History/ [accessed 23 Nov. 2012]).

[29] Ibid.

call them gardeners. Because in European concept, farms are huge so you don't call any place a farm, but a market garden. So the person running a place is a market gardener. So from history [there have been] some changes from the old days to today ... Formerly, before 1968, it was the Agricultural Department that took care of welfare of the farmers. Then in 1968, we start to license "farmers." We issue a license for a "farmer" but in the context of the Singapore 'farmer'—having a place which is used for farming and a tract of land which is used by him to carry out farming—so we let him apply for a license. [Interview in English]

The term "family farms" in this chapter refers to organizational structures where at least one-third of the farm labor is family based and there are no formal principles of accounting or labor recruitment.

Despite attitudes that these "farmers" were backward, over nine percent of the Singaporean population worked on these farms, often cloaked in a nationalistic-independence attitude. Their labor provided for remarkable developments in food production in Singapore from the late 1960s until the 1980s. These family farms were the cornerstone of food security. They promoted food self-sufficiency in a small, vulnerable island state by limiting vulnerability to increases in costs of imported food and curtailing dependence on outside sources for food supply that was subject to fluctuations in the international commodity pricing system.[30]

As a young graduate student, I observed, researched, and spoke with many of the people on these farms during fieldwork I carried out from June 1986 to January 1989 while a student at the National University of Singapore.[31] This was a poignant period when many farms were either waiting or already under official survey for resettlement compensation. Many farmers were therefore highly suspicious of authorities or persons bearing any kind of official letter. They complained about university researchers coming to their farms, as they felt these academics "asked too many questions and had taken up too much of [their] time away from [their] work." In view of these difficulties, I decided to employ a participant-observation approach in carrying out this historical ethnographic study. To carry out my fieldwork in as non-threatening a manner as possible, I simply walked into the farms and

---

[30] Please see the excerpts from the Primary Production Department's Annual Reports included in this volume.

[31] The interviews in this chapter are taken from the resulting Master's thesis: Cynthia Chou Gek Hua, "Farmers in Singapore: The Rural Sector in Transition," unpublished thesis, Department of Sociology, National University of Singapore, 1989.

introduced myself as someone who needed their help in writing "a book." By walking, I was able to explore some of the narrow and winding farm routes. It also impressed upon the farmers that I was not on official business. The fatigue that showed on my face sometimes won their sympathy, which often led to the beginning of our conversations. When rapport was established, I began to work alongside them. I met most of my informants through introductions, whereby one farmer would introduce me to other neighboring farmers, and so forth. Interviews on family farms were carried out in Teochew, Hokkien, Mandarin, and English. Unlike the informal manner in which I entered the family farms, I had to submit formal requests for my entry to the industrial farms and to interviews with government officials as well as state planners, usually by way of numerous official telephone enquiries and the presentation of several letters verifying my status as a researcher from the university. Data was also gathered by archival research—by reading official annual reports, parliamentary debates, speeches, newspaper articles, agricultural brochures, and pamphlets. Through this research, I gained insight into the role that agriculture played in the history of early independent Singapore, and how "farmers" living in rural areas of Singapore understood their role in society.

Unlike plantation owners, family farmers had no difficulty in identifying themselves as "farmers." Euphemisms were not needed. Farming activities that involved hands-on work were regarded as a "natural process" of life. As Mr. Sung, a fruit farmer in Lim Chu Kang explained in 1989, when the Primary Production Department was closing down these enterprises:

> Now, [the phasing out of farms] not proper system. Not natural. Natural one: grow district to district. Take away trees that bear a lot of fruit … you destroy … breaking natural resources. Farming natural … no need to learn. [Interview in English]

Family farmers referred to themselves according to what was raised on their farms—for example, "raise chickens ducks people," "grow vegetables people," and "rear cows people."[32] Their identity rested deeply in the way they perceived their farming activities. They saw themselves interacting in harmony with the ecological system, enhancing it to bring out its abundant food supply to support and sustain human life, not altering it. As Ang Ah

---

[32] In Teochew, and using the modern transliteration system into English, the phrase is: "*qi7 goi1 ah4 gai5 nang5, zeng3 cai3 gai5 nang5 or qi7 ghu5 gai5 nang5.*"

Bee, a pig farmer in Jalan Kayu lamented in 1989 when her farm was being phased out:

> It is good to farm. We can plant the basic necessities in our own land here and even help others in need. If this were not the case, we would all have died during the Japanese occupation. We helped each other survive. It is also cheap and fresh. So you tell me, what is going to happen when we face another dangerous situation? During the war, we provided the soldiers with vegetables. What is going to happen now? We are going to die! Soon, they will take away my land. There will not be enough land to grow our basic necessities. [Translated from Teochew]

Family farmers saw themselves as contributors toward putting the nation-state of Singapore in a more independent and less vulnerable position in which the country no longer had to rely totally on outsiders for its food needs, an important ideal in a rapidly decolonizing world. Even though they faced stigmatization because of the "rough work" they did as compared to the "gentlemen farmers" of the plantations, they legitimated their hands-on work by claiming to be patriotic protectors of a nation who till the soil to feed the people, especially in crisis situations, allowing the nation to develop food security. They also saw themselves as providing the people with reasonably priced basic needs, local produce, exotics, and quality produce.

Although family farmers were enjoying high profits, they were not without problems. Monsoons and bad drainage flooded lowland farms, epidemics of pests, price fluctuations in vegetable seeds from China and Thailand, and onion bulbs from Madras, the prohibition of pig rearing in the municipal area in addition to the increasing demand for housing land were but some of the challenges they had to overcome. Family farmers intensified their farming operations to attain higher returns per unit area. In fact, in spite of these difficulties, family farms survived during the period 1947–56 largely because of the considerable profits obtained, which further attracted people to farming. Singapore relied mainly on the family farmers for its supply of fresh vegetables, root crops, fruits, pigs, poultry and eggs.[33]

In the face of adversities, family farmers persisted in their search for ways to ensure the survival of their farms for reasons beyond mere economic gains. The authorities, working on rational bureaucratic principles, slighted

---

[33] *Annual Report of the Agricultural Department, 1950* (Singapore: Government Printing Office, 1951), p. 3.

these efforts as "superstitious" and "traditional." Religion played a vital role in the work activities of family farmers as well as in the way they interacted with the environment. The gods of the environment interacted with them by becoming the providers in times of difficulty. Rather than exercising domination over the environment, family farmers considered it necessary to work harmoniously with it. Altars were often found on their farms. Most Chinese farmers had an altar for the Chinese deity Grand Uncle Lord (大伯公) on their farms.[34] Farmers who tilled the land worshipped Earth Ancestor (地祖), the landlord god.[35] Vegetable farmers usually placed an altar for Earth Ancestor in the open facing their farm, which they would consult on the varieties of vegetables to be grown in the farm. In addition, the first and fifteenth of every month on the lunar calendar would be celebrated in honor of Earth Ancestor. Fruits also had different origins and thus had to be given due respect. Mr. Sung, a former fruit farmer, explained this in great length:

> Chinese pray for luck. Never mind which god. We pray to fruit god for more fruits. When my grandmother die, must tie white cloth to all the durian tree planted by her, so all the tree must mourn or will die. If anyone die, durians most important to mourn. Durians most *pantang* [prohibitions by taboo]. You can give urine to durians, but if you give cat, dog or people shit, they die. You can't play the fool with any plant. Why? I tell you story of how all fruits started. Story is can't pray to durian tree because durian are shit of Three Treasures (三寶公, or 'of the Buddha'), a Chinese god, who hate Malays so used his shit to trick them.[36] That's why durians look like shit. Also, can't pray to guava. This is the story. Soul/Spirit (靈): playboy god.[37] One day, the goddess took him back and killed him. But Soul/Spirit, a naughty god said that even if I die, my generation will live on. So Soul/Spirit put a lot of seeds in the guava. That's why guava grow in two by two representing human testes. That's why cannot give this fruit to gods. But now that got guava, it show that generation of this god still around. The starfruit like a star. When a child is born, child is given a new star in the sky. So we can't pray with

---

[34] *Dua7 beh4 gong1* (Grand Uncle Lord) is a local god who is believed to take care of the family and their farming activities. Vivienne Wee, "Religion and Ritual among the Chinese of Singapore: An Ethnographic Study," unpublished Masters in Social Science thesis, Department of Sociology, University of Singapore, 1977.

[35] In the modern transliteration system, "Earth Ancestor" is *Di7 zou2*. In the original, the speaker said the names of the various gods and spirits that follow in local dialect.

[36] In the modern transliteration system, "Three Treasures" is *Sa1 bo2 gong1*.

[37] In the modern transliteration system, "Soul/Spirit" is *Leng5*.

starfruit. I tell you another story. Now got land and grass. Some people say: bird shit, then grass grow. No! What happened is this. Jade Emperor in heaven tell a general in heaven to come down and give people rice and grass. This general naughty. He tell people must walk three footsteps to get one grass; walk three miles then get one rice. Then he went back. People short of rice *lah* ... because three footsteps get one grass. Land all grass. Nothing to eat. After investigation, Jade Emperor punished the general who said that he cannot do anything so general become a cow. Went down to earth to eat all the grass and do work for the rice field. Cows eat all sorts of grass so that won't grow so much grass. So cows do this two type of work. That's why we never eat beef. So actually people pity and respect the general. The cow is something like a Chinese god. So we pray and not eat him—or the other gods will not like you and will not hear your prayers. Cow become proud and big, so even the gods respect him. [Interview in English]

Remarkably, family farms benefitted from the industrialization program that many nations, including Singapore, embarked on in the 1960s. Primary among these benefits was the development of innovations in industrially manufactured fertilizers and machinery that enabled family farms to intensify their agricultural output. An increasing population in Singapore meant that all of the island's agricultural production had to focus by sheer necessity on the needs of the home-market, rather than on exports. Industrialization also brought forth increased investment possibilities outside agriculture. Plantation agriculturalists who could no longer draw a profit from their scale of farming began to move their investments away from agriculture and toward other more profitable industrializing sectors. Furthermore, as the labor supply no longer worked on the credit ticket system after the Second World War, plantation owners could no longer secure cheap labor. To compensate for this shortfall, farms deployed family labor and therefore did not have to pay regular wages. Although industrialization also offered employment opportunities outside the farm, many family farmers who lacked education preferred to remain self-employed. The improvement in transport possibilities also offered opportunities for family farmers to settle and establish farms further inland and to grow highly perishable crops.

Cultivators ensured continuity of family farms through kinship ties and a deep sense of belonging. Family farms were perceived as family heirlooms; marriage alliances were forged with other families to strengthen farming networks; and, farming skills were closely guarded and transmitted from one generation to the next within the family. In his study of family farms in Singapore, Rodolphe De Koninck revealed significant correlations between the various categories of family size, farm size, and type.[38] He showed that for reasons of historical settlement, the longer established families held larger farms and were more inclined to concentrate on livestock rearing or mixed farming. This was because contacts and credentials for obtaining proper capital could only be obtained over time. To the family farmers, the farm was an environment that encompassed both home and workplace, as expressed by Mr. Tai, a chicken farmer speaking in 1989 from his farm in Choa Chu Kang:

> This is my birthplace. When I wake up each morning, I know I have decent work to do. I also enjoy strolling around my farm during my leisure hours. Even if it rains for a whole week, I must carry on working, but it is because I want to work. [Translated from interview in Teochew]

Similar sentiments were echoed by other family farmers such as Mr. Lim, a chicken and vegetable farmer in Choa Chu Kang:

> Naturally, I have sentiments towards the land ... No words can express how I feel. Do you know how much this land means to me? My father had nothing except this piece of land to make a living. Who doesn't treasure his father's heritage? [Translated from interview in Mandarin]

A sense of loyalty to both their family and farm motivated them to identify their land as their source of life. All of these factors thus contributed greatly to the survival and success of family farms.

The total amount of vegetables family farms produced between 1960 and 1967 increased from 39,350 tons to 40,200 tons, despite decreasing acreage under cultivation from 7,720 to 7,180. The production of fruits, whose acreage decreased from 5,000 to 4,510 over the same period of time, also experienced an increase, from 3,260 to 4,510 tons. By 1968, family farms were producing 40,200 tons of vegetables, 935,000 pigs, 23 million fowl, 1.5 million ducks, 3,500 cattle, 2,000 goats and 315 million eggs with a total value of S$285 million, thus releasing an enormous sum of foreign exchange that would have otherwise been spent on imports.[39]

---

[38] Rodolphe De Koninck, "Chinese Farmers of Singapore: A Study in Social Geography," unpublished PhD dissertation, Department of Geography, University of Singapore, 1971.

[39] See the *Annual Report* of the Primary Production Department (Singapore: Government Printing Office, 1960–67); in addition, see the excerpts from these reports, of later years, included in this volume.

In spite of limited land resources, family farms achieved self-sufficiency (or close to it) in pigs, poultry, and eggs from 1964 until 1990. In fact, there was such an overproduction of pigs in 1971 and 1972 that it caused a decrease in their price. Family farms were also meeting 50 percent of the nation's vegetable needs and 30 percent of its fish needs.[40] Many kinds of leafy vegetables were harvested in quick succession throughout the year for the local market. Unlike plantation agriculture, small-scale family farms could practice crop rotation more easily to preserve soil fertility, as this is usually practiced on family farms in hilly areas. The usual order of rotation between one year to one and a half years is: leafy vegetables, followed by tobacco and fruit vegetables (for example, cucumber and bitter gourd). Mixed farming was also common amongst family farmers where pigs and poultry were kept in conjunction with food crop cultivation. In spite of land limitations, agricultural production increased.[41] Beginning in 1971, efforts were even made to find new markets for the export of canned meat and meat products. These agricultural efforts continued throughout the 1970s, and well into the 1980s, and were tremendously successful (see Table 8.1). In a January 1984 article in *The Straits Times*, the role of these family farms in development strategies was stated very clearly: "self-sufficiency in food has become a priority."[42] This would rapidly change.

Table 7.1 Singapore food production in 1982[43]

	Number	*Self Sufficiency*
Pigs	895,000	95%
Hens' eggs	524.9 mil	100%
Chickens	32 mil	70%
Ducks	4.39 mil	70%
Fish	18,000 tons	25%
Vegetables	40,150 tons	25%

[40] Puah, "Pig Farming and the State."

[41] *Annual Report of the Primary Production Department* (Singapore: Government Printing Office, 1971).

[42] Evangeline Gamboa and Lillian Chew, "Singapore Sets its Sights on Feeding Itself," *The Straits Times*, 17 Jan. 1984, p. 22.

[43] Gamboa and Chew, "Singapore Sets Its Sights on Feeding Itself."

The Phasing Out of Family Farms

Singapore had become, and remained, self-reliant in selected agricultural products throughout the 1980s. The pursuit of independence—food security—from external suppliers and the consequent reduction in the country's vulnerability to price increases of imported food was a point of government pride. Moreover, family farms were clearly well-developed and efficient. In January 1984, however, Prime Minister Lee Kuan Yew appointed "government trouble-shooter" Goh Keng Swee to be the Director of the Primary Production Department. Goh was an eminent official in the Singaporean government, having served in various capacities as First Deputy Prime Minister, Minister of Education, and Chairman of the Monetary Authority of Singapore throughout his tenure in the government. As the new Director of the Primary Production Department, he was tasked with paying particular attention to the economic aspects of agricultural production with a view toward generating still more revenue; getting the most food out of the island's limited agricultural land at the lowest prices; and, reducing the nation's food dependence on other countries for food supplies. Instead, Goh advocated that farms be phased out. This was in direct contradiction to the government's pre-1984 policy that regarded achieving self-sufficiency in food production as a national priority. The reverse in policy was so abrupt that it surprised many state officials, including Ngiam Tong Tau, the previous Director of the Primary Production Department.[44]

Being a major figure in the country's modernization efforts, Goh had a different approach to understanding the environment. In his view, agriculture, the farmer, and the rural environment all represented peasantry and back-wardness and, therefore, had no place in Singapore's modernization program. The environment had to be transformed to create an island city-state. His views about the place of farmers were clear:

> It is better to leave the peasant and his quaint ways to the anthropologist. For those who are interested in the modernization process, the crucial area of study lies in the cities. It is here that the transformation is taking place and the interaction between old cultural systems and values and new ones take on the most acute form. It is here that the breakthrough to modernity for the whole nation will take place through the accumulation of wealth and the earning of surplus value on an ever-increasing scale by the application of modern science and technology.[45]

---

[44] Ibid.; Puah, "Pig Farming and the State," pp. 33–40.
[45] Goh Keng Swee, *The Economics of Modernization and Other Essays* (Singapore: Asia Pacific House, 1972), p. 16.

Goh assumed his new responsibility over the Primary Production Department on 17 January 1984. Although he would retire from government service by the end of the year, he took on his new task with vigor. On 13 March, he reworked the policy of self-sufficiency, deciding to initially focus on pig farms as they created a tremendous amount of pollution, potentially sullying waterways and water supplies. Later, he extended his argument to include the phasing out of all other types of farms, including vegetable and fruit farms. He pointed out that the agricultural policy would be reworked so that it was no longer Singapore's aim to achieve self-sufficiency in primary produce, believing it was better to focus on what the nation could do best—producing goods and services in which it had a competitive edge over others.[46]

In the case of pig farming, Goh presented an argument that the estimated costs for treating pig waste was too high to be acceptable, and that more stringent pollution controls in the future would push the cost still higher. While there was some truth in this, his argument ignored prospects of cost savings. There is documented evidence that treated waste can be put to good use, thus offsetting some waste treatment costs. Waste treatment can even prove profitable.[47] Moreover, the regulations set by the authorities for family farmers to clean up pig waste were not expected to cause any sharp increase in the market price of pigs. Although the added costs were likely to range from S$10 to S$15 a year per pig according to the Primary Production Department, this added cost was still cheaper than imported pigs. It was estimated that the cost of production for local pigs was S$234.50 per 100 kilograms at 1984 land rental rates. For imports from Thailand, the cost was between S$316 per 100 kilograms—the breakdown being S$220 per 100 kilograms for production and S$96 for transportation. A waste-treatment plant for 6,000 pigs was estimated to cost S$105,000 annually. As farms produced at least two cycles of pigs annually, waste treatment cost could be reduced from S$17.50 to S$8.75 per pig. Waste treatment could even lead to biogas, a valuable by-product obtainable to generate electricity, which would further reduce the cost per pig to S$5.50.[48]

Despite such arguments, the policy had been set. The Agrotechnology Promotion Unit of the Primary Production Department of the Ministry of

---

[46] "Self-Sufficiency Not the Aim," *The Straits Times*, 18 Mar. 1984, p. 9.

[47] Puah, "Pig Farming and the State," pp. 38–9.

[48] Evangeline Gamboa, "Clean Up Costs of Pig Farms," *The Straits Times*, 28 Jan. 1984, p. 15.

National Development was tasked with opening investment opportunities for the development of agrotechnology projects and services in aquaculture, horticulture, livestock, and other services. Singaporean authorities quickly worked toward transforming all farmlands into agrotechnology parks for high-technology farming and consultancy services. The parks were to serve as demonstration sites for potential investors, and to allow for the development of expertise that would enable local professionals to market their agricultural knowledge and skills throughout the world, especially in tropical regions. The plans called for the development of ten agrotechnology parks, with the smallest taking up two hectares.[49]

Interestingly, the reworking of the entire agricultural policy in 1984 mirrored the development of plantation agriculture in Singapore. Like plantation agriculture, which concentrated on the cultivation of export crops, the goal of these industrial agrotechnological farms was to establish money-making ventures aimed at the production of high-value produce for export or for consumption in a local specialized market. The focus was thus not on producing for domestic needs. With this export orientation, industrial agrotechnological products would also be subject to the international pricing system as was the case with plantation produce. Finally, just as plantation agriculture received the support of colonial governments, industrial agrotechnological farms were only established after the government offered tax and financial incentives—such as pioneer service incentive, investment allowance incentive, operational headquarters incentive, export services incentive, and financial assistance schemes—to promote industrial farming.

The similarities between agrotechnological farms and plantations of the earlier period in Singapore's history of agriculture were a reversal of the pre-1984 agricultural policy of supporting the development of family farms. This reversal, however, can also be interpreted as re-integrating the agricultural sector into the mainstream ideology of a knowledge economy and moving Singapore from the stage of national capitalism to global capitalism. According to S. Rajaratnam, a key voice in the Singaporean government:

> The new capitalism is a global capitalism as distinct from national capitalism which is really a throwback of the old capitalism.
>   … the new global capitalism which is already in our midst must emerge victorious simply because it is the only capitalism which can

---

[49] *Singapore Services: A Key Area of Growth* (Singapore: Economic Development Board, 1989).

organize globally and use effectively the fabulous new technologies that are already here and the many more new technologies now taking shape in the laboratories and in the imagination of thousands of scientists and technologists throughout the world.

Eventually, national capitalisms must go ... This is because all national capitalisms, big and small, today live and prosper by tapping the world market that global capitalism is creating and expanding. Without the world market, national capitalisms will wither away.[50]

Global capitalism would be triumphant in Singapore.

With the shift away from family farmers, Singaporean officials now had to convince people of the economic rationality of such a move. More importantly, they had to construct a new image of what it meant to be a farmer and how people should interact with their environment and vice versa. One of the greatest problems was the term "farmer" itself which was too closely associated with living in rural areas, with the involvement of the family unit, and with people lacking formal education. Indeed, it was a term that the planners themselves had long created to denote low occupational prestige. The term generated prejudice, having taken on the stigma of "no career prospects" in an industrialized Singapore, crystallizing barriers and hindering people from moving into agriculture in Singapore. The authorities, therefore, were now confronted with the necessity of creating more complimentary job designations with which to persuade a new group of people to move into agrotechnological farming. New terms were constructed to suit the needs of this newly created agricultural sector, just as had been done in the language of commerce, science, and technology. In other words, this linguistic play was considered necessary to reconstruct farming as a middle class profession in a new environment. To connote glamour and professionalism, when tertiary graduates were encouraged to go into farming, they were told of job opportunities in the farming industry not as "farmers," but as "managers, zoologists, botanists, nutritionists, geneticists, microbiologists, veterinarians and specialists in horticulture and acquaculture" because "[i]n the eyes of a scientist, farms are excellent research laboratories."[51]

The phasing out of what the Primary Production Department termed as "traditional farmers," also led to a disappearance of the "rural sector" in

[50] S. Rajaratnam, "Global Capitalism is Wave of the Future," *The Straits Times*, 16 Aug. 1989, p. 25.

[51] *National University of Singapore Gazette 1987*, 1–7 (1987): 69.

Singapore. These areas included Mandai, Lim Chu Kang, Choa Chu Kang, Sembawang, Old Tampines, and Punggol—that is, the outskirts of the city area. Although these very same areas housed agrotechnology farms, they were not "rural," as the term connoted ideas of being backward, traditional and divorced from the industrialized city center. While they may be "rural," the "agrotechnology parks" became clearly situated in a configuration of a Singaporean economy focused on high technology and industrialization.

With shifts in the ideology of Singapore's state planners, it soon became difficult to define and identify who and what was farming in Singapore. State planners and people working on industrial farms both acknowledged that "farming" was carried out in high-technology farms, but experienced difficulty in identifying who the "farmers" were in such industrial operations. Below are abstracts of three interviews carried out in the late 1980s with officials that reveal the root of the problem.

> **Mr. Kee H.S.**: It is very difficult to define who the 'farmer' is in an agrotechnology farm. It is because of culture. It is whether the people themselves identify themselves as farmers. I don't know how to answer your question [as to who the farmer is in the case of high-technology farming]. (Telephone interview in English with a Primary Production Department official who was overseeing the introduction of industrial agrotechnological farms in 1989)

> **Mr. Poh**: Those doing the actual farming are those in Lim Chu Kang … places like that. They do the watering of vegetables, planting and all that. But for those in the high-tech farming, when we categorise them for our labour force survey, it depends on which company they work for. They are not categorized under farmers. They call themselves professionals, not farmers. Like technician in biochemistry, manager in pig-farming. You see, if they are graduates, they are 'qualified farmers', so that they are called chemists, managers, technical or research officers because they are doing a lot of research work also. Because the company that they are in may be developing more on biological chemical than actual farming although they may also grow things. Perhaps the labourers are the farmers. So when we do our listing, we categorize them under occupation and industry. There isn't really an occupation as a farmer in such industries. So our code for farmers will be much more reduced through the years. When we can't categorize them, we put them under the 'others' category until the next review when we create a new category for these people. This is because this category cannot be too big. (Telephone interview in English with a statistician involved in occupational categorizing at the Department of Statistics, National Development Board)

Mr. Choo L.W.: The licensee is the farmer. That means that he takes the land to farm. However, if it is a company that takes up the license which is also possible, then the company is the licensee. (Interview with an official at the Primary Production Department headquarters in charge of issuing farm licenses)

Since state planners felt uncomfortable with designating the term "farmer" to agrotechnologists because of the low status they accord to this term, agrotechnologists felt this discomfort too. Furthermore, as farm work in industrial farms became defined and categorized in such a way, it created increased alienation among the workers from the farming process. For the agrotechnologists, "farming" came to mean an integrated activity that involves a range of activities from experimental cultivation to making decisions on selling and marketing. To perform only one task in this range of activities was not seen as farming per se.

According to agrotechnologist Ms Toh, a "farmer" at a high technology farm could only mean someone working in the operations and research departments:

> The actual farmers in traditional terms would be in the nursery—the gardeners only. In modern terms, the whole operation department are farmers. I would call the research department as very high-class farmers (laughs) because they deal with farming techniques as well, except that they deal with the highly sophisticated technical farm … and the research department would be farming. (Interview in English)

The rest of the administrative staff were so divorced from the nursery that neither they themselves nor others would be able to regard their job as farming.

Interest in agrotechnogical farms never sparked off. In the late 1990s, there were some expressions of interest in biotechnology and genetically modified food production. This was quickly dissipated, however, in the advent of fervent protests in Europe and the United States over genetically modified food. These parks, however, still exist in the early 21st century. They do produce profits for investors, but also act as sites of tourism and educational outreach programs for urban Singaporean children. Their main products for export are aquarium fish and ornamental flowers, particularly orchids.[52]

---

[52] "Agrotechnology Parks," at http://www.ava.gov.sg/AgricultureFisheriesSector/ FarmingInSingapore/AgroTechParks/ [accessed 15 Nov. 2012]. The focus on aquarium fish export also provides further insight into the difficulties with fish exports and the issue in the mid-1980s. See Goh Hong Yi's contribution to this volume.

Today, agriculture is an insignificant part of Singapore's economy, accounting for just 0.2 percent of Gross Domestic Product and employing 0.2 percent of the workforce, while private entrepreneurs invest in the agricultural sector in Indonesia, Malaysia, Thailand, and China with the goal of exporting products to Singapore.[53] Agriculture and the end of farming in Singapore is a poignant story about a conscious decision based upon how the island's state leaders have interacted with and understood their environment.

---

[53] http://www.nationsencyclopedia.com/economies/Asia_and_the_Pacific/Singapore_AGRICULTURE.html [accessed 15 Nov. 2012].

SOURCE 8

"Wildlife and Singapore": An Assessment from the 1980s[1]

There is a prevailing view in Singapore that since Singapore has not much wildlife of its own left to protect, issues such as wildlife conservation are none of its concern.

Indeed, this view was recently expressed officially, in writing, to the Singapore Branch of the Malayan Nature Society, in a letter from the Ministry of Trade and Industry, attempting to explain why Singapore had not yet signed the Convention on International Trade in Endangered Species (CITES). Needless to say, the Branch will be replying and pointing out that one of the objectives of this Convention is to assist others, including friendly Asean neighbours in Singapore's case, to protect their own very abundant wildlife by limiting trade in it—it has little to do with protecting domestic wildlife, in Singapore's case.

This position is probably doubly false in that not only does Singapore need to be vigilant in monitoring its own possible role in regional wildlife trade (considering it is an important communications, transportation and trading crossroads), but it also probably has more wildlife left than Singaporeans themselves realise. Certainly, with pressures of continuing urbanisation and development, the few remaining nature reserves will need constant protection and monitoring.

A very necessary element of conservation work in Singapore is the education of the public to realise the value of what we do have left, and to inform them of the laws which do exist to protect it. Too few Singaporeans realise the existence of a local Wild Animals and Birds Act, for instance, and for various reasons, some understandable (such as manpower shortages), some sections of the law are not rigidly enforced either.

The Singapore Branch recently undertook to curb the number of quite blatant wildlife trade advertisements in the Classified Advertisements columns of the English-language daily, the Straits Times. That they were so blatant indicated that neither the general public nor the executives in the advertising division had ever considered

---

[1] This article originally appeared in *Malayan Naturalist* (May 1982): 38–40. We would like to thank the author, Ilsa Sharp, as well as the editors and members of the Malaysian Nature Society for allowing it to be reprinted here.

the moral issues which could underlie such ads and were ignorant of the law. We took it as much as an educational exercise as anything to inform both parties of the real situation.

We had been much assisted by our keen and tireless member, Mr Lee Toh Ming, who fed us countless examples of such ads. We are now monitoring them ourselves. Such as these ads:

- Sunday Times, May 31, 1981 (under 'For Sale— Others'):

  '**STUFFED LEOPARD**—Just imported from Indonesia at a cost of $3,500. Owner now selling at $2,500. Beautiful and realistic. A real bargain for stuffed animal enthusiast. Tel: 7778231'

- Straits Times, April 8, 1981 ('For Sale— Others'):

  '**RARE NATURAL SKIN** rugs available. Contact Tel: 2227045. David.'

- Sunday Times, January 18, 1981 ('Antiques'):

  '**RARE RHINOCEROS HORNS**. Very, very expensive. Written offers only. Offer per ounce. No callers. Address Robin, 72 Huddington Avenue, S'pore 1955.'

- Straits Times, May 12, 1981 ('Display Ads'):

  'Wholesale dealer wanted for

  HORNPOWDER AND OTHER NATURAL PRODUCTS

  Write to Dr. Mats Pihl
  Gunnarskarsvargen 13
  663 00 Skoghall, Sweden
  Telephone: Sweden— 054-27200'

- Sunday Times June 1 1980:

  '**One Baby Eagle**. Giant-sized breed. Brown colour. Price $500 o.n.o. Mrs. Tan 9 a.m. to 5 p.m. 4423852.'

Singapore's authorities are believed to be pretty efficient in controlling the importation of live animals from overseas. These ads however reflect the more fluid situation when it comes to parts of dead animals (covered by CITES) and with some strictly local trading among local collectors, especially aviary and caged bird enthusiasts.

The Singapore Branch Conservation Sub-Committee (comprising a lawyer lecturing at the National University of Singapore's Law Faculty, Mrs Lim Lin Heng, Mr Bernard Harrison, Director of the Singapore Zoological Gardens and myself, a freelance journalist) then wrote to the Classified Advertisements department at the Straits

Times, reminding them of the existing laws and expressing our general concern over the possible effect of such blatant trading on our immediate neighbours' attempt to conserve wildlife:

"While the mere insertion of an advertisement in the newspapers cannot legally constitute an 'offer', but only 'an invitation to treat', and your paper is thus not guilty of abetting any offence, the publication of such advertisements is damaging to wildlife conservation in the following ways:

1. It provides a medium for the marketing of wildlife and their by-products, enabling the purveyors to profit from such activities.
2. It correspondingly creates a demand for these products.
3. The net effect is that the trapping and slaughter of these creature is accelerated, for not only is there a ready market, the market is easily reached through a reputable newspaper …

We urge your paper to help us in this effort of conservation by refusing to print advertisements of this nature. This discretion lies in your hands. We are aware that this may entail a loss in revenue, but such loss is minimal and the gain to mankind is much greater. We wish to emphasise that this prohibition does not apply to advertisements for domestic animals, nor does it apply to horses, cattle, sheep, goats, domestic pigs, poultry and ducks …"

To our pleasant surprise, the Classified Advertisements executives at the Straits Times agreed to meet us to discuss this issue, and a most cordial meeting ensued. It was agreed that they would indeed make sterner checks on their advertisements in this area and reject where necessary. To assist them, we ourselves typed up a simple checklist of which animals or by-products to avoid, as it would be far too tedious for them to read through the many laws and conventions already tabled, most of which also use the complicated scientific names for wildlife.

This checklist draws mainly on CITES Appendix I & II, and the Malaysian Wildlife Department's Schedule I & II for the Protection of Wild Life, as well as the Singapore Animal and Birds Act.

The advertisements section has been reminded that it is fundamental to check whether any would-be advertiser and owner of any wild animal is in possession of the legally required import licence and/or wild animal licence, both issued by the Primary Production Department within the Ministry of National Development.

It has also been informed that trading in rhinoceros horn, elephant ivory, crocodile skin, monitor lizard and python skin, turtle shell, skins of all big or small wild cats and the pangolin is completely prohibited in Singapore unless either a valid export/import licence can be produced, or they have been captive bred, which fact must be supported by authentic documentation.

Birds such as hawks and eagles, drongos, orioles and kingfishers are locally protected and of grave local status.

Birds are smuggled into Singapore by traders—once here, the PPD does not confiscate but also does not allow export, and local trading is often allowed to continue. Although the curbing of this kind of advertisement may admittedly lead only to "underground" trade, we think this was a worthwhile project, in that it made a point with an important institution like the Straits Times. It also means that the Classified Advertisements staff will be doing some of our own educational work every time they explain to a probably innocent and ignorant would-be seller of wildlife exactly why they cannot place their ad in the Straits Times.

Our Conservatoin Sub-Committee intends now to move to more investigation of the CITES issue, and to physically monitor trade as far as possible, in particular by personally contacting some of the people who do advertise wildlife, animal-stuffing facilities, etc., to find out more about them and their activities.

Ilsa Sharp
Freeland journalist with a special interest in conservation

CHAPTER 8

The Nature Society, Endangered Species, and Conservation in Singapore

Goh Hong Yi

In 2006, Prime Minister Lee Hsien Loong articulated the official stance of the government with regard to nature and its role in the Singaporean worldview at the annual Clean and Green Week when he stated, "Leafy trees, colourful blooms and clean waterways are features that set Singapore apart from other cities." In the same speech, he emphasized that the government would continue to transform Singapore into a "city of gardens and water," so that it "stays something special and precious which we can be proud of."[1] As Lee's speech suggests, nature, in the form of roadside trees and well-maintained gardens, is a part of a Singaporean identity. This emphasis on the natural environment has been an important theme in the narrative of Singapore's progress since 1965. In his memoirs, Lee Kuan Yew also expressed this clearly when he wrote, "To achieve First World standards in a Third World region, we set out to transform Singapore into a tropical garden city." A "Green" Singapore has become an essential part of nation building, a powerful national symbol of identity and pride.[2]

The flip side to this narrative of development is that the greenery that came to characterize the new nation was built upon the destruction of nature from an older Singapore. Since the 1960s, reclamation and infrastructural

---

[1] "PM's Call: Make Singapore a City of Gardens and Water," *The Straits Times* [hereafter *ST*], 6 Nov. 2006, p. 6.
[2] Lee Kuan Yew, *From Third World to First—The Singapore story: 1965–2000* (Singapore: Singapore Press Holdings, 2000), p. 201; Victor Savage, "Singapore's Garden City: Translating Environmental Possibilism," in *City and the State: Singapore's Built Environment Revisited*, ed. Ooi Geok Ling (Singapore: Oxford University Press, 1997), p. 196.

development have caused the extent of built-up area on the island to double at the expense of swamps, forest, and agricultural land. Simultaneously, the resettlement of the population from rural *kampongs* to public flats limited opportunities for Singaporeans to interact with nature. This physical transformation of Singapore's landscape caused a shift in people's attitudes toward the natural environment. A study conducted on youth perceptions of nature in 1999 found that many in Singapore have little affinity with nature. Growing up in a highly urban environment, Singaporean youths are familiar with nature only in the form of manicured parks and gardens. They are thus "predisposed" to accept the state-directed, utilitarian discourse that nature has to be sacrificed for economic development and human needs. Yet, the state's interpretation of nature has not been unchallenged. Since independence from Malaysia, Singaporeans have expressed concerns that engineered landscapes have replaced a natural heritage of mangroves, rainforests, and coral reefs. Conservationists find such greened urban spaces a poor substitute for naturally occurring environments and these have became contested sites for people who place different values on nature.[3]

This contest became prominent in the 1990s, when the Nature Society (Singapore) (NSS) carried out a series of campaigns to prevent the development of Singapore's remaining natural areas. While their success was limited, their ability to gather, on one occasion, the support of 25,000 people for a petition to conserve a bird sanctuary at Senoko demonstrated that nature conservation was able to capture the attention of a significant portion of the population. Beyond ethical or ecological motivations, nature conservation in Singapore is a fight "to secure a sense of place" and to foster a "broader sense of identity among the citizenship."[4] Nature conservation, thus, represents an alternative strand of nation building from below where people come together in the civic sphere to protect their vision of what "home" means.

Few historians have studied the history of nature conservation in post-1965 Singapore. Various academics in the disciplines of Geography and

---

[3] Peggy Teo, Brenda Yeoh, Ooi Giok Ling, and Karen Lai, *Changing Landscapes of Singapore* (Singapore: McGraw-Hill Education, 2004), pp. 22–3, 43; Lily Kong, Belinda Yuen, Navjot S. Sodhi, and Clive Briffett, "The Construction and Experience of Nature: Perspectives from Urban Youths," *Tijdschrift voor Economie en Sociale Geographie* 90, 1 (Feb. 1999): 8–16; see also Timothy P. Barnard and Corinne Heng's and Cynthia Chou's contributions to this volume.

[4] "25,000 Appeal for Senoko Bird Habitat to be Saved," *ST*, 21 Oct. 1994, p. 3; Harvey Neo, "Challenging the Developmental State: Nature Conservation in Singapore," *Asia Pacific Viewpoint* 48, 2 (Aug. 2007): 187.

Political Science, however, have analyzed the contests over natural spaces to identify patterns of government-NGO (non-governmental organization) relationships and challenges of conservation in Singapore. Among the scholars examining the subject has been Harvey Neo, who has discussed how the state's monopoly on the discourse of development obstructs conservation efforts. The developmental state's principle that "collective economic interests should have primacy over non-economic individual ones" rejects views of nature that are based on extra-economic values. From the state's response to conservation struggles for Marina South Duck Ponds in 1992 and Senoko Bird Sanctuary in 1994, Neo argues that the state evoked developmental ideologies to justify the clearing of natural areas. By pronouncing conservationists' protests as "irrational" and "emotional," the state implied that they should be excluded during decision-making.[5]

In the same vein, political scientist Maria Francesch-Huidobro has focused on the relationship between the government and civil society with regard to environmental issues in modern Singapore. She argues that NGOs such as the NSS are not equal partners with the government but are instead co-opted and subordinated by the state while retaining a limited space for semi-autonomous action. Looking at incidents when the NSS managed to stop the government's developmental plans, she identified two approaches environmental NGOs took: "the power of persuasion" in the preservation of Sungei Buloh wetlands in 1988 and "the power of protestation" for the case of Lower Peirce Reservoir.[6]

While these studies provide useful frameworks of analysis, it is striking that the case studies referred to developments in the 1990s. Most refer to the NSS' endeavor to save Sungei Buloh in 1988 as the first local initiative for nature conservation and there is a consensus that nature conservation became popular only recently.[7] At the core of these arguments is the

---

[5] Ibid., pp. 188–9.

[6] Maria Francesch-Huidobro, *Governance, Politics and the Environment: A Singapore Study* (Singapore: Institute of Southeast Asian Studies, 2008), pp. 7, 165, 221.

[7] A lecture on nature conservation at the National University of Singapore by November Tan in 2008 included a timeline of conservation efforts in Singapore starting from 1988, at http://www.slideshare.net/micamonkey/nature-conservation-in-singapore [accessed 1 Mar. 2012]; the National Parks Board's timeline of conservation in Singapore, at http://www.nparks.gov.sg/cms/index.php?option=com_content&view=article&id=124&Itemid=126 [accessed 1 Mar. 2012], is similarly silent about the period from 1951 to 1990.

assumption that the anxiety over economic survival and bread-and-butter issues like housing and employment in the early years of independence meant there was little interest in environmental conservation. It seems incongruous that there were no conservation activities in Singapore until the 1990s given that conservation movements had already gained momentum both in the region and worldwide by the 1970s. Although the NSS was already an active society under their previous name of the Malayan Nature Society (Singapore Branch) (MNS), no mention has been made of any conservation efforts until the Sungei Buloh incident.

This chapter will focus on this silence in Singaporean environmental history and public policy by examining people's perception of nature in the post-independence period prior to 1990 and how interest in conservation began. It follows the development of the MNS, the earliest conservation group in Singapore, as a way to look at the state's attitude toward the environment and civil society. Instead of the conservation of natural areas, the focus will be on the relationship between the Malayan Nature Society (Singapore Branch) and the Singapore government in the realm of wildlife trade and conservation, which led to the signing of the Convention on International Trade in Endangered Species of Wild Fauna and Flora (CITES) in 1986. This episode reflects how Singapore negotiated its position on nature conservation in the larger context of state-civil society interactions and international environmental cooperation. It is argued that local initiatives for nature conservation began earlier than the 1990s, although the state's suspicions of conservation and their indifference toward environmental protection undercut local conservationists' attempts to express an alternative vision of nature in Singapore. The events that happened in the 1990s are part of a gradual expansion of public interest in nature and continue from these earlier conservation efforts.

Transition and Growth in the Malayan Nature Society

The Malayan Nature Society was a legacy of the colonial past. British civil servants, who were interested in the flora and fauna of the tropics, founded the organization, and its name reflected the geographical extent of its membership as the first committee consisted of members from both Malaya and Singapore. According to a newspaper article that heralded its formation in 1940, it was created "so that amateur naturalists and observers of natural life can get together and exchange notes, arrange lectures and organise field exhibitions for nature study."[8] The first President was E.O. Shebbare, Chief Game Warden of British Malaya.

The Singaporean branch of the Malayan Nature Society (henceforth MNS) was established in 1954. It soon became one of the most active branches of the Society. As a sign of the close relationship between the Singapore branch and the parent society in Kuala Lumpur, there was an informal consensus that the Vice-President of the Malayan Nature Society Council, which oversaw the activities of all branches, was to be from Singapore. Most members prior to 1965 were British army personnel and civil servants whose attitude toward nature shifted between "curiosity and concern"—concern over the People's Action Party's housing and industrialization plans during the period of self-government, but limiting their actions to discussing and documenting the state of the natural environment.[9]

The post-independence period was a time of transition for the society —when it changed from a small group consisting of mostly foreigners to a much larger organization with local participation and broader objectives that included nature conservation. The MNS was loosely structured with a main committee of around eight members who organized and coordinated all activities for the branch as well as liaised with the Malayan Nature Society Council in Kuala Lumpur. The committee met monthly and the meeting minutes are an untapped reserve of information for scholars working on the history of environmental conservation in Singapore.[10]

Working alongside the main committee, volunteers led sub-groups, such as the Bird Group, Butterfly Group or Photo Group, and organized extra activities in their areas of interest. These sub-groups were quite fluid, often fading away when members found other interests and revived when another leader came forward.[11] This informal structure of the early MNS was advantageous as it accommodated the varied interests of its members and

---

[8] "Malayan Nature Society Publishes New Journal," *ST*, 26 Sep. 1940, p. 8; some MNS members trace the origins of this society even further back to 1921, when the Singapore Natural History Society was formed for the "friendly intercourse between local naturalists." This society, however, faded into oblivion by 1928. "Singapore Natural History Society," *ST*, 13 Aug. 1921, p. 9; P.N. Avadhani, personal interview, 21 Feb. 2012.

[9] P.N. Avadhani, personal interview, 21 Feb. 2012.

[10] Malayan Nature Society (Singapore Branch) Committee Meeting Minutes [hereafter MCMM], NA2088 (Singapore: National Archives of Singapore, 1972–86).

[11] Wee Yeow Chin, personal interview, 18 Jan. 2012.

allowed the society to organize more projects than its small main committee could have managed. For example, under the committed leadership of Ng Soon Chye, the Bird Study Group initiated two major projects in 1976: an ecological study of Bukit Timah Nature Reserve (BTNR), and a bird study at the Serangoon Sludge Treatment Works.[12] The loose structure of the MNS continued until the society was reorganized into the NSS in the mid-1990s—the Singaporean branch broke away in 1992 as The Nature Society (Singapore)—when a more hierarchical and formal organization was introduced.

In 1966, MNS membership numbered only a few hundred.[13] Between 1972 and 1981, MNS activities usually attracted a turnout of 10 to 30 members. The number of members grew slowly but steadily for the first decade and a half until it nearly doubled in 1982. If membership in the MNS could be taken as an indicator of people's interest in nature, it was clear that by the mid-1980s, "nature-lovers" in Singapore were no longer rare. A key formative period for the MNS was in the 1980s, when its membership saw an eightfold increase from the start to the end of the decade. Beginning in 1982, meeting minutes reflected a gradual increase in turnout for MNS

Table 8.1 MNS membership by year[14]

Year	Membership
1974	140
1977	107
1978	128
1981	187
1982	326
1983	440
1984	711
1985	741
1986	840

[12] Malayan Nature Society (Singapore Branch) Annual General Meeting Minutes [hereafter MAGMM], NA2088 (Singapore: National Archives of Singapore, 1976).
[13] "Society to Save Man from that Sad Day when Nature's Treasures Fade Away," *ST*, 20 Mar. 1966, p. 10.
[14] Compiled from MNS Committee Meeting and AGM Minutes from the respective years.

activities, averaging at least 40 to 60 for each event. The actual number of people participating in MNS activities would likely be larger than the official membership as members could, and regularly did, invite their friends and family to the events.

Beyond membership size, the composition of MNS membership also became more local and less exclusive during this period. In the 1960s and 1970s, most members were expatriates as well as local elites and professionals such as university professors, scientists and directors of private companies, which may have discouraged some Singaporeans from joining.[15] Out of the eight-member main committee in 1972, for example, there were four biology lecturers from the University of Singapore, as well as an arborist and a mycologist from the Botanic Gardens.[16] There was an especially close link with the University of Singapore (the precursor to the National University of Singapore), from whose Biology Department many MNS members originated.

Links with the University of Singapore were important when the society was small and lacked resources. The MNS did not have its own premises; the official address of the society for much of this period was the office of P.N. Avadhani, a member since 1960, in the university's Botany Department. Meetings were held at the Bukit Timah campus and mail was directed there as well.[17] The expertise of the staff with regard to plant and animal life also allowed these members to organize enriching activities for others. This expertise and knowledge was also an asset that government statutory boards recognized and valued, giving rise to many platforms of collaboration and consultation between the state and the MNS.

Although academics were prominent in the MNS, there were also "amateur naturalists" who shared their knowledge with other members. For example, Ng Soon Chye, leader of the Bird Study Group in the 1970s, was a gynecologist by profession and much of his knowledge about birds was self-taught. The number of amateur naturalists in the MNS was to grow gradually as interest in nature grew among the larger public. In 1983, an article in *The Straits Times* celebrated the passion of MNS "amateurs" who published a book on tropical insects despite having no scientific

---

[15] As a journalist noted in 1966: "interested amateurs with no special training in biology or botany fear that they would find themselves among a crowd of 'experts'." "Society to save man from that sad day when nature's treasures fade away."

[16] MAGMM, 1972.

[17] P.N. Avadhani, personal interview, 21 Feb. 2012.

qualifications. The same article mentioned that "a noticeable influx of fresh, young, local blood in recent years has made the overall membership today more than 60 per cent local."[18]

The gradual shift to a more local and broad-based membership in the 1980s can be seen as a natural progression as the nation developed. The increase in membership and the popularization of nature could be attributed to three reasons: the growth of a middle class informed on environmental issues, the effect of urban high-rise living, and, lastly, greater publicity of MNS activities in the media. If the immediate post-independence period was one in which economic survival became a priority, and a dominant aspect of public discourse, by the 1980s more Singaporeans began to explore their interest in the natural environment. Such an explanation was congruent with the government's pro-development rhetoric and also parallels many studies that link higher socioeconomic status and environmentalism.[19] While the MNS became more inclusive, it was still associated with the middle class. It appealed to the young and educated as they had grown up in public housing flats—in an artificial urban environment—and began to perceive nature as something rare and exciting. The organization also held an appeal among the young and educated at this time as the activities, ranging from talks to walks, were conducted in English at this time.[20]

Beginning in the 1980s, there was also expansion in the coverage of the MNS, and nature-related topics, in the local media. The addition of journalists from *The Straits Times*, particularly Nancy Byramji (late 1970s) and Ilsa Sharp (1980s), to the MNS committee not only raised the profile of the society significantly but also drew the public's attention to issues of nature appreciation and protection. Notices for upcoming events, accounts of MNS outings, and articles featuring MNS volunteers, as well as opinion pieces about the state of the natural environment, began to appear regularly in the press in Singapore.

---

[18] Ng Soon Chye, "From Birds to Babies and Beyond: A Chat with One of Singapore's 'Fathers' of IVF," *LIFE*, 16 Mar. 2007, pp. 12–5; "Four Smitten by 'Love Bug'," *ST*, 5 June 1983, p. 1.

[19] Denton E. Morrison and Riley E. Dunlap, "Environmentalism and Elitism: A Conceptual and Empirical Analysis," *Environmental Management* 10, 5 (1986): 582; Wee Yeow Chin, personal interview, 18 Jan. 2012.

[20] Ilsa Sharp, personal interview, 18 Jan. 2012; "Eager Singaporeans Keep Nature Society Throbbing," *ST*, 31 May 1987, p. 2; "More Take a Closer Walk with Nature," *ST*, 6 Oct. 1983, p. 6.

The coverage of environmental issues also expanded into radio and television in the early 1980s. In 1983, the Singapore Broadcasting Corporation began production on two nature programs: the radio program "Nature World" and a children's television program named "Naturama."[21] Both featured the MNS and focused on the protection and enjoyment of nature in Singapore. In later years, Lynn Sa'don, a deejay at Singapore's Radio One and member of the MNS, regularly invited Sharp to her show "Your Host Tonight" to discuss nature-related issues. In Sharp's opinion, the radio programs were very effective in engaging the public and getting them interested: "People would call us to ask about all sorts of issues regarding wildlife, even on how to deal with bats roosting in their houses! Several also called and asked to join after they heard about us from the program."[22] Such publicity and programs suggested that nature was becoming more popular and contributed to the increase in MNS membership in the 1980s.

The activities the Nature Society organized during this period, however, give the impression that it was largely a recreational organization, which could be characterized in the words of Ilsa Sharp as "hobby not lobby."[23] Indeed, conservation was not the primary objective of the society in the first couple of decades after independence. As such, it echoed the original ethos of the society's colonial founders. This would begin to change by the early 1980s.

From Hobby to Lobby: Wildlife Trade and CITES

As membership of the Nature Society expanded in the 1970s and 1980s, particularly among Singaporean citizens, and their efforts gained greater publicity, leaders of the organization began to play a more prominent role in raising awareness on nature-related issues and in conservation in larger society. While the recreational and social function of the MNS did constitute a large portion of their activities, the society also worked on projects in collaboration with the government and international conservation bodies to further nature appreciation, public education, and wildlife research. Indeed, activities could fulfill twin functions of both recreation and research. For example, while the Bird Study Group's bird watching sessions were often

---

[21] "Radio Series about Nature and Wildlife," *ST*, 7 Mar. 1983, p. 11; "Discovering Nature's Bounty," *ST*, 19 Apr. 1983, p. 12.

[22] Ilsa Sharp, personal interview, 18 Jan. 2012.

[23] Ibid.

quite recreational, the information on the type and number of birds spotted was recorded to assess the health of the biodiversity of the area, or in one case, helped identify bird migration patterns in collaboration with a team of scientists from the World Wildlife Fund (WWF).[24] On other occasions, the society organized exhibitions and public seminars on issues to which the public could relate. The MNS' seminar, "Nature in Urban Singapore" in 1983, for example, taught the public where they could still appreciate and enjoy nature without harming it. The seminar had a full turnout of close to 300 participants.[25]

The society's unique strength, with its team of both professional and amateur naturalists, was its knowledge of the flora and fauna of Singapore and this knowledge was valuable to the government as well. In 1979, the MNS proposed to the Nature Reserves Board that sign-posted walking trails be developed to encourage more people to participate in nature-related activities. The rationale was to "inculcate nature consciousness and respect for environment among the youth, if only to wean them away from the coffee shop culture."[26] The Nature Reserves Board received the proposal with interest and invited MNS representatives to join them to work on the suggestions. MNS also contributed by designing a pamphlet on the animals and plants of the Bukit Timah Nature Reserve to educate visitors. This collaboration was an example of how the MNS took the initiative to engage the larger Singaporean community and proposed constructive plans to promote nature and improve existing nature parks. It was at this time that Roland Sharma, ex-chairman of the MNS, urged his committee to do more in the way of education, to "prove itself as more than a social club."[27] In 1981, a three-person Conservation Committee was set up within the MNS, comprising Ilsa Sharp, Lye Lin Heng—the society's legal advisor—and Bernard Harrison, Director of the Singapore Zoological Gardens. It was clear that in addition to education, conservation and wildlife protection, which had fallen under the purview of the Society by the 1970s, would now be a focus of activities in the MNS.[28]

---

[24] "Night Watch on the Flight to the South," *ST*, 1 Oct. 1983, p. 1.

[25] MCMM, 7 Feb. 1983.

[26] Proposal for the Popularisation of Nature Reserves in Singapore, MCMM, 24 Sep. 1979.

[27] MCMM, 1 Dec. 1980.

[28] MCMM, 26 Aug. 1981; *Malayan Naturalist, Malayan Nature Society* 35, 3 (May 1982): 41; Leo Tan Wee Hin, personal interview, 4 Jan. 2012.

In Singapore, unlike other countries where wildlife is harvested as a resource, direct exploitation was not a major threat to the ecology of the island as the nation's small size and highly urbanized environment excluded the possibility of wildlife constituting a viable domestic industry. Wildlife conservation in Singapore centered on violations of the Wild Animals and Birds Act, which prohibited the killing, taking or keeping of any wild animals or birds without a license—the exception being the house crow, which been an issue since the colonial era.[29] As there was a paucity of local wildlife, nature lovers turned their attention to the import of endangered animals from other countries into Singapore. Being the only environmental NGO at the time, the MNS frequently received tips and letters of concern about this issue from their own members and concerned members of the public. In 1977, for example, members expressed concern over the killing of *musang* (civet cats) in Bugis Street for sale as medicine. Similar complaints also arose regarding hawkers in Sago Lane who kept wild animals, like water monitors and pythons, for slaughter and consumption.[30] For such cases, the MNS carried out investigations on the dealers in question and reported them to the authorities.

The Nature Society also scrutinized the local pet business. Concerns over the trapping of wild birds for pets were expressed in an article in *The Straits Times* that condemned bird dealers for trapping birds from Singapore's natural stocks for sale to bird-fanciers. Lamenting the inadequate enforcement of the Wild Animals and Birds Act, Ng Soon Chye encouraged Singaporeans to appreciate birds in their natural habitats instead of caging them, emphasizing that certain bird species cannot survive in captivity and should be left alone. Trapped birds found during MNS outings would also be rescued and reported to the Primary Production Department (PPD). Overall, this led the MNS to conclude that it had by and large "achieved considerable success in promoting conservation and acting as a general watchdog over a number of nefarious activities" in 1978.[31]

The MNS found it more difficult to deal with the hidden face of the international wildlife trade in Singapore. Although the MNS knew that the

---

[29] See Fiona Tan's contribution to this volume. Lye Lin Heng, "Wildlife Protection Laws in Singapore," *Singapore Journal of Legal Studies* 288 (1991): 291.

[30] MCMM, 11 Apr. 1977 and 9 Oct. 1977.

[31] MAGMM, 1978; MCMM, 11 June 1979; "Save These Birds from Extinction," *ST*, 16 Oct. 1977, p. 12.

illegal import and re-export of wildlife was becoming a growing concern, they were hesitant to act because they did not understand the laws involved. As early as 1976, the MNS noted that there were international complaints about exports of animals from Singapore. The Malayan Nature Society Council in Kuala Lumpur also raised this issue in 1978, when it requested that the Singapore branch investigate the depletion of marine aquarium fish from coral reefs in Singapore for sale overseas.[32] Accordingly, MNS members visited the suspect dealers and concluded that a major aquarium fish dealer was importing rare marine fishes from Indonesia and Philippines in bulk. As no local conservation laws were infringed, the MNS took no further action despite discussing the issue for months.[33] Another incident, which convinced the Society that the illegal smuggling of wildlife through Singapore was serious, occurred in 1979 when Singapore Airlines was sued for "cruelty to crocodiles."[34] According to the International Union for Conservation of Nature and Natural Resources (IUCN), a shipment of 43 baby crocodiles bound for Taiwan from Papua New Guinea were seized from the hold of a Singapore Airlines jet. As the crocodiles were on the non-trading list of CITES—an international treaty that regulates wildlife trade—the shipment was illegal. Following this incident, the Malayan Nature Society Council contacted the MNS to ask whether the branch would contact local authorities to ask that something be done about the wildlife trade going through Singapore or should the Council do it. Again, the MNS was hesitant and decided to first consult their legal advisor before acting.[35]

The wildlife trade continued to occupy the agenda of the main committee in 1980 and it was clear that the MNS was cautious and unsure of how to proceed, as members were not optimistic that legislation would be used to regulate trade in endangered species. The consensus was that because the animals in transit did not originate from Singapore, the government would be reluctant to act. Even while continuing to look into the legal aspects of wildlife trade, the committee concluded that "Singapore will probably not be a signatory to any such international agreement, the meeting was of the opinion that it would be better to channel matters through ASEAN by way of the Council."[36]

[32] MCMM, 10 Aug. 1976 and 16 Jan. 1978.
[33] MCMM, 20 Feb. 1978.
[34] MCMM, 20 Aug. 1979.
[35] *IUCN Bulletin*, Mar. 1979, p. 21; MCMM, 24 Sep. 1979.
[36] MCMM, 14 Jan. 1980 and 25 Aug. 1980.

By the end of 1980, members of the society were on the verge of writing the government to request that it sign CITES as the first step to regulate wildlife trade and demonstrate Singapore's commitment to global biodiversity conservation. At the same time, an article appeared in *The Straits Times* announcing the MNS' intention to petition the government to sign CITES, which also served to raise public awareness about the treaty. The article explained that even though Singapore did not have enough wildlife to export, "a major advantage in signing the agreement would be better inter-governmental cooperation in the regulation of wildlife trade."[37] Before this letter could be sent, however, the committee agreed internally that "nothing could be written to the government or the press until research has been completed extensively."[38] It seemed that having established its value to the government as a credible society, the MNS did not want to jeopardize its standing with the authorities.

Pressure was also on the MNS to take action as active members had been supplying information and tip-offs on infringements of wildlife trade and have been "anxious to see action on this issue."[39] While the letter to the government was being drafted, the MNS committee also tried to use other non-legislative methods to curb the sale of wildlife products in Singapore. One way was to circumvent the public advertisement of such products. Rhino horns, rare parrots and eagles, arowana fish and gibbons were just some of the "products" that occasionally appeared in *The Straits Times* Classified Ads. The Conservation Committee of the MNS managed to successfully negotiate with the newspaper to monitor wildlife advertisements more closely and restrict those that were inappropriate.[40]

Throughout 1980 and 1981, the MNS continued its role as a "watch-dog" for those who perpetuated the trade in wildlife products. The committee realized, however, that simply monitoring and reacting to signs of wildlife trade would not be enough to help in their conservation unless legislation was instituted to regulate the import and export of wildlife and their products through Singapore. With that in mind, in October 1981, the MNS sent a

---

[37] "Society to Petition Govt on Wildlife Pact," *ST*, 17 Jan. 1981, p. 17.

[38] Among the issues to be investigated included details about CITES, fees that Singapore would have to pay upon joining, as well as writing to the IUCN for a list of endangered species and wildlife products that are traded in Singapore. MCMM, 16 Feb. 1981.

[39] MCMM, 19 May 1981.

[40] MCMM, 7 Dec. 1981.

letter to the Ministry of National Development (MND) and the Ministry of Trade and Industry (MTI) asking why Singapore had not signed CITES and requested that the government join the Convention. Three months later, in January 1982, MTI responded to the letter. It was a short reply, saying that there was no point in signing the Convention as Singapore had little wildlife of its own to protect and existing local laws were sufficient to protect that which existed.[41] Disappointed, the committee decided to write again, urging that Singapore should do its part to protect regional wildlife. This response was sent to the two ministries in March 1982.

Seeking to develop a wider interest in the matter, the MNS decided to "go public" when their second appeal was sent to the government. Avadhani explained in *The Straits Times* that because Singapore had not signed CITES, it has become "the unwitting channel for illegal trade in wildlife and its by-products," and reassured readers that signing the Convention would not mean a total ban on wildlife trade but rather ensure that trade would be regulated. The MNS stated that the government had taken a "restricted view of the situation and missed the point of the wildlife conservation issue"—protecting nature is the concern of all nations and Singapore should act in the spirit of ASEAN solidarity since Malaysia and Indonesia had already signed it.[42] The article also expressed concern that existing laws were inadequate to protect local wildlife, as the penalties were not severe enough to deter poachers.

The government's response to this public disagreement of its policy appeared in the newspapers in June. Although the critique of the government had been mild, the government's response was blunt. Officials reiterated the government stance that Singapore would not become a party to CITES. A spokesperson stated that while the MNS' appeal had been carefully considered, the government had "valid reasons" for not signing CITES. He declined to explain what these reasons were.[43]

Following the letter to *The Straits Times*, MNS committee members found themselves receiving strong but indirect messages which they believed originated with the authorities. A friend hinted to Avadhani that he should lay off the issue to avoid trouble. Another past MNS committee member interpreted this as a threat that the Chairman could be forced to retire from Singapore should he persist in taking up the matter. As the MNS was

---

[41] MCMM, 8 Jan. 1982.
[42] "Group Seek Govt Rethink on Wildlife," *ST*, 6 Apr. 1982: 14.
[43] "Ministry Reiterates Stand on Wildlife Pact," *ST*, 4 June 1982, p. 10.

affiliated with Malaysia, committee members imagined the government was suspicious that foreign parties were trying to hinder Singapore's development. By "going public," it seems the MNS had inadvertently alarmed a state that was not accustomed to challenges from civil society.[44]

With the threat and public rejection from the government, the MNS backed down. In the same article in which the government stated its stand, Avadhani clarified that the MNS "had never pressed for the government to sign—it merely advised that it was in Singapore's interest to be a party to CITES."[45] As the minutes of the Nature Society's meeting at this time stated succinctly, "CITES Dialogue: The government has replied that it will not sign. The matter is closed."[46]

The government's unwillingness to negotiate effectively obstructed MNS' first attempts to advocate and influence state policy in conservation. The MNS continued with its efforts in monitoring advertisements and incidents involving the sale of endangered animals and their products but ceased to demand that Singapore sign CITES. Reflecting on the MNS' limitations during the CITES petition, Ilsa Sharp recognized that the government was "largely unmoved." In her opinion, the society had an impact, even if it was "a sort of nuisance and inconvenience effect, but obviously not enough to change the government's mind or get them to act for change."[47]

This impact could be seen in how the government's reticence and refusal to explain its reasons for not signing CITES drew public and international sympathy to the Nature Society. An unnamed member of public wrote in response to the ministry's stand on CITES, stating that he was "very disturbed by the report" and argued that a truly caring society should do its part for nature conservation. The article also postulated that "the reason for not signing is essentially based on materialistic considerations" and asked MND to explain its stand.[48] The International Primate Protection League, an international NGO, also expressed its disappointment at the government's refusal to join CITES and added its support for the MNS. The League was more openly critical in its analysis of the situation: "the sad assumption to

---

[44] Avadhani was a Permanent Resident of Singapore, but a citizen of India. Wee Yeow Chin, personal interview, 18 Jan. 2012.
[45] "Ministry Reiterates Stand on Wildlife Pact."
[46] MCMM, 3 May 1982.
[47] Ilsa Sharp, email interview, 15 Mar. 2012.
[48] "A Caring Society Also Cares for Animals," *ST*, 14 June 1982, p. 13.

be made from Singapore's refusal to join the convention is that it wishes to retain the right to trade in smuggled wildlife in order to make money."[49] As the letter from the International Primate Protection League reveals, others were also monitoring the illegal wildlife trade through Singapore. While the government largely ignored these admonishments, the CITES issue was to arise again a few years later.

CITES, Diplomacy, and a "Notorious" Country

The Convention on International Trade in Endangered Species of Wild Fauna and Flora (CITES) is an international agreement between governments, which was first signed in 1973, and entered into force in 1975. Its primary aim is to ensure that international trade in wild animals and plants does not threaten their survival.[50] The International Union for Conservation of Nature and Natural Resources (IUCN) initiated the program in 1963, when there were growing concerns that wildlife populations worldwide were shrinking at an unprecedented rate due to uncontrolled exploitation— such as the hunting of animals for their fur, the capture of primates for medical research and crocodiles for their skins. As demands for wildlife and their products crossed national boundaries, the IUCN promoted the concept that "international cooperation is essential for the protection of certain species of wild fauna and flora against over-exploitation through international trade."[51]

A common misconception of CITES is that it prohibits trade in endangered species entirely. In fact, CITES seeks to regulate and prevent illegal trade rather than eliminate it. Under the CITES framework, trade in selected wildlife species are subjected to import, export, and re-export controls. The level of trade permitted is differentiated according to the degree of protection the species requires. Species are assigned to one of the three Appendices, based on the IUCN Red Data Books (see Table 8.2) and amendments to the Appendices can be proposed during the Conference of Parties held every two years. The permit system also requires that state-

---

[49] "Sorry S'pore Didn't Ratify Pact," *ST*, 5 Aug. 1982, p. 15.
[50] "What is CITES?" at http://www.cites.org/ [accessed 22 Feb. 2012].
[51] Chris Huxley, "CITES: The Vision," in *Endangered Species, Threatened Convention: The Past, Present and Future of CITES*, ed. Jon Hutton and Barnabas Dickson (London: Earthscan Publications, 2000), pp. 5–6; Preamble to the Convention of on International Trade in Endangered Species of Wild Fauna and Flora, 3 Mar. 1973.

designated managing authorities in each signatory ensure that "the specimen was not obtained in contravention of the laws of that State for the protection of fauna and flora."[52]

Table 8.2 CITES Appendices[53]

Appendix I	Species threatened with extinction.	Trade permitted only in exceptional, non-commercial circumstances. Requires import and export permits.
Appendix II	Species that may become threatened with extinction unless trade is strictly controlled.	Trade for commercial purposes permitted so long as it is not detrimental to species' survival. Requires export permits.
Appendix III	Species protected in at least one state, which requires the assistance of other countries to control trade.	Trade from a state that included the species in Appendix III requires an export permit.

CITES is not a comprehensive conservation strategy. As one critic argues, "When weighed against habitat-destruction, the wildlife trade is an insignificant cause of species decline."[54] Debates between conservationists, who support sustainable use of wildlife resources, and preservationists, who believe that all wildlife trade should be banned, remain a controversial topic for the Convention and reflect the different values that parties place on nature.[55] Nevertheless, within its limited objectives and notwithstanding issues of non-compliance among member countries, CITES has succeeded in establishing an internationally recognized framework to regulate wildlife trade.

As a tool for regulating wildlife trade across countries, states that are not parties to the Convention pose a problem for its effectiveness. The Convention allows for trade with non-party states provided that authorities

---

[52] Convention of on International Trade in Endangered Species of Wild Fauna and Flora (CITES), 3 Mar. 1973, art. III (2).

[53] "How CITES Work?" at http://www.cites.org/ [accessed 22 Feb. 2012].

[54] *IUCN Bulletin*, Jan./Feb. 1981, p. 123.

[55] Saskia Young, "Contemporary Issues of the Convention on International Trade in Endangered Species of Wild Flora and Fauna (CITES) and the Debate on Sustainable Use," *Colorado Journal of International Environmental Law and Policy* 14 (2003): 82.

in the non-party state issue comparable documentation. Unfortunately, this effectively allows traders to circumvent the Convention and "indirectly encourages and actually rewards non-parties" as it "bestows upon them a virtual monopoly in wildlife trade."[56] CITES member-states thus often perceive non-party states as "problem states" whose non-cooperation undermines their conservation efforts.

For its small size and highly industrialized economy, it is surprising that Singapore attracted so much attention among CITES member-states. In 1979, the *IUCN Bulletin* listed Singapore among other developing countries, such as Columbia, Mexico and Tanzania, as "prolific traders in wildlife." Singapore had a particularly bad reputation and was described as being "notorious as a 'laundering' port for illegal wildlife trade."[57] Eric McFadden, in evaluating the participation of Asian nations in CITES, stated that "Singapore has traditionally been the principal supplier of saltwater crocodile hides, an Appendix I species" to Western Europe.[58] The extent to which Singapore was a perpetuator to illegal wildlife trade was demonstrated in 1984, when the CITES Secretariat requested "all parties to take immediate action to prohibit and prevent any trade in ivory with Singapore" as they had received information that more than 40 tons of illegal ivory had been shipped from Africa to the nation-state. Just two years later, Singapore was again singled out. The Secretariat cautioned parties that a "very substantial trade" in the skins of snakes listed in Appendix II has been smuggled from India to Singapore, where the country of origin was falsely declared and re-exported. While actual numbers of what was exported are not available, a snippet of the volume of trade reported in *The Straits Times* is shocking. From 1980 to 1982, "Singapore exported 424,000 water monitor lizard skins, 82,246 reticulated python skins and 48,766kg of unworked tortoise shells. In 1981, it exported 30,000 pangolin skins."[59]

---

[56] Alan Schonfeld, "International Trade in Wildlife: How Effective is the Endangered Species Treaty?," *California Western International Law Journal* 15 (1985): 139; CITES, 3 Mar. 1973, art. X.

[57] *IUCN Bulletin*, Mar. 1979, p. 17; Gary Meyers and Kyla Bennett, "Answering the 'Call of the Wild': An Examination of U.S. Participation in International Wildlife Law," *Pace Environmental Law Review* 9 (1989): 103.

[58] Eric McFadden, "Asian Compliance with CITES: Problems and Prospects," *Boston University International Law Journal* 5 (1987): 317.

[59] "Plugging a S-E Asian 'Loophole'," *ST*, 5 Aug. 1984, p. 15; Rosalind Reeve, *Policing International Trade in Endangered Species: The CITES Treaty and Compliance* (London: Earthscan Publications Ltd, 2002), p. 129.

It was perhaps all the more frustrating to the CITES Secretariat that most countries in the region were already signatories to the Convention.[60] Singapore was a "loophole" that allowed smuggling to go on unchecked. A British visitor to Singapore expressed his disappointment with this state of affairs in 1980 after observing tourist shops in Singapore that sold stuffed animals and wildlife products such as stuffed pangolins and tiger skins. As a sharp rebuke to the Singaporean government, he commented that "while surrounding Asian countries become increasingly enlightened, Singapore remains backward as far as legislation on the trade in endangered wildlife is concerned" and this "encourages illegal poaching in Indonesia and Malaysia."[61]

Throughout the early 1980s, the CITES Secretariat "wooed" Singapore to sign CITES.[62] Environment Minister Ong Pang Boon even announced during the 1984 ASEAN Ministerial Meeting on the Environment that Singapore would sign CITES. Almost echoing the appeal made by the MNS two years earlier, he stated that "it is timely for us to give additional support to the call within ASEAN and the international community to combat the danger arising from the growing trade in endangered species."[63] The press speculated that Singapore would sign CITES in time to participate in the next Conference of Parties in early 1985. This did not occur. Much to the dismay of many local and international observers, the press was still speculating on the issue in 1986, and it was becoming an increasingly sticky diplomatic issue. Prince Philip, consort of Queen Elizabeth II of Britain, personally wrote to Prime Minister Lee Kuan Yew to request that Singapore sign CITES.[64] The prolonged uncertainty and anticipation over when Singapore would eventually sign the Convention was to end in an emotional international confrontation that forced the Singaporean government to re-evaluate its stand toward conservation.

On 25 September 1986, the United States unilaterally imposed a ban on wildlife and tropical aquarium fish imports from Singapore. The US Fish and Wildlife Service ordered the ban because Singapore was not able to

---

[60] ASEAN countries that joined CITES before Singapore: Malaysia (1978), Indonesia (1979), Philippines (1981), and Thailand (1983). McFadden, "Asian Compliance with CITES," p. 313.

[61] "Tourist Shops that Trade in Rare Wildlife," *ST*, 8 Mar. 1980, p. 15.

[62] "Plugging a S-E Asian 'Loophole'."

[63] "Singapore to Sign Endangered Species Treaty," *ST*, 30 Nov. 1984, p. 42.

[64] "Singapore to Sign Wildlife Pact," *ST*, 10 Mar. 1986, p. 3.

produce CITES-comparable documentation detailing the country of origin for its wildlife exports. Even though ornamental fish exported are not listed in Appendices I and II of CITES, under the Lacey Act, import of wildlife, including tropical fish, to the US was prohibited "unless acceptable assurance is provided that such items were lawfully taken from the country of origin." Singapore had not been able to authenticate the information provided on the export documents.[65] The implication was that unless Singapore joined CITES, it would have to bear the loss of the US as a partner in the lucrative trade in aquarium fish.

In 1986, Singapore's tropical fish exports totaled $50 million, and 40 percent went to America. The trade in other animal products amounted to another US$3–5 million. For the 200 exporters and approximately 1,000 fish farmers in Singapore, this was an unforeseen crisis. Objecting to the US sanctions, the Aquarium Fish Exporters' Association emphasized that "almost all of Singapore's exports of tropical fish to the US are farm-bred." The Association also urged the government to resolve the issue immediately, as many fish exporters and farmers were "hitting the panic button."[66] According to its representative, the embargo would also create heavy losses for airlines, which collected a similar amount for each dollar of fish exported in their freight. Denouncing the sanctions as "unfair," the Association asked that American authorities be held responsible for losses. Fish traders also announced that they were considering a court injunction against the US ban and argued that while the US banned farm-bred fish from Singapore, it was "accepting tropical fish exports from South America and Africa which are 100 percent caught in the wild." In retaliation, the fish exporters threatened to appeal to the General Agreement on Tariffs and Trade (GATT).[67]

The Singaporean government was similarly alarmed. In addition to contacting the American Embassy to express regret over the embargo, officials spared no effort to convince local and international observers that Singapore was serious about conservation. The government's public statements early in the crisis revolved around two points: Singapore had

---

[65] "An 'Early Solution' in Sight," *ST*, 3 Oct. 1986, p. 14.
[66] "US Ban on Aquarium Fish," *ST*, 2 Oct. 1986, p. 1; Reeve, *Policing International Trade*, p. 130. For further contextual information on fish farms and Singaporean agricultural policies in the 1980s, see Cynthia Chou's contribution to this volume.
[67] "Exporters and Airlines Also Hit," *ST*, 3 Oct. 1986, p. 14; "US Fish Ban: Global Body May Seek a Court Injunction," *ST*, 4 Oct. 1986, p. 36; "Fish Ban: Exporters Can Appeal to GATT," *ST*, 5 Oct. 1986, p. 10.

already indicated its willingness to join CITES; and thus, the American government's actions were high-handed and unreasonable. It was no coincidence that an article affirming Singapore's decision to sign CITES appeared alongside the first announcement of the ban in *The Straits Times*. In the article, a Ministry of National Development spokesperson stated that "Singapore has always supported CITES even though it is not a signatory" and asserted that Singapore had officially informed the CITES Secretariat that it has decided to join CITES three days before the ban took place. Besides deflecting American allegations, this announcement was also calculated to reassure the fish breeders that their business would resume once the paperwork for CITES was completed. Foreign Affairs Minister S. Dhanabalan referred to the ban as "absurd" and a "bureaucratic tangle" that the government would resolve soon.[68]

Following these announcements, the US Fish and Wildlife Service acknowledged that its primary concern was wildlife from other countries being re-exported from Singapore, not aquarium fish. According to an American official, the US government had "repeated its warning of a ban at least three times" since March 1986. Frustrated at Singapore's rebuttal that it had officially informed the CITES Secretariat of its intention to sign the treaty on 22 September, the official argued that "Singapore has been saying that for the past 10 years." To lift the ban, American officials needed "real assurance that Singapore intends to co-operate" and conform to CITES requirements.[69]

After intensive negotiations, a partial and temporary removal of the ban was enacted on 9 October 1986 and the export of tropical fish to the US resumed. Other wildlife and wildlife products, however, were still banned until the Americans were "satisfied that Singapore is complying with the rules and regulations of CITES." The US also required Singapore to ban the trade in rhinoceros horn products and cooperate with investigations into illegal wildlife trade.[70] While this seemed like a lengthy list of demands, Singapore was willing to comply. Yet, despite these diplomatic negotiations, it appeared that others were scrutinizing Singapore's every move. Influential

---

[68] "S'pore Backs Endangered Species Pact," *ST*, 2 Oct. 1986, p. 10; "Fish Ban 'Will Be Lifted by Year-End'," *ST*, 6 Oct. 1986, p. 9.
[69] "2 million of These Darlings Could Go Down the Drain," *ST*, 5 Oct. 1986, p. 1; "US Fish Ban: Global Body May Seek a Court Injunction," *ST*, 4 Oct. 1986, p. 36.
[70] "Americans Lift Embargo on S'pore Fish," *ST*, 10 Oct. 1986, p. 1.

conservation groups like the WWF openly stated that they would pressure the US government to re-impose the ban if Singapore failed to implement CITES. The conservation group "Monitor" also warned that, "Singapore is still in the hot seat" and that they "were considering a grassroots economic boycott of the Republic, particularly in the tourism trade."[71]

The boycott of Singaporean products, however, did not materialize as new regulations were soon implemented. The PPD briefed the relieved fish breeders on the new export forms that included the scientific names and country of origin of their fishes. Two weeks later, a government order came into effect prohibiting the trade in rhinoceros horn products. Although existing stocks in Chinese medicine shops were not confiscated and could still be sold locally, the import and export of the horn was banned.[72]

While the Singapore government complied with American demands, officials were naturally not pleased. Ministry representatives used terms like "high-handed," "provocative," and "illegal" when describing the situation. One official pointed out that the PPD had been working hard to set up the administrative machinery for CITES for over nine months, while also asserting that Singapore "will not hesitate to fight the US in GATT" if the ban is re-imposed and that the ban "is a serious encroachment of the sovereignty of the Singapore government."[73] In another interview, an officer in Singapore's Foreign Service reflected that the issue showed how Singapore is handicapped in international trade, as it had no means to "retaliate" against the US. In her opinion, the American government, being the ones who played a major role in establishing GATT, had failed to observe its rules and this "undermine[d] confidence in the international trading system."[74] In a self-vindicating report, the government stressed that it has been using administrative action to prevent trade in certain endangered species for many years even without CITES. Under the Control of Imports and Exports Act, the trade in *orang utans*, birds of paradise, and monkey-eating eagles was banned even before the establishment of CITES.[75]

---

[71] "Warning of Wider Ban if Illegal Wildlife Trade isn't Curtailed," *ST*, 12 Oct. 1986, p. 2.

[72] "New US Ruling for Aquarium Fish Exporters," *ST*, 11 Oct. 1986, p. 32; "S'pore Bans Trade in Rhino Horns," *ST*, 25 Oct. 1986, p. 1.

[73] "S'pore Still Smarting from US Fish Ban," *ST*, 15 Oct. 1986, p. 15.

[74] "Singapore Poser on Effectiveness of GATT," *ST*, 5 Nov. 1986, p. 10.

[75] "Trade in Some Wildlife Blocked," *ST*, 11 Nov. 1986, p. 13.

On 30 November 1986, Singapore finally became a signatory to CITES with the PPD being appointed the Management and Scientific Authority responsible for its implementation. Singapore, however, declared reservations on three species of crocodiles and alligators, pointing out in its press release that other countries such as Switzerland and Japan had also entered reservations on a number of species. The new regulations and provisions under CITES were to be implemented in stages over the following 90 days to allow traders time to adjust to the new requirements. Although Singapore sent a diplomatic note to the US asking that the ban be lifted fully the day after the Convention was signed, US officials responded that the ban would remain until they carried out a review with the CITES Secretariat. The US government only announced the complete lifting of the embargo on 1 January 1987. Stating that Singapore has taken "a number of positive steps to demonstrate a good-faith effort," they were assured that "acceptable" documentation would be provided for Singapore's exports. As a conclusion to the saga, American officials expressed their hope that Singapore "will continue to fulfil its responsibilities as a responsible trading nation in wildlife and wildlife products."[76]

During the last few months of 1986, the local press covered the CITES issue extensively. Compared to when the MNS raised the issue of CITES four years earlier, the US sanctions provoked a flurry of comments, articles, and responses on conservation and Singapore's position in global conservation efforts. In a lengthy article in *The Straits Times*, Liak Teng Kiat, a correspondent stationed in Washington, tried to put into perspective American motivations with regard to Singapore and CITES. The article suggested that wildlife protection was an issue most Americans would not dispute. Sketching out the history of the conservation movement in the US, he argued that environmental organizations such as the Sierra Club were able to influence US government policy. Another journalist discussed how joining CITES would impact local reptile skin and bird dealers and their businesses. Other public figures like Lim Boon Heng, then assistant secretary-general of the National Trade Union Congress, publicly ticked off the US for "imposing unreasonable measures on Singapore." He argued that "the zoo's success in

---

[76] "US Lifts All Curbs on Wildlife Imports," *ST*, 1 Jan. 1987, p. 36; Press Release, "Accession to CITES: Singapore's Concern for Wildlife Survival," Ministry of Communications and the Arts, 29 Nov. 1986; "Partial US Ban on S'pore Wildlife Won't Be Lifted Yet," *ST*, 3 Dec. 1986, p. 14.

breeding about 15 species of endangered animals was proof that Singapore cared for the preservation of wildlife" and that the US should be encouraging the zoo instead.[77]

It was perhaps fitting that after Singapore became a signatory of CITES, its first advocates—the Nature Society—took charge of organizing a one-day forum focusing on CITES and local wildlife conservation laws on 24 May 1987. The forum, titled "Conservation and You," included talks by officials from the PPD, WWF, as well as various wildlife experts on how they could contribute to conservation efforts and how the new treaty would affect Singapore.[78] It was a strange triumph for MNS members; four years after their efforts had begun the Singaporean government had become a signatory of CITES.

Local Initiatives versus International Pressure

On the present-day NSS website, the accession of Singapore to CITES in 1986 is listed as one of the "causes adopted and fought to a successful conclusion by the NSS."[79] However, its role in persuading the government to sign CITES was arguably limited. In Wee Yeow Chin's opinion, "the Nature Society had little influence in the government's decision to sign CITES; it was international pressure which made them change their mind."[80] It took the US embargo on aquarium fish to convince the government that this was no longer an issue they could brush aside. Why then, did the government reject the MNS' petition to sign CITES in 1982 but succumbed to international pressure in 1986?

The government was able to dismiss the MNS' appeal in 1982 with little difficulty as the organization was then still very much seen as a foreign-dominated fringe group. As discussed earlier, the MNS was just beginning to expand in membership and the scope of its activities in the early 1980s; it only had 187 members when it first tried to request the government sign CITES in 1981. It was only from the following year onward that their

[77] "Why Americans are Concerned about Wildlife" and "Wildlife Accord Will End Lucrative Trade in Reptile Skins," *ST*, 14 Dec. 1986, pp. 17–8; "Zoo's Breeding Efforts Show We Care," *ST*, 16 Nov. 1986, p. 12.

[78] "Forum on Conservation and You," *ST*, 12 May 1987, p. 14.

[79] "History and Accomplishments," at http://www.nss.org.sg/index.aspx [accessed 9 Mar. 2012].

[80] Wee Yeow Chin, personal interview, 18 Jan. 2012.

membership saw a substantial increase—doubling to more than 300 by the end of 1982 and double that again to reach near a thousand at the end of 1986—when CITES was eventually signed. Being such a small group, their voices were easily ignored, even if the group consisted of professional scientists and experts.

Even though the MNS was small, it was not totally alone in its hope that Singapore did its part for wildlife conservation in the early 1980s. Several Singaporean non-members were concerned enough to make their opinions heard through newspaper forums. Among those who wrote to support the MNS in 1982 was a student who expressed hope that Singapore would sign CITES and that the government act to stop the illegal trade in wildlife. He had come to know of the issue from *Reader's Digest*, which had highlighted how Singapore was a major stumbling block to Indonesia's efforts to curb wildlife smuggling.[81] Indeed, even when Singapore was not a member, the local press regularly published news on CITES and conservation efforts in other countries and there were people sympathetic with the MNS' cause.

According to personal interviews with past MNS committee members, there were also people from government agencies who shared the MNS' concerns with wildlife protection. On the CITES issue, Ilsa Sharp acknowledges that, "we not only wrote to the government, but there were also negotiations with PPD officers behind-the-scenes. While some of them did sympathise with the cause, their main concern was with enforcement if Singapore did join the Convention."[82] Indeed it was evident that even before the US ban was imposed, government agencies like the PPD were not oblivious to illegal trade in wildlife going through Singapore. The PPD investigated and exposed smuggling cases involving endangered wildlife and their products, often with the help of the Nature Society. For example, in 1983, the PPD successfully seized a shipment of cheetah skins worth $100,000 and charged the culprits under the Wild Animals and Birds Act. In the same year, at the request of the CITES Secretariat, the PPD has also agreed to reject import and export permits for rare tropical fish. On both occasions, the PPD stressed that even though Singapore was not a party to CITES, it supported its aims and objectives.[83] With that in mind, one may consider the defensive public

---

[81] "Vanishing Like the Tiger," *ST*, 16 Apr. 1980, p. 15.
[82] Ilsa Sharp, personal interview, 18 Jan. 2012.
[83] "$100,000 Cheetah Skins Seized," *ST*, 11 Feb. 1983, p. 38; "Don't Buy or Sell This Fish," *ST*, 5 Jan. 1983, p. 1.

statements government officials made during the American embargo as not mere rhetoric. While their efforts might not have matched the expectation of international observers in CITES, the PPD tried to control the illegal wildlife trade in its own way.

The course of action taken by the MNS, in making the issue public through the newspapers, most likely contributed to the rejection in the early 1980s. CITES was the first instance where the MNS publicly disagreed with and questioned the government's decision on an important policy. In the second decade after independence, the priority on economic survival and development meant that civil society interference in decision-making was discouraged. As Simon Tay describes in his periodization of civil society in Singapore, the dominance of the PAP in the 1970s and 1980s was a time when the "space for civil society shrank."[84] The MNS, with its professional knowledge and experience in nature and biodiversity issues, was valuable as a civil society partner for the government. It was co-opted in government projects and its members sat on committees of the Nature Reserves Board and the Parks and Recreation Department. Yet, like other civil society groups, the MNS had to function within set boundaries under the government and not challenge them. Francesch-Huidobro describes this as the "master and freed-slave" relationship, where NGOs were subordinate to the government in an unequal partnership.[85] Although PPD officials were not against the MNS, the matter was taken out of the PPD's hands when the MNS made their petition public. Ministry officials were forced to make a public response that they had considered the request but had decided against it. In openly disagreeing with the "master," the MNS had to be reminded of its place and resulted in investigations and warnings that were given to Avadhani. Reflecting on the incident in a recent interview, Avadhani said: "I have come to realize that the best way of influencing policy was not to confront them in public, but give them the information, seed the idea in them and let them decide for themselves that this is what they want."[86]

In speaking of the tension between confrontation and negotiation, Avadhani's comment not only applies to the CITES incident, but in the later conservation struggles for Lower Peirce Reservoir, Marina South Duck Ponds

---

[84] Simon Tay, "Towards a Singaporean Civil Society," *Southeast Asian Affairs* (1998): 247.
[85] Francesch-Huidobro, *Governance, Politics and the Environment*, p. 290.
[86] P.N. Avadhani, personal interview, 21 Feb. 2012.

and Senoko. In a way, the MNS' petition for CITES set a pattern which would be repeated in a different social-environmental context. Ten years after the MNS publicly challenged the government to sign CITES, the Society carried out a public campaign to oppose the golf course planned at Lower Peirce Reservoir. The government reacted in the same way, intimidating the leaders and publicly arguing against the merits of conservation in their attempt to reassert control. In the larger context of state-civil society relations, the Nature Society can be seen as to be precariously wavering at the boundary that defined the government's expectations for civil society groups that wanted to offer constructive criticism.[87]

In their public disagreement with the government on their decision not to sign CITES, the MNS was mild in its criticism, and took care not to offend. But, in the less permissive political landscape of the 1980s, they were met with a rebuff from the government and a flat refusal to accede to their request. In contrast, 10 years later in the Lower Peirce Reservoir confrontation, the increased awareness and support for the MNS' cause and the MNS' confidence in the legality of their campaign led Wee Yeow Chin and his committee to "take on" the government. Even though the government had to back down in that incident due to the many moral, legal and scientific arguments leveled against the golf course plan, it wasted no opportunity to make up for this "loss" in subsequent land-use conflicts. Another interviewee explained that although the government had not planned to develop the whole of Senoko, "they took the whole place to reassert their power after having conceded the golf course."[88] Conservation in Singapore was political and not just dependent on economic versus ecological benefits.

In dealing with the MNS, the government rhetoric centered around two contentions. The first was the priority of economic development over nature conservation; the second was the MNS' affiliations with foreign governments. Unlike the land-use confrontations of the 1990s where the rational voice of the developmental state expounded on the economic necessity of developing the contested natural site, the government could not openly claim to have profited off the trade in endangered animal products during the CITES incident. Instead, it alleged that the MNS was advocating

---

[87] Tay, "Towards a Singaporean Civil Society," p. 255; Nature Society, *Proposed Golf Course at Lower Peirce Reservoir: An Environmental Impact Assessment* (Singapore: Nature Society, 1992).

[88] Leo Tan Wee Hin, personal interview, 4 Jan. 2012.

for CITES as part of a Malaysian ploy to undermine Singapore. Its largely expatriate membership in the early 1980s—or at least the impression of it—did not help its cause. Even though the society consisted of more Singaporean than foreign members by 1992, the MNS' foreign links to Malaysia and other international conservation bodies provided justification for the government to ignore or reject its proposals. This was to remain a liability to their conservation efforts until the Society formally separated from the Malaysian parent association in 1992.

The state's objection to the MNS' foreign links was part of the prevailing belief that conservation was a foreign agenda designed for the West to retain control over the developing world. This was not a view unique to Singapore but also held in many developing countries. In a book on conflicts between Asian nations and environmental law, Roda Mushkat describes how developing countries perceived "concern for threats to biological diversity, voiced mainly by so-called specialists from developed/industrialized Western countries" as "yet another form of disguised imperialism, and that to bow before such concern would merely bring about an unwelcome neo-colonial-style intrusion upon their own national development policies."[89] An interviewee explained the skepticism the government had toward MNS conservation activities (not CITES) in simpler terms, "they [government officials] asked why we were doing this. They said that we are just being used by the white men and we should not be so foolish!"[90] The government could not conceive that nature conservation could be a legitimate agenda that locals take up but instead viewed them with a deep suspicion.

The CITES saga in Singapore illustrates this phenomenon well. While the IUCN is nominally an international body, Western nations are its main champions and its initiatives are "drafted solely from a developed country's perspective."[91] Having experienced a loss of wildlife, developed countries were concerned that the biodiversity-rich tropics would likewise squander their natural resources. But for many developing countries, wildlife is a

---

[89] Roda Mushkat, *International Environmental Law and Asian Values: Legal Norms and Cultural Influences* (Vancouver: UBC Press, 2004), p. 32.

[90] Leo Tan Wee Hin, personal interview, 4 Jan. 2012.

[91] Timothy Swanson, "Developing CITES: Making the Convention Work for All of the Parties," in *Endangered Species, Threatened Convention: The Past, Present and Future of CITES*, ed. Jon Hutton and Barnabas Dickson (London: Earthscan Publications, 2000), p. 150.

much-needed economic resource. Barnabas Dickson argues that the idea of CITES was born in the context of decolonization in Africa and the concern among European conservationists that the existing system of conservation would collapse with the withdrawal of colonial administrations. By pressing former colonies to join the international treaty, CITES represented an attempt on behalf of Western nations to "shore up the colonial approach to conservation in a post-colonial world." It was expected that "with their greater resources and experience," these nations "would be able to shape the direction and operation of the treaty."[92]

The American government employed such an approach when the enacted a trade embargo on Singapore aquarium fish to pressure Singapore, a non-party state, to join the Convention and adopt the regulatory mechanisms Western conservationists had developed. While trade is "a highly effective tool of international persuasion," especially when used against Singapore, it could also be criticized as "environmental imperialism."[93] This brings into question the right of states to determine their own environmental and conservation policy. Government officials in Singapore used such rhetoric when they described the American approach as "high-handed" and "unreasonable," and the embargo as "an encroachment on the sovereignty of Singapore."

Through the resented American ban, Singapore was, in the words of past MNS member, "dragged kicking and screaming into the 'civilised world'."[94] Singapore signed CITES because it was too costly not to do so. With fish breeders, exporters, and airlines severely affected, conservation was finally assigned an economic value that it had previously lacked. The administrative obstacles had not changed since the MNS first raised the issue in 1982, but when faced with such losses, these obstacles had to be overcome in as short a time as possible. This suggests that the main reason Singapore delayed signing CITES for so long, despite local concerns and persistent requests from international observers, was inertia and the belief that conservation was simply not important enough an issue in a country that prioritized economic development.

---

[92] Barnabas Dickson, "Global Regulation and Communal Management," in *Endangered Species, Threatened Convention: The Past, Present and Future of CITES*, ed. Jon Hutton and Barnabas Dickson, p. 166.
[93] Mushkat, *International Environmental Law and Asian Values*, p. 90.
[94] Ilsa Sharp, email interview, 15 Mar. 2012.

Within the persistent push for economic development, there were some voices in the government that were unsympathetic with how the Singaporean government handled the issue. Among these countervailing voices was prominent Singaporean diplomat Tommy Koh who proclaimed, "I felt that Singapore should do the right thing without being pressured into doing so. That we should have on our own volition become a party to CITES. But as usual, our bureaucracy dragged their feet and said that it was not in our national interest, the obligations are onerous and so on." While he did agree that the American action was high-handed, Koh—who became the official patron of the NSS when they separated from Malaysia—questioned "How much do you lose by prohibiting trade in endangered species of flora and fauna? We don't want to have that reputation anyway."[95]

Conclusion

The CITES incident acts as an important entry point to look at the history of not only the Nature Society but also how Singapore has come to terms with nature conservation. Unlike more recent conservation struggles when there was increased public awareness and demands for governmental accountability on nature-related issues, the CITES debate occurred at a time when the Nature Society was beginning to expand and experiment with advocacy. At a time when nature conservation was not yet popular, the government could afford to reject well-meaning petitions and decline to give explanations for an issue it assumed was of peripheral interest to the majority of Singaporeans.

The US embargo on aquarium fish, however, forced the government to re-evaluate its stance toward CITES and the island-state's international standing toward environmental protection. As Tommy Koh pointed out, it was better for Singapore to be seen as voluntarily subscribing to such international environmental cooperation platforms than having to be forced through other means to comply. The CITES incident was a turning point for how the Singaporean government portrayed itself internationally, even if not domestically. At the 1992 Earth Summit, Singapore presented its first ever Green Plan to outline policy directions to make Singapore a model green city in 2000. More recently, the Singaporean government committed itself

---

[95] Tommy Koh Thong Bee, "The Civil Service: A Retrospection," interview transcript by Oral History Centre, The National Archives, 23 May 1998, p. 100.

to develop the "City Biodiversity Index," an evaluation tool for parties to the Convention of Biological Diversity as its contribution to the Convention.[96] Today, Singapore spares no efforts to portray itself as a responsible member of the global community of nations with regard to nature conservation.

Within Singapore, debates related to nature conservation also changed after the CITES episode. While in general still serving to report and monitor cases of wildlife abuse and smuggling, the MNS gradually moved on to focus on the conservation of natural habitats in the late 1980s. As its membership grew and signs of increasing development encroached on people's need for space and a natural environment, the MNS, and its successor the NSS, undertook campaigns for their conservation in a more confident manner. It was only in the late 1990s, when a more radical activist faction left the society, that the NSS began to re-establish closer working relations with the government on conservation issues.

Because of the focus on the land-use tussles in the 1990s, there is no mention of the MNS' earlier efforts to advocate for wildlife conservation in existing literature on the Nature Society. The Nature Society's promotion of CITES and the debates raised were largely forgotten. The focus shifted to American intervention and the Singaporean government's compliance to avoid economic sanctions. These sanctions took agency away from the local civil society that had earlier championed the same cause. In looking at this period of activities in the Malayan Nature Society (Singapore) Branch, it can be seen that nature conservation is not a recent phenomenon. Today's conservation landscape, with its multitude of diverse environmental NGOs, should not be seen as the result of a sudden explosion of interest in the natural environment brought on by the West. Instead, the development of environmental consciousness is a mix of a variety of factors, ranging from a colonial era society that developed its own voice following independence, allowing it to work against, and alongside, a government focused on economic practicalities. While their advocacy efforts may have been limited in effectiveness in the 1970s and 1980s, the efforts of the dedicated individuals in the Nature Society, who organized activities and programs to present an alternative vision of a Singapore that could coexist with nature, were instrumental in creating an environmental consciousness among Singaporeans today.

---

[96] "City Biodiversity Index," at http://www.cbd.int/authorities/gettinginvolved/cbi. shtml [accessed 4 Mar. 2012].

"And That Was Good": A Brief History of the Greening of Singapore

"Plant a Tree" Drive in S'pore

A tree planting campaign was ordered by Mr. Lee Kuan Yew today to help bring rain. The target: 10,000 a year. The Government will plant 5,000—along new roads, on traffic circuses, in housing estates, school grounds and parks ... The Premier estimated that only one tree was planted for every 10 felled for building sites. To prevent vandalism, particularly on housing estates, he suggested that young trees be guarded by barbed wire. Singapore was becoming barren of trees, he said. To plant more would not only increase the island's water supply—trees encourage cloud formation and retain moisture that would otherwise be lost—but would make Singapore a pleasanter place to live in, he said. Mr Lee is expected to plant the first tree under this campaign on his tour of rural constituencies this weekend.

—*The Straits Times*, 12 June 1963, p. 9

...

Good Response for Big Tree Planting Drive

The tree-planting campaign launched by the Prime Minister, Mr. Lee Kuan Yew, is meeting with good response from the public. The Curator of the Botanic Gardens, Mr. A.G. Alphonso, said today his staff had been receiving telephone inquiries about suitable saplings. He said: "We don't normally have calls from the public about trees. But now the telephone rings almost all the time."

—*The Straits Times*, 24 June 1963, p. 3

I think the parks and recreation work started in earnest when our Prime Minister, at the beginning of the sixties, told the people that we must plant trees, we must green up the environment as we along with urbanisation and industrialization ... Lee Kuan

Yew had this very far-sightedness to say that unless we green up the environment, we will have a lot of problems, glares, dust, fumes and things like that. And with that as a kind of guideline to our government department, we went ahead to plan our work, so that streets are lined with trees, more parks created for the recreational activities of the population.

—Wong Yew Kwan
National Archives [Singapore] Oral History Centre, 001379, Reel 1

...

House is Told of "Floral Mile" Scheme

Plans are under way to develop a "floral mile" stretching from Newton Circus to Clementi Circus and nurseries are invited to do this. This was one of the number of "make Singapore beautiful" projects announced by the Minister for Law and National Development, Mr. E.W. Barker, during question time in Parliament today. Other projects are: Competitions in tree-planting and gardening in schools, contests and best-kept premises among commercial establishments, like petrol stations, and trees and shrubs for all road circuses. Flower trees will also be planted along the highways between Newton Circus and Woodlands while flower-boxes and plant shrubs will be put up in dividers on the main roads and at bus-shelters.

—*The Straits Times*, 9 Sep 1967, p. 10

We [the Singapore Botanic Gardens] got instructions to beautify the island, grow more trees. And so ... we were not at that time amalgamated with the National Parks yet ... We used to get these chaps form the PWD [Public Works Department], Architect Department and all that, and he [Howe Yoon Chong, a senior civil servant, who at the time was assigned to the Ministry of National Development] took great interest in the beautification work. He used to go twice a week ... Gets a big bus, takes all these fellows from PWD, Gardens and he drives them around, and he gives them what to do. Even roads ... They were just starting to build the roads and he says, "Yeah, you can start planning now, even before the roads are up!"

—Arthur George Alphonso
National Archives [Singapore] Oral History Centre, 002522, Reel 7

It started as a very modest unit under the Public Works Department. At the time it was called the Parks and Trees Unit, within the Public Works Department. Then it became sort of a division. It was changed to Parks and Recreation Division, still under the Public Works Department. But sometime, in perhaps 1973 or so, the Botanic Gardens was in fact roped into the Parks and Recreation Division also ... It was fortunate that the government was quite liberal in allowing this expansion to bring in a lot of officers with different expertise. For example, we needed botanists, we needed agronomists, we needed people who know something about pest and disease control. All these people we had or we still have within the Parks and Recreation Department. We planted trees, planted shrubs, created parks.

—Wong Yew Kwan

National Archives [Singapore] Oral History Centre, 001379, Reel 1

...

"Garden City" Float among Eight for N-Day Parade

Among the highlights of Singapore's ninth National Day parade will be eight gaily decorated and lighted floats that will follow the route march through the city at night ... The STPB [Singapore Tourist Promotion Board]'s float is expected to be among the most colourful items at the parade—a "Garden City" showing Singapore's skyscraper skyline interspersed with flowers of all varieties and hues. A group of 100 girls dressed in leaf green, flashing red and yellow board would precede the float followed by 12 stilt-walkers, who took part in the Chingay parade earlier this year.

—*The Straits Times*, 4 July 1974, p. 22

...

By round about 1978, the Parks and Recreation Department planted altogether something like 600,000 trees, and something like two to three million shrubs ... It is some sort of an achievement in a very urbanised environment. One has got to know that in the urbanised situation, it is not easy to look after trees. To plant a tree is one thing; to make sure it grows up is quite another matter altogether.

—Wong Yew Kwan

National Archives [Singapore] Oral History Centre, 001379, Reel 1

At that time, of course, they wanted results. So, we planted a lot of Angsanas. These Angsanas, you don't have to plant the seedlings. You can plant 10-foot stumps and they grow straight away. So we used these Angsanas for roadside planting. Of course, we used other trees—Yellow Flame, then we had Rain Trees. Mainly Rain Trees, but flowering trees as well. For different roads, we had different trees.

—Arthur George Alphonso

National Archives [Singapore] Oral History Centre, 002522, Reel 7

As the Garden City Action Committee, our job was to make sure the city is planted up, make sure the vegetation is growing well, make sure that in any new development, adequate tree planting is done. So it's an on-going action effort ... We sent teams overseas to Brazil, to all the other countries with compatible climates and they will gather the leaves of the plant varieties and tried them out here. So some of the trees here are from that type of effort ... When they built Changi Airport, they planted the trees before the road. That's why when the road came, all the trees already there. This was the era of the instant tree also. You know, the Angsana where you just cut and then you transplant anywhere. That was a very fast growing tree ... The Angsana was mainly when you want to have shade in a hurry. You can't wait years and years.

—James Koh Cher Siang
National Archives [Singapore] Oral History Centre, 002847, Reel 4

...

When Conservationists Do Not See People for the Trees

... Is it sound to say the island has no environment to talk about, let along destroy? That kind of talk discomforts me. Looking back, there were moments when I felt Singapore could have done things differently, when there should have been more circumspection before we bulldozed through our natural and architectural heritage. Yes, I include architectural conservation as an environmental concern because buildings are the natural environment of an urban landscape.

To me, some of the most painful examples are the loss of part of the jungle to build the Bukit Timah Expressway; the partial destruction of the habitat for animals and plants because of the quarrying at Bukit Timah; the destruction of the coral reef formations at some parts of Singapore's coastline ... Singapore may not be able to replace what it has lost, but it can avoid repeating mistakes. I hasten to add that I am no kneejerk opponent of whatever officialdom does to the environment, the very charge I levelled at some Green activists earlier.

In a city with a well-deserved reputation for being clean and green, the Government must be given full credit for its determined effort to mix green with the concrete grey of an urban environment ...

What I am urging is a matching of this effort of artificial creation (which is marvellous) with a greater awareness of natural preservation.

—M. Nirmala, *The Straits Times*, 26 Nov 1989, p. 32

...

We have evolved into the city in the garden. Remember, it's a completely different concept. It was a Garden City, not it is the City in the Garden. Singapore Island is a garden; it's not just a city. But, we grow a city within the garden. It's different from putting a garden into a city....

[Responding to criticism that it is "contrived"] Yes, that part I share a lot. I always tell them, I said, "When you create a park, it must try to look as natural as possible." But they tell me very honestly also, they get a lot of flak from CDC [Community Development Councils], MPs [Members of Parliament], and all because they in turn get a flak from the residents. "Oh, the muddy grass patch outside my house when it rains makes the whole place dirty. And the cleaners come and complain to the CDC, everyday I have to cleanup, why don't we just concretise the whole place?" ... NParks [The National Parks Board] cannot satisfy everybody, but certain areas we have to look out for ... So, I may set aside some manicured parks for you but go to Sungei [Buloh]. Then I would set up some other park that lets it grow as nature intended.

For Bukit Timah forest, as natural as possible. Keeping MacRitchie [Reservoir] by and large lush but providing a boardwalk so that you don't disturb the lush area, so we keep to the track. Please, if you want the orderly stuff, go to East Coast Park if you want an ordered park. Or you love to run your dogs, go to Bishan, West Coast Park. You want adventure? Pasir Ris and West Coast Park. But, West Coast Park is big by Singapore standards. I would keep the original mangrove for those who want the serenity and quietness of a non-orderly area. But, when we say non-orderly somebody would write to the press, "Aiyah, mosquitoes breeding in such an ugly looking rough hedges.".... We cannot force people to like nature or to dislike nature, but be realistic. Don't expect Singapore to be like an Amazon forest. We are too small ...

—Leo Tan Wee Hin
National Archives [Singapore] Oral History Centre, 002204, Reel 5

The exercise in greening Singapore has gone on for many, many years. It's not just something that happened in the last five or 10 years. That's why the trees are all grown bigger. So I think there was always an effort and the PM [Prime Minister] always led the way in making sure that people don't forget. He always says, "We don't want cement. If you plant trees, you can help lower the temperature." And it's true for tropical cities. The more trees you have, the temperature can be lowered. And that was good.

—James Koh Cher Siang
National Archives [Singapore] Oral History Centre, 002847, Reel 4

CHAPTER 9

A City in a Garden

Timothy P. Barnard and Corinne Heng

The nation-state of Singapore in the early 21st century consists of a bit more than 700 square kilometers. It hosts one of the highest population densities in the world, and is home to modern, high-rise residences and office buildings, all connected through a vast network of roads and expressways. Despite the presence of so much concrete, asphalt, and glass, and two centuries of constant pressure placed on the natural vegetation, it is a very green island. In 2011, botanists estimated that vegetation covered 56 percent of the ground area in Singapore. Approximately 27 percent of this was actively managed in lawns, gardens, and parks; the other 29 percent was classified as "spontaneous vegetation."[1] All of this greenery, however comforting and lovely it may be, is not natural or spontaneous. Its presence is the result of human activities, and often-deliberate plans.

Humans have shaped the natural environment of Singapore to suit their economic and social goals as long as they have been present on the island. The intensity of this transformation accelerated in the few decades following the appearance of English East India Company officials in 1819, when newly arrived immigrants cut down much of the forest that covered the island to make way for plantations. When these lands became exhausted in the second half of the 19th century, combined with the frequent rise-and-fall of prices for gambier and pepper and the shift of production to the Malay Peninsula, the island came to be covered in vast stands of *lalang* grass (*Imperata cylindrica*). After which it transitioned into rubber and agricultural

---

[1] A.T.K. Yee et al., "The Vegetation of Singapore: An Updated Map," *Gardens' Bulletin* (Singapore) 63, 1/2 (2011): 205–12.

plantations in the first half of the 20th century. Since the mid-20th century, the ecological transformation of Singapore has continued, mainly through the construction of large housing blocks to accommodate a rapidly expanding population that grew from around 900,000 following the Japanese occupation to over five million in the early 21st century. These various pressures on the land resulted in the clearing of at least 95 percent of the primeval forest in Singapore for agriculture or development in the past 200 years, with most of the damage done before 1900.[2]

In the second half of the 20th century, Singapore underwent a massive project to ensure the presence of vegetation throughout the island that reflected the tropical fecundity of much of Southeast Asia combined with the planning of the modern developmental state. Government programs supporting these goals have gone by a variety of titles, often containing combinations of the words "garden," "city," or "green." These programs, as well as the action of thousands of civil servants and officials enacting them, often are credited to the nation's dominating first Prime Minister, Lee Kuan Yew. As recounted in his autobiography—and quasi-narrative history of the state—these efforts originated in the early 1960s, when he proposed a tree-planting program to ensure that Singapore would become an "oasis in Southeast Asia." It was a program that Lee considered to be one of his proudest legacies.[3] Government agencies, including the Singapore Botanic Gardens, were enlisted in this effort, which, despite constant economic development and change, has resulted in Singapore becoming a developed, highly urbanized nation-state with more than half of its landscape covered in vegetation. This project was initiated not only to beautify the landscape but was linked to economic progress and social engineering during Singapore's early years of independence, and it has been wildly successful.

---

[2] The only remaining stands of original vegetation appear in very limited areas of the Bukit Timah Nature Reserve and Central Catchment Nature Reserve. In addition, in 1883 Nathaniel Cantley estimated that only seven percent of original forest remained. Nathaniel Cantley, *Report on the Forests of the Straits Settlements* (Singapore: Government Printing Office, 1883); Richard T. Corlett, "The Ecological Transformation of Singapore, 1819–1990," *Journal of Biogeography* 19, 4 (1992): 411–20; see also Tony O'Dempsey, Nigel Taylor, and Cynthia Chou's contributions to this volume for further details on these developments in Singaporean environmental history.

[3] Lee Kuan Yew, *From Third World to First—The Singapore Story: 1965–2000* (Singapore: Singapore Press Holdings, 2000), p. 199.

More importantly, until today, it serves as "a power symbol of many things, as advertisement for tourists, [and] also of identity and pride among Singaporeans."[4]

There is a background, a history, to these programs that influence the lives of everyone living in Singapore today. And, as is true with almost all of history in this small nation-state, it is linked to not only Lee and his focus on managing Singapore but also colonial era policies. The development of greening programs from the colonial era to the modern, independent government will be the focus of this chapter. In their efforts to create this oasis, Singaporean leaders, bureaucrats, and workers have manipulated the natural environment to reflect their vision of a planned green, urban landscape. In the process, they have created a city within a garden. Nature has flourished, but it has also been contained, disciplined, and manipulated to point that conservation and state control have become one in the same. Nature has become a human construct.

The Garden City

A garden is an area for growing flowers, fruit, or vegetables, and it can be used as a pleasure ground. Gardens have been in existence since ancient times, and have played a central role in the aesthetic character of a wide range of societies including the Mughal Empire, the Byzantium Empire, and various Chinese dynasties for several millennia. Just as the concept of a garden serves a particular vision of a green Singapore, these historic gardens served different purposes for their own societies. For example, Hellenistic Egypt focused on "market-gardening," where foods such as olives and nuts for commercial production were grown within the garden. In other societies, gardens were for the pleasure of the upper classes and their often-extravagant designs reflected their wealth, like the Hanging Gardens of Babylon. As "natural" as gardens are to one's imagined oasis of fresh flora and greenery, one common factor is that they are very much man-made constructs. Plants are manipulated to serve a purpose, whether for visual pleasure or for more pragmatic interests.[5]

---

[4] Lui Thai Ker, "Towards a Tropical City of Excellence," in *City and the State: Singapore's Built Environment Revisited*, ed. Ooi Giok Ling and Kenson Kwok (Singapore: Oxford University Press for Institute of Policy Studies, 1997), pp. 195–6.

[5] Christopher Thacker, *History of Gardens* (Berkeley, CA: University of California Press, 1979), pp. 13–5.

Planned gardens existed in Singapore prior to colonial rule, in the small gambier gardens present when Raffles landed in 1819, which reflect an attempt to shape the natural vegetation to the needs and goals of the pre-colonial society. Upon the arrival of the East India Company rule, the scale of these plantations—a large-scale form of a garden—expanded at breathtaking rate to encompass much of the island. Beyond these plantations, a small, functional botanic garden was built on Fort Canning Hill, and by the middle of the 19th century the current Singapore Botanic Gardens had come into existence. In addition to these formal gardens, British officials and other residents also constructed parks and private gardens. The development of parks and green spaces in areas such as Fort Canning Hill, as well as lining the roadside along Orchard Road with bamboo to provide shade for pedestrians, supplemented these transformed green spaces in rural areas. Businessman, such as Hoo Ah Kay, better known as Whampoa, also created large exquisite private gardens, while in most *kampongs* people planted fruit trees and flowers to beautify their surroundings.[6] Singapore was green, but there was a growing discomfort throughout the 19th century with how quickly it was transforming from an idealized fecund tropical island to one with less socially appealing flora as the Municipality—which consisted of the urban core around the port—grew increasingly crowded and the rural areas became noticeably deforested.

Efforts to maintain greenery in Singapore have their roots in a British understanding of nature and gardens, as well as a concern following the abandonment of gambier and pepper plantations in the 19th century. The rural areas of Singapore outside the Municipality remained covered in vegetation, although it had been massively disturbed. The subsequent secondary growth horrified colonial officials who turned to Nathaniel Cantley, Superintendent of the Singapore Botanic Gardens in the early 1880s, to propose a solution. In the report Cantley submitted, he estimated that only seven percent of original forest remained and advocated their preservation in the Straits Settlements, which included Penang and Melaka. To address this loss, he called for the development of Forest Reserves and nurseries to supply plants and trees for areas throughout the Straits Settlements. In Singapore, this resulted in the establishment of reserves around Bukit Timah Hill and the Central Catchment area, as well as a program promoting the planting of 1,000 trees in the "Chinese areas." The success of this proposal led to the

---

[6] William Warren, *Singapore: City of Gardens* (Singapore: Periplus, 2000).

creation of a green central region in Singapore, which has been maintained since the late 19th century.[7]

The Municipality of Singapore and the regions outside of the Forest Reserves were not the focus of greening efforts during the colonial era. The amount of greenery in the urban area was not considered a problem, as it reflected basic understandings of life in a modern city and the plantations were considered to be a pragmatic method to gain profit out of the land. These basic understandings, however, were beginning to transform in the West, with the development of public parks in industrialized cities and the creation of plans to make urban settlements more livable.

Any increasing focus on urban greenery among colonial officials was strongly rooted in the culture of the colonial overlord, Britain, and changing understandings of a livable environment. The key figure in many of these developments was Ebenezer Howard, a stenographer working in the English Parliament who had spent part of his youth in the United States and lived in Chicago following the Great Fire, thus observing its renewal as a modern city. In the late 19th century, there was a growing concern over the social effects of the Industrial Revolution, and officials directed their attention toward alleviating the terrible social conditions in the urban centers of England, where air pollution and overcrowding plagued increasingly unsanitary cities. Due to his familiarity with the works of his contemporaries, such as influential economist Alfred Marshall and his concept of decentralized industrial districts, Howard promoted a solution that came to be known as the "garden city." In his 1902 book, *Garden Cities of Tomorrow*, which was originally published in 1898 as *To-Morrow: A Peaceful Path to Reform*, Howard envisioned humans living in harmony with nature in new urban landscapes that would become "an alternative to the overgrown and congested industrial city and the depressed depopulated countryside."[8] These new urban landscapes would consist of a "permanent girdle of open

---

[7] Cantley, *Report on the Forests of the Straits Settlements*. See also Tony O'Dempsey's and Nigel Taylor's contributions to this volume.

[8] Robert H. Kargon and Arthur P. Molella, *Invented Edens: Techno-Cities of the Twentieth Century* (Cambridge, MA: Massachusetts Institute of Technology, 2008), pp. 1–20; Stephen V. Ward, *The Garden City: Past, Present, Future* (London and New York: E&FN Spon, 1992), p. 28; Stephan V. Ward, "Ebenezer Howard: His Life and Times," in *From Garden City to Green City: The Legacy of Ebenezer Howard*, ed. Kermit C. Parsons and David Schuyler (Baltimore, MD: The Johns Hopkins University Press, 2002), pp. 16–8.

and agricultural land" that would encircle a town, and bring people closer
to nature through the designation of greenbelts in smaller self-contained
towns, which would be established in rural areas. The populace could then
enjoy the benefits of a "city" and at the same time enjoy Mother Nature. This
doctrine eventually developed into dogma in England, where it can be most
clearly seen in the post-War development of London and the New Towns
Act of 1946.[9]

Colonial officials after the Second World War transferred the concepts
of developing a more livable green space that remained true to Howard's
vision from the metropole to the rapidly industrializing city of Singapore
during the late 1940s and 1950s. Land use was shifting from rubber plantations to agricultural food production in rural areas, while the continuing
development of the municipal area and industrialization resulted in more
trees being cut. To counteract these developments, the Rural Branch of the
Public Works Department began a tree-planting program in Singapore
during the 1950s. As part of this scheme, workers beautified the new Changi
Coast Road and Tanah Merah Besar Road in an announced "major new tree-
planting scheme" in 1955, which focused mainly on areas outside the urban
core.[10] The results in rural areas were impressive. By the end of the decade,
residential areas and the agricultural hinterland were increasingly green.
The urban core of Singapore, however, remained "barren" and took on the
appearance of a "concrete jungle," although much effort during this period
was put into horticulture, with the Singapore Gardening Society and the
Botanic Gardens often working together to hold increasingly popular public
talks in which they provided gardening tips to the public.[11]

Due to the continued loss of greenery and trees in urban areas in the
late 1950s and early 1960s, there was a growing concern that Singapore
would become a sterile, grey terrain in which concrete and asphalt dominated
and social problems multiplied. These fears echoed Lewis Mumford's theories
with regard to living in urban spaces. In his influential 1961 book, *The City*

---

[9] Ebenezer Howard, *Garden Cities of To-Morrow* (London: Faber and Faber, 1947),
pp. 50–7, 138–47.
[10] "Sacred Bo Tree of Paya Lebar Again Flourishing," *The Singapore Free Press*, 11 Aug.
1955, p. 5; "She Adores Singapore," *The Singapore Free Press*, 28 Jan. 1957, p. 11.
[11] John Ewart, "More People Hear Gardening Talks," *ST*, 31 Mar. 1955, p. 4; Azhar
Ghani, "Success Matters: Keeping Singapore Green," *IPS Update*, Apr. 2011, p. 2;
Warren, *Singapore*, pp. 14, 25.

of History, Mumford argued that problems in society were rooted in the structure of modern cities, which would only become sustainable if there was a balance with nature, which would result in the creation of an "organic city."[12] The call for reform from the leading urban architects and advisors of the time appealed to the energetic young politicians running the largest city in the newly formed nation of Malaysia. New efforts at social engineering and the transformation of the environment and its relationship to modern technology were needed if they were to create a sustainable, modern city.

The greening campaign thus entered a new phase in 1963, when Lee Kuan Yew, then Prime Minister, initiated a tree planting campaign that echoed many of Howard's, as well as Mumford's, goals. It was envisioned that these efforts would help transform the city-state into a "natural haven amidst the concrete, material trappings of economic progress," which would accompany its own industrial transformation.[13] At the time, much of Singapore was under construction. According to newspaper accounts of the time, Lee was concerned that the development of Singapore was displacing too many trees—according to his calculations, ten trees were destroyed for every one planted at the time. On 16 June 1963, Lee planted a young Mempat (*Cratoxylum formosum*) tree in Farrer Circus to counter these developments symbolically and begin a new phase in Singaporean environmental history.[14]

This initial phase of the modern greening of Singapore lasted four years. The number of trees planted increased significantly with, for example, the planting of 2,668 trees in 1963 versus 440 trees in 1962. After a few years, the planting campaign began to spread to the rural areas of Singapore with a particular focus placed on planting along newly constructed road-

---

[12] Lewis Mumford, *The City in History* (New York: Harcourt, Brace and World, 1961); Kargon and Molella, *Invented Edens*; Victor Savage, "Singapore's Garden City: Reality, Symbol, Ideal," *Solidarity* 131–132 (1991): 73; Peter Crane, "Botanic Gardens for the 21st century," *Gardenwise* 16 (Jan. 2001): 7.

[13] Howard, *Garden cities of To-morrow*; Robert Freestone, "Greenbelts in City and Regional Planning," in *From Garden City to Green City: The Legacy of Ebenezer Howard*, ed. Kermit C. Parsons and David Schuyler (Baltimore, MD: Johns Hopkins University Press, 2002), p. 72; Lee Sing Kong and Chua Sian Eng, *More Than a Garden City* (Singapore: Parks and Recreation Department, 1992), p. 2.

[14] The circus was located at the intersection of Farrer Road and Holland Road. The tree no longer exists. "Lee Begins the Tree Campaign," *ST*, 17 June 1963, p. 7; "'Plant a Tree' Drive in S'pore," *ST*, 12 June 1963, p. 9.

Plate 9.1 Prime Minister Lee Kuan Yew launching the Tree Planting Campaign in June 1963 (Source: Ministry of Communications and Information Collection, courtesy of the National Archives of Singapore).

sides, such as Changi Road, Mandai Road, and Jurong Road, where the developing industrial and residential areas of the island were located.[15] The Tree-Planting Campaign, as it was known, however, was not entirely successful as the results were less than ideal. While up to 10,000 trees were planted annually, it was mainly done without a concern for the species of trees planted, and their location. This was most likely due to the lack of people within the government who were "experts in the field." In addition, there was little support from the public. This lack of public support took many forms, even coming from within the government. In 1964, for example, officials oversaw the cutting of more trees than necessary— following the normal practice of the time to clear-cut an area—during the construction of a school in the Alkaff Gardens, resulting in letter writers complaining about government hypocrisy. To prevent such "vandalism," Lee Kuan Yew even proposed that young trees be wrapped in barbed wire. After four years of sputtering attempts at tree planting, government officials decided that the entire program needed to be re-launched, with the populace trained to act responsibly around nature.[16]

To counter these initial setbacks in the effort to create a green Singapore, the government introduced the "Garden City" program in May 1967. Among the most important developments was the creation of a newly formed Parks and Trees Unit within the Public Works Department, under the leadership of Chong Toh Goo, an engineer. The goal of this new Unit, and the Garden City campaign, was to make Singapore "a city beautiful with flowers and trees," and went beyond the greening of Singapore to include efforts to limit rubbish and waste. Like many of the campaigns to come in Singapore, Lee Kuan Yew proposed it as a combined "administrative exercise"—involving the planting of trees and clearing of rubbish—and an effort to discipline the public so "that the people of Singapore be trained not to undo the good work the Government hopes to accomplish."[17]

---

[15] Anonymous, *Annual Report of Parks and Recreation, 1963* (Singapore: Parks and Recreation Division, 1964), p. 4; Anonymous, *Annual Report of Parks and Recreation, 1966–1967* (Singapore: Parks and Recreation Division, 1968), p. 6.

[16] "'Plant a Tree' Drive in S'pore"; "Body to Make People Care for Trees," *ST*, 19 Apr. 1967, p. 13; Nature Lover, "Vanishing Parkland at Alkaff Gardens," *ST*, 23 May 1964, p. 17; "When Trees Must Make Way for New Schools," *ST*, 6 June 1964, p. 15.

[17] "Garden City," *ST*, 13 May 1967, p. 10; "S'pore to Become Beautiful, Clean City Within Three Years: PM Announces Two-Stage Plan," *ST*, 12 May 1967, p. 4.

The "Garden City" program that began in 1967 consisted of numerous projects to address a variety of issues regarding Singaporean cleanliness and ecology, and it expanded rapidly. Fines for littering were increased—from $5 to $150 for a first offence—and the Government distributed dustbins, which only half of Singaporean homes had in 1967. In the first six months, workers from the Public Works Department planted over 9,000 trees to "beautify the Republic." Within a year, over a dozen related projects were being undertaken. Expanding beyond roadside planting, the banks of the Alexandra, Geylang, Bedok, and Bukit Timah canals became the focus of tree-planting efforts, and flower boxes even appeared in the central dividers of Alexandra Road and Bukit Timah Road. Traffic islands, as well as circuses, throughout the city underwent "treatment." The Public Works Department also turned its attention to the urban environment of concrete by supplying plants to offices and promoting the transformation of the frontage of buildings to allow for shrubs and ornamental plants. The government also created plant nurseries in Yio Chu Kang, Woodleigh, and Ulu Pandan to supply the city with trees and shrubs, while "model nurseries" were constructed along Dunearn Road to encourage people to purchase plants and participate in their own way. In the campaign promoting these efforts, emphasis was placed on the many benefits of having such vegetation, which included preventing "pedestrians from jaywalking along these busy highways."[18]

These early efforts were not without their critics or skeptics. The program initially limited the choice of plants to 40 species, which created a fear that this would lead to monotonous vegetation along the roadsides, and reduce the diversity of flora that naturally occurs in tropical areas.[19] In addition, the efforts of bureaucrats in beautifying the city met some stinging feedback in Parliament. As *The Straits Times* depicted the debate, "Ministries are not usually responsible for anything aesthetically pleasing," but went on to add that initial effort was off to a "promising start" by the end of 1967. These projects, along with fines and cleanliness campaigns, continued for the next several years, and resulted in an increasingly green—and disciplined—urban

---

[18] "Transforming S'pore into a 'Garden City'," *ST*, 20 Oct. 1967, p. 7; "House is Told of 'Floral Mile' Scheme," *ST*, 9 Sep. 1967, p. 10; Yap Neng Chew, "Garden City: The Need for Planning," *ST*, 29 Jan. 1968, p. 10; Cheong Yip Seng, "Big Strides Taken to Make S'pore a Garden City," *ST*, 21 July 1968, p. 6.

[19] Antony Santiago, "Garden City: Planting with Imagination from the Widest Choice … and Checking on the Red Tape," *ST*, 4 Nov. 1967, p. 14.

space in Singapore that led one letter writer to *The Straits Times* to opine that Singapore had "become very pleasant."[20]

To keep the momentum going, Tree-Planting Day—7 November—was established in 1971 to "help maintain the citizens' interest and efforts at keeping Singapore green and beautiful."[21] The designation of tree-planting day reflects much of the calculation that was going into the program. The choice of the date coincided with the beginning of the rainy season, thus reducing the need for watering and allowing the plant a chance to survive. In addition, it allowed the government to mobilize Cabinet Ministers as well as Members of Parliament in a public display of support for the program. During the first Tree-Planting Day, Deputy Prime Minister Goh Keng Swee symbolically planted the first tree, a Rain Tree (*Albizia saman*), on Mount Faber. This was the first of over 30,000 plants placed in the ground that day, in a frenzy of planting that included 7,000 trees and over 14,000 shrubs, a tradition that has continued ever since, although perhaps not at this initial level.[22]

To promote the greening of Singapore even further, the government merged the Singapore Botanic Gardens with the Parks and Tree Unit under the Ministry of National Development in 1973. Two years later, this new unit was named the Parks and Recreation Department. The justification for these moves was to elevate the garden city concept to the next level by bringing in experts who understood vegetation, and not just continue the practice of planting trees for the sake of planting trees. The union of the Singapore Botanic Gardens with the Parks and Trees Unit was tenuous initially, as personnel from both departments had to adjust to new expectations. This was especially true for those who worked at the Singapore Botanic Gardens. The greening campaign—while a worthy cause—forced employees of an institution that was by-and-large autonomous before independence to shift from their original pursuit of purely scientific research and academic work to the maintenance of plants to serve the nation. In the words of government officials at the time, the Singapore Botanic Gardens would now support

---

[20] "Floral Way," *ST*, 21 Dec. 1967, p. 12.
[21] "Tree-Planting Day to Keep the City Clean, Green," *ST*, 16 Oct. 1971, p. 30; Nature Lover, "A Happier Feeling Now with More Greenery," *ST*, 3 Oct. 1970, p. 20.
[22] "Dr Goh Plants Tree to Launch T-Day," *ST*, 8 Nov. 1971, p. 17; Ghani, "Success Matters," p. 4.

efforts to "naturalise" the city, and it was necessary to avoid "blooming mistakes" that had occurred due to the "crash planting" of so many trees in the ten years following the initial tree-planting ceremony in 1963.[23]

Despite the tensions and difficulties between the Singapore Botanic Gardens and the government, the Gardens' staff nonetheless played their role to lessen the impact of industrialization in Singapore and contributed to the greening efforts. Their most prominent contribution was knowledge of the floral world. The original Parks and Trees Unit worked mostly by trial and error to see which types of plants were suitable for planting around the island, with rapidity of growth often being the primary consideration. In the 1960s and early 1970s, this approach resulted in the Angsana (*Pterocarpus indicus*) being the main tree found along thoroughfares in Singapore as it was easy to transplant, grew quickly, and provided shade with its large canopy. In the subsequent decades, the tree grew less popular among officials as it went into decline due to "Angsana wilt," which is a fungal disease that is spread through spores ambrosia beetles carry. One consequence of the "wilt" was weakened trees, which further exacerbated the dangers of the brittle branches of Angsana trees. This occasionally caused tree limbs to fall onto roads, and even hit automobiles, resulting in officials in the Parks and Recreation Department appearing in court to defend their efforts at greening Singapore. By the early 1990s, the fungus was killing almost 30 trees a month, finalizing a shift in the species of trees chosen. Among the most popular trees to replace the Angsana were the Rain Tree and the Yellow Flame (*Peltophorum ptercarpum*). Each of these trees grows quickly, has a wide canopy, and reaches heights of over 20 meters, making them ideal for the rapid greening project that the Singaporean government was promoting.[24]

The staff of the Singapore Botanic Gardens also played an important role in the creation of a variety of gardens and parks in Singapore. Among the first were the Chinese Garden and adjacent Japanese Garden, which

---

[23] William Campbell, "Pooling Talent to Avoid 'Blooming Mistakes'," *ST*, 25 Sep. 1973, p. 12; "New Dept to Develop Garden City," *ST*, 28 Feb. 1973; Bonnie Tinsley, *Singapore Green: A History and Guide to the Botanic Gardens* (Singapore: Times Book International, 1983), p. 53; Bonnie Tinsley, *Visions of Delight: The Singapore Botanic Gardens Through the Ages* (Singapore: The Gardens, 1989), p. 39.

[24] Timothy Auger, *Living a Garden: The Greening of Singapore* (Singapore: National Parks Board and Editions Didier Millet, 2013), pp. 31–4; Wee Yeow Chin, *A Guide to Wayside Trees of Singapore* (Singapore: The Centre, 1989), p. 7; James Koh Cher Siang, National Archives [Singapore] Oral History Centre, 002847, Reel 4.

were constructed in 1974–75 to bring some greenery to Jurong, the most industrialized area of Singapore. Parks, such as those in Bishan and Toa Payoh, soon became a common feature of Housing and Development Board (HDB) satellite towns over the next few decades. Also, six nurseries to provide the relevant shrubs and trees to be planted were developed to ensure there was a sufficient supply of trees throughout Singapore. Finally, to ensure that expertise in this exercise would be readily available, the Singapore Botanic Gardens launched programs to train personnel in horticulture and botany.[25]

While these changes took place on the ground, new laws and committees were promulgated to support the greening of Singapore in the halls of government. Primary among these was the establishment of the Garden City Action Committee to formulate policies related to the natural environment. One of the main tasks of committee members was to coordinate the often at-odds ministries to bring together a more cohesive initiative to green Singapore. The results of this cooperation were manifested in the combining development efforts with greenery. This was accomplished partly through the creative promotion of the growing of plants along concrete structures and the introduction of flowering plants, often in boxes placed on overhead bridges. In addition, major thoroughfares were constructed with at least a 1.5-meter gap in the middle to allow for light and rain to reach plants, which could then flourish in the allowed space. Concrete throughout the city was also treated with stucco, or given a rough surface, to allow climbing plants to take root. These coordinated efforts to beautify the developing nation-state extended to cleanliness campaigns, which included the removal of illegal dwellings and forced repair of dilapidated buildings, to make the island "clean and green." Greenery was even used to cover up illegal squatter colonies in areas along Rochor Road and Ophir Road that officials considered to be "slums."[26]

---

[25] William Campbell, "The Chinese Garden," *ST*, 2 Dec. 1973, p. 12; "New Unit Planning a Variety of Landscaped Gardens," *ST*, 21 Sep. 1973, p. 10; Lee and Chua, *More Than a Garden City*, pp. 119–23; National Parks Board, *Annual Report 2007/2008*, p. 52; Auger, *Living in a Garden*; Singapore Government, *Year Book for 1973* (Singapore: Government Printing Press), p. 236.

[26] Min Geh and Ilsa Sharp, "Singapore's Natural Environment, Past, Present and Future: A Construct of National Identity and Land Use Imperatives," in *Spatial Planning for a Sustainable Singapore*, ed. T.C. Wong et al. (London: Springer with the Singapore Institute of Planners, 2008), p. 187; Lee and Chua, *More Than a Garden City*, p. 127; Auger, *Living in a Garden*, pp. 40–1.

Plate 9.2 Discussions and meetings beginning in the 1960s, often under the leadership of Prime Minister Lee Kuan Yew, focused on the various greening campaigns that would create a Garden City. This meeting, from 1963, was among the first (Source: Ministry of Communications and Information Collection, courtesy of the National Archives of Singapore).

Thousands of people worked over several decades to create a green Singapore. These officials ranged from Howe Yoon Chong, a permanent secretary in the Ministry of National Development, who visited sites and helped oversee plantings in the 1970s, to Clayton Lee, an arborist in the early 21st century who inspects trees and determines their health.[27] The policies, and labor, of this army of people resulted in the planting of millions of trees and shrubs in Singapore, transforming a highly urbanized state into green oasis with vegetation covering more than 50 percent of the land, in comparison to an estimate of 36 percent in 1986. The results were remarkable, and Singapore had become a more livable city.[28]

---

[27] Auger, *Living in a Garden*, p. 77; Arthur George Alphonso, National Archives [Singapore] Oral History Centre, 002522, Reel 7.

[28] To present it another way, between 1970 and 1992 over five million trees and shrubs were planted in Singapore. "City in a Garden," NParks Fact Sheet, 17 Mar. 2012, at http://www.nparks.gov.sg/ [accessed 19 Aug. 2013].

The role of officials, and the formations of these committees as well as the quantification of results, reflected the bureaucratic and administrative approach that the Singaporean government took with regard to nature. The head of this bureaucracy was Lee Kuan Yew, and he took a personal interest in the various environmental programs to the point that he was a micro-manager. He often wrote letters to the Ministry of National Development to urge the planting of more trees, and developed a personal knowledge of plants and soil from all around the world. Furthermore, he prioritized funding to ensure that it was sufficient to beautify the surroundings. By doing this, Lee wanted to project his image as the "chief gardener" of Singapore to show that he was capable of running the nation efficiently.[29] In official accounts of this period, Lee Kuan Yew has been portrayed as taking control of a Third World country, including its natural environment, and willing it into First World status. As a journalist for *The Straits Times* wrote in 2011, Lee "seeded a civilised garden in an unruly land."[30] Such quotes reflect how nature was coming to be seen in Singapore, and becoming part of the national narrative. Beyond making it a more pleasant place to live, the greening program played a role in disciplining the society to fit the hopes of the government. Nature had become a metaphor for Singaporean development. It was to be tamed and directed, much like the populace.

Disciplining Nature, Disciplining Society

Aggressive tree-planting began in Singapore in the 1960s. In 1963, government officials justified the launch of the Tree Planting Campaign as necessary to maintain the environment of rapidly industrializing Singapore. The newly planted trees not only provided shade and shelter; they also ensured that dust would be contained, especially in industrial areas while also reducing noise for public housing dwellers. There was also a need to ensure an abundance of vegetation. With more concrete than trees, officials

---

[29] Ghani, "Success Matters: Keeping Singapore Green," p. 9; Lee, "High Five for LKY; Singapore's Chief Gardener," *The Straits Times*, 28 May 2011; Neo Boon Siong, June Gwee, and Candy Mak, "Growing a City in a Garden," in *Case Studies in Public Governance: Building Institutions in Singapore*, ed. June Gwee (Abingdon, Oxon; New York: Routledge, 2012), p. 13.

[30] Lee, "High Five for LKY"; the emphasis on Lee's role can be found in almost any account of greening in Singapore. For example, see Lee, *From Third World to First*; Auger, *Living in a Garden*.

feared that the reduced concentration of oxygen in the air would lead to air pollution, a phenomenon that plagues many newly industrializing cities. The reasoning for such environmental measures, however, shifted with the beginning of the Garden City project in 1967. The greening of Singapore after this point took on an importance for nation-building purposes in terms of economic and social relevance. Lee wanted to ensure that the image of Singapore was not one of "general dilapidation and ... unkempt gardens," but of a beautiful, orderly landscape that would convey the image of a nation that was economically vibrant and disciplined.[31]

The economic benefits of the various greening policies arose from the engineered landscape, a feature of a garden city in which not only buildings were planned, but nature as well. This careful planning implied a control over nature as technocrats ranging from architects and landscape engineers decided which plants to select and where to put them. This resulted in neat rows of trees along the roads as well as always trimmed and well-maintained shrubs along the sidewalks. This well-organized landscape became central to urban development policy in Singapore. The desire to create a well-ordered landscape was weaved into almost all policies related to urban development and the environment. This can be seen in various regulations passed during the period. For example, in the mid-1970s the government began to provide tax relief to homeowners who maintained a garden as well as fines to property developers who did not properly maintain trees on their land. To further support these policies, the Parks and Trees Act was put in force in 1975. It ensured that developers did not cut down trees without the permission from the government and gave the government the right to plant or replant trees. Every tree planted or uprooted was accounted for, reflecting the level of control the government had over the environment and, by extension, the people. It sent a message to the citizens that the government enforced social discipline and bureaucratic administration with regard to the environment, and these efforts showcased official dominant rule.[32]

---

[31] Lee, *From Third World to First*, p. 202; Lui, "Towards a Tropical City of Excellence," in *City and the State: Singapore's Built Environment Revisited*, ed. Ooi and Kwok, p. 189.

[32] The amount of tax relief was between $100 and $300 a year, and 80,000 properties were eligible. "Garden City Concept Gets Lift," *ST*, 10 Apr. 1972, p. 14; "New Guidelines for Aeration of Trees," *ST*, 14 Feb. 1974, p. 11; "Laws to Preserve 'Garden City' Image," *ST*, 21 Mar. 1975, p. 7; Lui, "Towards a Tropical City of Excellence," in *City and the State: Singapore's Built Environment Revisited*, ed. Ooi and Kwok.

The presentation of an orderly Singapore, even down to the level of the natural environment, contributed to the impression that the nation-state was a stable location for investors. This perception most dramatically presents itself to new arrivals to the nation, as foreigners saw—and continue to see—nothing but beautiful flowers, shrubs, and trees while exiting the airport. This was a deliberate move. The East Coast Parkway and Bedok areas—lined with beautiful and orderly vegetation to impress visitors and residents as they head into town—are a particular point of pride as is often pointed out in interviews with Lee Kuan Yew and other officials who oversaw the planting.[33] Lee believed that if Singapore was dirty and disorganized, investors would not be interested in establishing businesses in the growing city-state, and thus the theme of cleanliness, progress, and the environment became the focus of numerous speeches. In a 1965 speech, for example, Lee said that he "had visions of a beautiful garden, [with] everybody passing by admiring the flowers and trees and so on. And at the same time the garden would be bearing gold and silver underneath, invisible to all sight as cars went whizzing by."[34] This aspect of the greening campaign was clearly a success, particularly as the nation emerged as one of the "Four Asian Tigers" by the 1990s. The greening of Singapore was a long-term achievement for the government in terms of economic nation building, and Lee remarked that it was the "most cost effective project [he had] launched." It made Singapore stand out from other countries because "most countries in Asia then paid little or no attention to greening."[35]

Apart from the contributions to economic nation-building, the Garden City project had another aim that was targeted at the social aspect of nation-building. The government was hoping that it would enhance the quality of life for citizens in Singapore. Gardens helped to invoke the "*kampong* spirit" that was lost when Singaporeans moved into HDB flats from the late 1960s onwards and gave citizens the feeling of "garden living" or "island living." Also, it reduced the impact that relocation had on the

---

[33] James Koh Cher Siang, National Archives [Singapore] Oral History Centre, 002847, Reel 4.

[34] Lee Kuan Yew, "To Survive and Prosper," 27 Nov. 1965, in *The Papers of Lee Kuan Yew: Speeches, Interviews and Dialogues*, Volume 3 (1965–1966) (Singapore: Gale Asia, 2012), pp. 233–7; Ghani, "Success Matters: Keeping Singapore Green," p. 7; Luk Van Wassenhove, "Singapore-City in a Garden: A Vision for Environmental Sustainability," INSEAD, 2013, p. 3.

[35] Lee, *From Third World to First*, pp. 203, 205.

populace.[36] To ensure that citizens retained a sense of belonging and "neighbourliness," which was reminiscent of the *kampong* days, the government tried to keep something "familiar" for Singaporeans in light of the rapid transformation of Singapore's landscape in a short space of time of about 20 years.

There was also a corresponding aim of beautifying the environment and changing the social habits of Singaporeans. The Parks and Recreation Department was concerned about the overall aesthetic appearance of the plants in the 1980s and this marked the start of a new phase in the greening project. With 300,000 trees and 3 million shrubs already planted, the aggressive tree-planting project had been mostly fulfilled. The green landscape now had to be adorned with flowers and even fruit trees to make it more appealing to the senses of people and enhanced the overall beautification of the landscape in a fast growing city. Projects to beautify the urban landscape also shifted to cleaning the Singapore River and Kallang River. Beyond these programs, the most important element in improving the landscape was applied to the people as a way to "adjust" the behavior and habits of Singaporeans. "Brown issues" such as littering and old habits such as trampling on grass and plants were a cause of concern for the government in the 1980s. These problems obstructed the vision of a Garden City, especially if "heaps of rubbish were uncollected, gathering flies and harbouring disease vectors. And these stink."[37]

Concern over these issues created a need to educate citizens to respect the environment and landscape. The government began much of this "education" among the young by allowing students to bring home a flower or seedling to plant at their house, which helped spread the green message to their families.[38] This approach tweaked the behavior of Singaporeans with the goal of eradicating "bad" habits and encouraging "good" habits. Furthermore, the Garden City project helped to avert the instillation of

---

[36] Daniel Goh Pei Siong, "Defending Nature in the 'Garden City': Environment and Social Power in Singapore," unpublished Master's thesis, Department of Sociology, National University of Singapore, 2000, p. 71.

[37] Victor R. Savage and Lily Kong, "Urban Constraints, Political Imperatives: Environmental 'Design' in Singapore," *Landscape and Urban Planning* 25 (1993): 37–52; Lee and Chua, *More Than a Garden City*, p. 10; Evangeline Gamboa, "The Making of a Garden City: How S'pore Tackled Its Environmental Problems," *ST*, 27 Dec. 1983, p. 20.

[38] "Making Children Aware of Trees," *ST*, 17 May 1982, p. 13.

Plate 9.3 Support for greening programs could be found throughout all government agencies, including the Post Office, which issued a special stamp collection, "Wayside Trees of Singapore," in 1976 (Courtesy of the Postal Services Department, Singapore, and the National Archives of Singapore).

"ugly" Singaporeans, because the government believed that the level of civilization of a country was reflected not only by the landscape but also the people living within the landscape. After all, the development of the Garden City in Singapore was a "testimony of a people's ethos, cultural attainment [and] aesthetic taste," for only people who developed gardens and maintained them were of "high social and educational standards."[39] The ultimate goal of these greening campaigns was to showcase Singaporeans as a people who were not only concerned with the material aspects of life, but also cared about nature and the environment.

The government justified much of the campaign for a greener Singapore as an attempt to engineer social habits and increase revenue for the economy. In this regard, they were successful. The campaigns, however, also gave Singaporeans an unconscious sense of pride in their country as a Garden City. The clean, flawless cityscape came to be compared to other countries when Singaporeans travelled abroad. The Garden City project was an example of a successful nation-building approach that happened to involve nature, and had meanings on a number of levels. The nation, its citizenry, and environment had been disciplined.

Nature Contained

Following the success of campaigns to create a green, clean, and disciplined nation-state in the 1970s and 1980s, issues related to the environment began to shift in Singapore. Although campaigns continued—with new announcements, such as the development of "green corridors" connecting parks and the creation of a Heritage Trees Scheme in 2001 to preserve mature trees, still being made on a regular basis—the focus was now on how the green space was managed, leading to occasional tensions between the government and environmental groups in Singapore, such as the Nature Society.[40] At the

---

[39] Lui, "Towards a Tropical City of Excellence," in *City and the State: Singapore's Built Environment Revisited*, ed. Ooi and Kwok, p. 196; Van Wassenhove, "Singapore-City in a Garden: A Vision for Environmental Sustainability," p. 5.

[40] For a discussion of events leading up to the debates over nature reserves, please see Goh Hong Yi's contribution to this volume. Geh and Sharp, "Singapore's Natural Environment;" Harvey Neo, "Challenging the Developmental State: Nature Conservation in Singapore," *Asia Pacific Viewpoint* 48, 2 (Aug. 2007): 186–99; Leo Tan Wee Hin, National Archives [Singapore] Oral History Centre, 002204, Reels 5 and 6.

center of these tensions was contrasting definitions of "nature," "conservation," and "garden city" between environmentalists and government officials. As Victor Savage and Harvey Neo—both geographers at the National University of Singapore—and many others have pointed out, environmentalists chaffed at the "deliberate beautification" of the environment in which every tree was planned, located, and monitored to an amazing degree. They did not consider such an approach "natural" at all, as it had more to do with development than conservation. Instead, it was "controlled tropicality" in the words of Nature Society stalwarts Min Geh and Ilsa Sharp.[41] While the amount of vegetation was comforting and welcomed, the "complacency" toward the "artificial creation" of the environment had set in and became discomforting for many.[42]

A dialogue between the government and environmentalists over these issues began to emerge in the mid-1980s following requests from the Nature Society to designate Sungei Buloh, a 318-hectare mangrove swamp area in northwestern Singapore that is host to migrating birds (particularly from September to April), as a nature reserve. Sympathetic government officials—particularly S. Dhanabalan, Mah Bow Tan, and Tommy Koh—helped steer the proposal through government channels, and in April 1988 the government designated an 87-hectare site as a bird sanctuary. The development of Sungei Buloh led to more in-depth discussions between the government and citizens, influencing a number of new initiatives, ranging from the National Parks Act 1990, an inventory of all nature reserves in the 1990s, and the publication of the Singaporean Green Plan in 1993, all of which were done with the support of various non-governmental organizations.[43] Much of this cooperation focused around attempts to create less planned natural spaces throughout Singapore, and has resulted in the preservation of some peripheral areas, such as Chek Jawa and Labrador.

---

[41] Savage, "Singapore's Garden City"; Geh and Sharp, "Singapore's Natural Environment," p. 185; Neo, "Challenging the Developmental State," p. 190.

[42] M. Nirmala, "When Conservationists Do Not See People for the Trees," *ST*, 26 Nov. 1989, p. 32.

[43] Since the 1980s, Sungei Buloh Wetland Reserve has expanded to 130 hectares. Maria Francesch-Huidobro, *Governance, Politics and the Environment: A Singapore Study* (Singapore: Institute of Southeast Asian Studies, 2008); Geh and Sharp, "Singapore's Natural Environment," pp. 192–3; Lee Swee Hoon, "Bird Lovers Submit Proposals for 300-ha Nature Reserve," *ST*, 14 Dec. 1987, p. 14; Aziz Hussin, "Govt Gives Green Light for Bird Sanctuary," *ST*, 9 Apr. 1988, p. 12; "Yishun Sanctuary for Night Herons Proposed," *ST*, 24 Oct. 1989, p. 23.

The rhetoric of greening also entered official discourse by the early 21st century. Examples of this can be found in almost any statement government officials made with regard to construction, even in the most important political speeches given every year. In his 2011 National Day Rally Speech, Prime Minister Lee Hsien Loong, for example, announced that new HDB estates such as Punggol 21 and Treelodge@Punggol would be "different" because they would not simply be residences but part of urban landscape as there would be "greenery all around it."[44] This also culminated in the declaration from the National Parks Board that Singapore is a "City in a Garden" in late 2011. The "vision" of this latest government program is to "surround homes with greenery and biodiversity" so that Singaporeans are able to "step out into an islandwide network of exciting parks, nature areas, streetscapes, and park connectors." Singapore would continue to develop within a cityscape of planned vegetation.[45]

The cooperation between environmentalists and the government, and even attempts at biodiversity, however, had limits. Any developments promoting nature in Singapore had to be done without hindering economic development. For example, the government delayed any reclamation projects at Chek Jawa—a 100-hectare wetland ecosystem on the southeastern tip of Pulau Ubin—for ten years "as long as it is not needed for development."[46] Tan Wee Kiat articulated this approach most clearly in the late 1990s when he was the Chief Executive Officer of National Parks Board, stating that "socio-economic and political priorities had prevailed over nature conservation," rendering any criticism of government policies "moot." The dismissal of any criticism—or, at times, even suggestions—related to the natural environment was because it was not longer natural. Nature had become a "human construct" in Singapore, Tan argued, as the creation of parks and gardens in the highly urbanized landscape of Singapore required that "each blade of grass and each shrub and tree has had to be brought to the site and put into place by horticulturalists."[47] Calls for more natural vegetative

---

[44] http://www.news.gov.sg/public/sgpc/en/media_releases/agencies/mica/press_release/P-20110814-1.html. [accessed 19 Aug. 2013].

[45] Neo, "Challenging the Developmental State"; Leo Tan Wee Hin, National Archives [Singapore] Oral History Centre, 002204, Reels 5 and 6; Lee and Chua, *More Than a Garden City*, p. 25.

[46] Geh and Sharp, "Singapore's Natural Environment," p. 195.

[47] Tan Hsueh Yun, "Garden City's Critics Barking Up Wrong Tree," *ST*, 21 Apr. 1999, p. 37; Harvey Neo, "Challenging the Developmental State: Nature Conservation in Singapore," *Asia Pacific Viewpoint* 48, 2 (Aug. 2007): 190.

growth, according to Tan, were unrealistic in such a context. The government would determine where every tree was located, and monitor it to an amazing degree. Although officials took pride in the greening campaigns, the relationship to nature, and civil society, remained very controlled.

In the highly engineered landscape of Singapore, one project has come to epitomize the attitude of government officials toward nature in the nation-state. It is the Gardens by the Bay, which Tan Wee Kiat steered from conception to completion. One of the newest parks in Singapore, and one of the largest, it is a "people's garden," in which visitors can enjoy a huge expanse of greenery for free, although there are entrance fees for large domed biospheres within the park.[48] These biospheres are the Flower Dome, which replicates a mild, dry climate that is normally found in arid regions, and the Cloud Forest, which imitates the cool, moist conditions of tropical mountain regions that altitude-challenged Singapore is unable to naturally reproduce. The presence of these biospheres points to its inspiration, the Eden Project in Cornwall, United Kingdom, which has "super-plant conservatories focusing on different themes such as the Rainforest Biome and Mediterranean Biome," that the Gardens by the Bay attempts to emulate.[49] To develop this state-of-the-art garden and park, including the biospheres, the government allocated 101 hectares of reclaimed land in the Marina Bay area with 8.1 kilometers of waterfront in the early 2000s. This commitment also highlights the economic priorities of the government with regard to the environment, as the Gardens by the Bay cost over S$1 billion to construct, with annual operating costs estimated at over S$50 million.[50]

Opened to the public at the end of 2011, the Gardens by the Bay represents the culmination of the greening projects that have existed in Singapore since 1963. It showcases high horticulture technology and is a model for the "amalgamation of a multitude of disciplines ranging from

[48] National Parks Board, "Media Factsheet," National Parks Board, 17 Feb. 2012, p. 1.

[49] Koh Buck Song, *Perpetual Spring: Singapore's Gardens by the Bay* (Singapore: Marshall Cavendish Editions, 2012), p. 38; for more information on the Eden Project, see http://www.edenproject.com/ [accessed 14 Aug. 2013].

[50] National Parks Board, *Annual Report 2009/2010*, p. 10; "Final Cost for Gardens by the Bay within Budget: Khaw," *AsiaOne*, 15 Oct. 2012, at http://news.asiaone.com/News/Latest+News/Relax/Story/A1Story20121015-377822.html [accessed 19 Aug. 2013]; "Gardens by the Bay," NParks Fact Sheet, 17 Mar. 2012, at http://www.nparks.gov.sg/ [accessed 19 Aug. 2013].

Plate 9.4 Gardens by the Bay, Singapore (Courtesy of Christopher Yong).

architecture to bioengineering" that the government has used for greening Singapore. In addition, the park reflects larger national building goals in its four heritage-themed gardens, which represent the four "races" in Singapore: Chinese, Indian, and Malay. (The fourth "race"—Eurasian—is not represented; a "Colonial" garden was built instead.) These heritage-themed gardens use plants as ethnic symbols. For example, in the Chinese-themed garden, there are numerous bamboo plants as it is considered a "Chinese" plant. The problems with a demographic project of using plants to represent ethnic groups are numerous; however, it does reflect not only the racial narrative of Singaporean policies, but also attempts to infuse this into surrounding natural environment for nation-building purposes.[51]

The Gardens by the Bay, thus, reflects the artificiality of much of the greening process over the past 50 years. This is a fruition of the efforts of the government to emphasize not only nature, but also urban structures and people together to make the garden concept in Singapore more meaningful. While it is supposed to epitomize the link between the "environment, history and heritage with recreation and other shared spaces, [thus] bringing the community together,"[52] the implementation and manipulation of nature at the Gardens by the Bay has made it a focus of much criticism, reflecting the larger tensions between environmental groups and government planners. As Joanne Leow commented in a widely-circulated essay on a popular website, it "is an imposed, artificial construct of nature and history," particularly as the government announced plans to begin the development of areas in the Central Catchment Reserve, specifically the lush secondary growth areas of the Bukit Brown Cemetery, a region that Cantley recommended be set aside as a forest reserve in the late 19th century.[53] As much as the government wants to create a natural oasis of seamless greenery in Singapore, the fact remains that it is man-made and engineered artificially, much like the Gardens by the Bay, and the government demands it accommodates the engineered development of an expanding society.

The greening of Singapore has come a long way since the Tree Planting Campaign that began in 1963, and even earlier colonial policies. It has

---

[51] Much of this can be found through an examination of the official website: http://www.gardensbythebay.com.sg/en/home.html [accessed 19 Aug. 2013].

[52] National Parks Board, *Annual Report 2011/2012*, p. 28.

[53] Joanne Leow, "On Supertrees, Neo-Colonialism and Globalisation," at http://yawningbread.wordpress.com/2012/07/05/on-supertrees-neo-colonialism-and-globalisation/ [accessed 24 Aug. 2013].

led to a drastic transformation of the landscape while becoming a nation-building project that few notice. Singaporeans see the numerous trees, flowers, and shrubs more as tools that beautify the country than a nation-building tool that has moved beyond economic benefits to inculcate values into Singaporeans and shape the identity of the nation. This is in line with the government's vision of transforming Singapore into a "seamless green matrix." These programs have been very successful, and it has made the nation a more pleasant place to live.

The various programs that began in the 1960s, however, have a history. Whether it was the development of gambier and pepper plantations in the 19th century, or the planned horticulture of the Singaporean Botanic Gardens, Singapore has been an island in which humans have contained nature to suit their purposes. Attitudes toward the natural environment also have been shaped during this process. Whether it was fear of tigers roaming the disturbed edges of 19th-century plantations or the prioritizing of economic trade of foreign animals in the following century, the nation has been home to a variety of understandings and approaches toward nature that reflect different stages of its development. In this sense, the natural environment has a rich history on this island, which is as vital as any tale within the Singapore Story.

Bibliography

Newspapers

Agence France Presse
Daily Express Sabah
Eliza Cook's Journal
Macphail's Edinburgh Ecclesiastical Journal and Literary Review
National University of Singapore Gazette
Reuters News
Punch, or the London Charivari
The Guardian
The Singapore Chronicle and Commercial Register
The Singapore Free Press and Mercantile Advertiser
The Straits Observer
The Straits Times
Straits Times Overland Journal
Today (Singapore)

Books and Articles

Abdullah, Munshi. *The Autobiography of Munshi Abdullah*, trans. W.G. Shellabear. Singapore: Methodist Publishing House, 1918.

Adas, Michael. *The Burma Delta: Economic Development and Social Change on an Asian Rice Frontier, 1852–1941*. Madison, WI: University of Wisconsin Press, 1974.

––––––. *Machines as a Measure of Men: Science, Technology and Ideologies of Western Dominance*. Ithaca, NY: Cornell University Press, 1989.

Alfred, Eric R. "The Zoological Collections of the National Museum 1957–1974." In *Our Heritage: Zoological Reference Collection: Official Opening Souvenir Brochure, 31 October 1988* (Singapore: National University of Singapore, Zoological Reference Collection, 1988), p. 5.

Andaya, Barbara. *Perak, The Abode of Grace: A Study of an Eighteenth-Century Malay State*. Kuala Lumpur: Oxford University Press, 1979.

Ang A. et al. "Low Genetic Variability in the Recovering Urban Banded Leaf Monkey Population of Singapore." *The Raffles Bulletin of Zoology* 60, 2 (2012): 589–94.

Anonymous. "Singapore Tigers." *The Singapore Naturalist* 3 (May 1924): 8–9.

————. *Singapore Rubber Centenary, 1877–1977.* Singapore: Rubber Centenary Committee, 1977.

————. *Singapore Services: A Key Area of Growth.* Singapore: Economic Development Board, 1989.

Asma, Stephen T. *Stuffed Animals and Pickled Heads: The Culture and Evolution of Natural History Museums.* Oxford: Oxford University Press, 2001.

Auger, Timothy. *Living a Garden: The Greening of Singapore.* Singapore: National Parks Board and Editions Didier Millet, 2013.

Baker, Daniel B. "Alfred Russel Wallace's Record of His Consignments to Samuel Stevens, 1854–1861." *Zoologische Mededeelingen* 75, 16–25 (2001): 254–341.

Bankoff, Greg. "Big Men, Small Horses: Ridership, Social Standing and Environmental Adaptation in the Early Modern Philippines." In *The Horse as Cultural Icon: The Real and Symbolic Horse in the Early Modern World*, ed. Peter Edwards, Karl Enenkel, and Elspeth Graham (Leiden: Brill, 2011), pp. 91–120.

Bankoff, Greg and Sandra Short, eds. *Breeds of Empire: The "Invention" of the Horse in Southeast Asia and Southern Africa, 1500–1950.* Copenhagen: Nordic Institute of Asian Studies Press, 2007.

Barnard, Timothy P. "Protecting the Dragon: Dutch Attempts to Limit Access to Komodo Lizards in the 1920s and 1930s." *Indonesia* 92 (2011): 97–123.

————. "Noting Occurrences of Every Day Daily: H.N. Ridley's 'Book of Travels'." In *Fiction and Faction in the Malay World*, ed. Mohamad Rashidi Pakri and Arndt Graf. Newcastle upon Tyne: Cambridge Scholars Publishing, 2012, pp. 1–25.

Bird, Isabella. *The Golden Chersonese and the Way Thither.* New York: G.P. Putnam's Sons, 1884.

Blom, Philipp. *To Have and to Hold: An Intimate History of Collectors and Collecting.* New York: The Overlook Press, 2002.

Boomgaard, Peter. *Frontiers of Fear: Tigers and People in the Malay World, 1600–1950.* New Haven, CT: Yale University Press, 2001.

————. "'Primitive' Tiger Hunting in Indonesia and Malaysia, 1800–1950." In *Wildlife in Asia: Cultural Perspectives*, ed. John Knight. London: Routledge-Curzon, 2004, pp. 185–206.

————. "The Making and Unmaking of Tropical Science: Dutch Research on Indonesia, 1600–2000." *BKI* 162, 2–3 (2006): 191–217.

Boomgaard, Peter, Freek Colombijn, and David Henley, eds. *Paper Landscapes: Explorations in the Environmental History of Indonesia.* Leiden: KITLV Press, 1997.

Brown, C.C., ed. *Malay Annals, translated by C.C. Brown from MS Raffles no. 18.* Kuala Lumpur: MBRAS, 2009.

Buck, Frank and Edward Anthony. *Bring 'Em Back Alive.* New York: Simon and Schuster, 1930.

Buckley, Charles Burton. *An Anecdotal History of Old Times in Singapore: From the Foundation of the Settlement under the Honourable East India Company on*

February 6th, 1819 to the Transfer to the Colonial Office as Part of the Colonial Possessions of the Crown on April 1st, 1867, 2 vols. Singapore: Fraser and Neave, 1902.

Bucknill, John A.S. and F.N. Chasen. *The Birds of Singapore Island*. Singapore: Government Printing Office, 1927.

Bunting, B., C.D.V. Georgi, and J.N. Milsum. *The Oil Palm in Malaya*. Kuala Lumpur: Department of Agriculture, Straits Settlements and Federated Malay States, 1934.

Burkill, H.M. "Protection of Wild Life on Singapore Island." In *Nature Conservation in Western Malaysia*, ed. J. Wyatt-Smith and P.R. Wycherley. Kuala Lumpur: Malayan Nature Society, 1961, pp. 152–64.

Burkill, I.H. "The Establishment of the Botanic Gardens, Singapore." *Gardens' Bulletin, Straits Settlements* 2 (1918): 55–92.

_____. "The Second Phase in the History of the Botanic Gardens, Singapore." *Gardens' Bulletin, Straits Settlements* 2 (1918): 93–108.

_____. *A Dictionary of the Economic Products of the Malay Peninsula*. Kuala Lumpur: Governments of Malaysia and Singapore, 1966.

Cameron, John. *Our Tropical Possessions in Malayan India: Being a Descriptive Account of Singapore, Penang, Province Wellesley, and Malacca; Their Peoples, Products, Commerce, and Government*. London: Smith, Elder, 1865.

Cantley, Nathaniel. *Report on the Forests of the Straits Settlements*. Singapore: Government Printing Office, 1883.

Chee, Lillian. "Under the Billiard Table: Animality, Anecdote and the Tiger's Subversive Significance at the Raffles Hotel." *Singapore Journal of Tropical Geography* 32, 3 (2011): 350–64.

Choo, Thereis. "Uncovering the History of the Bandstand." *Gardenwise* 39 (2012): 7–8.

Chou Gek Hua, Cynthia. "Farmers in Singapore: The Rural Sector in Transition." Unpublished Master's thesis, Department of Sociology, National University of Singapore, 1989.

Chua, Kevin. "The Tiger and the Theodolite; George Coleman's Dream of Extinction." *FOCAS: Forum on Contemporary Art and Society* 6 (2007): 124–49.

Cohn, Bernard. *Colonialism and Its Forms of Knowledge: The British in India*. Princeton, NJ: Princeton University Press, 1996.

Corlett, Richard. "Vegetation." In *The Biophysical Environment of Singapore*, ed. Chia Lin Sien, Ausafur Rahman, and Dorothy Tay B.H. Singapore: Singapore University Press, 1991, pp. 134–54.

Corlett, Richard T. "The Ecological Transformation of Singapore, 1819–1990." *Journal of Biogeography* 19, 4 (July 1992): 411–20.

Corner, E.J.H. "The Freshwater Swamp-Forest of South Johore and Singapore." In *Gardens' Bulletin Supplement, No. 1*. Singapore: Government Printing Office, 1978.

_____. *The Marquis. A Tale of Syonan-to*. Singapore: Heinemann Asia, 1981.

Crane, Peter. "Botanic Gardens for the 21st century." *Gardenwise: The Newsletter of the Singapore Botanic Gardens* 16 (January 2001): 4–8.

Crawfurd, John. *A Descriptive Dictionary of the Indian Islands and Adjacent Countries*. London: Bradbury and Evans, 1856.

Cribb, Robert. "Birds of Paradise and Environmental Politics in Colonial Indonesia, 1890–1931." In *Paper Landscapes: Explorations in the Environmental History of Indonesia*, ed. Peter Boomgaard, Freek Columbijn, and David Henley. Leiden: KITLV, 1997, pp. 379–408.

————. "Conservation in Colonial Indonesia." *Interventions* 9, 1 (2007): 49–61.

Dammerman, Karel Willem. *Preservation of Wild Life and Nature Reserves in the Netherlands Indies*. Weltevreden: Emmink, 1929.

Darwin, Charles. *Charles Darwin's Notebooks, 1836–1844*, ed. Paul H. Barrett et al. London: British Museum [Natural History], 1987.

————. *Charles Darwin's Notebooks from the Voyage of the Beagle*, ed. Gordon Chancellor and John van Wyhe. Cambridge: Cambridge University Press, 2009.

De Koninck, Rodolphe. "Chinese Farmers of Singapore: A Study in Social Geography." Unpublished PhD dissertation, Department of Geography, University of Singapore, 1971.

Desmond, Ray. *Kew*. Richmond: Royal Botanic Gardens, Kew, 1995.

Desmond, Ray and F. Nigel Hepper. *A Century of Kew Plantsmen. A Celebration of the Kew Guild*. Richmond: Royal Botanic Gardens, Kew, 1993.

Dhoraisingam, Kamala Devi, and D.S. Samuel. *Tan Tock Seng; Pioneer; His Life, Times, Contributions and Legacy*. Kota Kinabalu: Natural History Publications, Borneo, 2003.

Dinerstein, Eric et al. "The Fate of Wild Tigers." *BioScience* 57, 6 (2007): 508–14.

Donovan, D.G. "Cultural Underpinnings of the Wildlife Trade in Southeast Asia." In *Wildlife in Asia: Cultural Perspectives*, ed. John Knight. London: Routledge, 2004, pp. 88–111.

Ebenezer, Howard. *Garden Cities of To-morrow*. London: Faber and Faber, 1947.

Foong Thai Wu et al. "Roadmap of the School of Horticulture: 1972–1999." *Gardenwise* 13 (1999): 12–3.

Fox, Walter. *Guide to the Gardens*. Singapore: Singapore Botanic Gardens, 1889.

Francesch-Huidobro, Maria. *Governance, Politics and the Environment: A Singapore Study*. Singapore: Institute of Southeast Asian Studies, 2008.

Frost, Mark Ravinder and Yu-Mei Balasingamchow. *Singapore: A Biography*. Singapore: Editions Didier Millet, 2009.

Fry, Edward. "On the Relation of the Edentata to the Reptiles, Especially of the Armadillos to the Tortoises." *Annals and Magazine of Natural History* 18 (1846): 278–80.

Fujinuma, Junichi and Rhett D. Harrison. "Wild Pigs (*Sus scrofa*) Mediate Large-Scale Edge Effects in a Lowland Tropical Rainforest in Peninsular Malaysia." *PLoS ONE* 7, 5 (2012): e37321.

Gates, G.E. *The Earthworms of Burma*. Cambridge, MA: Harvard University Press, 1934.

Geertz, Clifford. *Agricultural Involution: The Process of Ecological Change in Indonesia*. Berkeley, CA: University of California Press, 1963.

George, Wilma. "Alfred Wallace, the Gentle Trader: Collecting in Amazonia and the Malay Archipelago 1848–1862." *Journal of the Society for the Bibliography of Natural History* 9, 4 (1979): 503–14.

Gibson, James Jerome. *The Ecological Approach to Visual Perception*. Boston: Houghton Mifflin, 1979.

Goh Pei Siong, Daniel. "Defending Nature in the 'Garden City': Environment and Social Power in Singapore." Unpublished Master's thesis, Department of Sociology, National University of Singapore, 2000.

Goss, Andrew. "Decent Colonialism?: Pure Science and Colonial Ideology in the Netherlands East Indies, 1910–1929." *Journal of Southeast Asian Studies* 40, 1 (2009): 187–214.

Grove, Richard H. *Green Imperialism: Colonial Expansion, Tropical Island Edens, and the Origins of Environmentalism, 1600–1860*. Cambridge: Cambridge University Press, 1995.

Gudeman, Stephen. *Economics as Culture: Models and Metaphors as Livelihood*. London: Routledge and Kegan Paul, 1986.

Gullick, John and Gerald Hawkins. *Malayan Pioneers*. Singapore: Eastern Universities Press, 1958.

Gwee, June. *Case Studies in Public Governance: Building Institutions in Singapore*. New York: Routledge, 2012.

Hall-Jones, John and Christopher Hooi. *An Early Surveyor in Singapore: John Turnbull Thomson in Singapore, 1841–1853*. Singapore: National Museum, 1979.

Hanitsch, R. *Guide to the Zoological Collections of the Raffles Museum, Singapore*. Singapore: Straits Times Press, 1908.

————. *List of the Birds, Reptiles and Amphibians in the Raffles Museum, Singapore*. Singapore: Straits Settlements Government Printing House, 1912.

————. "Raffles Library and Museum, Singapore." In *One Hundred Years of Singapore*, vol. 1, ed. Walter Makepeace, Gilbert E. Brooke, and Roland St. J. Braddell. London: John Murray, 1921, pp. 519–66.

Headrick, Daniel. *The Tools of Empire: Technology and European Imperialism in the Nineteenth Century*. New York: Oxford University Press, 1981.

Holttum, R.E. "The Society's Early Days." *Malayan Orchid Review* 22 (1988): 22–6.

Hong Lysa and Huang Jianli. *The Scripting of a National History: Singapore and Its Past*. Singapore: NUS Press, 2008.

Hornaday, William T. *The Experiences of a Hunter and Naturalist in the Malay Peninsula and Borneo*. Kuala Lumpur: Oxford University Press, 1993.

Hubback, Theodore. *Elephant and Seladang Hunting in the Federated Malay States*. London: R. Ward, 1905.

_____. *Three Months in Pahang in Search of Big Game: A Reminiscence of Malaya*. Singapore: Kelly and Walsh, 1907.

Huxley, Chris. "CITES: The Vision." In *Endangered Species, Threatened Convention: The Past, Present and Future of CITES*, ed. Jon Hutton and Barnabas Dickson. London: Earthscan Publications, 2000, pp. 3–12.

Ickes, Kalan. "Hyper-Abundance of Native Wild Pigs (*Sus scrofa*) in a Lowland Dipterocarp Rain Forest of Peninsular Malaysia." *Biotropica* 33, 4 (2001): 682–90.

Ingold, Tim. *The Perception of the Environment: Essays in Livelihood, Dwelling and Skill*. London: Routledge, 2000.

Jackson, James C. "Chinese Agricultural Pioneering in Singapore and Johore, 1800–1917." *Journal of the Malayan Branch of the Royal Asiatic Society* 38 (1965): 77–82.

_____. *Planters and Speculators: Chinese and European Agricultural Enterprise in Malaya, 1786–1921*. Singapore: University of Malaya Press, 1968.

Jayakumar, S. and Tommy Koh. *Pedra Branca: The Road to the World Court*. Singapore: NUS Press, 2009.

Johnson, Anisha Anne. "It's (about) Time for a Tiger: A Social History of Malayan Breweries Limited, 1931–1957." Unpublished Honours thesis, Department of History, National University of Singapore, 2010/11.

Kargon Robert H. and Arthur P. Molella. *Invented Edens: Techno-Cities of the Twentieth Century*. Cambridge, MA: Massachusetts Institute of Technology, 2008.

Kathirithamby-Wells, Jeyamalar. *Nature and Nation: Forests and Development in Peninsular Malaysia*. Honolulu, HI: University of Hawai'i Press, 2005.

_____. "Peninsular Malaysia in the Context of Natural History and Colonial Science." *New Zealand Journal of Asian Studies* 11, 1 (2009): 337–74.

Khan, M.K.M. "Tigers in Malaysia." *The Journal of Wildlife and Parks* 5 (1986): 1–23.

Khew, Gillian Su-Wen and Tet Fatt Chia. "Parentage Determination of *Vanda* Miss Joaquim (Orchidaceae) through Two Chloroplast Genes *rbcL* and *matK*." *AoB PLANTS*: 10.1093/aobpla/plr018.

Kiew, Ruth. "The Vanished Forests of Singapore Recaptured." *Gardenwise* 24 (2005): 28.

Koerner, Lisbet. "Carl Linnaeus in His Time and Place." In *Cultures of Natural History*, ed. N. Jardine, J.A. Secord, and E.C. Spary. Cambridge: Cambridge University Press, 1996, pp. 145–62.

Koh Buck Song. *Perpetual Spring: Singapore's Gardens by the Bay*. Singapore: Marshall Cavendish Editions, 2012.

Kong, Lily, Belinda Yuen, Navjot S. Sodhi, and Clive Briffett. "The Construction and Experience of Nature: Perspectives from Urban Youths." *Tijdschrift voor Economie en Sociale Geographie* 90, 1 (February 1999): 3–16.

Kohn, David. "Theories to Work by: Rejected Theories, Reproduction, and Darwin's Path to Natural Selection." *Studies in History of Biology* 4 (1980): 67–170.

Kwa Chong Guan, Derek Heng, and Tan Tai Yong. *Singapore: A 700-year History: From Early Emporium to World City.* Singapore: National Archives of Singapore, 2009.

Lam, T.J. "Foreword." In *Our Heritage: Zoological Reference Collection: Official Opening Souvenir Brochure, 31 October 1988.* Singapore: National University of Singapore, Zoological Reference Collection, 1988, p. 1.

Lamb, Christian. *This Infant Adventure: Offspring of the Royal Gardens at Kew.* London: Bene Factum Publishing, 2010.

Layton, Lesley. *Songbirds in Singapore.* Singapore: Oxford University Press, 1991.

Lee, Edwin. *Singapore: The Unexpected Nation.* Singapore: Institute of Southeast Asian Studies, 2008.

Lee Kuan Yew. *From Third World to First—The Singapore Story: 1965–2000.* Singapore: Singapore Press Holdings, 2000.

————. *The Papers of Lee Kuan Yew: Speeches, Interviews and Dialogues,* vol. 3 (1965–1966). Singapore: Gale Asia, 2012.

Lee Sing Kong and Chua Sian Eng. *More Than a Garden City.* Singapore: Parks and Recreation Department, 1992.

Levi, Giovanni. "On Microhistory." In *New Perspectives on Historical Writing,* ed. Peter Burke. University Park, PA: Pennsylvania State University Press, 1992, pp. 97–119.

Lewotin, Richard Charles. "Organism and Environment." In *Learning, Development and Culture,* ed. Henry C. Plotkin. Chichester: Wiley, 1982, pp. 151–70.

Liew, Clement. "The Roman Catholic Church of Singapore, 1819–1910: From Mission to Church." Unpublished Honours thesis, Department of History, National University of Singapore, 1994.

Lim, P. Pui Huen. *Tan Cheng Lock Papers: A Descriptive List.* Singapore: Institute of Southeast Asian Studies, 1989.

Logan, J.R. "The Probable Effects on the Climate of Pinang of the Continued Destruction of Its Hill Jungles." *Journal of the Indian Archipelago and Eastern Asia* 2 (1848): 534–6.

Low Mei Gek, Cheryl-Ann. "Singapore from the 14th–19th Century." In *Early Singapore 1300s–1819: Evidence in Maps, Texts and Artifacts,* ed. John N. Miksic and Cheryl-Ann Low Mei Gek. Singapore: Singapore History Museum, 2004, pp. 41–54.

Luo Shu-Jin et al. "Phylogeography and Genetic Ancestry of Tigers (*Panthera tigris*)." *PLoS Biol* 2, 12 (2004): 2275–93.

Lum, Shawn and Ilsa Sharp. *A View from the Summit: The Story of Bukit Timah Nature Reserve.* Singapore: Nanyang Technological University and the National University of Singapore, 1996.

Luyt, Brendan. "Collectors and Collecting for the Raffles Museum in Singapore: 1920 to 1940." *Library and Information History* 26, 3 (September 2010): 183–95.

Lye Lin Heng. "Wildlife Protection Laws in Singapore." *Singapore Journal of Legal Studies* 288 (1991): 287–319.

MacKenzie, John. *The Empire of Nature: Hunting, Conservation and British Imperialism.* Manchester: Manchester University Press, 1988.

————. "Empire and the Ecological Apocalypse: The Historiography of the Imperial Environment." In *Ecology and Empire: Environmental History of Settler Societies*, ed. Tom Griffiths and Libby Robin. Edinburgh: Keele University Press, 1997, pp. 215–28.

Marchant, James. "A Man of the Time: Dr. Alfred Russel Wallace and His Coming Autobiography." *Book Monthly* 2, 8 (1905): 545–9.

Marx, Karl. *Pre-Capitalist Economic Formations*, trans. J. Cohen, ed. E.J. Hobsbawm. London: Lawrence and Wishart, 1964.

Mayer, Charles. *Trapping Wild Animals in Malay Jungles.* New York: Duffield and Company, 1921.

Mazák J.H. and C.P. Groves. "A Taxonomic Revision of the Tigers (Panthera tigris) of Southeast Asia." *Mammalian Biology—Zeitschrift für Säugetierkunde* 71, 5 (2006): 268–87.

McCracken, Donald P. *Gardens of Empire: Botanical Institutions of the Victorian British Empire.* London: Leicester University Press, 1997.

McFadden, Eric. "Asian Compliance with CITES: Problems and Prospects." *Boston University International Law Journal* 5 (1987): 311–25.

Meyers, Gary and Kyla Bennett. "Answering the 'Call of the Wild': An Examination of U.S. Participation in International Wildlife Law." *Pace Environmental Law Review* 9 (1989): 75–116.

Milton, Giles. *Nathaniel's Nutmeg: How One Man's Courage Changed the Course of History.* London: Hodder and Stoughton, 1999.

Min Geh and Ilsa Sharp. "Singapore's Natural Environment, Past, Present and Future: A Construct of National Identity and Land Use Imperatives." In *Spatial Planning for a Sustainable Singapore*, ed. T.C. Wong et al. London: Springer with the Singapore Institute of Planners, 2008, pp. 183–204.

Moore-Colyer, R.J. "Feathered Women and the Persecuted Birds: The Struggle against the Plumage Trade, c.1860–1922." *Rural History* 11, 1 (2000): 57–73.

Morrison, Denton E. and Riley E. Dunlap. "Environmentalism and Elitism: A Conceptual and Empirical Analysis." *Environmental Management* 10, 5 (1986): 581–9.

Mumford, Lewis. *The City in History: Its Origins, Its Transformations, and Its Prospects.* New York: Harcourt, Brace and World, 1961.

Murray, Narisara. "From Birds of Paradise to Drosophila: The Changing Roles of Scientific Specimens to 1920." In *A Cultural History of Animals in the Age of Empire*, ed. Kathleen Kete. Oxford: Oxford University Press, 2007, pp. 113–34.

Mushkat, Roda. *International Environmental Law and Asian Values: Legal Norms and Cultural Influences.* Vancouver: UBC Press, 2004.

Nature Society. *Proposed Golf Course at Lower Peirce Reservoir: An Environmental Impact Assessment.* Singapore: Nature Society, 1992.

Neale, Fred Arthur. *The Old Arm-Chair: A Retrospective Panorama of Travels by Land and Sea*. London: Society for Promoting Christian Knowledge, 1854.

Neo, Harvey. "Challenging the Developmental State: Nature Conservation in Singapore." *Asia Pacific Viewpoint* 48, 2 (August 2007): 186–99.

_____. "Unpacking the Postpolitics of Golf Course Provision in Singapore." *Journal of Sports and Social Issues* 34, 3 (2010): 272–87.

Newbold, T.J. *Political and Statistical Account of the British Settlements in the Straits of Malacca, viz. Pinang, Malacca, and Singapore; with a History of the Malayan States on the Peninsula of Malacca*. London: John Murray, 1839.

Ng Soon Chye. "From Birds to Babies and Beyond: A Chat with One of Singapore's 'Fathers' of IVF." *LIFE* (16 March 2007): 12–5.

Ng, Peter K.L. and N. Sivasothi, eds. *A Guide to the Mangroves of Singapore, Volume 1: The Ecosystem and Plant Diversity*. Singapore: Singapore Science Centre, 1999.

North, Marianne. *A Vision of Eden: The Life and Work of Marianne North*. Richmond: Royal Botanic Gardens, Kew, 1993.

Nura Abdul Karim. "The Passing of Lady Yuen-Peng McNeice." *Gardenwise* 39 (2012): 2–5.

Oh, Terri. "Celebrating 150 Magical Years of the Gardens." *Gardenwise* 33 (2009): 2–3.

Ohn Set. "Beginning of the End." *Gardenwise* 24 (2005): 22–3.

Ooi Giok Ling and Kenson Kwok, eds. *City and the State: Singapore's Built Environment Revisited*. Singapore: Institute of Policy Studies, 1997.

Ooi Jin Bee. "Agriculture Change in Singapore." *Asian Profile* 1, 2 (1973): 365–76.

Osborne, Megan S. "Early Collectors and Their Impact on the Raffles Museum and Library." *The Heritage Journal* 3 (2008): 1–15.

Oxley, Thomas. "Some Account of the Nutmeg and Its Cultivation." *Journal of the Indian Archipelago and Eastern Asia* 2, 10 (1848): 641–60.

_____. "The Botany of Singapore." *Journal of the Indian Archipelago and Eastern Asia* 4 (1850): 436–40.

_____. "The Zoology of Singapore." *Journal of the Indian Archipelago and Eastern Asia* 3 (1849): 594–7.

Parsons, Kermit C. and David Schuyler, eds. *From Garden City to Green City: The Legacy of Ebenezer Howard*. Baltimore, MD: Johns Hopkins University Press, 2002.

Pascoe, Francis P. "Longicornia Malayana; or, a Descriptive Catalogue of the Species of the Three Longicorn Families Lamiidæ, Cerambycidæ and Prionidæ, Collected by Mr. A.R. Wallace in the Malay Archipelago." *Transactions of the Entomological Society of London* 3 (1864): 1–718.

Peltonen, Matti. "Clues, Margins and Monads: The Micro-Macro Link in Historical Research." *History and Theory* 40, 3 (October 2001): 347–59.

Pfeiffer, Ida. *A Woman's Journey Round the World from Vienna to Brazil, Chili, Tahiti, China, Hindostan, Persia and Asia Minor*. London: Ingram, Cooke, and Co., 1852.

Pilon, Maxime and Danièle Weiler. *The French in Singapore: An Illustrated History (1819–Today)*. Singapore: Editions Didier Millet, 2011.

Pitt, K.W. "From Plantations to New Town: The Story of Nee Soon." In *The Development of the Nee Soon Community*, ed. L.G. Lim How Seng. Singapore: The Grassroots Organisations of Nee Soon Community and National Archives, Oral History Department, 1987, pp. 193–225.

Puah You Kai. "Pig Farming and the State: Re-thinking Rural Development in Post-Independent Singapore (1965–1990)." Unpublished BA (Honours) thesis, Department of History, National University of Singapore, 2012.

Purseglove, J.W. "History and Functions of Botanic Gardens with Special Reference to Singapore." *Gardens' Bulletin, Singapore* 17 (1959): 125–54.

Pyenson, Lewis. *Empire of Reason: Exact Sciences in Indonesia, 1840–1940*. Leiden: E.J. Brill, 1989.

Raby, Peter. *Alfred Russel Wallace: A Life*. Princeton, NJ: Princeton University Press, 2001.

Reeve, Rosalind. *Policing International Trade in Endangered Species: The CITES Treaty and Compliance*. London: Earthscan Publications Ltd, 2002.

Reith, G.M. *Handbook to Singapore: With Map and Plans of the Botanic Gardens*. Singapore: The Singapore and Straits Printing Office, 1892.

Ridley, H.N. "Vanda Miss Joaquim." *The Gardener's Chronical* 13 (1893): 740.

_____. "The Mammals of the Malay Peninsula." *Natural Science* 6, 35–37 (February 1895): 23–9, 89–96, 161–6.

_____. "Flora of Singapore." *Journal of the Straits Branch of the Royal Asiatic Society* 33 (1900): 27–196.

_____. "The Oil Palm." *Agricultural Bulletin of the Straits and Federated Malay States* 6, 2 (1907): 37–40.

_____. *The Flora of the Malay Peninsula*, 5 vols. London: L. Reeve & Co., 1925.

Ridley, Henry N. *Spices*. London: Macmillan, 1912.

Ritvo, Harriet. *The Animal Estate: The English and Other Creatures in the Victorian Age*. Cambridge, MA: Harvard University Press, 1987.

_____. "Animal Planet." *Environmental History* 9, 2 (2004): 204–20.

Rookmaaker, Kees and John van Wyhe. "In Wallace's Shadow: The Forgotten Assistant of Alfred Russel Wallace, Charles Allen." *Journal of the Malaysian Branch of the Royal Asiatic Society* 85, 2 (2012): 17–54.

Rothfels, Nigel. *Savages and Beasts: The Birth of the Modern Zoo*. Baltimore, MD: Johns Hopkins University Press, 2002.

Rothfels, Nigel, eds. *Representing Animals*. Indianapolis, IN: Indiana University Press, 2002.

Rudwick, Martin J.S. *The Meaning of Fossils: Episodes in the History of Palaeontology*. Chicago, IL: University of Chicago Press, 1985.

Sanson, Veronique. *Gardens and Parks of Singapore*. Singapore: Oxford University Press, 1992.

Savage, Victor R. *Western Impressions of Nature and Landscape in Southeast Asia*. Singapore: Singapore University Press, 1984.

_____. "Singapore's Garden City: Reality, Symbol, Ideal." *Solidarity* 131–132 (1992): 67–75.

_____. "Singapore's Garden City: Translating Environmental Possibilism." In *City and the State: Singapore's Built Environment Revisited*, ed. Ooi Geok Ling. Singapore: Oxford University Press, 1997, pp. 187–202.

Savage Victor R. and Lily Kong. "Urban Constraints, Political Imperatives: Environmental 'Design' in Singapore." *Landscape and Urban Planning* 25 (1993): 37–52.

Schonfeld, Alan. "International Trade in Wildlife: How Effective is the Endangered Species Treaty?" *California Western International Law Journal* 15 (1985): 111–60.

Sekhon, Isher Singh. "Agriculture in Singapore (1819–1959)." Unpublished Academic Exercise, Department of Geography, University of Malaya, Singapore, 1961.

Sharma, Roland E. "The Zoological Reference Collection. The Interim Years 1972–1980." In *Our Heritage: Zoological Reference Collection: Official Opening Souvenir Brochure, 31 October 1988*. Singapore: National University of Singapore, Zoological Reference Collection, 1988, p. 10.

Sharp, Ilsa. *The First 21 Years: The Singapore Zoological Gardens Story*. Singapore: Singapore Zoological Gardens, 1994.

Sheets-Pyenson, Susan. *Cathedrals of Science: The Development of Colonial Natural History Museums during the Late Nineteenth Century*. Montreal: McGill-Queen's University Press, 1988.

Shweder, Richard. "Cultural Psychology—What is It?" In *Cultural Psychology: Essays on Comparative Human Development*, ed. James W. Stigler, Richard A. Shweder, and Gilbert Herdt. Cambridge: Cambridge University Press, 1990, pp. 1–43.

Smith, Simon. *British Relations with the Malay Rulers from Decentralization to Malayan Independence 1930–1957*. Oxford: Oxford University Press, 1995.

St. John, James Augustus. *Views in the Eastern Archipelago: Borneo, Sarawak, Labuan*. London: T. McClean, 1847.

Strickland, H.E. "Description of a Chart of the Natural Affinities of the Insessorial Order of Birds." *Report of the Thirteenth Meeting of the British Association for the Advancement of Science Held at Cork in August 1843, Notices and Abstracts of Communications* 13 (1844): 69.

Swanson, Timothy. "Developing CITES: Making the Convention Work for All of the Parties." In *Endangered Species, Threatened Convention—The Past, Present and Future of CITES*, ed. Jon Hutton and Barnabas Dickson. London: Earthscan Publications, 2000, pp. 134–52.

Tagliacozzo, Eric. *Secret Trades, Porous Borders: Smuggling and States along a Southeast Asian Frontier, 1865–1915*. New Haven, CT: Yale University Press, 2005.

Tan, Hugh T.W. et al. *The Natural Heritage of Singapore*. Singapore: Prentice Hall, 2010.

Tan Kee Soon. "The Chinese Names of Streets and Places in Singapore." *Journal of the Straits Branch of the Royal Asiatic Society* 46 (1906): 195–213.

Tan, Leo W.H. "In transit ... National Museum ... Science Centre ... National University ... Stop!" In *Our Heritage: Zoological Reference Collection: Official Opening Souvenir Brochure, 31 October 1988*. Singapore: National University of Singapore, Zoological Reference Collection, 1988, p. 7.

Tannebaum, Jerrold. "Animals and the Law." In *Animals and the Law: Property, Cruelty, Rights*, ed. Arien Mack. Columbus: Ohio State University Press, 1999, pp. 125–93.

Tanner, Adrian. *Bringing Home Animals: Religious Ideology and Mode of Production of the Mistassini Cree Hunters*. New York: St. Martin's Press, 1979.

Tarulevicz, Nicole. "History Making in Singapore: Who is Producing the Knowledge?" *New Zealand Journal of Asian Studies* 11, 1 (2009): 402–25.

Tate, D.J.M. *Straits Affairs: The Malay World and Singapore, Being Glimpses of the Straits Settlements and the Malay Peninsula in the Nineteenth Century as Seen Through the Illustrated London News and Other Contemporary Sources*. Hong Kong: John Nicholson Ltd., 1989.

Tay Eng Pin et al. *A Pictorial Guide to The Singapore Botanic Gardens*. Singapore: Singapore Botanic Gardens, 1989.

Tay, Simon. "Towards A Singaporean Civil Society." *Southeast Asian Affairs* (1998): 244–61.

Taylor, Nigel. "Singapore Botanic Gardens: A Living and Growing Heritage." *BeMUSE* 5, 3 (2012): 24–9.

Templer John C., ed. *Private Letters of Sir James Brooke, K.C.B., Rajah of Sarawak, Narrating the Events of His Life, from 1838 to the Present Time*, 3 vols. London: Bentley, 1853.

Teo, Peggy, Brenda Yeoh, Ooi Giok Ling, and Karen Lai. *Changing Landscapes of Singapore*. Singapore: McGraw-Hill Education (Asia), 2004.

Thacker, Christopher. *History of Gardens*. Berkeley, CA: University of California Press, 1979.

Thomson, J. *The Straits of Malacca, Indo-China, and China, or Ten Years' Travels, Adventures, and Residence Abroad*. New York: Harper and Brothers, 1875.

Thomson, J.T. "General Report on the Residency of Singapore, Drawn Principally with a View of Illustrating Its Agricultural Statistics." *Journal of the Indian Archipelago and Eastern Asia* 4 & 5 (1850): 27–41, 102–6, 134–43, 206–21.

Thomson, John Turnbull. *Account of the Horsburgh Light-house, Erected on Pedra Branca, Near Singapore*. Singapore: G.M. Fredrick, 1852.

———. *Some Glimpses of Life in the Far East*. London: Richardson and Company, 1864.

Tinsley, Bonnie. *Singapore Green: A History and Guide to the Botanic Gardens*. Singapore: Times Book International, 1983.

———. *Visions of Delight: The Singapore Botanic Gardens through the Ages*. Singapore: Singapore Botanic Gardens, 1989.

———. *Gardens of Perpetual Summer: The Singapore Botanic Gardens*. Singapore: National Parks Board, Singapore Botanic Gardens, 2009.

Tregonning, K.G. "Tan Cheng Lock: A Malayan Nationalist." *Journal of Southeast Asian Studies* 10, 1 (March 1979): 25–76.

Trocki, Carl. *Prince of Pirates: The Temenggongs and the Development of Johor and Singapore, 1784–1885.* Singapore: NUS Press, 2007.

Turnbull, C.M. *The Straits Settlements 1826–67: Indian Presidency to Crown Colony.* London: Athlone Press, 1972.

_____. *A History of Singapore, 1819–1988.* Singapore: Oxford University Press, 1989.

Tweedie, M.W.F. "Zoology in the Raffles Museum, 1932–1957." In *Our Heritage: Zoological Reference Collection: Official Opening Souvenir Brochure, 31 October 1988.* Singapore: National University of Singapore, Zoological Reference Collection, 1988, p. 2.

Tweedie, Michael. "Obituary: Frederick Nutter Chasen." *Ibis* 88, 4 (October 1946): 527–8.

van Wyhe, John and Kees Rookmaaker. "A New Theory to Explain the Receipt of Wallace's Ternate Essay by Darwin in 1858." *Biological Journal of the Linnean Society* 105, 1 (2012): 249–52.

_____. "Wallace's Mystery Flycatcher." Manuscript to be published.

Wallace, A.R. "Letter Dated 9 May 1854, Singapore." *Zoologist* 12, 142 (1854): 4395–7.

_____. "Letters from the Eastern Archipelago" *The Literary Gazette, and Journal of the Belles Lettres, Science, and Art* 1961 (1854): 369.

_____. "Notes on the Localities Given in Longicornia Malayana, with an Estimate of the Comparative Value of the Collections Made at Each of Them." *Transactions of the Entomological Society of London* (ser. 3) 3, 7 (1869): 691–6.

_____. "Introduction." In "A Catalogue of the Aculeate Hymenoptera and Ichneumonidae of India and the Eastern Archipelago." *Journal of the Linnean Society, Zoology* 11 (1873): 285–96.

Wallace, Alfred R. "On the Ornithology of Malacca." *Annals and Magazine of Natural History* (ser. 2) 15, 86 (1855): 95.

Wallace, Alfred Russel. *The Malay Archipelago: The Land of the Orang-Utan, and the Bird of Paradise. A Narrative of Travel, with Studies of Man and Nature.* London: Macmillan and Co., 1869.

_____. *My Life: A Record of Events and Opinions.* London: Chapman and Hall, 1905.

_____. *Alfred Russel Wallace Letters and Reminiscences,* ed. James Marchant. London: Cassell, 1916.

Ward, Stephen V., ed. *The Garden City: Past, Present, Future.* London: E & FN Spon, 1992.

Warren, James Francis. *Ah Ku and Karayuki-san: Prostitution in Singapore, 1870–1940.* Singapore: Singapore University Press, 2003.

Warren, William. *Singapore: City of Gardens.* Singapore: Periplus, 2000.

Wee, Vivienne. "Religion and Ritual among the Chinese of Singapore: An Ethnographic Study." Unpublished Master's in Social Science thesis, Department of Sociology, University of Singapore, 1977.

Wee, Yeow Chin. *A Guide to Wayside Trees of Singapore*. Singapore: The Centre, 1989.

Wee Yeow Chin and Richard Corlett. *The City and the Forest: Plant Life in Urban Singapore*. Singapore: Singapore University Press, 1986.

Wee Yeow Chin and Richard Hale. "The Nature Society (Singapore) and the Struggle to Conserve Singapore's Natural Areas." *Nature in Singapore* 1 (August 2008): 41–9.

Wheatley, Paul. "Land Use in the Vicinity of Singapore in the Eighteen-Thirties." *Malayan Journal of Tropical Geography* 2 (1954): 63–6.

White, Richard. "Environmental History: The Development of a New Historical Field." *Pacific Historical Review* 54 (1985): 297–335.

Whitmore, T.C. *Tropical Rain Forests of the Far East*. New York: Oxford University Press, 1984.

Worster, Donald, ed. *The Ends of the Earth: Perspectives on Modern Environmental History*. Cambridge: Cambridge University Press, 1988.

Worster, Donald. *The Wealth of Nature: Environmental History and the Ecological Imagination*. Oxford: Oxford University Press, 1993.

Yang, C.M. "The Reunion of the Zoological Reference Collection." In *Our Heritage: Zoological Reference Collection: Official Opening Souvenir Brochure, 31 October 1988*. Singapore: National University of Singapore, Zoological Reference Collection, 1988, p. 12.

Yee, A.T.K. et al. "The Present Extent of Mangrove Forests in Singapore." *Nature in Singapore* 3 (2010): 139–45.

Young, Saskia. "Contemporary Issues of the Convention on International Trade in Endangered Species of Wild Flora and Fauna (CITES) and the Debate on Sustainable Use." *Colorado Journal of International Environmental Law and Policy* 14 (2003): 167–89.

Contributors

Timothy P. Barnard (editor) is an Associate Professor in the Department of History at the National University of Singapore, where he focuses on the environmental and cultural history of island Southeast Asia. His publications include "Protecting the Dragon: Dutch Attempts at Limiting Access to Komodo Lizards in the 1920s and 1930s," *Indonesia* (2011); and, *Multiple Centres of Authority: Society and Environment in Siak and Eastern Sumatra, 1674-1827* (2003).

Cynthia Chou is an Associate Professor in the Department of Cross-Cultural and Regional Studies at Copenhagen University. Her research focuses on marginalized ethnic groups in Island Southeast Asia as well as food studies. Her publications include *Indonesian Sea Nomads: Money, Magic and Fear of the Orang Suku Laut* (2003), and *The Orang Suku Laut of Riau, Indonesia: The Inalienable Gift of Territory* (2010).

Mark Emmanuel is an independent scholar of Singapore who is interested in cultural and social issues. His publications include "Viewspapers: The Malay Press of the 1930s," *Journal of Southeast Asian Studies* (2010); and "The Malaysia Cup: Soccer and the National Imagining of Singapore, 1965–1996," *Journal of the Malaysian Branch of the Royal Asiatic Society* (2011).

Goh Hong Yi is a history teacher in Singapore. Her research interests stem from her love for nature and her experience volunteering with Singaporean environmental groups.

Corinne Heng is a history teacher in Singapore. Her research interests focus on post-1965 Singapore with a particular focus on issues concerning nature and the built environment.

Tony O'Dempsey is a GIS and remote sensing expert as well as an amateur naturalist, and has been participating in NParks fauna surveys in Singapore for the past 15 years. He has a keen interest in the history of development in Singapore and its effects on the natural environment and is currently undertaking a study of the land use history of the Central Catchment Nature Reserve.

Fiona L.P. Tan is an Assistant Archivist at the National Archives of Singapore. Her prior attachments with various local museums and libraries has cultivated an interest in the history of museums and nature in colonial Singapore. Her publications include "Of Birds and Beasties," in *Camping and Tramping through the Colonial Archive: The Museum in Malaya*, ed. Tan Li-Jen and Shabbir Hussain Mustafa (Singapore: NUS Museum, 2011).

Nigel P. Taylor is the Director of the Singapore Botanic Gardens. He began his career at the Royal Botanic Gardens, Kew, as a horticultural taxonomist and led a team that saw Kew Gardens inscribed as a UNESCO World Heritage Site in 2003. He is currently working on the same objective for the Singapore Botanic Gardens. He is the author of six books and more than 200 publications.

John van Wyhe is a historian of science, with a focus on Charles Darwin and Alfred Russel Wallace. He is a Senior Lecturer in the Department of History and the Department of Biological Sciences at the National University of Singapore, where he oversees the Wallace Online Project (http://wallace-online.org/). He has published eight books and lectures and broadcasts around the world.

Index